Kent & Sussex

timeout.com

Time Out Guides Ltd
Universal House
251 Tottenham Court Road
London W1T 7AB
United Kingdom
Tel: +44 (0)20 7813 3000
Fax: +44 (0)20 7813 6001
Email: guides@timeout.com
www.timeout.com

Published by Time Out Guides Ltd, a wholly owned subsidiary of Time Out Group Ltd.
Time Out and the Time Out logo are trademarks of Time Out Group Ltd.

© Time Out Group Ltd 2011

10 9 8 7 6 5 4 3 2

This edition first published in Great Britain in 2011 by Ebury Publishing.
A Random House Group Company
20 Vauxhall Bridge Road, London SW1V 2SA

Random House Australia Pty Ltd 20 Alfred Street, Milsons Point, Sydney, New South Wales 2061, Australia

Random House New Zealand Ltd 18 Poland Road, Glenfield, Auckland 10, New Zealand

Random House South Africa (Pty) Ltd Isle of Houghton, Corner Boundary Road & Carse O'Gowrie,
Houghton 2198, South Africa

Random House UK Limited Reg. No. 954009

Distributed in USA by Publishers Group West
1700 Fourth Street, Berkeley, California 94710

Distributed in Canada by Publishers Group Canada
250A Carlton Street, Toronto, Ontario M5A 2L1

For further distribution details, see www.timeout.com.

ISBN: 978-1-84670-239-6

A CIP catalogue record for this book is available from the British Library.

Printed and bound in India by Replika Press Pvt. Ltd.

The Random House Group Limited supports The Forest Stewardship Council (FSC®), the leading international forest certification organisation. Our books carrying the FSC label are printed on FSC® certified paper. FSC is the only forest certification scheme endorsed by the leading environmental organisations, including Greenpeace. Our paper procurement policy can be found at www.randomhouse.co.uk/environment

Time Out carbon-offsets all its flights with Trees for Cities (www.treesforcities.org).

MIX
From responsible
sources
FSC® C016779

Published by

Time Out Guides Limited
Universal House
251 Tottenham Court Road
London W1T 7AB
Tel +44 (0)20 7813 3000
Fax +44 (0)20 7813 6001
email guides@timeout.com
www.timeout.com

Editorial

Author Daniel Neilson
Editors Sarah Guy, Cath Phillips, Elizabeth Winding
Researchers William Crow, Jamie Warburton
Proofreader John Pym
Indexer Jackie Brind

Managing Director Peter Fiennes
Editorial Director Sarah Guy
Series Editor Cath Phillips
Business Manager Daniel Allen
Editorial Manager Holly Pick
Assistant Management Accountant Ija Krasnikova

Design

Art Director Scott Moore
Art Editor Pinelope Kourmouzoglou
Senior Designer Kei Ishimaru
Group Commercial Designer Jodi Sher

Picture Desk

Picture Editor Jael Marschner
Acting Deputy Picture Editor Liz Leahy
Picture Desk Assistant/Researcher Ben Rowe

Advertising

New Business & Commercial Director Mark Phillips
International Advertising Manager Kasimir Berger
Advertising Sales Gail McKay, Gemma Still

Marketing

Sales & Marketing Director, North America & Latin America
Lisa Levinson
Senior Publishing Brand Manager Luthfa Begum
Group Commercial Art Director Anthony Huggins
Marketing Co-ordinator Alana Benton

Production

Group Production Manager Brendan McKeown
Production Controller Katie Mulhern

Time Out Group

Chairman & Founder Tony Elliott
Chief Executive Officer David King
Group Financial Director Paul Rakkar
Group General Manager/Director Nichola Coulthard
Time Out Communications Ltd MD David Pepper
Time Out International Ltd MD Cathy Runciman
Time Out Magazine Ltd Publisher/MD Mark Elliott
Group Commercial Director Graeme Tottle
Group IT Director Simon Chappell

Contributors Sarah Bolland, Alison Bourke, Ruth-Ellen Davis, Jamie Warburton.

Thanks to Tim Arthur, Daryl Bailey, Lydia Bartlett (Amplifier Group), Lynnette Crisp & Julie Edwards (Visit Kent), Dan Dufeu, Pete Fiennes, Judy Kneen, Anna Norman, Adam Monaghan, Adam McNaught-Davis, Ros Sales, Will Salmon, Cat Scully, George Shaw, Stuart Still, Jemma Vanderbil, Mark Williams.

Maps pages 22, 136 Kei Ishimaru, page 217 JS Graphics (john@jsgraphics.co.uk).

This product contains mapping from Ordnance Survey with permission of HMSO. © Crown Copyright, all rights reserved. License number: 100049681.

Cover photography Dave Porter/Britain on View/Photolibrary.com

Back cover photography Britta Jaschinski; CA Harrrington

Photography Adam Monaghan except : pages 11, 16, 17, 19, 66, 67, 69, 76, 121, 131, 154 (top right), 155 (top right), 176, 181 (top), 182, 189, 192, 198 (bottom right), 199 (bottom right), 204 (bottom), 206, 212, 257 (bottom), 272 (bottom right), 273 (top and bottom right), 275, 279 (second top right), 291, 292 Daniel Neilson; pages 12, 23, 46, 47 (bottom), 79 (bottom), 177 Alamy; pages 20, 64, 65, 72, 73, 108, 109, 137, 139, 140, 141, 143, 242, 243, 246, 252 Britta Jaschinski; page 32 James Brittain; page 33 Chris Mansfield; pages 34, 35, 36, 39 Visit Maidstone; page 42 Paul Wilkinson; pages 45, 52 (top & bottom) Jael Marschner; pages 52 (centre right), 85 (top), 148, 158, 293 Lance Bellers; page 52 Russ Witherington; page 53 Mark Yuill; page 54 Kent Tourism; pages 59, 92, 160 (left) English Heritage Photo Library; pages 71, 240, 245 (bottom) Heloise Bergman; pages 79 (top), 85 (bottom) Snowshill; pages 96, 128 vitek12; page 100 (top & centre) Thierry Bal; pages 100 (bottom), 154 (bottom right) David Fowler; pages 101, 104 www.centralphotography.com; pages 110, 115, 116 Ady Kerry; page 113 Living Architecture; pages 125, 199 (top & bottom left), 217, 221 (top & bottom right), 237, 245 (top), 247, 269, 271, 277 Jonathan Perugia; page 129 Markabond; page 145 Jan Baldwin; pages 151, 154 (left) David Young; page 160 (right) Andy Poole; page 163 Chamomille; page 165 Darren Ciolli-Leach; page 166 Richard Donovan; page 170 Gallimaufry; page 174 George Green; page 193 Chris Mole; page 198 Maria Gioberti; page 204 (top) Chris Jenner; pages 208, 209 John Dominick; page 210 John R. Smith; pages 9 (bottom right), 43, 213 Chris Pierre; pages 219, 220 (top left & bottom) Richard Rowland; page 249 Laurence Gough; page 255 tiorna; page 257 (top) Britain on View/Photolibrary.com; page 268 Nick Hawkes; page 284 (top) George Selwyn; pages 284 (bottom), 289 (top & right) Mike Caldwell; page 287 Peter Durant/arcblue.com; page 296 Basphoto.

The following photos were provided by the featured establishments : pages 15, 26, 28, 29, 30, 38, 41, 47(top), 48, 50, 56, 57, 68, 80, 82, 83, 86, 88, 91, 94, 97, 98, 99, 102, 103, 118, 122, 123, 124, 126, 149, 153, 164, 178, 190, 198 (bottom left), 200, 201 203, 214, 225, 231, 232, 234, 235, 258, 260, 272, 273, 279, 280, 285, 286, 287 (middle), 289 (left).

About the guide

Kent & Sussex is one in a new series of Time Out guides covering Britain. We've used our local knowledge to reveal the best of the region, and while we've included all the big attractions, we've gone beneath the surface to uncover plenty of smaller, hidden treasures too.

The landscape is timelessly lovely, from the tranquil beauty of the Weald, stretched out between the chalk escarpments of the Downs, to the splendid sweep of the coast. Shingle beaches, dune-backed sands and boat-filled harbours are interspersed with classic seaside resorts, from genteel Broadstairs to bohemian Brighton; beyond the wetlands of Romney Marsh, Dungeness has its own bleak, windswept beauty.

Inland are ancient castles and romantic gardens, unspoilt villages and cosy country pubs, along with the cathedral cities of Canterbury and Chichester. Both counties also have vibrant cultural scenes, taking in opera and music festivals, architectural gems and world-class art galleries – not least the new Turner Contemporary and Towner, testament to the south coast's talent for reinvention.

TELEPHONE NUMBERS

All phone numbers listed in this guide assume that you're ringing from within Britain. If you're calling from elsewhere, dial your international access code, then 44 for the UK; follow that with the phone number, dropping the first zero of the area code.

OPENING TIMES

Part of the charm of the countryside is that it's not like the city. But this means beware opening times; places often close for the winter months, or open only at weekends, and some shops still shut for lunch. If you're eating out, many places still finish serving at 2pm sharp for lunch and at 9pm for dinner. So if you're making a journey, always phone to check. This goes for attractions too, especially outside the summer holiday season. While every effort has been made to ensure the accuracy of the information contained in this guide, the publisher cannot accept any responsibility for errors it may contain.

ADVERTISERS

The recommendations in *Kent & Sussex* are based on the experiences of Time Out's reviewers. No payment or PR invitation has secured inclusion or influenced content. The editors choose which places to include. Advertisers have no influence over content; an advertiser may receive a bad review or no review at all.

FEEDBACK

We hope you enjoy the guide. We always welcome suggestions for places to include in future editions and take note of your criticism of our choices. You can email us at guides@timeout.com.

Contents

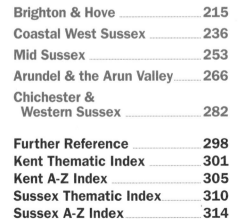

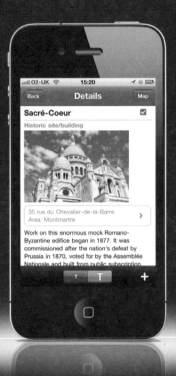

Festivals & Events

Kent

APRIL

Planet Thanet Easter Beer Festival
www.easterbeerfestival.org.uk. Date mid Apr.
Swap chocolate eggs for pints of ale at this popular
Easter beer festival at the Winter Gardens in Margate.
Live music features on both days, and there's a giant
pub quiz on Saturday evening.

Rochester Sweeps' Festival
Date late April-early May.
Morris dancers come jingling from far and wide for this
five-day May celebration. The festival centres on the
traditional May Day holiday for chimney sweeps, which
involved a street parade and the dawn waking of the
seven-foot-tall Jack-in-the-Green character.

JUNE

Rochester Dickens Festival
www.rochesterdickensfestival.org.uk. Date early June.
Characters from Dickens' much-loved works come to
life in a combination of music, dance and drama at
Rochester's twice-yearly tribute (also see December).

South of England Show
www.seas.org.uk. Date mid June.
Staged annually by the South of England Agricultural
Society at its Ardingly grounds, this show has grown
from traditional agricultural roots to include equestrian
exhibitions, cavalry parades and a funfair. There is
also an emphasis on regional food, with cookery
demonstrations and a large market area.

Broadstairs Dickens Festival
*01843 861827, www.broadstairsdickensfestival.co.uk.
Date 3rd week June.*
The UK's most comprehensive celebration of the
author, this delightful festival spans Victorian markets,
costume exhibitions and even a Victorian bathing party,
with participants sporting suitably modest attire.

Folkestone Triennial
*www.folkestonetriennial.org.uk. Date June-Sept 2011
& 2014.*
A host of high-profile artists create new works of art
for the streets, squares and beaches of Folkestone
in this ground-breaking festival, which was launched
in 2008; Tracey Emin and Tacita Dean were among
the artists who took part.

JULY

Hop Farm Festival
*020 7644 1445, www.hopfarmfestival.com.
Date early July.*

South of England Show

Whitstable Oyster Festival

Held at the 90-acre Hop Farm in Paddock Wood, this up-and-coming music festival only started in 2008, but has already seen the likes of Bob Dylan and Van Morrison take part. Festival-goers enjoy two days of music, funfair rides, food stalls and good camping facilities, with no corporate branding across the site.

Lounge on the Farm
www.loungeonthefarm.co.uk. Date early July.
This charming little festival on Merton Farm in Canterbury has bags of character and plenty of local cider. Past headliners have included the Super Furry Animals and the New York Dolls.

Ramsgate Carnival Weekend
www.visitthanet.co.uk. Date late July.
A colourful procession takes to Ramsgate's Royal Esplanade, while family-friendly entertainment over the carnival weekend includes a funfair.

Ramsgate Week
www.ramsgateweek.com. Date late July.
The Royal Temple Yacht Club's well-attended annual regatta at Ramsgate Harbour involves various races and entertainment.

Tonbridge Castle Festival of Music & Fireworks
www.tmbc.gov.uk. Date late July.
Crowds picnic on the lawns of Tonbridge Castle to enjoy live music and firework displays.

Whitstable Oyster Festival
01227 862066, www.whitstableoysterfestival.com. Date late July.
Mollusc-related festivities take over the harbour town of Whitstable for a week in July. Events include the ceremonial landing of the oysters and the Oyster Parade, led by the Lord Mayor.

AUGUST

Broadstairs Folk Week
01843 604080, www.broadstairsfolkweek.org.uk. Date Aug.
Broadstairs is particularly attractive during this summery week of folk music, and there's a convivial atmosphere. Various venues in the town get involved, and a campsite is available just ten minutes from the main concert marquee.

Whitstable Regatta
01227 274313, www.whitstablelionsclub.org.uk. Date mid Aug.
As the Oyster Festival closes, the Whitstable Regatta springs into action; alongside water sports there are fairground rides, circus performances, craft stalls and fireworks. The exact date changes every year, as a high tide is needed for the yacht race on Saturday.

Herne Bay Festival
www.hernebayfestival.co.uk. Date late Aug.
Herne Bay revels in nine days of music and entertainment. It's a community festival, with bands and workshops – gumboot dancing lesson, anyone?

Sandwich Festival
www.sandwichfestival.org.uk. Date late Aug.
See Sandwich at its most lively during festival week, with a lengthy programme of events that takes in a boat parade, concerts and a barn dance in the street.

SEPTEMBER

Faversham Hop Festival
www.thehopfestival.com. Date 1st weekend Sept.
This lively local event in Faversham town centre encompasses music, arts and crafts, and Morris dancers. Everything goes with a swing, thanks to the Shepherd Neame beer.

Art in Romney Marsh
www.artinromneymarsh.org.uk. Date end Sept-Oct.
An experimental and contemporary arts collaboration by various artists, displayed in several of Romney Marsh's medieval churches over four weekends.

OCTOBER

Canterbury Festival
www.canterburyfestival.co.uk. Date Oct.
Canterbury's autumn arts festival features more than 200 events, with categories ranging from theatre, literature and comedy to world music and film.

DECEMBER

Rochester Dickensian Christmas Festival
www.rochesterdickensfestival.org.uk. Date 1st weekend Dec.
A seasonal look at the author, with a mistletoe ball, street theatre and much merriment.

Sussex

JANUARY

Wassail Evening
01323 811411, www.middlefarm.com. Date early Jan.
Warm your cockles with a mulled cider and a hearty jig at this winter celebration at Middle Farm, traditionally held on Twelfth Night. Music, dancing, feasting and ale should banish the January blues.

Brighton Tattoo Convention
www.brightontattoo.com. Date late Jan.
A colourful affair at Brighton Racecourse, where tattoo artists from around Europe congregate to show off their inking skills. Bands take to the stage, and there's usually an after-party at a Brighton venue.

FEBRUARY

Rye Bay Scallop Festival
www.ryebayscallops.co.uk. Date mid Feb.
Plump scallops steal the spotlight for a week. Rye's eateries offer scallop-focused menus, and there are tastings, cookery classes and markets at various locations. Look out for the hotly contested 'What a

Load of Scallops' event, in which entrants race wheelbarrows of scallop shells from the fisheries to the Ship Inn.

Brighton Science Festival
01273 777628, www.brightonscience.com. Date mid Feb-early Mar.
One of the UK's largest science events, with talks, experiments and hands-on workshops. The Bright Sparks Day and Wet Sounds experience are among the highlights.

See Festival
01273 227700, www.seefestival.org. Date late Feb.
Documentaries are the focus of this film festival, which showcases both established and up-and-coming talents in a series of screenings, workshops and premières.

MARCH

Clown Convention
www.bognorregistc.org.uk. Date early Mar.
Clowns from around the country slap head to Bognor for a foolish few days. Events take place at Butlins and in the town centre, culminating in a clown parade.

Sussex Beer Festival
www.sussexbeerfestival.co.uk. Date mid Mar.
Beers, ciders and wines, plus great food, friendly staff and a fantastic atmosphere at Hove Town Hall.

APRIL

Spring Harvest Food Festival
www.brightonfoodfestival.com. Date early Apr.
Such is the popularity of the Brighton Food Festival in September that its organisers launched this spring event. Find scores of food-related events across town.

Brighton Marathon
www.brightonmarathon.co.uk. Date mid Apr.
An increasingly popular race, taking in the best of the city and its coastline; the last mile is along the seafront road, ending at Madeira Drive.

London to Brighton Jaguar Run
www.brightonrun.co.uk. Date mid Apr.
One of several classic car runs that finishes on Madeira Drive; Jaguar cars of all ages complete a scenic route from London to Brighton's seafront.

MAY

Hastings Jack in the Green
www.hastingsjack.co.uk. Date late Apr-early May.
May Day is a big deal in Hastings. Expect music, Morris dancers, storytelling and theatre, culminating in a procession through the old town and along the seafront.

Artists' Open Houses Festival
www.aoh.org.uk. Date weekends in May.
Peek inside the homes and studios of Brighton artists at the most extensive free arts event in the UK. More than 1,000 artists exhibit their work at around 200 locations across the city.

Brighton Festival
www.brightonfestival.org. Date May.
Brighton Festival presents an impressive programme of theatre, dance, music, literature, family shows and outdoor spectacles, kick-started by the Children's Parade. In past years, the illustrious likes of Anish Kapoor and Brian Eno have acted as guest curators.

Brighton Fringe
01273 764900, www.brightonfestivalfringe.org.uk. Date May.
This is the third largest Fringe Festival in the world, offering a heady mix of cabaret, comedy, classical concerts, club nights, theatre and exhibitions, as well as street performance.

Great Escape
020 7688 9000, www.escapegreat.com. Date mid May.
This innovative music festival showcases local, national and international bands at locations across Brighton. An eclectic line-up ensures there is something for all musical tastes.

Brighton Kite Festival
www.brightonkiteflyers.co.uk. Date late May.
Held in Stanmer Park, this wholesome family event has been brightening the skies of Brighton for more than 30 years. Arena events might feature team flying displays and Indian fighting kites.

Charleston Festival
www.charleston.org.uk. Date late May.
Its enjoyable annual festival keeps Charleston's literary past alive, and attracts some illustrious speakers. Big names in attendance have included Bill Bryson, Alan Bennett, Zadie Smith, Max Hastings, Philip Pullman and David Dimbleby.

Sands of Time Seaside Festival
www.sandsoftime.co.uk. Date late May.
Bogner Regis, the sunniest place in Britain, is just the place for this two-day hymn of praise to the seaside. Alongside the all-important sandcastle competition, there are donkey rides and a vintage car rally. The date changes yearly to allow for a low tide during the sandcastle contest.

Glyndebourne Festival
www.glyndebourne.com. Date late May-Aug.
Each summer a programme of six operas are performed at this internationally renowned festival, alongside a range of talks and workshops, Although it remains a formal affair, moves are being made to open it up to a wider audience with cheaper tickets for shows early in the season. There are two restaurants, but most opt for champagne-fuelled picnics on the expansive lawns.

JUNE

Brighton Fashion Week
www.brightonfashionweek.co.uk. Date 2nd week June.
Catwalk shows, great parties and shopping discounts at a host of events showcasing future design stars.

FESTIVALS & EVENTS

Sandwich Festival. See p13.

AEGON International tennis
01323 412000, www.lta.org.uk. Date mid June.
Eastbourne's Devonshire Park hosts this world-class tennis event, with top names battling for supremacy on the courts.

London to Brighton Bike Ride
www.bhf.org.uk/london-brighton. Date mid June.
Held in aid of the British Heart Foundation, this annual 54-mile bike ride from the capital to the coast is the UK's largest charity bike ride, with 27,000 riders.

JULY

Petworth Festival
01798 344576, www.petworthfestival.org.uk. Date July.
Classical music and Shakespearean theatre are two of the mainstays at this respected event.

Paddle Round the Pier
www.paddleroundthepier.com. Date early July.
A free Brighton festival featuring the best in beach culture, extreme and street sports, plus live music and family fun. Proceeds go to charity.

Bognor Bird Man
www.birdman.org.uk. Date mid July.
Folk compete with their self-made flying machines by jumping off Bognor Pier into the blue, generally dressed in wacky costumes. There's a £25,000 jackpot for the furthest flight.

Med Fest
www.westdean.org.uk. Date mid July.
A weekend of Mediterranean food and drink, live music and dancing in the lovely setting of West Dean Gardens. Check the website for details of other events held here.

Soundwaves Festival
www.soundwaves-festival.org.uk. Date mid July.
Dip into an alternative world of cutting-edge new music, sound-art installations and participatory experiences in venues around Brighton.

Lammas Festival
01323 737809, www.lammasfest.org. Date late July.
This fantastic Eastbourne festival showcases local talent in traditional music and dance, while raising money for the RNLI.

Rox Festival
www.the-rox.org. Date late July.
The Rox is a charitable organisation that puts on classical concerts, theatre productions, comedy events and gigs throughout the year; in July, it stages a music and arts festival in Bognor Regis.

AUGUST

August Festival at Brighton Racecourse
www.brighton-racecourse.co.uk. Date early Aug.
Watch the races, sip champagne, have a flutter and admire the hats on Ladies Day.

Brighton Pride
www.brightonpride.org. Date early Aug.
The biggest free Pride festival in the UK celebrates everything LGBT in a week of events and parties, culminating in a spectacular parade through the city.

Airbourne
www.eastbourneairshow.com. Date mid Aug.
Eastbourne's four-day airshow features ground and air displays, Sunday-night fireworks and plenty of daredevil aerial stunts.

Vintage at Goodwood
www.vintageatgoodwood.com. Date mid Aug.
A three-day festival celebrating music, fashion, film, art, dance and design from the 1940s to the '80s. Among other attractions, there are five clubs, a rock 'n' roll stage, the world's biggest vintage clothes market and several hair salons. Dressing up is a must.

Arundel Festival
www.arundelfestival.co.uk. Date late Aug.
Enjoy a wealth of theatre, music and cinema at this lovely late summer festival, which has been running since 1978.

Brunswick Festival
www.brunswickplaceresidents.org.uk. Date late Aug.
An annual festival in celebration of the diverse community of Brighton's Brunswick neighbourhood. Expect a mix of street theatre and bands, as well as bric-a-brac, food and craft stalls.

Shoreham Airshow
www.shorehamairshow.co.uk. Date late Aug.
A Royal Air Force Association airshow with a five-hour flying display of RAF, aerobatic and historic aircraft. Look out for the show's renowned 'Scramble' scenario featuring Spitfire, Hurricane and Messerschmitt planes in a thrilling re-enactment.

Coastal Currents
www.coastalcurrents.org.uk. Date late Aug-Sept.
One of the largest annual arts festivals in the south, Coastal Currents events stretch along the coastline, from Bexhill in the west to Rye in the east. Strands include visual arts, performance, an open studios event, talks and workshops.

SEPTEMBER

Brighton & Hove Food and Drink Festival
www.brightonfoodfestival.co.uk. Date Sept.
A celebration of the best food and drink in Sussex, featuring cooking demonstrations, a farmers' market and lots of tasting.

Rye Festival
www.ryefestival.co.uk. Date Sept.
This arts festival includes a wealth of literary events, plus classic, world and popular music events.

Brighton Speed Trials
www.brightonandhovemotorclub.co.uk.
Date 2nd weekend Sept.

Britain's oldest motor racing event – first staged in 1905 – showcases a wide range of cars and motorbikes, racing over a quarter of a mile along Brighton seafront.

Wisborough Green Hot Air Balloon Festival
01403 700346, www.wisboroughgreen.org. Date 2nd weekend Sept.
An annual hot-air balloon festival raising money and awareness for CHASE hospice. Passengers are asked to donate £90 for a trip in one of around 25 balloons that fly from Wisborough Green over the weekend (book in advance). Non-flyers can take in the colourful spectacle over a picnic.

Ace Café Reunion
www.ace-cafe-london.com. Date mid Sept.
Some 40,000 motorbikes descend on Brighton's seafront in celebration of biking, and the original Ace Café on London's North Circular Road.

Goodwood Revival
www.goodwood.co.uk. Date mid Sept.
Retro motors are the name of the game at this acclaimed annual Goodwood get-together.

Seafood and Wine Festival
www.visit1066country.com. Date mid Sept.
Hastings celebrates local flavours with a programme of music, street entertainment and cookery demonstrations from local chefs and restaurateurs.

Brighton Art Fair
www.brightonartfair.co.uk. Date late Sept.
The largest art exhibition on the south coast brings painters, printmakers, photographers, sculptors and Sussex-based galleries to the Corn Exchange.

OCTOBER

Brighton Comedy Festival
www.brightoncomedyfestival.com. Date Oct.
Lots of laughs from some the UK's finest comedians, at the Brighton Dome.

City Reads
www.cityreads.co.uk. Date Oct.
An annual citywide initiative championing the love of books. Each year, one book is chosen for the community to read, discuss and engage with in a series of special events around Brighton and Hove.

World Pea Throwing Championship
01273 473152, www.thelewesarms.co.uk. Date 1st weekend Oct.
The idea is pretty simple: contestants hurl peas as far as they possibly can along Castle Ditch Lane, outside the Lewes Arms pub in Lewes.

Apple Festival
01323 811411, www.middlefarm.com. Date mid Oct.
Celebrate the humble apple at Middle Farm's much-loved Apple Festival. Find music, dancing, and scores of apple-related products – including, of course, gallons of cider.

Arundel Food Festival
www.arundelfoodfestival.org.uk. Date mid Oct.
Most pubs and restaurants in Arundel host some sort of event in honour of the festival, from foraging walks or butchery demonstrations to cupcake masterclasses.

Battle of Hastings re-enactment
www.english-heritage.org.uk. Date mid Oct.
Held on the battlefield of the 1066 clash, this spirited historical re-enactment is an extraordinary spectacle.

Taste of Rye
01797 229049, www.tasteofrye.org.uk. Date mid Oct.
This celebration of local produce features special dinners, markets and cookery classes.

Eastbourne Beer Festival
www.eastbournebeerfestival.co.uk. Date late Oct.
Over a weekend in October, Eastbourne's Winter Garden sees over 120 alcoholic brews, local bands and pub games.

White Night
www.whitenightnuitblanche.com. Date last Sat Oct.
An evening of festivities signalling the end of British Summer Time, with an array of cultural events across Brighton and Hove.

NOVEMBER

London to Brighton Veteran Car Run
www.lbvcr.com. Date early Nov.
An annual event attracting hundreds of vehicles from the UK and abroad, as well as thousands of spectators.

Lewes Bonfire Night
www.lewesbonfirecouncil.org.uk. Date Nov 5.
Bonfire societies parade through Lewes' streets, with burning effigies, oil drums and chants. After the parades, there are some cracking fireworks displays. Outsiders are discouraged from attending, though, to keep crowd numbers at manageable levels; see the website for more details. For more on the south coast's bonfire societies, see right.

CineCity Film Festival
www.cine-city.co.uk. Date mid Nov-early Dec.
The south coast's best celebration of film, featuring premières, previews, arthouse cinema, talks, archive treasures and special events.

Christmas Artists Open Houses
www.aoh.org.uk. Date weekends late Nov-Christmas.
More than 100 artists participate in the Chistmas Open House event. Invest in some art, or simply browse over a mince pie and mulled wine.

DECEMBER

Burning the Clocks – Winter Solstice Parade
www.burningtheclocks.co.uk. Date late Dec.
Home-made paper and willow lanterns are paraded through Brighton and burned on the beach to mark the winter solstice and the end of the year, and there are spectacular pyrotechnic displays.

The rekindling of the bonfire societies

Lewes's celebrated November 5th celebrations attract thousands of revellers for a spectacle that features 17 burning crosses (each commemorating a Protestant martyr from the town, burned alive by Mary I), followed by hundreds of torch bearers, wearing striped sweaters (smuggling garb) or the dress of a Tudor or Civil War soldier. The street appears engulfed in flames. Some participants drag barrels of burning tar, others set off bangers and fireworks – the small town is transformed.

Lewes may have the most famous bonfire night celebrations, but in towns and villages across Sussex (and parts of Kent), members of bonfire societies light torches, dress up and parade the streets on most weekends between the first procession, at the Uckfield Carnival in September, to the Robertsbridge and Barcombe parades in the third week of November. There are more than 30 bonfire societies in Sussex, including ones from the villages of Firle, Newick, Barcombe, Lindfield, Mayfield, Chailey and Robertsbridge, and the towns of Hastings, Rye, Battle, Hailsham, Shoreham, Littlehampton and Eastbourne. Lewes alone has six bonfire societies.

In the 21st century, the bonfire festivities are going from strength to strength. Today, the events are mostly family affairs (though Lewes can get rowdy, and is not recommended for younger children), but just under the surface lies a dark history.

Mary I was vehemently Catholic, and her reign saw many Protestants burned at the stake, earning her the sobriquet 'Bloody' Mary. The 17 Protestants from Lewes who died in this way between 1555 and 1557 became martyrs, as did people from many villages across Sussex. Some of the villages were already commemorating the martyrdoms with bonfires, but after 5 November 1605 (when Guy Fawkes and a group of Catholics attempted to blow up the House of Lords and James I), the day became cemented in public consciousness and enshrined in law under the Observance of 5th November Act as a thanksgiving for the plot's failure. It was the only public holiday that survived Cromwell's Puritan purge of festivals (Christmas didn't). The festivities were often drunken, riotous affairs where effigies of the Pope were burned. However, through the issue of public disturbance orders, they were gradually dampened through the 17th and 18th centuries. It wasn't until 1851, and the publication of Mark Anthony Lower's *The Sussex Martyrs, their Examinations and Cruel Burnings in the time of Queen Mary*, that the cult of the Sussex martyrs began. 'Bonfire Boyes' across Sussex began again to commemorate the events with added fervour. The anti-papist undertones remained, but it was more often, as it is today, an opportunity to get drunk and set fire to things – across villages in the South-east, the flames of the societies are still burning bright.

Kent

Dungeness. See p105.

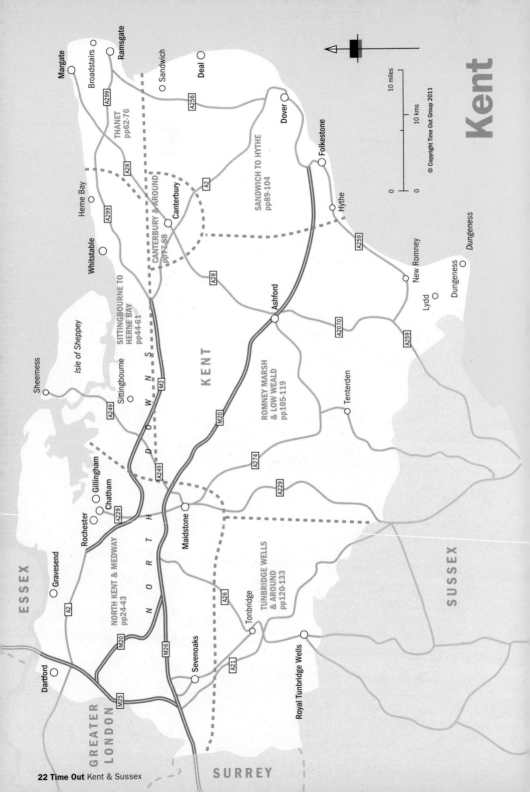

Kent

© Copyright Time Out Group 2011

10 miles

10 kms

THANET
pp62-76

CANTERBURY & AROUND
pp77-88

SANDWICH TO HYTHE
pp89-104

SITTINGBOURNE TO
HERNE BAY
pp44-61

KENT

ROMNEY MARSH
& LOW WEALD
pp105-119

NORTH KENT & MEDWAY
pp24-43

TUNBRIDGE WELLS
& AROUND
pp120-133

NORTH DOWNS

Margate
Broadstairs
Ramsgate
Sandwich
Deal
Dover
Folkestone
Herne Bay
Hythe
New Romney
Dungeness
Dungeness
Lydd
Canterbury
Whitstable
Isle of Sheppey
Sheerness
Sittingbourne
Ashford
Tenterden
Gillingham
Chatham
Rochester
Gravesend
Maidstone
Tonbridge
Sevenoaks
Dartford
Royal Tunbridge Wells

ESSEX

GREATER
LONDON

SURREY

SUSSEX

A299
A28
A299
A256
A2
A28
A2
A259
A259
A2070
A249
M2
A249
A274
A229
M20
A229
A26
A21
A2
M20
M26
M25

Kent

North Kent & Medway

The nautical history of the north Kent coast has played a huge role in the history of England, all of which is outlined in one of Kent's most popular attractions: Chatham Historic Dockyard. Major towns on or near the coast include Gravesend, Rochester, Chatham and Gillingham, but there are also the wide open spaces of the Hoo Peninsula, which divides the estuaries of the River Thames (to the north) and the Medway (to the south).

Inland, the River Medway carves a valley through the chalk North Downs to Maidstone and towards West Sussex. Sevenoaks is at the heart of this lovely region – one marred only by the network of motorways, but otherwise full of country homes, castles and parkland (many under the auspices of English Heritage or the National Trust). Chartwell, Down House, Ightham Mote, Knole and Leeds Castle are among the stellar attractions.

GRAVESEND & HOO PENINSULA

Gravesend

Although not a tourist hotspot, Gravesend is not short of attractions, particularly for historians. The Thames riverfront and the streets leading down to it from the train station are attractive, with uneven paving, old shop fronts and river views. On the pedestrianised High Street, look out for the 19th-century Old Town Hall and the Borough Market, one of the earliest chartered markets in England, dating from 1268 and still trading today.

St George's Church (*see p26*) by the river has a statue of Pocahontas outside it. Pocahontas, the 17th-century Native American who was taken captive by English colonial settlers (later marrying one and moving to London) is buried in Gravesend. She died in 1617 on a ship anchored off Gravesend on what would have been her return voyage to Virginia.

On the riverside, explore the area by walking from the Rum Puncheon (*see p31*) on West Street to the Ship and Lobster (Mark Lane, 01474 324571, www.shipandlobster.co.uk) at the end of the river wall. You pass pleasant Elizabeth Gardens, then come to the recently restored Town Pier – the oldest cast iron pier in the world, erected in 1834. It marks the start of the Saxon Shore Way, which traces the Kent coastline for 140 miles to Hastings in Sussex. By the pier is the Three Daws (*see p31*); continuing east along Crooked Lane is St Andrew's Gardens. Get closer to the Thames by continuing from the gardens on to Royal Pier Road, where you'll find the Mission House, which started life in 1840 as a tavern; but was put in to more wholesome use use from 1871 as a reading room for the children of the poor. The ground floor is now part of the Thames House B&B (*see p31*). Along this road is also Clarendon Royal Hotel, now being redeveloped, and Gravesend Blockhouse, one of five artillery barracks built in the area by Henry VIII. Royal Pier Road will bring you to Royal Terrace Pier, erected in 1842 for day-trippers coming from London by steamer.

Continue from Royal Pier Road on to the Terrace to see the former Customs House built in 1812. Then walk onward toward the promenade and the Riverside Leisure Area. With the Thames spread out before you, you'll see the oldest building in Gravesend: Milton Chantry, which was founded in 1322 as a chapel and went through various incarnations before becoming the Chantry Heritage Centre (Milton Place, 01474 337600, open Apr-Sept Sat, Sun). Return down Canal Road and Norfolk Road to end at Mark Lane.

Hoo Peninsula

The Hoo Peninsula appeals to those with a love of wildlife (particularly birds), an interest in history, or even a fondness for the novels of Charles Dickens, some of which have their roots in this marshy landscape.

Hoo forms a part of two protected areas known as the Thames Estuary and Marshlands, and the Medway Estuary and Marshes, both Sites of Special Scientific Interest. There are two RSPB reserves – at Northward Hill, High Halstow (*see p26*) and at Cliffe Pools (Salt Lane, 01634 222480, www.rspb.org.uk); the peninsula is a meeting place for migratory and nesting waterfowl. The Cliffe Pools Reserve is the place to spy on the water birds that skim, swim and wade in the lagoons of the Thames Estuary. Nature trails crisscross the reserve.

The village of Cliffe has various ancient buildings. St Helen's church (Church Street, 01634 220210, www.cliffechurch.org, open 1st & 3rd Sat of mth) dates from around 1260, with alternating layers of Kentish ragstone and squared black flint. The Grade II-listed 16th-century barn at Rye Farm in Common Lane has a traditional hipped roof and an ancient wagon porch. On the edge of the wetlands, Cliffe Fort was built in the 1860s. A Brennan Torpedo station was also built on the site in 1890; it's now pretty much inaccessible, having been claimed by the wilderness. The landscape stood in for Vietnam's paddy fields during the filming of Stanley Kubrick's *Full Metal Jacket*.

Places to visit

GRAVESEND & HOO PENINSULA

Cooling Castle
Cooling, ME3 8DT.
This castle was built in the 1380s by Sir John de Cobham. It was situated on the edge of the Cooling marshes to defend the area against invasion, particularly from the French who had raided much of Kent, as far as Gravesend. The castle has thick stone walls, a moat and two sturdy drum towers at the gateway. Nontheless, it was successfully stormed by Sir Thomas Wyatt in 1554 during the Kentish uprising against Queen Mary. It's now a private residence (owned by Jools Holland), but visitors are welcome to take a look at the impressive gatehouse.

RSPB Northward Hill
High Halstow, ME3 8DS (01634 222480, www.rspb.org.uk). Open dawn-dusk daily. Admission free.
A new walking trail showcases the UK's largest colony of herons and egrets. The three-mile trail is set amid the gentle marshland of the Hoo Peninsula, and wellington boots are recommended. Woodpeckers, tits, nightingales, turtledoves and warblers are all resident, but the stars of the show are the herons (some 200 pairs). They are out and about for most of the year, but spring – when the young birds learn to fly – is prime time for visits.

St George's Church
Church Street, Gravesend, DA11 0DJ (01474 534965, www.stgeorgesgravesend.org.uk). Open 11am-3pm Tue.
A lovely church, St George's is best known for the woman immortalised in a statue outside its door. Pocahontas, the Native American chief's daughter famous for helping colonial settlers at Jamestown, Virginia, is buried somewhere in the vicinity. If the church is closed, a member of staff from Towncentric, the visitor information centre (18A St George's Square, 01474 33 76 00) may be available to show you around.

St James's Church
Main Road, Cooling, ME3 8DG (01634 220565). Open 7.30am-4pm daily.
To stand by the tiny graves at St James's Church, surrounded by miles of desolate marshland, is to find yourself transported into the pages of *Great Expectations*. This is widely considered to be the place in which Pip encountered the convict Magwitch, next to the 'little stone lozenges' where his five brothers are buried. The graves actually belong to two families whose children died in the 18th and early 19th centuries, possibly struck down by 'marsh ague', a form of malaria prevalent at the time. The 13th-century church is open to visitors.

Shorne Woods Country Park
Brewers Road, Shorne, DA12 3HX (01474 823800, www.kent.gov.uk/kentcountryparks). Open 9am-9pm (or dusk if earlier) daily. Admission free.
The park covers 174 acres and is both an Area of Outstanding Natural Beauty and a Site of Special Scientific Interest. It contains woodland, meadow,

Dickens World

heathland, wetland and garden, not to mention an arboretum with almost every species of tree native to Kent. There's also a visitors' centre.

ROCHESTER, CHATHAM & GILLINGHAM

Darland Bank
Darland Avenue, Gillingham, ME7 3ER (01622 662012, www.kentwildlifetrust.org.uk).
This is a great area to tramp through, full of woodland, flowers and butterflies. At 45 hectares, it is the largest countryside site in Medway.

Dickens World
Leviathan Way, Chatham Maritime, ME4 4LL (01634 890421, www.dickensworld.co.uk). Open 10am-4.30pm Tue-Fri; 10am-5.30pm Sat, Sun. Admission £13; £8-£11 reductions; £40 family.
Dickens World opened in 2007 and recreates his characters and locations with animatronics and actors. The ramshackle clapboard buildings are peopled with a cast of pickpockets, barmaids, flower sellers, policemen and rat-catchers. Visitors can take a peek at a traditional schoolroom in the style of Dotheboys Hall, be mildly frightened by the ghosts in Ebenezer Scrooge's house and follow Magwitch's ill-fated escape in the Great Expectations boat ride.

Guildhall Museum
High Street, Rochester, ME1 1PY (01634 848717, www.medway.gov.uk). Open 10am-4.30pm Tue-Sun. Admission free.

The history of Rochester is covered in this 17th-century building, though most people make a beeline for the Dickens Discovery Rooms. Here, visitors are taken on a journey through the writer's intriguing life and times. Playing on the cult of celebrity that surrounded Dickens, the centerpiece of the collection is a series of mock-ups of different newspapers and magazines exploring his appeal. The exhibition also features artefacts such as his pen and walking stick, plus a rare collection of family portraits.

Historic Dockyard Chatham ★
Dock Road, Chatham, ME4 4TY (01634 823807, www.thedockyard.co.uk). Open Apr-Oct 10am-5pm daily. Feb, Mar, Nov 10am-4pm daily. Admission £15; £7.50-£12.50 reductions; £42.50 family.
Britain's ships have been built, repaired and manned at Chatham from the time of the Spanish Armada right up until the Falklands War, and it's the most complete example of an historic dockyard from the 'age of sail'. With three historic warships to explore and galleries bringing 400 years of maritime history to life, there's plenty to see. Excellent temporary exhibitions range from paintings to a collection of robots. There are indoor picnic facilities (with a soft play area) as well as a restaurant.

Rochester Castle
Rochester, ME1 1SW (01634 335882, www.english-heritage.org.uk). Open 10am-4pm daily. Admission £5.00; £3.50 reductions; £13.50 family.
Carving an unmistakable shape on Rochester's skyline, this fortress is one the best preserved in the UK. It stands at 113 feet, towering over the banks of the River Medway, and you can climb to the top to see for miles around. The building is an unusual combination of one round tower set against three square towers, a defensive structure designed in the aftermath of the 1215 siege of the castle by King John.

Rochester Cathedral
High Street, Rochester, ME1 1SX (01634 843366, www.rochestercathedral.org). Open 7.30am-6pm Mon-Fri, Sun; 7.30am-5pm Sat. Tours 10am-4.30pm Mon-Fri, Sun; 10am-2pm Sat. Admission free. Tours £4.
The cathedral was founded in 604 by Bishop Justase. Behind the Romanesque façade, look for the Norman architecture of the nave and parts of the crypt. There's also the remarkable 14th-century Chapter Library door, which can only be seen by special appointment. Interactive trails, audio trails and visual projections will help you unravel the history of this place of worship and pilgrimage.

Royal Engineers Museum
Prince Arthur Road, Gillingham, ME4 4UG (01634 822839, www.remuseum.org.uk). Open 9am-5pm Tue-Fri; 11.30am-5pm Sat, Sun. Admission £7.50; £5 reductions; £20 family.
The story of the Royal Engineers is fascinating: as well as being innovators in flying, photography and transport, the Sappers made a huge contribution to modern Britain's infrastructure. Displays include a Harrier Jump Jet, and the museum often hosts historic re-enactments.

AROUND MEOPHAM
Camer Country Park
Camer Park Road, Meopham, DA13 0AL (01474 337449). Open 24hrs daily.
This country park is a designated Area of Outstanding Natural Beauty. The 45 acres covers parkland and woodland; there's also a café.

Cobham Hall
Cobham, DA12 3BL (01474 823371, www.cobhamhall.com). Open times vary; check website for details. Admission £5.50; £4.50 reductions. No credit cards.
This country house is used as a girls' boarding school for most of the year, so is only open to the public at certain times. It's a beautiful house, worked on at various times by James Wyatt, Inigo Jones and the Adam brothers, and the grounds were shaped by landscape designer Humphry Repton. The magnificent Gilt Hall has an 18th-century Snetzler organ.

Owletts
The Street, Cobham, DA12 3AP (01304 207326, www.nationaltrust.org.uk/main/w-owletts).
This National Trust property is also a family home, occupied and run by a descendant of the donor: the architect Sir Herbert Baker. It was built in 1683, with a north wing added in 1794. The house is remarkable for its grand plasterwork and imaginative furniture, some of which was collected by Baker and some of which he commissioned. The house is closed for 2011; check the website for details of when it will reopen.

Trosley Country Park
Waterlow Road, Meopham, DA13 0SG (01732 823570, www.kent.gov.uk/kentcountryparks). Open 9am-9pm (or dusk if earlier) daily. Admission free.
This area of woodland and grassland is a Site of Special Scientific Interest. It's crisscrossed with trails, as well as having what Kent Country Park calls Trim Trails (a kind of outdoor exercise equipment station with instructions). There's an eco-friendly visitor centre with a living green roof and a café.

SEVENOAKS & AROUND
Chartwell ★
Mapleton Road, Westerham, TN16 1PS (01732 868381, www.nationaltrust.org.uk/main/w-chartwell). Open times vary; check website for details. Admission House, garden & studio £10.60; £5.30 reductions; £29.50 family. Garden & studio only £5.30; £2.65 reductions; £13.25 family. Winter garden & exhibition (Jan-Mar, Nov, Dec) £2.70; £1.35; £7.50 family.
Not only was Winston Churchill the pre-eminent British political figure of the 20th century, but he was also a Nobel Prize-winning author and a talented amateur painter. Much of his writing and painting took place at his beloved Chartwell, where he lived from 1924 until his death in 1965. Inspiration was provided by the glorious views over the Weald and lovely gardens. Visitors can see the lakes he created, the water garden where he fed his fish, Lady Churchill's rose garden and the Golden Rose Walk (a golden wedding anniversary present from the couple's children).

KENT

Inside, the house has been left much as it was in Churchill's day, filled with his books, maps, pictures and personal effects.

Charts Edge Garden

Hosey Hill, Westerham, TN16 1PL (01959 565541, www.heartofkent.org.uk). Open mid Apr-mid Sept 2-5pm Fri, Sun. Admission £4; free-£3.50 reductions. No credit cards.

These ten acres hold numerous rare plants and bold displays of rhododendrons, magnolias and azaleas. A Victorian folly, terraced water garden, bog garden and sculpture trail also feature.

Down House ★

Luxted Road, Downe, BR6 7JT (01689 859119, www.english-heritage.org.uk). Open July, Aug 11am-5pm daily. Apr-June, Sept, Oct 11am-5pm Wed-Sun. Feb, Mar 11am-4pm Wed-Sun. Admission £9.90; £4.95-£8.90 reductions; £25 family.

Charles Darwin's home for 40 years was extensively refurbished in 2009 to celebrate 150 years since the publication of *The Origin of Species*, and the simultaneous bicentennial of Darwin's birth. It's a joy to visit, and gives a real sense of the life of one of the world's greatest scientists: a jar of earthworms sits on his wife Emma's cherished rosewood piano, a skeleton lies on the billiard table and trailing plants and bees fill the greenhouses. Downstairs, the restored rooms feature as much original furniture as possible, including Darwin's study chair, the board he laid across his lap to handwrite *The Origin*, the backgammon set used for twice-daily games with Emma, and the signed copy of *Das Kapital* on his bookcase. David Attenborough describes Darwin's life and work in a hand-held multimedia tour. The immaculately tended grounds served as Darwin's own personal outdoor laboratory. You can walk in his footsteps, following the 'thinking' sand walk that he himself constructed and walked around three times a day, whatever the weather.

Emmetts Garden

Ide Hill, nr Sevenoaks, TN14 6BA (01732 751509, www.nationaltrust.org.uk). Open Mar-Oct 11am-5pm Mon-Wed, Sat, Sun. Admission £5.90.

There are wonderful views from this delightful garden. It was laid out in the late 19th century and contains many exotic and rare trees and shrubs, and is full of colour – the bluebell bank is spectacular.

Ightham Mote

Mote Road, Ivy Hatch, Sevenoaks, TN15 0NT (01732 810378, www.nationaltrust.org.uk). Open House June-Aug 11am-5pm Mon, Wed-Sun. Mar-May, Sept, Oct 11am-5pm Mon, Thur-Sun. Nov-mid Dec 11am-3pm Thur-Sun. Shop, restaurant & garden June-Aug 10.30am-5pm Mon, Wed-Sun. Mar-May, Sept, Oct 10.30am-5pm Mon, Thur-Sun. Nov-mid Dec 11am-3pm Thur-Sun. Feb 11am-3pm Sat, Sun. Estate dawn-dusk daily. Admission £10.40; £5.20 reductions; £26.30 family.

Like many early Tudor manors, Ightham Mote was built in a hollow and surrounded by a moat. The half-timbered manor house has a Great Hall, crypt and a chapel with a hand-painted Tudor ceiling. It also features what must be the only Grade I-listed dog house in the country. There are also tranquil gardens and woodland walks to enjoy.

Knole

Sevenoaks, Kent TN15 0RP (01732 450608, www.nationaltrust.org.uk). Open House Mar-Oct noon-4pm Wed-Sun. Shop, tearoom, visitor centre, Orangery & courtyards Apr-Sept 10.30am-5pm Tue-Sun. Mar, Oct 10.30am-5pm Wed-Sun. Nov, Dec 11am-4pm Wed-Sun. Garden Apr-Sept 11am-4pm Tue. Admission House £10.40; £5.20 reductions; £26 family. Garden £5; £2.50 reductions.

This imposing Kentish ragstone house, surrounded by a 1,000-acre deer park, was once the Sackville's ancestral home. It's called a calendar house, with 365 rooms, 52 staircases, 12 entrances and seven

Squerryes Court

Lullingstone Roman Villa
Lullingstone Lane, Eynsford, DA4 0JA (01322 863467, www.english-heritage.org.uk). Open Apr-Sept 10am-6pm daily. Oct, Nov 10am-4pm daily. Jan, Dec 10am-4pm Wed-Sun. Admission £5.90; £3-£5 reductions; £14.80 family.
When fragments of a Roman mosaic were unearthed here in 1939, it swiftly became apparent that this was one of the most notable Roman villa sites in England. Today, Lullingstone Roman Villa is a fascinating place in which to view mosaics, wall paintings and one of the country's earliest known Christian chapels. Children can get into the spirit of the era by playing Roman games and trying on a selection of costumes.

Quebec House
Quebec Square, Westerham, TN16 1TD (01732 868381, www.nationaltrust.org.uk/main/w-quebec house). Open House Mar-Oct 1-5pm Wed-Sun. Nov-mid Dec 1-5pm Sat, Sun. Garden & exhibition Mar-Oct noon-5pm Wed-Sun. Admission £4.20; £1.50 reductions; £10 family.
This 16th-century red-brick house was the childhood home of British army officer General James Wolfe, a key military figure in British battles with the French in Canada. The Grade I-listed building has been restored to appear much as it did when occupied by the Wolfe family; the coach house features an exhibition on the 1759 Battle of Quebec.

Riverhill Himalayan Gardens
2 miles south of Sevenoaks on the A225,TN15 0RR (01732 459777, www.riverhillgardens.co.uk). Open mid Mar-Sept 10.30am-5pm Wed-Sun. Admission £6.25; £3.95-£5.60 reductions; £17.50 family.
Seeds from the world's most famous mountain range have been nurtured at this burgeoning park, alongside a bevy of native blooms. Visitors can wander the Everest trail, scramble around the Himalayan hideout and play area, and find their way through the hedge maze, based on designs from Tibetan woodcarvings. Everest Viewpoint offers glorious vistas, stretching for 20 miles.

Squerryes Court
Westerham, TN16 1SJ (01959 562345, www. squerryes.co.uk). Open House Apr-Sept 12.30-5pm Wed, Sun & bank hols. Gardens Apr-Sept 11.30am-5pm Wed, Sun & bank hols. Admission House & gardens £7.50; £4-£7 reductions; £16 family. Gardens only £5; £2.50-£4.50 reductions; £9.50 family.
A collection of Old Master paintings is the focus inside this stately manor house, which was built in 1680 by Sir Nicholas Crisp. The house was acquired in 1731 by a John Warde, and it is his family's paintings, together with furniture, porcelain and tapestries, that can be seen today. The house is surrounded by formal gardens that echo the design of the grounds as they were in the 18th century.

MAIDSTONE & AROUND

Great Comp Garden
Comp Lane, Platt, TN15 8QS (01732 885094, www.greatcompgarden.co.uk). Open Apr-Oct 11am-5pm daily. Admission £5.50; £1-£5 reductions.

courtyards. Vita Sackville-West grew up here, and wrote, 'It has the tone of England; it melts into the tawnier green of the park, into the blue of the pale English sky.' One of the last medieval deer parks in England, perhaps Knole's greatest charm is that it has remained virtually unchanged through the centuries; the Sackvilles resisted the 18th-century fashion for Capability Brown-style landscaping, believing the grazing deer, now a 600-strong herd of fallow and sika deer, to be quite picturesque enough. Sadly, nearly three-quarters of Knole's ancient trees were felled by the storm of 1987, but many hornbeam, oak and ash trees still stand.

Lullingstone Castle & World Garden
Eynsford, DA4 0JA (01322 862114, www.lullingstone castle.co.uk). Open House noon-5pm bank hols only. Tours by appointment Wed, Thur. World Garden Apr-Sept noon-5pm Fri-Sun & bank hols. Admission £7; £4-£6.50 reductions; £18 family. No credit cards.
Lullingstone Castle (actually a manor house) is one of England's oldest family estates, with the house and the gatehouse being built in 1497. It was the subject of BBC TV's *Save Lullingstone Castle*, and has indeed been saved, thanks to the introduction of the World Garden. This was set up by Tom Hart Dyke, the 20th incumbent of the house. Plant hunting is his passion, and on an expedition to Panama in 2000, he was kidnapped for nine months; during the ordeal he came up with the idea for the garden, featuring rare plants from all over the globe.

Lullingstone Country Park
Kingfisher Bridge, Castle Road, Eynsford, DA4 0JF (01322 865995, www.lullingstonecastle.co.uk). Open 9am-9pm or dusk daily. Admission free.
The magnificent ancient trees here include oak, ash, sweet chestnut and hornbeam, some with life spans of over 800 years. Summer sees meadows bloom with wild flowers and a flurry of orchids. For an informative visit, arrange a guide for a 6.5-mile circular walk through the park. There's a visitor centre with café.

Places to visit

Keen gardeners will find much of interest at this seven-acre garden, the backdrop to a mellow 17th-century manor house. Expansive lawns give way to rare and exotic blooms, terraces and a woodland garden; in summer, the salvias are particularly glorious. There's also a gift shop, nursery and tearoom, serving lunches and afternoon teas.

Leeds Castle ★
Maidstone, ME17 1PL (01622 765400, www.leeds-castle.com). Open Apr-Sept 10am-6pm daily (last entry 1hr before closing). Oct-Mar 10am-5pm daily (last entry 1hr before closing). Admission £18.50; £11-£16 reductions (tickets are valid for a year).
Set on two grassy, interconnected islands on the River Len in Kent, Leeds Castle is often described as England's loveliest castle. Surrounded by water, it boasts a magnificent and much-photographed medieval exterior, with a mighty gatehouse and tall, crenelated towers and battlements. The interiors are largely the work of the castle's last private owner, Lady Baillie, who bought it in 1926 and refurbished it in opulent fashion.

The outdoor aviary is remarkable, holding more than 100 exotic bird species, while stately black swans glide around the moat. The grounds take in various gardens; planted with lupins, roses, lads' love and neat box hedges, the Culpepper Garden is particularly lovely. The yew maze, meanwhile, was planted in 1988; explorers make their escape via a dramatic underground grotto, adorned with eerie carvings of mythical beasts. The castle's dog collar museum adds a final quirky touch, with a collection spanning five centuries – from no-nonsense spiked iron bands to lavish velvet creations.

Maidstone Museum & Bentlif Art Gallery
St Faith's Street, ME14 1LH (01622 602838, www.museum.maidstone.gov.uk). Open 10am-5.15pm Mon-Sat; 11am-4pm Sun. Admission free.
Taking in Japanese fine art, shells from Pacific islands, and Egyptian mummies, the Maidstone Museum is an unexpectedly global affair. It has expanded since 1858, and now has several additional wings to the Elizabethan manor at its heart. The museum's 574 oil paintings are thought to be the largest public collection in Kent, and the watercolour and drawing collection totals over 2,500 works. A particularly impressive corner is the Egyptian Collection, which features a 2,700-year-old mummy.

Museum of Kent Life
Lock Lane, Sandling, ME14 3AU (01622 763936, www.kentlife.org.uk). Open Apr-Oct 10am-5pm Mon-Fri; 10am-6pm Sat, Sun. Jan-Mar, Nov, Dec 10am-4pm daily. Admission Summer £8.50; £6.50-£7.50 reductions. Winter £5; £3-£4 reductions.
Delve into the history of the county, browsing period buildings, finding out about farming traditions and meeting the animals. This 28-acre plot is part animal park, part restored buildings, with an assortment of farmyard animals and a birdhouse, alongside such buildings as a 1940s house. There are also donkey rides and junior quad biking. Arrive in style aboard the *Allington Belle* paddle boat (*see p38*) from Maidstone town centre.

Museum of Kent Life

Further east, All Hallows village is clustered around All Saints church, the only Grade I-listed building on the peninsula. Built of flint and stone, it has a lead roof, a wooden west tower and north and south porches to the nave (look at the west end for the oldest stone laid).

During the 19th century, the peninsula was well known for its links with smuggling. Tales include reports of contraband hidden on the island of Gantlebor near Yantlet creek, and of secret tunnels passing below the Hogarth Inn (High Street, 01634 270025) in the neighbouring village of Grain.

Cooling, a hamlet overlooking the North Kent Marshes, is one of the most atmospheric places on the peninsula. St James's (see p26), an abandoned 13th-century church set on bleak marshland, was the scene of Pip's meeting with the convict Magwitch in Great Expectations. At the edge of the marshes, 14th-century Cooling Castle (see p26) is also enchanting.

Where to eat & drink

Riva
Town Pier, West Street, Gravesend, DA11 0BJ (01474 364694, www.rivaonthepier.com). Open noon-midnight Mon-Sat; noon-8pm Sun. Lunch served noon-3pm Mon-Sat; noon-4pm Sun. Dinner served 6-10.30pm Mon-Sat.
Eat at the end of the oldest surviving cast iron pier in the world. Huge glass windows wrap around the restaurant, allowing views of the Thames – particularly lovely in the evening. The restaurant serves bistro dishes such as lamb shank with rosemary mash or seafood tagliatelle, while the bar offers snacks and a range of cocktails.

Rum Puncheon
87 West Street, Gravesend, DA11 0BL (01474 353434). Open 11am-11pm Mon-Fri; noon-11pm Sat; noon-10.30pm Sun. Lunch served noon-3pm daily. Dinner served 8-10pm Fri, Sat.
After a major refurbishment the pub is now decked out prettily with chandeliers, wrought iron lamps and dark wood. It's a cosy place to hunker down, with a variety of ales and a short menu of pub grub. Morning coffee and afternoon teas are also served by friendly and efficient staff.

Three Daws
7 Town Pier, Gravesend, DA11 0BJ (01474 566869, www.threedaws.co.uk). Open 11am-1am Mon-Sat; noon-1am Sun. Lunch served 11am-3pm Mon-Thur; noon-4.30pm Sun. Dinner served 6-9pm Mon-Thur. Food served 11am-9pm Fri, Sat.
Once a smugglers' haunt, the attraction of the Three Daws today lies in its position and views over the water. A simple menu (chilli con carne and rice; steak, kidney and ale pie) is the backdrop to a selection of real ales.

Where to stay
Accommodation in the area consists chiefly of chain hotels or small B&Bs such as Briars Court (90 Windmill Street, Gravesend, 01474 363788, www.briarscourt.talktalk.net), which has three clean, comfortable rooms.

Stable Cottages
Fenn Croft, Newlands Farm Road, St Mary Hoo, Rochester, ME3 8QS (01634 272439, www.stable-cottages.com). Rates 2-bedroom cottage £300-£550 per week. 4-bedroom cottage £600-£1,000 per week. No credit cards.
This complex of two- and four-bedroom self-contained cottages is set on 20 acres of quiet farmland on the Hoo Peninsula, tucked away down a private lane. There's also an indoor pool and sauna on site.

Thames House
29 Royal Pier Road, Gravesend, DA12 2BD (07805 477973, www.thameshouseandb.com). Rates £70-£85 double incl breakfast. No credit cards.
A lovingly maintained Grade II-listed building overlooking the Thames. Upstairs are three elegant, light-filled bedrooms, and downstairs is a warm kitchen where breakfast comes with home-made bread and jam, and eggs from the owners' hens. The rooms are stocked with little sewing kits and complimentary toiletries, and the town is right on your doorstep.

CHATHAM, GILLINGHAM & ROCHESTER

Chatham
The town's big tourist attraction is the Historic Dockyard Chatham (see p27), which has breathed new life into Chatham by transforming the dockyard into a wonderful museum, complete with three historic warships. (In fact, there's not much to see away from the waterside.) Wander the boat-strewn docks and look out to 16th-century Upnor Castle (Upper Upnor, 01634 718742, www.english-heritage.org.uk, open Apr-Oct), so close to the river it gives the illusion of floating.

Fort Amherst (Dock Road, 01634 847747, www.fortamherst.co.uk), a Napoleonic fortress used to protect the former Royal Dockyard and the route to London from attack, is also worth a visit. Pause for sustenance at the Blueberry Park sandwich bar (5 Military Road, 01634 832634, closed Sun), or one of the many eateries in and around the Dockside Outlet Centre (Maritime Way, 01634 899389, www.docksideshopping.co.uk), a converted Victorian boiler house.

Otherwise, there's always the Dickens World theme park (see p26). The author lived in Chatham as a child from 1817 to 1822, while his father worked at the dockyard as a clerk for the Royal Navy.

Gillingham
Like Chatham, Gillingham was once a naval hub – the majority of Chatham Dockyard is actually within Gillingham's town boundary. One of the area's most dramatic skirmishes was in 1667, when the Dutch sailed up the River Medway to invade Gillingham in what is remembered as the Raid on the Medway. The realisation of the vulnerability of the dockyard led to the construction of the Chatham Defence Lines: fortifications that ran across the dockyard peninsula from Chatham Reach to Gillingham Reach and included Fort Amherst (see above).

For wide open spaces without any military connection, Capstone Farm Country Park (Capstone Road) comprises 114 hectares of meadow, hedgerow and ancient woodland, and is a good place to stretch your legs or attempt the mountain bike course. Riverside Country Park (Lower Rainham Road, 01634 337432), a Site of Special Scientific Interest that includes the Motney Hill (www.rspb.org.uk) and Berengrave (www.friendsofberengrave.btik.com) nature reserves, is another welcome green space.

Back in town, Medway Park (Mill Road, 01634 336655, www.medwaypark.org.uk) has indoor pools, a gym, a dance studio, sports halls and a trampolining centre. There's also the Ice Bowl skating rink (Ambley Road, 01634 388477, www.theicebowl.co.uk) and a ski slope at Chatham Ski and Snowboard Centre (Capstone Road, Alpine Park, 01634 827979, www.chathamskislope.co.uk). The Strand Leisure Park (Pier Approach Road, 01634 573176) is good for a family day out, with an outdoor leisure pool, a miniature railway, a nine-hole golf course, a play area and a tearoom.

Rochester

Rochester had a huge influence on Charles Dickens, and celebrates that connection in the twice-yearly Dickens Festival (see p11). There are numerous plaques around town commemorating areas significant to Dickens' time in Rochester, and many of the places that inspired him can be visited. He gave Restoration House (17-19 Crow Lane, 01634 848520, www.restorationhouse.co.uk, open June-Sept Thur, Fri) the name 'Satis House', and made it the home of Miss Havisham in Great Expectations. The Six Poor Travellers House (97 High Street, 01634 845609, open Mar-Oct), a 16th-century almshouse, was claimed for The Seven Poor Travellers tale. Eastgate House on the High Street,

now a wedding venue, appeared in The Pickwick Papers (renamed as Westgate House), as did Rochester Castle (see p27) and Rochester Cathedral (see p27). The Guildhall Museum (see p26) has a Dickens Discovery room.

If you don't fancy following in Dickens' footsteps, details of various walking and ghost tours can also be found at the Medway Visitor Information Centre (95 High Street, 01634 843666, www.medway.gov.uk/tourism). Alternatively, leave dry land behind and climb aboard a steamship – the paddle steamer Kingswear Castle (01634 827648, www.pskc.freeserve.co.uk, Easter-mid Oct) offers river trips on the Medway and the Thames from Rochester and Chatham.

The town's most interesting shop is Baggins Book Bazaar (19 High Street, 01634 811651, www.bagginsbooks.co.uk), with its vast stock of second-hand books.

Where to eat & drink

Elizabeth's of Eastgate
154 High Street, Rochester, ME1 1ER (01634 843472, www.elizabethsofeastgate.co.uk). Lunch served noon-2pm Tue-Sun. Dinner served 6.30-9.30pm Tue-Sun.
Elizabeth's of Eastgate is mentioned as the home of Pip's Uncle Pumblechook in Great Expectations. The 16th-century building is located just a few minutes from Rochester Cathedral and Castle. It's a smart place, serving such dishes as game terrine with a port reduction, followed by grilled rump of Romney Marsh lamb with lyonnaise potato and rosemary jus.

Topes
60 High Street, Rochester, ME1 1JY (01634 845270, www.topesrestaurant.com). Lunch served noon-2.30pm Wed-Sun. Dinner served 6.30-9pm Wed-Sat.

Chatham Docks. See p31.

KENT

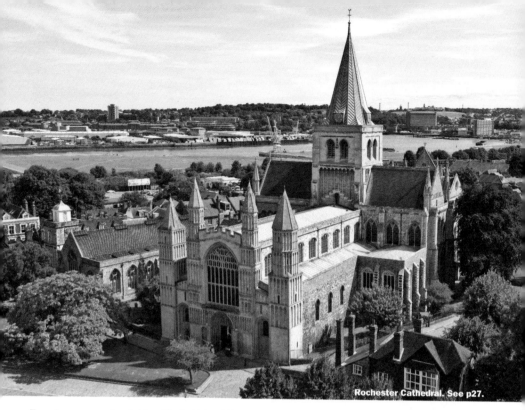

Rochester Cathedral. See p27.

Topes has a more modern feel than Elizabeth's (*see left*), but the building is old. Good-value set lunches might feature potted crab and shrimp with brioche loaf and lime crème fraîche, followed by rosemary and honey-glazed gammon with swede mash, curly kale and piccalilli.

Where to stay

Dockyard Bed & Breakfast
10 Officers Terrace, Historic Dockyard, Chatham, ME4 4LJ (07858 384712, www.dockyardbandb.com). Rates £60 double incl breakfast. No credit cards.
This one-room B&B is part of a Georgian terrace previously occupied by senior officials from Chatham Dockyard. Sensitively restored, the en suite room can work as a single, double or family room. Breakfasts (full english, with the choice of kippers) are served in the dining room. Guests have the use of a snooker table, and free parking at the end of the terrace.

Ship & Trades
Maritime Way, Chatham Maritime, ME4 3ER (01634 895200, www.shipandtradeschatham.co.uk). Rates £75 double incl breakfast.
A Shepherd Neame hotel, pub and restaurant in the shell of what was once dockyard offices and an engineering shop. The decor plays on this nautical heritage, with rough rope weaved around mirrors and wall-mounted prints of the docks and their water traffic. There are 11 simple en suite rooms. It's a good location for exploring the Chatham waterside, right on the waterfront (with Upnor Castle sitting

prettily on the other side of the River Medway) and close to Dickens World and the Historic Dockyard. The Dockside Outlet Shopping Centre, with its shops, eateries and cinema, is next door.

Sovereign
29 Medway Bridge Marina, Manor Lane, Borstal, ME1 3HS (01634 400474, www.thesovereignbb.co.uk). Rates £70-£85 double incl breakfast. No credit cards.
An unusual B&B: six snug rooms on a 1930s Rhine passenger ferry, moored permanently at the Medway Bridge Marina. There's a lounge with big windows looking on to the river. Sovereign is run by friendly couple who serve a breakfast almost large enough to sink the boat.

AROUND MEOPHAM

Meopham
Meopham, a village ranged along the A227, is an agreeable, quiet place with one of the longest village streets in England (around seven miles). Meopham Valley Vineyard is here (Wrotham Road, 01474 812727, www.meophamvalleyvineyard.co.uk; tours May-Sept), but Meopham is best known for its open spaces, specifically Camer Country Park, Trosley Country Park (for both, *see p27*) and the cricket ground.

There are four main greens in the parish: Culverstone Green, Harvel Green, Hook Green and, the best known, Meopham Green. Cricket has been played here since 1778, and it's one

Leeds Castle. See p30.

Things to do

River Medway and Millennium River Park

GRAVESEND & HOO PENINSULA

Wealdway Walk
www.ldwa.org.uk
This long-distance path starts at Town Pier in
Gravesend and continues south across the Weald,
an Area of Outstanding Natural Beauty. If you see
the walk through to the end, you'll cover 80 miles
and find yourself in Eastbourne on the Sussex coast,
via Tonbridge, Tunbridge Wells and Uckfield.

ROCHESTER, CHATHAM & GILLINGHAM

Buckmore Park
*Maidstone Road, Chatham, ME5 9QG (01634
201562, www.buckmore.co.uk). Open Mar-Oct 8am-
11pm Mon-Fri; 8am-9pm Sat; 10am-8pm Sun. Jan,
Feb, Nov, Dec 8am-10pm Mon-Fri; 8am-9pm Sat;
10am-8pm Sun. Rates vary; check website for details.*
This outdoor kart circuit has the biggest fleet of karts
for hire in the country. Its 1,200m circuit is available
to drivers from the age of four upwards, and was once
the practice ground of internationally renowned British
Formula 1 drivers Lewis Hamilton and Jenson Button.
As well as karts, there are quad bikes, Argocats,
Powerturn buggies and Laser Tag.

Diggerland
*Roman Way, Medway Valley Leisure Park, Strood,
ME2 2NU (0871 227 7007, www.diggerland.com).
Open times vary; check website for details. Admission
£17; £8.50 reductions.*
Budding Bob the Builders, *Scrapheap Challenge*
fans and anyone who digs diggers and dumpers,
take note: excavation heaven is here. Gouge
enormous holes out of the ground (and fill them
in again), drive construction machinery, race JCBs,
or watch, bemused, as formation diggers dance to
music. Kids can drive bulldozers and dumper trucks,
or zoom off on the Young Driver Experience – if they're
not too busy swinging in a giant JCB scoop or digging
for buried treasure.

Rochester Dickens Festival
*www.rochesterdickensfestival.org.uk.
Dates early June; 1st weekend Dec.*
A celebration of the author's life and work. Many
enthusiasts dress up in Victorian costume or as one
of his well-known characters, such as Oliver Twist,
Magwitch or Miss Havisham, with Ebenezer Scrooge
to the fore during the Christmas parade. There are
craft stalls and street entertainers, as well as grand
balls (one for each festival).

AROUND MEOPHAM

Brands Hatch Circuit
*Fawkham, Longfield, DA3 8NG (01474 872331,
www.motorsportvision.co.uk). Open by appointment.
Driving Experience from £99 adult; £79 children.*
Numerous international motoring firsts have taken
place here, such as the first British Touring Car race,
Nigel Mansell's first Grand Prix victory and Ayrton
Senna's first motor racing win.
    Over 30 events are held every year, including
DTM, British Superbikes and the FIA Formula 2
Championship. Amateurs can also take the wheel,
with the Driving Experience package.

MAIDSTONE & AROUND

Allington Belle Paddle Boat
*Mortar Inn, Allington Lock, Maidstone, ME14 3AU
(01622 661064, www.allingtonbelle.co.uk). Open
Easter-Oct 11am-4pm daily. Fare £5; £2 reductions.
No credit cards.*
Leaving from near the Millennium River Park, the
Allington Belle chugs along a six-mile stretch of the
River Medway, through Teston Country Park to the
Museum of Kent Life (*see p30*). It takes an hour.

KENT

of the best-kept cricket grounds in the country. It's overlooked by a Grade II-listed windmill: this is the current headquarters of the Parish Council but visits are possible in summer through the Windmill Trust (01474 813518).

Other buildings of note include the church of St John the Baptist on Wrotham Road. Built on the site of a Saxon church it dates back to 1325. In 1382 an earthquake caused the aisles to collapse, but these were rebuilt in 1386 and the church has remained in remarkably good shape since then. Look out for the beautiful stained glass windows. Just over a mile north, the 14th-century church of St Mildred in Nurstead (often referred to as 'the Little Church in the Field') is also worth a look.

Luddesdown

Luddesdown, east of Meopham, is a charming rural parish on the North Downs. It's on the Wealdway Walk (see left), and many walkers take a detour for refreshments at the 18th-century Cock Inn (Henley Street, 01474 814208, www.cock luddesdowne.com).

The parish takes its name from a settlement of houses and farms around Luddesdown Court Manor. The privately-owned Manor, which dates back to about 1100, is thought to be the oldest continuously inhabited house in England. St Peter and St Paul's Church (Luddesdown Road, www.cobham-luddesdowne.org) is a tiny structure, built in the Manor's grounds in the 13th century.

Close to Luddesdown is the site of a village wiped off the map by the Black Death in 1349. The only remnant of what was once the village of Dode (or Dowde) is a small deconsecrated Norman chapel (DA13 0XF, www.dodevillage.com), built in 1100. It's now a licensed civil wedding venue and also hosts memorial services and other ceremonies. Two cottages have also been built as 'a place of solitude and peace for those wishing to escape the world for a few days' (see below).

Cobham

Nearby, the handsome village of Cobham is a conservation area. The main thoroughfare is the Street, where you'll find St Mary Magdalene church, Owletts house and garden (see p27), three pubs and the quaint Cobham Village Store.

Charles Dickens was very fond of Cobham, and would often walk the grounds of Cobham Hall (see p27) and prop up the bar at the Leather Bottle, sometimes plucking scenes from the village for his novels. One of the landmarks that made it into print is the Old College, a set of beautifully preserved almhouses at the back of the church. They are thought to be Titbull's Almshouses in The Uncommercial Traveller.

Around the village are acres of woodland, including Cobham Park (surrounding Cobham Hall), Shorne Woods Country Park (see p26) and Jeskyns Community Woodland and Greenspace (Henhurst Road, 01474 825118, www.forestry.gov.uk).

This lovely countryside was the scene of one of Cobham's more grisly episodes – on 28 August, 1843, the painter Richard Dadd murdered his father, believing him to be the devil. His father's body was found at a chalk pit called Paddock Hole, since named Dadd's Hole, in the woodland just outside Cobham.

Where to eat & drink

George Inn ★
Wrotham Road, Meopham, DA13 0AH (01474 814198). Open 11am-11pm Mon-Sat; noon-10.30pm Sun. Lunch served noon-3pm Mon-Fri; noon-4pm Sat. Dinner served 6-10pm Mon-Sat. Food served noon-8pm Sun.

A characterful old pub with a heavy oak door, low ceiling and wonky wooden floors (plus a new extension; try to sit in the old part if you can). The bar serves Shepherd Neame ales and pub grub; more formal meals can be had in the restaurant. The George used to be a court room; today's car park is where the stocks were set up to punish offenders.

Green Man
Hodsoll Street, TN15 7LE (01732 823575, www.greenmanpub.com). Open 11am-2.30pm; 6pm-11pm Mon-Thurs; 11am-11pm Fri-Sat; noon-10.30pm Sun. Lunch served noon-2pm Mon-Fri; noon-3pm Sat. Dinner served 6.30-9.30pm Mon-Sat. Food served noon-8.30pm Sun.

Although a little hard to find, especially in the dark, the Green Man is worth it. (Coming from Meopham follow Wrotham Road and look out for the turning into the pretty hamlet of Hodsoll Street on the right, then follow the street to its end.) There's a friendly atmosphere, a fine choice of ales and decent pub fare (steak with pepper sauce, say, or beer battered cod). It's popular with walkers, who enjoy the open fire in winter and the garden in summer. Monday is quiz night, and occasionally there's live music too.

Twig & Spoon Bistro ★
Woodlands Garden Centre, Ash Lane, Ash, TN15 7EG (01474 852788, www.twigandspoon.co.uk). Open 9.30am-4.30pm Mon-Sat; 10am-4pm Sun.

A cut above the average garden centre café, with floor to ceiling windows and an attractive plant-lined courtyard. The menu is a revelation too: brunch options include kidneys and bacon on toast; light bites feature chicken liver pâté with red onion confit, while larger feeds include apple cider pork belly with butter beans. Nearly everything served at the Twig & Spoon is made on the premises, and much of the menu is sourced from the locality.

Where to stay

A peaceful getaway is guaranteed in two timber-framed cottages (wowww.hideaways.co.uk/holiday-cottage/hillview-H763) on the site of the abandoned village of Dode (see left); both sleep two.

The Darnley Arms (40 The Street, Cobham, 01474 814218) has three B&B rooms and serves a good english breakfast.

Beechfield Cottages
Little Beechfield Farm, Heron Hill Lane, Meopham, DA13 0QL (01474 815818, www.cottagecompany. co.uk). Rates from £500 per week. No credit cards.

Hengist. See p42.

These lovely cottages, set on three acres of land, each have a kitchen, lounge and bathroom, plus TV and DVD player, Wi-Fi, and views of the valley. Choose between the pretty Olde Chicken Shed Cottage or the Railway Cottage. Both can accommodate up to five people and are self-catering, though a continental breakfast is provided.

Leather Bottle

54-56 The Street, Cobham, DA12 3BZ (01474 814327, www.theleatherbottle.co.uk). Rates £69-£86 double incl breakfast.

Charles Dickens boarded in room six of this 17th-century inn, later describing it in *The Pickwick Papers* as a 'clean and commodious village ale-house'. There are six rooms in all, two of which have four-poster beds. Dickens memorabilia, including his death certificate, is dotted about the place. Pub grub classics are served in the bar and restaurant; real ales and a large garden complete the picture.

SEVENOAKS, WESTERHAM & EYNSFORD

Sevenoaks

Sevenoaks is a pleasant commuter town that has retained many characterful buildings. Knole (*see p28*), with its splendid house and 1,000-acre park, is on the south-east edge of the town. St Nicholas Church on Rectory Lane, opposite the entrance to the grounds of Knole, dates from the 13th century, although the majority of it was built in the 15th. John Donne was rector here in the 17th century, and two of Charles Dickens' daughters are buried in the churchyard.

From the church, walk down the right branch of the High Street to Chequers, a Grade II-listed coaching inn. Right on Buckhurst Lane, the Kaleidoscope (01732 453118, www.kent.gov.uk/sevenoakslibrary) is a library, local history museum and gallery. Along London Road is the Stag Community Arts Centre (01732 450175, www.stagsevenoaks.co.uk) a cinema, theatre and music venue. The Tourist Information Centre (01732 450305, www.sevenoakstown.gov.uk, closed Sun) is also in the complex.

Among the many nature reserves in the area are Kemsing Downs (01622 622012, www.kentwildlifetrust.org.uk) on the North Pilgrims Way just north of Sevenoaks; Dryhill Local Nature Reserve (Dryhill Lane, 01732 823 570, www.kent.gov.uk), in a former quarry; and Sevenoaks Wildlife Reserve (01622 622012, www.kentwildlifetrust.org.uk), a 55-hectare mixed habitat area that attracts a variety of birds. The Jeffery Harrison Visitor Centre here details the history of the site and has dioramas of local habitats.

On the southern edge of Sevenoaks, the North Downs Way and Greensand Way both pass by Riverhill House (*see p29*).

Eynsford

North of Sevenoaks is the valley of the River Darent and Eynsford (pronounced 'Ainsford'). It's a delightful stretch, and home to the Hop Farm (near Shoreham, 01959 523219, www.hompshop.co.uk) family farm and shop. The village of Eynsford is prepossessing, with a narrow, 450-year-old stone bridge leading over the Darent; larger vehicles have to traverse the ford.

Just off the High Street are the remains of Eynsford Castle (www.english-heritage.org.uk). It was built by William de Eynsford, who was at the centre of the argument between Thomas Becket and Henry II that led to the Archbishop of Canterbury's murder in 1170 (Thomas Becket excommunicated Eynsford, offending Henry II, who overruled the decision). Through the ford and under a viaduct is Lullingstone Roman Villa (*see p29*).

Also along this road is Eagle Heights (Hulberry Farm, Lullingstone Lane, 01322 866577, www.eagleheights.co.uk, closed Mon-Fri winter), a bird of prey centre with more than 150 resident raptors. Just beyond the villa, meanwhile, is Lullingstone Castle (*see p29*).

KENT

Westerham

To the west of Sevenoaks is Westerham, an upmarket commuter town that's full of Range Rovers and BMWs. On the village green are statues of the town's two most famous residents: Sir Winston Churchhill (who owned nearby Chartwell, *see p27*) and General James Wolfe (celebrated at Quebec House; *see p29*). Westerham is also within easy reach of Squerryes Court (*see p29*) and Charts Edge Garden (*see p28*).

There's good shopping to be had too. The Design Gallery (5 The Green, 01959 561234, www.designgallery.co.uk) specialises in Arts and Crafts furniture and art deco pieces. Also overlooking the green is Judy French (3 The Green, 01959 562575, www.judyfrench.com, closed Sun) a small boutique; next door Amelia Rose (2 The Green, 01959 565104, www.amelia-rose.co.uk, closed Sun) sells handbags. Manuka Shoes (15 High Street, 01959 565644, www.manukashoes. com, closed Sun) has belts, scarves and jewellery alongside the shoes.

There's also a well-attended farmers' market (www.westerhamkent.org.uk) on the first and third Sunday morning of each month, held in the town's Market Square.

Where to eat & drink

In Sevenoaks, the White Hart (Tonbridge Road, 01732 452022, www.brunningandprice.co.uk/ whitehart) is a reliable bet for decent food and real ales. To the east of Sevenoaks in Godden Green, the Bucks Head (01732 761330, www.buckshead goddengreen.co.uk) has a more Mediterranean menu and a welcoming atmosphere.

In Westerham, Food for Thought (19-20 the Green, 01959 569888, www.foodforthought.eu) is a pleasant spot for tea and cakes, overlooking the green. For liquid refreshment, the 16th-century coaching inn the George & Dragon (Market Square, 01959 563071, www.george-and-dragon-pub-in-westerham.co.uk) is a cosy option. The Kings Arms (Market Square, 01959 562990, www.kingsarms-westerham-kent.co.uk), an imposing 18th-century hostelry frequented by Churchill, has been modernised over the years and feels a little bland, but does have 17 spruce bedrooms to offer.

George & Dragon

The Street, Ightham, TN15 9HH (01732 882440, www.harrisinns.co.uk/the-george-and-dragon). Open 11am-11pm Mon-Thur; 11am-midnight Fri, Sat; noon-10.30pm Sun. Lunch served noon-4pm Mon-Thur, Sun. Dinner served 6-9pm Mon-Thur. Food served noon-9pm Fri, Sat.
There's a lot of history (Guy Fawkes and Elizabeth I are among the names dropped) attached to this snug rural inn; what matters today is the setting (open fires and exposed beams) and the food and drink. Food is substantial, seasonal fare; local venison sausages with garlic mash and red onion gravy, perhaps, or an upmarket ploughman's lunch. Ales are Shepherds Neame.

Plough

High Cross Road, Ivy Hatch, TN15 0NL (01732 810100, www.theploughivyhatch.co.uk). Open noon-3pm, 6-11pm Mon-Fri; 10am-11pm Sat; 10am-6pm Sun. Lunch served noon-2.45pm, dinner served noon-2.45pm Mon-Fri. Food served noon-9.30pm Sat; noon-6pm Sun.
The USP of this refurbished village inn is the pancake menu. The sweet pancake is given a decidedly Kentish flavour, with cider-poached pear and clotted cream, while savoury options include chicken, mushroom and shallot, or smoked bacon, roast tomato, goat's cheese and pesto. On the main menu are such dishes as baked smoked haddock with new potatoes, spinach, wholegrain mustard sauce and poached egg; the bar menu has an own-made steak burger

KENT

Archbishop's Palace. See p40.

with chips, classy sandwiches and a ploughman's. Drinks include real ales and local wines. There's a cosy bar, a dining room, gardens and a terrace.

Where to stay

Comfortable rooms and friendly staff in a convenient high street location can be had at the Royal Oak Hotel in Sevenoaks (High Street, 01732 451109, www.the-royal-oak-hotel.co.uk), and the Kings Arms (*see p39*) in Westerham.

Good B&Bs include the 16th-century Old Farm House (430 Main Road, Westerham Hill, 01959 571003, www.theoldfarmhousewesterham.co.uk), which has four rooms, and Cabbages & Kings (Old Post Office, Church Road, Halstead, 01959 533054, www.cabbages-and-kings.co.uk), which has three. The latter is an old flint house, once the post office and village store of Halstead.

Starborough Manor

Marsh Green, Edenbridge, TN8 5QY (01732 862152, www.starboroughmanor.co.uk). Rates £130 double incl breakfast. Apartment £800-£1100 per week.
Starborough Manor offers three smart bed and breakfast rooms (also available as a self-catering apartment). All rooms have lovely views over the grounds. Breakfast includes full english or scrambled eggs with smoked salmon or kippers.

MAIDSTONE & AROUND

Maidstone

Maidstone was built up around the River Medway and has been a market town since 1549. The centre of Maidstone is marred by a multi-storey car park, a shopping centre and other unsightly constructions. Down by the river, however, are some beautiful buildings and a good riverside walk.

Although it's hard to imagine today, in the tightly knit centre, pedestrianised Gabriel's Hill was a key site of the Battle of Maidstone during the English Civil War. More than 300 Royalists were killed here. Also of note on Gabriel's Hill is the Golden Boot (nos.25-31, 01622 752349, www.thegoldenboot. co.uk, closed Sun). Established in 1790, it's the UK's oldest family-owned shoe shop. When this shop first opened, Maidstone was a lively town that saw hops, wool and, increasingly, paper being transported along the Medway.

More history is revealed on nearby Earl Street. Mayor of Maidstone Andrew Broughton was the person who, as the High Court Justice, declared the death sentence on Charles I. A plaque on Earl Street where he used to live states: 1603-1688 Mayor & Regicide.

West down the High Street is the Tourist Information Centre (High Street, 01622 602169, closed Sun). Running parallel to the High Street is Bank Street. Look up to see original façades of the 17th-century shops. At the end, walk south down Mill Street to the oldest part of Maidstone. From here you can admire the exterior of the Archbishop's Palace (now the Register Office).

TEN KENT CHURCHES

All Saints, Waldershare

Aside from the delightful rural setting, in a villlage near Dover, the highlight of this Norman church is the memorials, especially one to the Bertie family in the. south chapel, which features life-size figures of husband and wife holding hands. In the north chapel there's a monument to Sir Henry Furnese, which rises in tiers to the ceiling. A Victorian nave and Victorian stained glass are other features.

All Saints, West Stourmouth

This charming ragstone and flint church near the River Stour is no longer used for worship, but the wooden bell-cote, Georgian box pews and finely carved Jacobean pulpit make for fascinating viewing. This remote building has Saxon roots, but alterations over the years have left their mark; the church suffered particular damage in an earthquake in 1382, and was largely rebuilt.

Canterbury Cathedral

Archbishop Thomas Becket met a brutal end beneath its roof, and thousands of pilgrims have made their way here (as depicted by Geoffrey Chaucer in *The Canterbury Tales*). Today, Canterbury Cathedral is the seat of the head of the Church of England, the Archbishop of Canterbury. See the Romanesque Water Tower, admire the gothic nave, and hear the oldest of its 21 bells, Bell Harry, chime at 8am and 9pm each day to mark the opening and closing of the cathedral. *See p80.*

Rochester Cathedral

Rochester is a particularly venerable cathedral, being second only in age to Durham. It was founded in 604 by Bishop Justus, and is an exceptional example of a Norman church. The doorway of the western entrance is much revered, depicting the figures of Christ, Justus and King Ethelbert of Kent. *See p27.*

St Benedict, Paddlesworth

Scores of weary pilgrims have said their prayers in this tiny church on the Pilgrims Way, near Snodland. This is a modest place comprised of a chancel and a nave, set amid 18th-century red-brick farmhouses, with the North Downs providing a striking backdrop.

Mulberry Tree. See p43.

St Clement, Knowlton

This may be a small church, set between the main house and outbuildings of grand Knowlton Court (www.knowltoncourt. co.uk), but the monuments and stained glass make for something special. Note the fine tomb thought to be by English sculptor Grinling Gibbons, honouring the sons-in-law of renowned naval officer Sir Cloudesley Shovell.

St James, Cooling

St James' churchyard, and its eerie marsh-side location, is believed to have inspired the setting for the meeting between Pip and the convict Magwitch in *Great Expectations*. Inside the church, impressive stonework dates back to the late 13th century. A minute 19th-century vestry is lined with cockleshells – the emblem of St James – and monuments include a brass effigy of the wife of Lord Cobham of Cooling Castle, Lady Feyth Brook. *See p26.*

St Mary's, Luddenham, Faversham

A modest church that hasn't been used for services since the early 1970s. To the south of the River Swale, tucked away on a patch of farmland, St Mary's is a collage of ages, from the west doorway's zigzag pattern dating back to the early 12th century to the little brick tower built in 1806.

St Mary the Virgin, Fordwich

This unassuming church is over 900 years old, and features a shingled spire, box pews and 17th-century rails. Also here are the Royal Arms and Commandments (painted on the plaster) from 1688, a 12th-century font of Bethersden marble, and the Fordwich Stone, a chunk of limestone, carved in 1100 in the semblance of a tomb.

St Peter's, Sandwich

St Peter's is at the heart of Sandwich (*see p89*), and still earns its keep with the occasional service and a host of public events, including exhibitions and recitals. It is of Norman origin, but with Dutch design and brickwork in the tower and the gable – evidence of Sandwich's role as a bolthole for Protestant refuges from the Netherlands; they helped to repair the church when part of it collapsed in the 1600s.

Aylesford

KENT

Opposite is the Tyrwhitt-Drakes Museum of Carriages (Mill Street, 01622 602838, www.museum.maidstone.gov.uk/tyrwhittdrake). It closes during the winter and faces an uncertain future, so call ahead.

A footpath links the Palace and All Saints Church (Mill Street, 01622 843298, www.maidstoneallsaints.co.uk, open Easter-Sept Tue-Sat). It was built in 1398, and largely untouched. Next to the church is the College of All Saints, built around the same time as the church. By the river is the Lockmeadow Millennium footbridge, the start of a six mile-walk to Allington Castle and the Museum of Kent Life; the *Allington Belle* (*see p36*) can also be found near here.

Aylesford

Ignore the unattractive industrial estates around the M20 north of Maidstone, and head straight for Aylesford, an exquisitely preserved riverside village over which a Norman church presides. It was the location of the Battle of Aylesford in 455, a conflict between the Britons and the Anglo-Saxons led by Hengist (after which Richard Phillips' restaurant is named; *see right*).

Take time to wander the village and along the riverbank to the Old Bridge, parts of which date back to 1250. There's a lovely view from the riverside patio in the Chequers (High Street, 01622 717286). On the outskirts of the town is the Friars (01622 717272, www.thefriars.org.uk), an ancient priory. More than 200,000 pilgrims a year still arrive at its gates. The grounds are open year round (admission is free), and there's also a book and gift shop and a tearoom.

Just north of Aylesford is Kits Coty House, a Neolithic tomb. Diarist Samuel Pepys described it best: 'Three great stones standing upright and a great round one lying on them, of great bigness, although not so big as those on Salisbury Plain. But certainly it is a thing of great antiquity.'

Where to eat & drink

In Maidstone, the most characterful pub is the crooked, Tudor building of Ye Olde Thirsty Pig (Knightrider Street, 01622 755655). Fortify Café (32 High Street, 01622 670533, www.fortifycafe.co.uk) is a vegetarian eatery with a good reputation. Oak on the Green (Bearsted Green, 01622 737976, www.oakonthegreen.com) in Bearstead, a suburb of Maidstone, is a charming free house with dry hops hanging from the ceiling.

The best places to eat are outside of Maidstone city centre; most are also handy for visits to Leeds Castle. The Pepperbox Inn (Windmill Hill, Fairbourne Heath, 01622 842558, www.thepepperboxinn.co.uk) has a welcoming atmosphere, Shepherd Neame beers and the best food in the vicinity.

Just over five miles away in Headcorn is the George & Dragon (01622 890239), a characterful pub with good beers and ciders. It also serves food – though you might be lured in by the Headcorn Teashop (01622 890682) instead, with its array of own-made cakes.

Hengist ★
7-9 High Street, Aylesford, ME20 7AX (01622 719273, www.hengistrestaurant.co.uk). Lunch served noon-2.30pm Tue-Sat; noon-4.30pm Sun. Dinner served 6.30-10.30pm Tue-Sat.
Co-owned by chef Richard Phillips (who also has Thackeray's of Tunbridge Wells and Chapel Down of Tenterden in his stable), Hengist has gained a reputation for fine dining with such dishes as slow roasted pork belly with parsnip and sage terrine, creamed savoy cabbage and

apple and sage compote. The food is superb, beautifully presented and served in elegantly designed rooms that are sympathetic to the 16th century building's original features. Jazz musicians play on Thursday nights.

Kits Coty Brasserie
15 Old Chatham Road, Bluebell Hill, Aylesford, ME20 7EZ (01634 684445, www.kitscoty.co.uk). Lunch served noon-2.30pm Tue-Fri, Sun. Dinner served 7-9.30pm Tue-Sat.
Far-reaching views complement this contemporary dining space on Bluebell Hill. Start with Scottish scallops and black pudding on pea risotto, move on to grilled swordfish, followed by plum and amaretti crumble. Vegetarians are well catered for, with baked mushroom and goat's cheese pie with saffron sauce a particular highlight.

Mulberry Tree
Hermitage Lane, Boughton Monchelsea, ME17 4DA (01622 749082, www.themulberrytreekent.co.uk). Lunch served noon-2pm Tue-Sat; noon-2.15pm Sun. Dinner served 6.30-9pm Tue-Thur; 6.30-9.30pm Fri, Sat.
A sleek restaurant with a menu featuring Glassenbury Estate partridge with a parfait of livers and carrot purée, or ham hock terrine with pineapple pickle, fried quail's egg and chips. Puddings are equally enticing: milk chocolate torte with Kentish cherry jelly and honeycomb, for example. An extensive wine list includes some local names. On warm days, all this can be enjoyed from the terrace or garden.

Where to stay
Maidstone's location on the M20 means there's a wide range of chain hotels, including the Hilton Maidstone (Bearsted Road, 01622 734322, www.hilton.co.uk/maidstone), Ramada Maidstone (0844 815 9045, www.ramadajarvis.co.uk/maidstone) and Marriott Tudor Park (Ashford Road, 01622 734334, www.marriott.co.uk).

Black Horse Inn
Pilgrims Way, Thurnham, nr Maidstone, ME14 3LD (01622 737185, www.wellieboot.net). Rates £85-£90 double incl breakfast.
The Black Horse is a lovely country pub, located three miles from Maidstone, with dry hops hanging from the ceiling, a log fire and brick floors. The pet-friendly B&B accommodation is in an annexe. The 30 neat rooms each have TV, Wi-Fi and tea and coffee making facilities. It's nothing fancy, but this place offers more character than the chain hotels on the M20.

Welsummer ★
Chalk House, Lenham Road, Harrietsham, ME17 1NQ (01622 844048, www.welsummercamping.com). £12-£20 per pitch, plus £3 adult, £1 child (3-13 years).
This lovely campsite is named after a breed of chicken, and is a welcoming, unpretentious place. The approach is on small country lanes, but the site is just south of the M20, and conveniently close to a couple of train stations. Welsummer is a small site – two fields and some woodland – dotted with fruit trees. The owner used to camp on this land with her family when she was a child, and it retains an appealingly intimate feel. The atmosphere is laid-back, with helpful staff and few rules – just enough to stop the site becoming unruly. Thoughtful touches include the hand basin at children's height in the shower block, and the fact that cars are parked in a large field away from the tents.

Welsummer

Sittingbourne to Herne Bay

Some of the most beautiful stretches of Kent can be found on the north coast, and there are some interesting towns too. The delights of Whitstable are well known: colourful fishermen's huts (now trendy accommodation, of course), oysters, independent shops and good restaurants. But less talked-about places can be just as fun to visit. Herne Bay, for example, a little further to the east, is what Whitstable used to be – an unpretentious seaside town. The coast is also generously peppered with fine examples of British architecture, from beautifully preserved pubs to sprawling country manors. A cluster are to be found in Faversham, and include Britain's oldest brewery, Shepherd Neame. The rest is all about quiet pleasures; historical towns, wild coastline and marshlands, and the kind of flourishing countryside that has given Kent its reputation as the garden of England.

ISLE OF SHEPPEY

The Isle of Sheppey, spurned by many because of its down-at-heel reputation, does get some tourist footfall. A loyal band of holidaymakers, mainly with young families, troop to traditional seaside resorts such as Sheerness and Leysdown every year. Then there are the naturalists, who comb the marshlands and coast for wildlife, and, well, the naturists, who head for one of Britain's few official nudist beaches at Leysdown-on-Sea.

Lying in the Thames Estuary, the Isle of Sheppey is made up of three main islands: Sheppey, the Isle of Harty and the Isle of Elmley. It's separated from the mainland of Kent by the Swale channel, and is accessible via the Sheppey Crossing Bridge and the Sheerness-Sittingbourne rail link. It's 36 square miles in area, and criss-crossed by little channels. This is marshy land, particularly in the south, but for fossil hunters and birdwatchers, there's much treasure in the damp, wild landscape.

At the southern wetlands of the RSPB site at Elmley Marshes (*see p48*), visitors hunker down in hides and watch curlews, teals, starlings, hen harriers, rough-legged buzzards and a few short-eared owls. The Swale National Nature Reserve (*see p48*) on the Isle of Harty also provides access to the wild, winged and wading creatures of coastal marshlands, including migrant moths, rare butterflies, waterfowl, barn owls and Montagu's harriers. Meanwhile, fossil hunters chip and sieve away at the shore between Sheerness and Warden Point, where a bounty of London clay has been known to offer up shark teeth and vertebrae, fossil worms, turtle shells, plant remains and snake bones.

For those who prefer lying on the coast, there are sand and pebble beaches, and plenty of affordable holiday homes in the north. The old naval town of Sheerness – the largest town on the island, tucked away in the north-west corner – offers plenty of holiday accommodation, as well as a Blue Flag beach (on Beach Street), Barton's Point Coastal Park (Marine Parade, www.bartonspoint.com), seaside shops and amusement arcades. There's a market (Rose Street car park, 8.30am-3.30pm Tue and Sat) and, for what it's worth, the largest freestanding cast-iron clock tower in Kent; set at the junction of the High Street and Broadway, it's 36 feet high.

Sheerness is also home to Blue Town, so-named for the blue wash the first houses were painted in the 1700s; dockers had stolen Admiralty blue paint. Many of the houses were later destroyed by fire, and new houses were built and the dockyard redeveloped, reopening in 1823. Find out more at the Sheerness Heritage Centre (Rose Street, 01795 663317, www.sheernessheritagecentre. com), housed in a 19th-century weatherboard cottage once inhabited by a docker.

West of Sheerness is the old harbour town of Queenborough, the last royal new town of the Middle Ages. Its church, built in 1366, is the only remaining building from that period, but its name, has survived. It was named for Queen Philippa, wife of Edward III, who between 1361 and 1377 built a castle here as a defence against French raids. Cromwell ordered its demolition in the early 1650s, but the castle's story lives on at the Guildhall Museum (01795 667295, open Apr-Oct Sat afternoons) in the High Street.

Leysdown, on the eastern tip of the island, is a traditional seaside resort with a sandy beach, holiday accommodation, amusements, pubs and clubs. Half a mile south-east of the main Shell Ness beach is one of the UK's few official naturist beaches. To get there, follow the signs for Shell Ness and head down a bumpy road (but be aware that the site has been known to suffer from 'meerkats', that is, gawpers).

Minster, on the north coast, occupies Sheppey's highest point and, in a landscape barely above sea

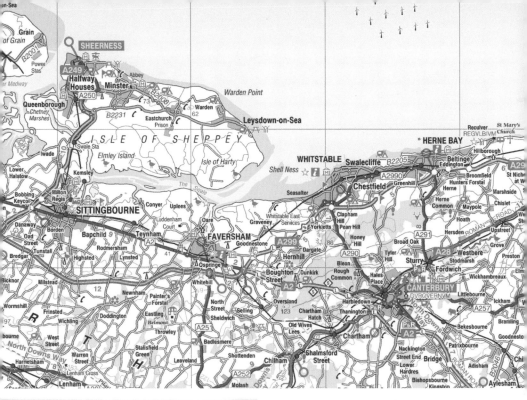

Whitstable. See p57.

level, is in the rare position of providing a raised view. Walk along the Minster cliff paths, home to rare orchids, plant and sea fossils, and horse grass. Minster Abbey, founded as a nunnery around 670, sits on the hilltop and has been a place of worship for more than 1,400 years. The old gatehouse is now the Minster Abbey Gatehouse Museum (01795 875111, open June-Oct Tue, Wed, Fri-Sun; Easter-May Wed, Sat), exhibiting fossils, wartime relics, Roman coins, Victorian costumes and other bits and pieces from the town's past. Occasional guided walks can be taken courtesy of Kent County Council; see www.guidedwalks.kent.gov.uk for details. The battlements, 200 feet above sea level, make a nice viewing platform from which to plot your next adventure across the island.

Where to eat & drink

Ferry House Inn

Harty Ferry Road, Harty, ME12 4BQ (01795 510214, www.theferryhouseinn.co.uk). Open 11am-3pm, 6.30-11pm Tue-Fri; 11am-11pm Sat; noon-6pm Sun. Food served noon-2.30pm, 6.30-9pm Tue-Sat; noon-9pm Sat; noon-4pm Sun.

This 16th-century inn seems very remote, surrounded by glistening marsh, chattering birds and open sky, but in fact it's quite an easy journey from London. The inn has moorings in the Swale Estuary and has become popular with people who moor their yachts and then row in for dinner. They come for excellent, unfussy food and the tranquillity of the location.

Isle of Sheppey. See p44.

Leysdown beach. See p44.

Places to visit

ISLE OF SHEPPEY

Elmley Marshes
Kings Hill Farm, Elmley, ME12 3RW (01795 665969, www.rspb.org.uk). Open 9am-9pm (or dusk if earlier) Mon, Wed-Sun. Admission free. Suggested donations for non-members £2.50; 50p-£1.50 reductions; £4.50 family. No credit cards.
This wilderness, far from the caravan parks, holiday homes and amusements of the coast, is one of the principal attractions on the Isle of Sheppey. Part of the National Nature Reserve managed by Elmley Conservation Trust, it's home to five hides and many birds, including buzzards, avocets, merlins, golden plovers, teals, hen harriers and pintails. A viewpoint at Capel Fleet, a few miles away, is said to be the best place in the UK for spotting birds of prey.

St Thomas the Apostle
Harty (01795 875146, www.hartychurch.org.uk). Open dusk-dawn daily.
Those attracted to the peace and quiet found in Sheppey's remoter parts often seek out this Norman church. Built in 1089, it stands serenely and virtually unchanged in the remote hamlet of Harty, lit by oil lamps and candles (there's no electricity). Notice the timber framing at the west end of the nave, which is the source of some mystery; many hold that it's a form of ancient lookout tower that predates the church. You'll also find the ornately carved Harty Chest, dating from the 14th century.

Swale National Nature Reserve
Shellness Road, Leysdown-on-sea, ME12 4RJ (0845 600 3078, www.naturalengland.org.uk). Open 24hrs daily. Admission free.
This reserve, a Special Protection Area, offers a different, saltier-watered Kentish landscape to Elmley Marshes. It can be found on a strip of coast in the Harty Marshes, running from Shell Ness in the east to the Ferry Inn (*see p45*) in the west. There are three hides – look out for waterfowl, rare butterflies and moths, and both short eared and barn owls. A nature trail takes in rare plants found on the mudflats, marshes and beach, including narrow-leaved and dwarf eel grass, grassworts, golden samphire and white sea kale.

MILTON REGIS & SITTINGBOURNE

Holy Trinity Church
Green Porch Close, Milton Regis, ME10 2HA (01795 472016, www.holytrinitymiltonregis.com). Open Apr-Oct 10am-4pm Sat and by appointment.
One of the oldest churches in Kent, founded around the arrival of St Augustine in 597, Holy Trinity is believed to have been built over a sacred pagan site. The theory is reinforced by what is thought to be a pagan altar stone in front of the porch, and tiles dating from Roman times on the walls. The church was altered under Norman influence, clearly seen in the thick-walled tower, built between 1310 and 1330.

Sittingbourne Heritage Museum
67 East Street, Sittingbourne, ME10 5ZZ (01795 471876, www.sittingbourne-museum.co.uk). Open Summer 10am-4pm Sat. Admission free.

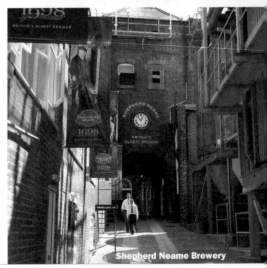

Shepherd Neame Brewery

This quaint little museum opened in 1999 – locals had been collecting memorabilia for it since the 1970s. As well as the artefacts donated by the town, the museum often organises displays of historical scenes in makeshift shops, houses and public buildings.

FAVERSHAM

Belmont House & Gardens
Throwley, ME13 0HH (01795 890202, www.belmonthouse.org). Open House & gardens Easter-Sept Sat, Sun. Guided tours 2.15pm, 2.45pm, 3.30pm. Gardens only 10am-6pm (or dusk if earlier) daily. Admission House & gardens £7; £4-£6 reductions. Gardens only £4; £1.50-£2 reductions. No credit cards.
Both the lovely house and gardens of the Belmont Estate, a ten-minute drive south of Faversham, are open to the public. The original house was built in 1769, but most of what exists today was constructed at the end of the 18th century to a neo-classical design by Samuel Wyatt. Belmont is notable for the collection of clocks amassed by the 5th Lord Harris. The grounds include a restored walled kitchen garden, acres of park and woodland and a lovely vista of the Kentish Downs. The cricket pitch is used for matches in summer.

Farming World
Nash Court, Boughton, ME13 9HY (01227 751144, www.farming-world.com). Open Mar-Oct 9.30am-5.30pm daily. Admission £6; £4-£5 reductions.
Pigs, ponies, pheasants, llamas, alpacas and birds of prey are found on this working and breeding farm, just east of Faversham. It's a big family attraction in the area, complete with play spaces, gardens, tractor rides and a full diary of events for kids. There is also a Mower Museum, housing the largest collection of lawnmowers in the South-east.

Mount Ephraim Gardens
Hernhill, ME13 9TX (01227 751496, www.mount ephraimgardens.co.uk). Open Easter-Sept noon-5pm Wed-Sun. Admission £5; £1-£2.50 reduction.
Ten acres of Edwardian gardens near Faversham, featuring rose terraces, yew hedges, a water garden, vineyard, lake and Japanese gardens. There are Edwardian tearooms and a gift shop too.

National Fruit Collection
Brogdale Road, Faversham, ME13 8XZ (01795 536250, www.brogdalecollections.co.uk). Open Mar-Oct 10am-5pm daily. Jan, Feb, Nov, Dec 10am-4.30pm daily. Guided tours £7; £3-£6.50 reductions; £17 family. Self-guided walk £5; £2.50-£4.50 reductions; £12.50 family.
Brogdale Farm is home to Britain's most extensive orchards. There are more than 2,000 types of apple (and 500 of pear) among its 4,000 varieties of fruit. One-hour guided walks through the orchards enable you to pick your own apples and learn about the varieties, and there's even a little railway. Visit in October for Apple Week, when there are apple displays and tastings, craft stalls and a hog roast. Other festivals are devoted to cherries (July) and cider (September).

Shepherd Neame Brewery ★
17 Court Street, Faversham, ME13 7AX (01795 532206, www.shepherdneame.co.uk). Open Shop 10.30am-4.30pm Mon-Sat. Tours check website for dates. Tours £10.75; £8.50-£10 reductions.
Britain's oldest brewer the handsome Shepherd Neame Brewery contains a shop and a bar as well as the brewery. The tour reveals Faversham's 850-year-old brewing history, and explains the brewing process – with tastings, of course.

WHITSTABLE

Horsebridge Centre
11 Horsebridge Road, Whitstable, CT5 1AF (01227 281174, www.horsebridge-centre.org.uk). Open 9am-6pm Mon-Sat; 10am-6pm Sun.
A purpose-built arts centre with a wide programme of events, the Horsebridge contains an art gallery, a performance space and a café.

Whitstable Castle & Gardens
The Gate House, Tower Hill, Whitstable, CT5 2BW (01227 281726, www.whitstablecastle.co.uk). Open Gardens 8am-1hr before dusk daily. Orangery Tea Room 10am-4pm Wed-Sun.
The castle and its grounds (a park with ornamental gardens and a playground) have been recently restored. Now run by Canterbury City Council, it's used for weddings, classes and community events. Also on site are a tearoom and an art studio and gallery.

Whitstable Museum & Gallery
Oxford Street, Whitstable, CT5 1DB (01227 276998, www.canterbury.co.uk). Open July, Aug 10am-4pm Mon-Sat; 1-4pm Sun. Jan-June, Sept-Dec 10am-4pm Mon-Sat. Admission free.
This small museum is filled with artefacts, paintings and photographs relating to local shipping, fishing, oyster-catching and diving. There are half a dozen special exhibitions per year.

HERNE BAY

Reculver Towers & Roman Fort
3 miles east of Herne Bay, CT6 6SS (www.english-heritage.org.uk.
About three miles east along the seafront from Herne Bay lie the impressive 12th-century towers of a ruined church (most of which was demolished in 1809), a Roman 'Saxon Shore' fort and a Saxon monastery. Take in the ruins and stay for a spot of birdwatching. Or gaze at the sun setting over the sea where Barnes Wallis secretly tested his famous bouncing bomb (as immortalised in the 1955 film *The Dam Busters*).

Wildwood
Off the A291, Herne Common, CT6 7LQ (01227 712111, www.wildwoodtrust.org). Open Apr-Sept 10am-6pm daily. Oct 10am-5.30pm daily. Mar 10am-5pm daily. Nov-Feb 10am-4pm daily. Admission £9.95; £7.95-£8.95 reductions; £32.50 family.
This wildlife park a few miles south of Herne Bay has an array of creatures, from red squirrels and badgers to wolves and Arctic foxes. There's also an adventure playground, an education centre and a restaurant.

Read's. See p55.

Nic's Restaurant

4 Railway Terrace, Queenborough, ME11 5AY (01795 661146). Lunch served 12.30-2.30pm (bookings only), dinner served 7-9pm Mon-Sat.

A nice little place serving tasty, own-made grub. The menu lists British and continental dishes that rely heavily on seasonal vegetables, local meat and fish fresh from the harbour. Under-12s eat for half price. Home-made fudge, jams and preserves are also for sale.

Old House at Home

High Street, Queenborough, ME11 5AA (01795 662463, http://web.mac.com/payre67/old_house/Welcome.html). Open noon-midnight Mon-Thur, Sun; noon-1am Fri, Sat. Food served noon-9pm Mon-Sat; noon-4pm Sun.

A local favourite thanks to friendly staff, a warm atmosphere, cask ales and decent pub food. The big window that frames sunsets over the sea is another plus. For a closer view, and a bit of banter, take drinks to the benches outside. Live music kicks off at 4pm on Sunday afternoon, and there are jamming sessions from 8pm on Wednesdays.

Where to stay

Along Sheppey's coast are plenty of caravan parks, campsites and B&Bs. Large concerns such as Ashcroft Coast Holiday Park at Minster-on-Sea (Plough Road, 0844 210 2013, www.park-resorts.com), Warden Springs Holiday Park at Eastchurch (Thorn Hill Road, 0844 210 2013, www.park-resorts.com) and Harts Holiday Park at Leysdown-on-Sea (Leysdown Road, 0845 815 9775, www.parkholidaysuk.com) have the monopoly on family holiday accommodation, but there's a good range of self-catering options across the island. Try Connetts Farm (Plough Road, 01795 880358, www.connettsfarm.co.uk) in Eastchurch, and Mulberry Cottages (01233 813087, www.mulberrycottages.com), which has choices in various locations. In Sheerness, the Royal Hotel (29 Broadway, 01795 662626, www.theroyalhotel-online.co.uk) has 14 simple rooms (£55-£80 incl breakfast) and is two minutes from the beach.

Muswell Manor

Shellness Road, Leysdown-on-Sea, ME12 4RJ (01795 510245, www.muswellmanor.co.uk). Rates £65 double incl breakfast.

Stay near the birthplace of British aviation: the first recorded aeroplane flight in Britain took off in 1909 from outside this Grade II-listed 16th-century building. It was also the site of the first headquarters of the UK Aero Club, and next to the site of the Short brothers' first factory. The Manor is close to the wildlife-rich Harty marshes, a bird sanctuary and the beachcombing heaven of Shellness. As well as a caravan park, there are three neat B&B rooms, a bar and a restaurant.

MILTON REGIS & SITTINGBOURNE

Milton Regis

Although Sittingbourne now counts Milton Regis as a village within its district, in medieval times it was the other way around: Sittingbourne came under the

FIVE KENT BREWERIES

Gadds' Ramsgate Brewery
www.ramsgatebrewery.co.uk.
Opened in 2002, Gadds is a fabulous little brewery that makes top-notch ales that are sold in pubs all over the county, but especially around Thanet (check the website for locations). Regular brews include the imaginatively named No.3, No.5 and No.7. The splendid Black Pearl bottled beer was created especially for Eddie Gilbert's fish restaurant (*see p76*) in Ramsgate.

Goacher's
www.goachers.com.
Based in Maidstone, this small producer has been in business for more than 25 years. It currently brews seven ales – using 100% malted barley and Kentish hops, without any sugar or additives – including the very popular Fine Light Ale and a rich barley wine, Old 1066 Ale, brewed in winter only. Check the website for pubs that serve Goacher's beers.

Nelson Brewery
www.nelsonbrewingcompany.co.uk.
'England expects every man to drink our beer' is the motto of the Nelson Brewery, based in the Chatham dockyard where the *Victory* was built. Regular brews include the award-winning Pieces of Eight, and the wonderfully named Friggin in the Riggin; there are speciality and seasonal ales too. Tours can be arranged on request.

Shepherd Neame Brewery
Founded in Faversham in 1698, Shepherd Neame is the oldest brewer in the country, and one of the biggest names in British brewing. Bestselling cask ales include Spitfire and Bishops Finger, and the bottled Whitstable Organic Ale is growing in popularity. Brewery visits are available, and there's a shop on site too. *See p49.*

Whitstable Brewery
www.whitstablebrewery.info.
Although established only in 2007, this boutique brewery supplies various pubs and restaurants in Whitstable, including the Hotel Continental, the Whitstable Brewery Bar and the Whitstable Oyster Fishery Company, as well as local supermarkets. Wheat Beer, Raspberry Wheat Beer, Oyster Stout and Pilsner Lager are sold in bottles; East India Pale Ale and Native Ale by the cask.

Whitstable. See p57.

KENT

control of the older and more powerful town and manor of Middleton Regis. Its past status is evident in the handsome houses and buildings, which include the 15th-century Court Hall on the High Street, now a museum (01795 478446, open Apr-Sept 10am-1pm Sat).

For a peep at the village's more recent history, head for the creek. In the 19th and early 20th centuries, Milton Regis relied heavily on this inlet, which generated the power for the area's paper mills. Once the paper was manufactured, the creek would then provide a means of transport for it and other materials coming in and out (including the bricks produced by the local brick works).

Sittingbourne

Sittingbourne's roots as a market town can be traced back to its location on the Roman Watling Street (now the A2), which was the main route from Dover to London and the most important road in Kent. In terms of trade, this was hugely significant, and throughout the 17th and 18th centuries many merchants would pass through the town's taverns and inns on their way to the capital. In 1858, the railway arrived and Sittingbourne lost its reputation as a lively road travellers' town. Instead, like Milton Regis, it became known for paper and bricks, both materials in high demand in an expanding Victorian London.

Many of those visiting Sittingbourne today do so to walk. It's a great base from which to strike out for surrounding villages such as Tunstall, Upchurch and Rodmersham, across acres of orchard and field, dotted with thatched houses and cosy pubs. Another wonderful stretch leads from nearby Tonge to Graveney on the east side of Faversham, and is part of the long-distance Saxon Shore Way. It's wild and desolate, particularly when the tide is out, revealing miles of mud flats, flocks of seabirds and the occasional hardy human. ·

Where to eat and drink

George Inn

44 The Street, Newnham, ME9 0LL (01795 890237). Open 11am-3pm, 6.30-11.30pm Mon-Sat; noon-10.30pm Sun. Lunch served noon-2.30pm Mon-Sat; noon-6pm Sun. Dinner served 7-9.30pm Mon-Sat; 7-9pm Sun.
The George Inn, once a farm building deep in the countryside, dates from the 1500s; it became a pub in 1718. It's a bit of a landmark in Newnham, which is about seven miles inland from Sittingbourne. Enjoy the warmth from the huge inglenook fireplace, while enjoying Shepherd Neame ale and hearty fare such as soups, steaks and pies.

Plough Inn

Lewson Street, ME9 9JJ (01795 521348, www.the ploughatlewsonst.com). Open 11.30am-3pm, 6.30pm-midnight Mon-Sat; noon-3pm, 7pm-midnight Sun. Lunch served noon-2.30pm Mon-Sat; noon-3pm Sun. Dinner served 7-9.30pm Mon-Sat.
A lengthy menu of traditional pub food and real ales are served at the Plough, handily located just off the A2. There's

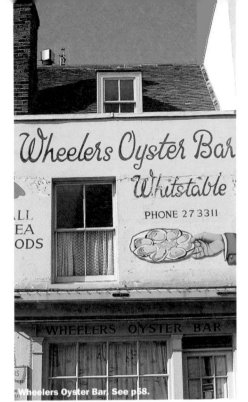

Wheelers Oyster Bar. See p58.

also a big garden, a space where motorhomes can park overnight and, on a Wednesday night, live music.

Where to stay

Beaumont

74 London Road, Sittingbourne, ME10 1NS (01795 472536, www.thebeaumont.co.uk). Rates £70-£80 double incl breakfast.
A handy location (right on the A2 and within walking distance of Sittingbourne town centre) makes the Beaumont a useful option. The main part of the building is a 300-year-old farmhouse; the nine rooms, although small, come with cable TV, free Wi-Fi, toiletries and tea- and coffee-making facilities. Breakfast is generous and served with a smile.

FAVERSHAM

Faversham, seven miles east of Sittingbourne along the A2, is the kind of town that invites exploration, with its historic marketplace and streets full of enticing houses, pubs, teahouses and shops (there are few chain stores here). Faversham's key industries – farming, brewing, fishing and gunpowder-making – have left their mark. The Chart Gunpowder Mills, for example, off Stonebridge Way, were founded in around 156; the firm's gunpowder was used at Trafalgar and Waterloo. In 1916, a gunpowder mill in Uplees, just north of Faversham, blew up, killing 108 people; many are buried in a mass grave in Faversham Cemetery on Love Lane.

For a quick walking tour, start off at Faversham train station on Railway Road, turning right on to Preston Street. Pass the Fleur de Lis Heritage Centre (01795 590726, www.faversham.org), or pop in – it holds tourist information, a museum, a gallery and a garden. Preston Street leads to Market Street, where you'll find the Guildhall (from 1574), the beating heart of Faversham and host to the town's market on Tuesday, Friday and Saturday. Market Street continues on to West Street, home to the handsome Sun Inn (see p56), and eventually to Stonebridge Pond, which leads to the creek. After the pond, turn right to Davington Hill for a glimpse of Davington Church or turn left to follow Stonebridge Way to Chart Gunpowder Mills (open Apr-Oct, 2-5pm Sat, Sun).

If you turn right at Market Street before it brings you on to West Street, you'll find yourself at Court Street. Stop off at the Shepherd Neame Brewery (see p49), or head to pretty Abbey Street. It's lined with timber-framed buildings – all uneven roofs, leaning walls and stooped doorways. Seek out Arden's House, one of the few surviving buildings of Faversham Abbey and scene of the notorious murder of Thomas Arden.

At the Anchor Inn (see right), turn left on to Standard Quay and the silent beauty of the water. There are boats leaning up against the dock walls, blackened timber buildings and, within some of these, an almost secret set of shops. Pick up antiques, vintage clothes and furniture, or tea and scones. On Sundays, Faversham's quirky flea market (www.favershamfleamarket.co.uk, 10am-3pm) is held in the Monk's Granary.

Beyond the town, the lush Kent Downs and the flatlands of the north Kent marshes spread out for miles. Just outside Faversham is the Stone Chapel, also known as the Church of Our Lady of Elwarton (01795 534542, www.faversham.org); not much is left, but its foundations are of Roman origin. Find the chapel, and the remains of a pagan shrine, in a copse about half a mile west of Ospringe.

Where to eat & drink

Real ale fans should make for the Elephant (31 The Mall, 01795 590157, closed Mon); for an Indian meal, try the Prince of India (17 Preston Street, 01795 535359). The Sun Inn (see p56) is a reliable Shepherd Neame hostelry, while the Phoenix (Abbey Street, 01795 591462, www.thephoenixtavernfaversham.co.uk) has a range of ales from several breweries, and also has good food.

Jitterbugs is a new café on Preston Street (no.18a, 01795 533121), serving coffee and snacks in a relaxed atmosphere with an open fire and lots of Penguin classics. Bread comes from the local Champion Bakery; sandwiches include portobello mushroom, goat's cheese and balsamic vinegar on walnut or spelt bread.

Macknade Fine Foods (Selling Road, 01795 534497, www.macknade.com) is a farm shop like no other, with a deli, a fishmonger, a butcher, a bakery and a range of imported foods, as well as a café.

Anchor Inn
52 Abbey Street, Faversham, ME13 7BP (01795 536471, www.theanchorinnfaversham.com). Open noon-11pm Mon-Thur; noon-midnight Fri, Sat; noon-11pm Sun. Food served 12.30-2.30pm, 6-9pm Mon-Fri; 12.30-3pm, 6.30-9pm Sat; 12.30-3pm Sun.
The Anchor Inn sits between two of the most charming parts of Faversham, Abbey Street and Standard Quay. It's a worthy landmark: a 300-year-old pub with beams said to be from the old Abbey that once stood up the road. There's a choice of real ales and superior pub grub, or fish and seafood from the Crab Shack restaurant. The Anchor is run by Hamish Stuart (ex Average White Band), who also has the Three Mariners in Oare (see p56); quite often there's live music on Sunday afternoons.

Dove Inn
Plum Pudding Lane, Dargate, ME13 9HB (01227 751360, www.thedoveinndargate.co.uk). Open noon-3pm, 6-11pm Tue-Thur; noon-midnight Fri; noon-3pm, 6pm-midnight Sat; noon-5pm Sun. Lunch served noon-2pm Tue-Sat; noon-2.30pm Sun. Dinner served 7-9pm Tue-Sat.
An ivy-clad Victorian pub with a roaring fire, this is picture postcard stuff. Great gastropub dishes include asparagus with black pudding and poached egg; Kentish pork and ale sausages with mash; and sticky toffee pudding. Don't let its sleepy image deceive you; book in advance – the Dove won Shepherd Neame Pub Restaurant of the Year in 2010. Dargate is a few miles east of Faversham, off the A299.

Read's ★
Macknade Manor, Canterbury Road, Faversham, ME13 8XE (01795 535344, www.reads.com). Lunch served noon-2pm, dinner served 7-9pm Tue-Sat.
Read's restaurant with rooms is based in a lovely Georgian manor, surrounded by equally handsome grounds, and sports a Michelin star, thanks to chef David Pitchford and his team. A typical meal might see roast breast of local pheasant with red cabbage braised with apples, game chips

Things to do

WHITSTABLE

Greta 1892
South Quay, Whitstable Harbour (01795 534541, www.greta1892.co.uk). Open Apr-Oct by appointment. Day trip £44-£49 per person.
Built in 1892, the Thames sailing barge *Greta* was used in the Dunkirk evacuation; now, under owner and skipper Steve Norris (and his two dogs), she takes visitors on six-hour trips from Whitstable into the Thames Estuary. Sights might include the wind farm and the strange-looking Maunsell sea forts at Red Sands, 12 miles offshore.

Whitstable Cycle Hire
Captain's House, 56 Harbour Street, Whitstable, CT5 1AQ (01227 275156, www.whitstable cyclehire.com). Rates One-day cycle hire £15. No credit cards.
All kinds of bikes are for hire, from children's and tandems to mountain bikes, either for the day or the week. Booking is recommended. Guided tours can also be arranged.

and brussels sprouts, followed by poached Kentish pear with sable biscuit, mascarpone mousse, butterscotch sauce and vanilla ice-cream. Upstairs are six luxurious bedrooms (£260-£290 double incl breakfast and dinner).

Rose & Crown
Perrywood, Selling, ME13 9RY (01227 752214, www.roseandcrownperrywood.co.uk). Open 11am-3pm, 6.30-11pm Mon-Sat; noon-4pm, 7-10.30pm Sun. Lunch served noon-2pm, dinner served 7-9pm Tue-Sun.
Six miles south of Faversham, surrounded by 150 acres of woodland (with plenty of footpaths) and encompassing a former woodcutter's cottage and stable, this is a charming 16th-century pub. There's a great range of drinks: real ales (there's always a guest beer), assorted ciders and a wine list that includes bottles from local vineyards. Hearty pub dishes feature game in season.

Shipwrights Arms
Hollow Shore, Oare, ME13 7TU (01795 590088, http://shipwrightspub.website.orange.co.uk). Open Apr-Sept 11am-3pm, 6-11pm Mon-Fri; noon-11pm Sat; noon-10.30pm Sun. Oct-Mar 11am-3pm Mon; 11am-3pm, 6-10pm Tue-Fri; 11am-4pm, 6-11pm Sat; noon-4pm, 6-10.30pm Sun. Lunch served Apr-Sept noon-2.30pm daily. Oct-Mar noon-2pm Mon-Fri; noon-3pm Sat; noon-4pm Sun. Dinner served Apr-Sept 7-9pm Tue-Sat. Oct-Mar 7-9pm Fri, Sat.
The Shipwrights Arms sits in the marshlands like a hermit with only an old boatyard and creek for company. It's difficult to track down, and once you've found it you'll see a plethora of signs telling guests how to behave. If you don't mind this kind of thing, you'll think this is one of the most characterful pubs in Kent: a weatherboard cottage tavern at least 300 years old, full of cubbyholes, narrow doorways and low-beamed ceilings. Pub food runs from sandwiches to steak pie and ham, eggs and chips. Book a table if you want more than a bar snack – otherwise find a nook, order a locally brewed real ale, and drink in the atmosphere.

Three Mariners
2 Church Road, Oare, ME13 0QA (01795 533633, www.thethreemarinersoare.co.uk). Open 11.30am-3pm, 6-11pm Tue-Thur; 11.30am-3pm, 6pm-midnight Fri; noon-midnight Sat; noon-7pm Sun. Lunch served noon-2.30pm Tue-Sat; noon-3.30pm Sun. Dinner served 6-9pm Wed, Thur; 6-9.30pm Fri, Sat.
Popular with walkers, and close to beauty spot Harty Ferry, this 17th-century pub sits squarely in Oare Marsh territory. This is an attractive landscape, full of creeks and bobbing boats, and the garden terrace of the Three Mariners offers a view of the marshes. The food is a cut above, and features locally caught fish in dishes such as skate wing with capers and brown butter. The ales are from Shepherd Neame, of course. The Three Mariners has a nice vibe; it's also a music venue and hosts its own weekend music festival every September; see www.moaremusic.co.uk for details.

Where to stay
Freedom Holiday Homes (01580 720770, www. freedomholidayhomes.co.uk) has properties all around Kent and Sussex, including some beautiful self-catering cottages in Faversham. The Victorian Railway Hotel on Preston Street (01795 533173, www.railwayhotelfaversham.co.uk) has seven comfortable en suite rooms (£65-£70 double incl breakfast). Read's (*see p55*) has six well-appointed rooms above its acclaimed restaurant.

Sun Inn
10 West Street, Faversham, ME13 7JE (01795 535098, www.sunfaversham.co.uk). Rates £70 double incl breakfast.
A welcoming 17th-century alehouse, right by Faversham's historic Market Square. There's a bar, and restaurant, a beer garden and eight neat en suite rooms. Traditional fare includes a roast on Sundays.

Sportsman. See p58.

WHITSTABLE

The image of Whitstable as a weekend bolt hole for London's middle classes is not undeserved, but this lovely old coastal town has enough character to withstand total gentrification – and it's still very much a working fishing town. To learn about the town's history, pop into Whitstable Museum (Oxford Street, 01227 276998, www.whitstable-museum.co.uk). Exhibits include a display devoted to the town's most famous fan, Peter Cushing, who bought a seafront house here in 1959. It includes film stills, props and examples of the actor-turned-painter's art.

Whitstable has smartened itself up for visitors – for example, many of the old fishermen's huts on the seafront have been fashioned into holiday retreats (see p58) and the Cheese Box (60 Harbour Street, 01227 273711, www.thecheesebox.co.uk, closed Tue) is a fantastic deli set up by a Londoner in 2008 – but it doesn't pander. Much of the town looks as it always has, from the Island Wall with its mid 19th-century cottages to the little alleys once used by fishermen to cut through the town to sea (Squeeze Gut Alley is so narrow that many have to walk through it sideways). The main streets, running north from Oxford Street to High Street to Harbour Street, all lead toward the seafront and harbour. Here you'll find a selection of small shops, galleries and cafés. Look out for Oxford Street Books (01227 281727, www.oxfordstreetbooks.com), where every nook and cranny is stuffed with second-hand books.

Continuing north from Harbour Street to Tower Hill, Whitstable Castle (see p49) sits on the border of Whitstable and the suburb of Tankerton. The newly restored castle and grounds has become a centre for community activities and is a good place to take in some sea air. If you climb to the top of the hill you'll come out opposite Tower Hill Tea Gardens (07780 662543), an idyllic and often quiet spot with sea views.

Running parallel to the shingle beach is Island Row, lined with pretty cottages; walk east to reach the harbour. Stand facing the sea and you'll see some of the 30 or so turbines of the Kentish Flats wind farm. Low tide reveals a natural spit of shingle on a clay bank, known as the Street. You can walk it for about half a mile, on the last of the town's land to the north, the rest having been eroded and swallowed by the sea. Keep an eye on the rising tide, though. Cyclists will enjoy the Crab & Winkle Way (see p87), a route to Canterbury along a disused railway line.

Whitstable has been praised for its oysters since Juvenal shucked a few here a couple of thousand years ago. These days, the oyster beds granted royal protection by Elizabeth I are no secret. The Royal Native Oyster Company, one of the earliest commercial ventures in Europe, was reconstituted as the Whitstable Oyster Fishery Company in 1896. A combination of overfishing and disease almost did for the industry in the 1920s, but it was revived in the '80s. These days, the WOFC runs many thriving businesses in town and has spearheaded Whitstable's gentrification. The Whitstable Oyster Festival (www.whitstableoysterfestival.co.uk) spans nine days in July; as well as oyster processions and fish dances, there's the Whitstable Regatta, on the festival's second weekend.

Where to eat & drink

In Whitstable it helps to know your oysters. Natives (grown in Whitstable, as well as Colchester and Helford) will cost you about £15 per half dozen. If you're paying about a fiver, chances are you're eating the less expensive pacific (also known as rock or gigas), which has a larger, longer shell. The Crab & Winkle (South Quay, 01227 779377, www.crab andwinklerestaurant.co.uk, closed Mon winter), the Pearson's Arms (Sea Wall, 01227 272005, www. pearsonsarms.com) and Williams & Brown Tapas (48 Harbour Street, 01227 273373, www.thetapas. co.uk, closed Tue, Wed winter) are all reliable places for fish and seafood. Local favourite Birdies (41 Harbour Street, 01227 265337, closed Tue) serves inventive dishes such as deep-fried bream with chillies.

Windy Corner Stores (Nelson Road, 01227 272955) is a chic boho café and general store, using lots of Kentish produce; the same owners also run a small restaurant, Salt Marsh (27A Oxford Street, 01227 272955).

There are plenty of takeaway options too – try the fish market on South Quay (01227 771245; there are barbecues here in summer). For fish and chips, VC Jones is a favourite (25 Harbour Street, 01227 272703, www.vcjones.co.uk, closed Mon).

The Whitstable Brewery Bar (East Quay, no phone) is a bar owned by the Whitstable Oyster Fishery Company that segues from easy-going beach bar into a club (Friday and Saturday nights only in winter).

JoJo's

2 Herne Bay Road, Tankerton, CT5 2LQ (01227 274591, www.jojosrestaurant.co.uk). Lunch served 12.30-2.30pm Wed-Sun. Dinner served 6.30-9pm Tue-Sat. No credit cards.

From small beginnings, JoJo's has moved into smart new seafront premises, complete with a coffee shop. The Mediterranean food comes in the form of various meze (a plate of chorizo or patatas bravas, say) and mains such as Monkshill mutton and feta koftas with spicy tomato sauce and tsatsiki or beer-battered pollack goujons with tartar mayo. The food is inexpensive; alcohol is BYO with £2 corkage. Booking is strongly advised.

Old Neptune
Marine Terrace, Whitstable, CT5 1EJ (01227 272262, www.neppy.co.uk). Open noon-11pm Mon-Thur; noon-12.30am Fri, Sat; noon-10.30pm Sun. Food served Summer noon-5pm daily. Winter noon-3pm daily.
This likeable, atmospheric pub with sloping wooden floors is practically on the beach. Food is simple stuff, competently done. In winter, cosy up with a pint and listen to live music, surrounded by whiskery dogs and fishermen; in summer, take advantage of the outdoor seating.

Samphire
4 High Street, Whitstable, CT5 1BQ (01227 770075, www.samphirerestaurant.co.uk). Food served 9am-10pm daily.
Even when is besieged by weekend crowds attracted by the reasonably priced, unfussy bistro menu, staff remain cheerful. There's no need to book for the big breakfasts of local bacon, sausage and eggs, or brunches and lunches of eggs benedict, stews and soups, but evenings can be busy. The menu changes every three months, but expect a choice of five starters and five mains that could include beetroot soup, slow-braised lamb, oxtail or venison sausages from the butcher down the road, and scallops from Rye Bay.

Sportsman ★
Faversham Road, Seasalter, CT5 4BP (01227 273370, www.thesportsmanseasalter.co.uk). Open noon-3pm, 6-10.30pm Mon; noon-3pm, 6-11pm Tue-Sat; noon-10pm Sun. Lunch served noon-2pm Tue-Sat; noon-2.30pm Sun. Dinner served 7-9pm Tue-Sat.
This renowned gastropub sits near the sea wall on the old coast road west of Whitstable. Located in the backwaters of the Seasalter marshes, it's a remote, somewhat bleak location, but the food is so good that people flock here. Expect local, seasonal ingredients in starters such as slip sole grilled in seaweed butter or mussel and bacon chowder, and mains like Monkshill Farm pork belly and apple sauce or seared thornback ray, brown butter, cockles and sherry vinegar dressing. Book well in advance.

Wheelers Oyster Bar ★
8 High Street, Whitstable, CT5 1BQ (01227 273311). Open 10.30am-9pm Mon-Tue; 10.15am-9pm Thur-Fri; 10am-10pm Sat; 11am-9pm Sun. No credit cards.
Fish comes fresh off the boats and into dishes such as skate cheek salad, seafood platter and steamed cod. Wheelers has been serving local oysters since 1856; they now come in a variety of ways, from plain to encased in Guinness batter. It's a quirky place, pink on the outside and small and simply decorated inside. It's BYO (no corkage charge).

Whitstable Oyster Fishery Company
Royal Native Oyster Stores, Horsebridge, Whitstable, CT5 1BU (01227 276856, www.oysterfishery.co.uk). Lunch served noon-2.30pm Mon-Fri. Dinner served 6.30-9pm

Tue-Thur; 6.30-9.30pm Fri. Food served noon-9.45pm Sat; noon-8.30pm Sun.
This handsome building, once home to the Royal Native Oyster Stores, occupies a prime position on the beach. The nautical-looking dining room is the setting for a meal that might run from half a dozen native oysters to a whole roast local wild seabass with garlic and rosemary. It's not cheap (locals say that prices are aimed at the DFL – Down from London – crowd), but a meal here feels like a treat. You can have a drink in the bar upstairs while you wait for your table – the Whitstable Brewery beer is worth tasting. Booking is essential.
Sister establishment, the more casual Lobster Shack (01227 772157, www.thelobstershack.co.uk, closed Mon-Fri winter) is located at the end of East Quay, in a 19th-century building once used for grading oysters. It's also worth a visit, for the likes of dressed crab or deep-fried squid, available to eat in or take out. Bookings are not taken.

Where to stay
Whitstable Cottage Company (01227 262173, www.whitstablecottagecompany.com) has a range of bright, well-maintained properties to let in Whitstable, Seasalter and Herne Bay.

Captain's House & Polly's Attic
56 Harbour Street, Whitstable, CT5 1AQ (01227 275156, www.thecaptainshouse.org.uk). Rates £95 double incl breakfast. No credit cards.
B&B accommodation in adjoining houses. The well-maintained Captain's House (sleeping up to four) has an en suite double bedroom, a living room with kitchen facilities and a double sofa bed, and plenty of old-fashioned charm. Polly's Attic is a bright white studio apartment, with a double bed and child-sized bunk beds.

Duke of Cumberland
High Street, Whitstable, CT5 1AP (01227 280617, www.thedukeinwhitstable.co.uk). Rates £70-£110 double incl breakfast.
You can't miss the Duke as you come into Whitstable. It's a massive Shepherd Neame boozer with good cheer glowing from its stained-glass windows. There are nine en suite rooms, simply furnished in understated neutral colours.

Fishermen's Huts ★
Hotel Continental, 29 Beach Walk, CT5 2BP (01227 280280, www.hotelcontinental.co.uk). Rates 2-person hut £260-£400 per weekend. Family hut £300-£500 per weekend.
Once used for storage by cockle fishers, these ten wooden huts have been transformed into upmarket and very popular holiday accommodation by the Whitstable Oyster Fishery Company. All (except hut 6) have great sea views, and all are right on the beach – so not for those looking for somewhere secluded. The newest hut (no.10) is bigger than the others, with space for four adults. There's also the Anderson Shed, a converted boat builder's shed that can take four adults and two children.

Hotel Continental
29 Beach Walk, Whitstable, CT5 2BP (01227 280280, www.hotelcontinental.co.uk). Rates £70-£145 double incl breakfast.

Reculver Towers & Roman Fort. See p49.

A 1930s hotel, refurbished in 1998 by the Whitstable Oyster Fishery Company, this has a prime position on the seafont. As well as 23 nicely updated rooms, there's a brasserie and a bar, both offering lovely views and a relaxed atmosphere. Apart from oysters, simple dishes such as pear, walnut and roquefort salad or beefburger with fries are served.

HERNE BAY

Herne Bay, with its slow pace of life and shabby yet elegant seafront, hasn't yet been rediscovered in the same way as Whitstable. The legacy of its heyday can be seen in the striking 80-foot clock tower (a gift from Londoner Ann Thwaytes in 1836), the grand promenade and the newly restored bandstand. Boats huddle within the small tidal harbour, and the remnants of what was once the town pier is still visible out at sea – most of it collapsed in a storm in 1978. These days the town has a large elderly population and not much in terms of entertainment; the shingle beach is popular with families, and there are good walks on the shore and nearby cliffs. Things get livelier in summer, when there's a two-week carnival, plus music festivals and art markets.

The Central Parade is the town's focal point. The bandstand has an ice-cream kiosk and information centre, and a programme of summer concerts. Also along the front are the flashing arcades of Sandancers Amusements, a seaside shop selling beach goods and bodyboards, and an outdoor mini golf centre.

Head to William Street to find the cinema (01227 365676, www.kavanaghcinema.co.uk), a swimming pool complex (01227 742102, www.activelifeltd. co.uk) and the Herne Bay Museum & Art Gallery (01227 367368, www.hernebay-museum.co.uk, closed Sun). It displays fossils and Roman finds, and a prototype bouncing bomb left over from those tested off the coast during World War II. There are two theatres: the King's Hall (01227 374188, www.thekingshall.com) and Herne Bay Little Theatre (01227 366004, www.hernebaylittletheatre.com).

Rummagers will appreciate the quality of the junk, second-hand and charity shops found all over town. Look out for Saxongate Antique & Design (75 High Street, http://saxongate.com, 07971 512203, closed Mon, Sun) located in Briggsy's Old Cinema.

The rest of Herne Bay's attractions can be found by wandering along the coast: if you're prepared to poke around in the mud, you might find fossilised shark teeth or ancient coins. Alternatively, stick to the well-beaten paths. A pleasant hour-long walk is to Reculver Tower and Roman Fort (see p49), heading east along the coast via Beacon Hill. Cyclists should check out the cycle route between Reculver and Whitstable, which passes through Herne Bay following the Saxon Shore Way; details on www.maritimeheritagetrail.co.uk.

Other sights are out at sea. As well as the pier head, you can see wind turbines and the Maunsell sea forts, a series of strange-looking towers built to protect the Thames estuary during World War II and now abandoned. They housed pirate radio stations, such as Radio Invicta, in the 1960s and have featured in episodes of Doctor Who.

KENT'S BEST BIRDWATCHING SITES

Blean Woods
Nr Canterbury (www.rspb.org.uk).
This woodland site offers five trails, up to eight miles long; a couple are suitable for wheelchairs and pushchairs. Woodpeckers, nightingales and nightjars are regularly seen.

Cliffe Pools
Rochester (01634 222480, www.rspb.org.uk).
On the north Kent coast, Cliffe Pools is home to breeding redshanks, avocets and common terns. There are a number of nature trails and newly improved visitors facilities. RSPB staff and volunteers can be found in the car park on weekends.

Dungeness
Lydd (01797 320588, www.rspb.org.uk).
The windblown landscape here is a unique birding spot. Despite its bleak appearance, it harbours a vast array of birdlife. Migrant species seen here include wheatears, swallows, martins and warblers.

Elmley Marshes
Isle of Sheppey (01795 665969, www.rspb.org.uk).
Elmley Marshes has the highest density of breeding waders in southern England. There are several hides in the wetlands, including one overlooking a shallow pool that's popular with avocets. Also seen here are curlew, golden plover, teal and pintail. See p48.

Hamstreet Woods National Nature Reserve
Ashford (www.naturalengland.org.uk).
This lovely patch of woodland was one of the first nature reserves in the country, and attracts a wide selection of birds and moths. It's a relaxing place for a stroll, with a network of footpaths and bridleways. There's also an easy-access route.

Where to eat & drink

Herne Bay is blessed with some fine pubs, including the Druid's Head (182 High Street, 01227 372751), where you'll find a pleasant beer garden. Macari's ice-cream parlour (54 Central Parade, 01227 374977) is the place to go for knickerbocker glories and coffee. For more substantial but equally traditional seaside fare, visit Ernie's Plaice Fish Bar (77 Central Parade, 01227 366471, closed Mon, Tue winter).

Butcher's Arms

29A Herne Street, Herne, CT6 7HL (01227 371000, www.micropub.co.uk). Open noon-1.30pm, 6-9pm Tue-Sat. No credit cards.

As long as you're not travelling with an entourage (they won't fit in), this former butcher's shop in the village of Herne, just inland from Herne Bay, is a fine place to sup a real ale. Said to be the smallest freehouse in England, it serves beer from all over England. The walls are festooned with local artefacts and curiosities, mostly beer related.

Le Petit Poisson

Pier Approach, Herne Bay, CT6 5JN (01227 361199, www.lepetitpoisson.co.uk). Lunch served noon-2.30pm Tue-Fri; noon-3pm Sat; noon-3.30pm Sun. Dinner served 6.30-9pm Tue-Fri; 6.30-9.30pm Sat.

Next to the pier pavilion, this fish restaurant was once the Sea View Bar, but has smartened up under the present ownership. Try potted shrimp or dressed crab to start, then move on to moules marinières or steamed wild sea bass. Seating is available indoors and out, and the location is nice and close to the beach.

Ship Inn

17 Central Parade, Herne Bay, CT6 5HT (01227 366636, www.theshiphernebay.com). Open 11am-11.30pm Mon-Sat; 11am-10.30pm Sun. Lunch served noon-2.30pm Mon-Sat; noon-4pm Sun. Dinner served 6-9pm Mon-Thur; 6.30-9.30pm Fri, Sat.

This congenial 18th-century building on Central Parade is one of the oldest in Herne Bay. The white weatherboarded Ship Inn has plenty of seating outside, with fine views of the sea. Inside, the walls are decked with smuggling memorabilia. Food is above-average pub grub.

Where to stay

For anything approaching boutique accommodation, *see p58* Whitstable. Fans of *Little Britain* might care to stay in Bay View Guest House (86 Central Parade, Herne Bay, 01227 741458, www.the-bayview-guesthouse.co.uk) – it's where 'lady' Emily Howard flounced.

Priory B&B

203 Canterbury Road, Herne Bay, CT6 5UG (01227 366670, www.thepriorybandb.co.uk). Rates £60-£65 double incl breakfast.

A mile from the beach, this Grade II-listed Georgian house is situated in the conservation area of Herne Bay, close to the Thanet Way. Six rooms (single, double and family sizes) offer comfortable en suite accommodation. A bright conservatory leads to the garden.

Nor Marsh & Motney Hill

Gillingham (01795 665969, www.rspb.org.uk).
This saltmarsh island in the Medway Estuary is a particularly important site for wintering waterfowl, including avocets, black-tailed godwits, dunlins, knots, shelducks and brent geese. There are good views of the reserve from the Saxon Shore Way footpath.

Riverside Country Park

Gillingham (www.kent.gov.uk).
Riverside Country Park covers 100 acres in the Medway Estuary near Gillingham, and includes a number of different habitats. Regular visitors are brent geese, pintails, shelducks and black-tailed godwits. There's a café and toilets on site.

Sevenoaks Wildlife Reserve

Sevenoaks (www.kentwildlifetrust.org.uk).
This large reserve, half land, half water, includes five lakes, a reed bed and woodland. The result is a wide variety of wildlife; amon the birds, you might spot little ringed plovers, lapwings, moorhens, coots and great crested grebes.

Tudeley Woods

Tunbridge Wells (01273 775333, www.rspb.org.uk).
More than 1,000 types of fungus and orchids have been recorded in this woodland site. There's a scheme to bring back Dartford warblers, and nightjars and tree pipits have already returned to join the lesser-spotted woodpecker.

Thanet

Sweeping sandy bays, majestic white cliffs, lush rolling fields; it's no wonder a succession of conquerors couldn't resist coming ashore on the Isle of Thanet to lay claim to its charms. The warriors guarded their prize with a liberal peppering of fortifications, some of which still stand. The river that made Thanet an island has long since silted up, but the area attracts plenty of visitors, as it has done ever since the Victorians established a string of resorts along the coast. Their elegant piers and bandstands remain, alongside more modern amusements.

Geographically, little separates the three towns of Margate, Ramsgate and Broadstairs, but in character they are a world apart. Margate, the naughty little sister, has seen its share of troubles. Once the holiday destination of middle-class Londoners, its fortunes fell in dramatic style when air travel became affordable. There are signs of a recovery, however, most noticeably in the form of the stunning new Turner Contemporary art gallery. Broadstairs is much more genteel, with higgledy-piggledly houses on higgledy-piggledly lanes. Its Dickens connection is also played upon – he was a regular visitor to the town. Ramsgate lies somewhere in between the two, and its lively fishing port and good seafood restaurants make it a worthwhile destination.

The main reason for the area's popularity as a holiday destination, though, is its beaches. In 2010 Thanet was awarded Blue Flag status for nine of its beaches: child-friendly Minnis Bay, St Mildred's Bay and West Bay in Westgate, Botany Bay, Stone Bay and Joss Bay in Broadstairs, as well as Ramsgate Main Sands and Margate's Main Sands and Westbrook Bay.

Pushing into the sea at the foot of the Thames Estuary, the peninsula likes to think of itself as removed from Kent, and proudly maintains its 'Isle of Thanet' moniker despite having being attached to the mainland for a century.

MARGATE & CLIFTONVILLE

Best known for binge-drinking and Tracey Emin, Margate is evolving into an arty enclave. But there's still old-school seaside fun to be had: candyfloss, waltzers and donkey rides, plus Margate Caves, a network of caverns once used by smugglers, and the curious Shell Grotto (*see p66*), covered with 4.6 million shells. Cliftonville is a quieter suburb of the town, with some attractions of its own.

Just how much the brand-new Turner Contemporary gallery (*see p67*) will lift Margate's fortunes remains to be seen. But it's clear Margate has the right ingredients: independent galleries, smart cafés and vintage accessories shops (still free of London magpies) have all opened in the last few years. Add a fantastic sandy beach, incredible sunsets – famously captured by JMW Turner – and a high-speed train link (which has reduced the trip from London to an hour and a half), and the promise of a revival no longer seems like developers' hyperbole. There's even a superb boutique hotel: the Reading Rooms (*see p69*).

The Turner Contemporary is undoubtedly the most important development in Margate, if not across Kent. Opened in April 2011, the £17 million gallery project will bring jobs, as well as a focal point for the considerable artists' community in the town. The building is a stunning addition to a pleasant skyline (marred only, but significantly, by the Arlington House tower block). Hopes are resting on the Turner, but early exposure has already shown it's providing what Margate needs most: a good news story.

But we can't pretend it's all good. There's the aforementioned Arlington House, boarded-up shops, empty amusement arcades and bored-looking teenagers. But there is also something refreshing about the town even as it currently stands, and it's not just the sea air; its seedy honesty and desolate beauty are a welcome change from over-exposed Whitstable and precious Broadstairs along the coast.

Funding for a new Dreamland amusement park (www.dreamlandmargate.com) has boosted the consensus that regeneration won't be wholly arts-based. Dreamland opened in 1920, and is home to the Grade II-listed Scenic Railway rollercoaster, Britain's oldest (and, until recently, operational) rollercoaster – the first listed amusement park ride in the country. With a plan to rescue vintage rides from defunct theme parks around the country, the new Dreamland, due to open in summer 2012, will be the first amusement park of its kind. Check the website for the latest developments.

That said, entertainment is not hard to find here. Margate has a handful of theatres including the second-oldest in Britain, the Theatre Royal (Addington Street, 0845 130 1786, www.theatre royalmargate.com), and the smallest, the Tom Thumb in Cliftonville (Eastern Esplanade, 01843 221791, www.tomthumbtheatre.co.uk). The Winter Gardens (Thorpe Crescent, 01843 296111, www.margatewintergardens.co.uk), which celebrates its 100-year history in 2011, also programmes shows and concerts.

Margate's most valued tourist draw, however, has to be the beach. The deep sandy strand, which you can practically step on to from the train station, has a tidal pool, bouncy castles, slides and a funfair.

From the Turner Contemporary, walk along Margate Harbour Arm (01843 260260, www.margate harbourarm.co.uk). Along this little stretch jutting out into the sea is the Margate Harbour Arm Gallery which mounts intriguing exhibitions. Here there are also two of the best places for a drink in Margate, the Lighthouse Bar and BeBeached (for both, *see p68*), a 'real food café'. Cruiser bikes, perfect for a jaunt along the promenade or on the expanse of sand, can be hired from Caitlin Beach Cruisers (Unit 8, 07956 395896, www.caitlinsbeachcruisers. com), as can tandems and skateboards.

In the town itself, there are some interesting shops and one quirky tearoom, the Mad Hatter (*see p68*). Margate is already gaining a reputation for vintage clothing and furniture stores – the area in front of the Turner building has even been dubbed the 'cultural quarter' by the tourist board. RG Scott's Furniture Mart (Bath Place, Grotto Hill, 01843 220653 www.scottsmargate.co.uk, closed Wed

and Sun) is a family business that stocks all manner of furniture and curios over three floors. No wonder film crews come knocking when they need some period pieces. Local gal Tracey Emin is a fan. Helter Skelter Boutique (13 Market Place, 01843 223474, www.helterskelterboutique.com, closed Mon-Wed, Sun) specialises in mid 20th-century and contemporary furniture, as well as jewellery and vintage mod gear. At 7 Market Place is Qing (01843 299055, www.qingart.co.uk, closed Wed), dedicated to high-quality Japanese furnishings, furniture and art. At no.2, Blackbird (01843 229533, www.blackbird-england.com, closed Mon-Wed) sells contemporary craft, stationery and artwork. Market Place is also home to Beeping Bush gallery (no.16, 01843 223800, www.beepingbush.co.uk), a space and studio for local artists and community groups, with an emphasis on digital media. Back on Market Street, Madam Popoff Vintage (no.3, 01843 447434) sells a wide range of fashions from the 1920s to the '90s.

Just off the Parade is Duke Street, along which is the Outside the Square Gallery (01843 571201, www.letsvisit.co.uk) opened by Tracey Emin in 2010. The large space holds paintings and sculptures by international artists. Marine Studios (17 Albert Terrace, 01843 282219, www.marinestudios. co.uk) is located in a grand Grade II-listed building overlooking the seafront; home to the museum design agency HKD, it also has an exhibition space and artists' studios.

Just a few minutes' walk along the coast from Margate is genteel Cliftonville, a determinedly traditional bucket-and-spade suburb of the Victorian seaside town. Its chief delights are its beautifully manicured lawns backing on to the parade, some

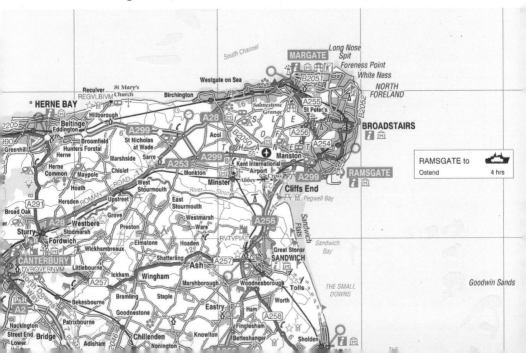

Botany Bay

Places to visit

MARGATE & CLIFTONVILLE

Drapers Windmill
St Peters Footpath, CT9 2SP (01843 291696, www.draperswindmill.com). Open Aug 2-4pm Sat, Sun. June, July 2-4pm Sun. Other times by appointment. Admission free.
This carefully restored windmill, built in 1845, has a small museum focused on the agricultural history of the area and including items related to the milling of Kent wheat. The mill is kept in working order.

Hornby Visitor Centre
Westwood Industrial Estate, CT9 4JX (01843 233525, www.hornby.com). Open 10am-5pm Thur-Sun. Admission £4; free-£2 reductions; £10 family.
Travel through the history of the model train at this shiny new visitor centre by model makers Hornby. The miniature railway specialist has opened its archive to the public, showing little trains and railway pieces from the beginning of last century, together with items from other toy manufacturers who have joined Hornby over the years, including Scalextric, Airfix and Corgi.

Quex Museum ★
Birchington-on-Sea, CT7 0BH (01843 842168, www.quexmuseum.org). Open Apr-Oct 11am-5pm Tue-Sun. Nov-Mar 1-4pm Sun. Admission £7; £5 reductions; £20 family. Gardens only £2; £1.50 reductions.
Located in Birchington, west of Margate, this is hard to define, but a must-visit. There's an old manor house and gardens, but the highlight is the idiosyncratic Powell-Cotton Museum. In the late 19th-century, Major Powell-Cotton hunted down all manner of exotic animals, then had them stuffed and put on display, grouped in approximations of their natural state. At the time, these spectacular dioramas became a standard for natural history museums around the world, and the Victorians flocked to see them. Today, it's a little incongruous, but fascinating, especially with the eccentric history of Powell-Cotton intertwined with it all – try to take one of the guided tours. After gawping at the surreal displays, take a woodland walk to Waterloo Tower, with its 12 bells. Quex Barn, by the entrance, is an excellent farm shop and café. The Thanet Island Music Festival is held in the grounds.

Shell Grotto
Grotto Hill, CT9 2BU (01843 220008, www.shellgrotto.co.uk). Open Easter-Oct 10am-5pm daily. Admission £3; £1.50 reductions; £8 family.
In 1835, a duckpond-digging local lowered his son Joshua into a hole that opened up, and the lad emerged with wild stories of tunnels covered in shells. The shell grotto remains an enigma to this day and is Grade I-listed. A twisting, 70-foot-long passageway leads to a subterranean chamber, covered with intricate mosaics made from over four-and-a-half million laboriously glued-on shells. First opened to the public in 1837, the grotto has bemused day-trippers ever since. Is it the meeting place of a secret sect, a pagan temple or simply a bizarre Regency folly? Even its age remains a mystery, as the soot from the oil lamps that lit it in Victorian times means it can't be carbon-dated.

KENT

Quex shop and café

Turner Contemporary ★
The Rendezvous, CT9 1HG (01843 294208,
www.turnercontemporary.org). Open Summer 10am-
5.30pm Tue-Sun. Winter 10am-4.30pm Tue-Sun.
Admission free.
The Turner Contemporary has a lot of weight on its
shoulders: the fortunes of Margate are inextricably
tied to its success. When it opens in April 2011, the
£17 million project will be the jewel of Thanet – its
dramatic silver structure certainly makes it look
like one. The opening exhibition, Revealed: Turner
Contemporary Opens (April-Sept 2011), will use one
of JMW Turner's paintings as the centrepiece for new
commissions by Daniel Buren, Russell Crotty, Ellen
Harvey and Conrad Shawcross, as well as selected
works by Teresita Fernandez and Douglas Gordon.
Nothing in the World but Youth (Sept 2011-Jan 2012)
will look at Margate's youth culture and how it is
reflected in art. Hamish Fulton (Jan-May 2012) will
be the first solo exhibition.

BROADSTAIRS & BOTANY BAY

Crampton Tower Museum
The Broadway, CT10 2AB (01843 871133,
www.cramptontower.co.uk). Open Mar-Oct 2-5pm
daily. Nov-Feb 1-4pm Sat, Sun. Admission £3; £1.50
reductions; £7.50 family. No credit cards.
Standing tall on the Broadway, crenellated Crampton
Tower has never seen action as a fortress; instead it's
a Victorian flint water tower, designed by the engineer
Thomas Crampton. The museum celebrates his life
from working with Brunel designing railway engines,
to his status as 'father of submarine telegraphy'.

Dickens House Museum
2 Victoria Parade, CT10 1QS (01843 861232,
www.dickensfellowship.org). Open June-Sept 10-5pm
daily. Apr-June 2-5pm daily. Jan-Mar, Oct-Dec 2-5pm
Sat, Sun. Admission £3.25; £1.90 reductions; £9
family. No credit cards.
Dickens House, now a small museum, was once
the residence of a Miss Mary Pearson, who inspired
the character of Miss Betsey Trotwood, David
Copperfield's great-aunt (in the novel, the house was
moved to Dover, to avoid embarrassment). The Tudor
building is filled with Dickensiana, from prints by HK
Browne (one of Dickens's illustrators) to letters written
by Dickens about Broadstairs (which he refers to as
'Our English Watering Place').

RAMSGATE & MINSTER

Hugin Viking Ship
Pegwell Bay, CT11 (01843 577577,
www.visitthanet.co.uk).
This Viking ship is a replica of one that sailed into
Pegwell Bay from Denmark in 1949 to celebrate the
1,500 years since Britain was invaded by Hengist
and Horsa. Fifty-three crew members rowed the boat
over in the 1940s, though only one was a professional
seaman. In keeping with Viking navigation of the day,
only a sextant was carried. Note that the ship can
only be viewed from the outside.

Minster Abbey
Church Street, CT12 4HF (01843 821254,
www.minsterabbeynuns.org). Tours May-Sept
2.45-4pm Mon-Fri; 11am-noon Sat. Jan-Apr,
Oct-Dec 11am-noon Sat. Also by appointment.
Admission free.
Minster Abbey is still a working abbey run by 13 nuns,
but tours of the ancient building and gardens are
possible. It was founded in 670 by St Domneva and
granted to St Augustine's Abbey in Canterbury by King
Canute in 1027. A Norman church was added between
1075 and 1150, but some buildings were demolished
during the Dissolution. It would be another 400 years
until, in 1937, it was bought by Benedictine nuns
and became a monastic house again. There is basic
accommodation for private retreats.

RAF Manston History Museum
Manston Road, CT12 5DF (01843 825224,
www.rafmanston.co.uk). Open Mar-Oct 10am-4pm
daily. Nov-Feb 10am-4pm Sat, Sun. Admission £1;
50p reductions.
Manston has been a working airfield since 1916,
but it gained fame in World War II as the base for the
Lancaster bombers that carried out the Dambusters
raid. It was also used by the USAF during the Cold
War. The RAF left in 1999 and the airfield has become
Kent International Airport, currently mainly used by
large cargo planes. In addition to learning about the
airfield's history, there are assorted planes to look
at, plus occasional Wings & Wheels days that feature
other military vehicles. Also on the site is the Spitfire
& Hurricane Memorial Museum (www.spifirememorial.
org.uk – admission free), which houses one of the
few surviving Spitfires that was used in World War II
and a 1944 Hurricane.

KENT

Ambrette

great art deco houses, a beautiful lido tower and, the showstopper, a terrific Arnold Palmer-designed miniature golf course.

Where to eat & drink

There are a couple of good cafés in the area around the Turner Contemporary. Café G (1 High Street, 01843 225600, www.cafeg.net) has Fairtrade products, excellent coffee and a wide selection of paninis, platters and salads. The Cupcake Café (4-5 Market Place, 01843 231300, www.thecupcake.biz) – catchphrase 'Keep Calm and Have a Cupcake' – captures the arty zeitgeist of Margate's cultural quarter. The most singular establishment, however, is the Mad Hatter (9 Lombard Street, 01843 232626, open Sat only), an archetypal English tearoom with an old piano and antique furniture. Tea and cake is served by the Mad Hatter himself, dressed in a waistcoat and top hat.

Ambrette ★

44 King Street, CT9 1QE (01843 231504, www.the ambrette.co.uk). Lunch served noon-2.30pm, dinner served 5.30-10pm Tue-Sun.
This Indian restaurant, formerly the Indian Princess, is hailed as one of the best in Kent. The freshest ingredients – including Kentish game and locally caught fish – are used in dishes such as Gressingham duck pan-grilled with spices in orange, fennel and cinnamon sauce by head chef Dev Biswal. Prices aren't low, but flavours are sensational, and the own-made breads have to be tried.

BeBeached

Margate Harbour Arm, CT9 1AP (07961 402612, www.bebeached.co.uk). Food served 11am-4.30pm Wed-Sun. Dinner served Summer 7.30-9.30pm Thur-Sat. Winter 7.30-9.30pm Fri, Sat.
BeBeached is in a great location, with views over the harbour and the town. Billed as a 'real food café', it serves only seasonal food, most of it organic. Typical dishes include leek and Kentish cheese crumble with new potatoes and puy lentils or spiced crisp-coated chicken with a fattoush salad. Prices are very reasonable, and it's a fine place in which to hang out.

Lighthouse Bar

Margate Harbour Arm, CT9 1AP (01843 291153, www.margateharbourarm.co.uk). Open noon-midnight daily. Tapas served noon-11pm daily. No credit cards.
A most pleasant place to have a drink, perched on the end of the Margate Harbour Arm. There are large windows giving expansive views; in winter a wood-burning stove makes it cosy. In the summer you can climb up to the lighthouse that stands next door and look at the skies Turner loved so much. Alongside snacks, there's an excellent wine list as well as beers and coffee.

Where to stay

Margate YHA

3-4 Royal Esplanade, Westbrook Bay, CT9 5DL (0845 371 9130, www.yha.org.uk). Rates £30 for 2 people.
This ex-hotel is right on the seafront, so it's perfectly placed for a bucket-and-spade holiday. The beach outside is gently shelving and sandy; Margate's main beach is a stroll down the prom. There are 60 beds, some in family rooms holding four or five beds. Most of the hostel has free Wi-Fi, the two lounges have TVs and DVD players, and there are laundry facilities. There's a cycle store too – handy given the number of cyclists doing the coastal route. Note that the YHA is self-catering only.

Reading Rooms ★

31 Hawley Square, CT9 1PH (01843 225166, www.thereadingroomsmargate.co.uk). Rates £135-£170 double incl breakfast.
Distressed, slate-blue walls, huge La Maison beds and antique chandeliers feature in the three rooms of this fabulous B&B. Massive bathrooms boast roll-top baths, walk-in showers, Ren toiletries and marble floors. Breakfast – freshly squeezed apple juice, smoked salmon and scrambled eggs and own-made muesli – is brought to your room in the morning at a time of your choosing. It's the best place to stay in Margate, and could be classed as a destination in itself.

Smiths Court Hotel

21-27 Eastern Esplanade, CT9 2HL (01843 222310, www.smithscourt.co.uk). Rates £55-£90 double incl breakfast. Self-catering from £300 per week.
Once part of the Court Hotels group, the refurbished Smiths Court on Cliftonville seafront is now owned and operated by Robert and Ann Smith and their family. There are bright, spick-and-span rooms as well as self-catering suites with fully equipped kitchenettes, dining areas and a daily maid service. There are the usual lounge facilities and a gym. The Orangery dining room serves English dishes using local produce where possible.

Walpole Bay Hotel & Living Museum

Fifth Avenue, CT9 2JJ (01843 221703, www.walpole bayhotel.co.uk). Rates £65-£145 double incl breakfast.
Part hotel, part museum, Cliftonvill'es Walpole was built as a genteel hotel by Louisa Budge in 1914 and extended in 1927; the hotel stayed in the family (and frozen in time) until 1995. Now, though the elegance remains, the Walpole has modern facilities such as en suite bathrooms and satellite TV. The antique features are unique, notably the 1920s ballroom, with its original sprung maple dancefloor and the 1927 Otis trellis-gated lift. Take a ride to the top floor to observe the original workings in action, then admire old photographs of early holidaymakers on the second floor, and the maids' sculleries with their ceramic sinks and wooden drainers and the old kitchens. Doubles and family rooms with a baby-listening service are available, and there are lovely views out to sea; many of the 36 rooms have balconies. Dogs are welcome. The restaurant offers traditional fare, including cream teas (2-5pm) and hearty Sunday roasts.

BROADSTAIRS & BOTANY BAY

Broadstairs

Charles Dickens loved Broadstairs, and it's easy to see why he declared it 'one of the fresh and free-est little places in the world'. Broadstairs is the quintessential faded English seaside town. It's got the cockles and whelks, the candyfloss and the ice-cream. The tiny streets are brimming with Victorian and Edwardian buildings in which quaint shops ply their trade, from the downright twee to splendid retro 1950s Italian coffee houses.

In fact, the Dickens connection can be seen all over the town, from the Olde Curiosity Shop café (9 Harbour Street) to the Dickens House Museum (*see p67*). Since 1937 the town has held an annual knees-up devoted to the writer (www.broadstairsdickensfestival.co.uk), which sees the resort overrun with enthusiasts for a week in June,

Lighthouse Bar

limbering up for the Victorian cricket match, attending an adaptation of one of the great man's novels at the Dickens House Museum or simply strolling around town in full Victorian regalia. It can come as a surprise for uninitiated visitors, as crinoline-clad ladies rustle by, passing gentlemen

Things to do

MARGATE & CLIFTONVILLE

Kent Scuba
274 Northdown Road, CT9 2PT (01843 297430, www.kentscuba.com). Open 10.30am-5.30pm Mon, Tue, Thur-Sat. Taster dive session £25.
This friendly centre offers PADI scuba diving training courses for all abilities. Courses include Open Water, Rescue Diver and speciality courses such as Wreck Diving and Digital Underwater Photography. The shop also has a formidable selection of diving equipment to keep enthusiasts warm and safe, and can arrange dive trips in the UK and abroad.

Ride Kite Surfing
07977 147115, www.ridekitesurfing.com. One-day course £120. No credit cards.
Learn to harness the sea breeze and let it propel you over the water under the tuition of an experienced instructor. The company kits out pupils in all the necessary gear, and once you've mastered the basics in a group, they offer one-on-one tuition for those who want to hone their skills. Courses take place on various beaches.

BROADSTAIRS & BOTANY BAY

Kent Surf School
Viking Bay, CT10 1QS (01843 866707, www.kentsurfschool.co.uk). Open Summer 10am-5pm daily. Winter by appointment. Starter course from £35.
Kent Surf School offers surf lessons for all ages and abilities, whether as an individual or in a group. If the weather isn't creating enough waves to make surfing viable, the instructors get the kayaks, surf skis and paddleboards out.

Turner & Dickens Walk
www.turneranddickenswalk.co.uk.
Tread the four-mile route between JMW Turner's stomping ground of Margate and Dickens' much-frequented Broadstairs. Scenes from the two figures' lives and works are displayed at various points, and there are intriguing landmarks such as Drapers Mill and Crampton Tower Museum.

RAMSGATE & MINSTER

Horizon Sea Safaris
Royal Harbour, CT11 8LN (07931 744788, www.horizonseasafaris.co.uk). One-hour seal watching £20; £15 reductions. No credit cards.
Top up on local knowledge, historical snippets and facts on local wildlife, all while riding the waves, on one of Horizon's sea ventures. Choose between options such as fishing trips, fast and furious powerboat trips, and excursions to the seal haven of Goodwin Sands.

politely doff their top hats, and stripey-suited bathers picnic on the sands.

Viking Bay is the main bay in Broadstairs. It's so-named because it's around here that the Viking marauder Hengist first landed in Britain. Horseshoe-shaped, with a small harbour, it has fishing boats, a sailing club, ice-cream kiosks, a small children's funfair and a café. The beach is easily accessible for all now that a lift has been installed (open daily from Whitsun to the end of September). Children can let off steam on trampolines and there is still a traditional Punch and Judy show in the summer. For scaled-down pitch and putt fun, Lillyputt Minigolf (01843 861500, www.lillyputt.co.uk) on Victoria Parade has child-sized clubs and a well-designed course. Put the ball through the right final hole to win a free game.

Even without the Victoriana, everything has an old-world charm and toy-town appeal, from the dinky Palace cinema (01843 865726, www.palacebroadstairs.co.uk) to the little streets criss-crossing the town, the fishermen's cottages and seven pretty beaches. And, of course, there's Morelli's (*see p73*), a splendid ice-cream parlour and the subject of one of photographer Martin Parr's defining shots.

The British folk revival of the 1950s and 1960s has left a lasting and substantial legacy in the town: Broadstairs Folk Week (01843 604080, www.broadstairsfolkweek.org.uk), which takes place in August. The emphasis is on traditional folk styles – so expect lots of fiddles and reels in pubs across the town.

The town also has a solid line in characterful shops. Several are gathered around the compact centre that stretches south from the station towards the promenade. On Charlotte Street is the Bottleneck (nos.7-9, 01843 861095, www. thebottleneck.co.uk, closed Sun), a carefully sourced collection of Australian and New Zealand wines. A few streets away on Harbour Street, the Herbal Apothecary (no.2, 01843 863096, www.herbal apothecary.co.uk, closed Sun) is stuffed with organic beauty brands, including Burt's Bees, Lavera and the hard-to-find A'Kin. Qualified herbalist Patina Blakeney is also on hand with a stash of natural remedies. Dolls' house enthusiasts can pick through the miniature homes and furnishings in Small World (9 York Street, 01843 448055, closed Mon, Sun). Time and Space on the High Street (No. 82, 01843 866006) with its stock of retro toys and games, is a joy, and everyone will enjoy a tea and cake at the Oscar's Festival Café (**15 Oscar Road, 01843 872442, closed Mon-Wed**).

Union Square, behind the Old Curiosity Shop on Harbour Street, is worth a look. The houses are around the square are some of the oldest in the town; Union Square was named for the union of Great Britain in 1703.

The bays of Broadstairs
Broadstairs has seven bays. Botany Bay is the most northerly, Kingsgate Bay has chalk cliffs and caves. and Joss Bay is popular with sunbathers and, when the wind and tide is right, surfers. Its large car park

KENT

Broadstairs

reflects its popularity. The North Foreland Lighthouse looks out over the sea from here – the lighthouse's cottages are now self-catering residences (*see p74*). Stone Bay, the setting for John Buchan's *The 39 Steps*, is reached via steps down the cliff or by walking along the promenade from Viking Bay. Louisa Bay, just round the southern headland of Viking Bay, is fairly quiet. The most southerly of the seven is Dumpton Gap. You can walk to Ramsgate from here at low tide, or along the clifftop if the tide is in.

Botany Bay, the prettiest of the seven, is a short drive from Broadstairs. All the bay are characterised by chalk cliffs – the longest continuous stretch in Britain – but Botany wins the prize for its much-photographed chalk stacks. The approach is through quiet suburban streets (from Broadstairs, follow the B2052, then turn off down Percy Avenue, Kingsgate Avenue or Botany Road). There are no fairground waltzers, no donkey rides, no chippies, no amusement arcades, no candyfloss, no doughnut dispensers. This is an old-fashioned beach, where you make your own entertainment. And that's its charm.

That, and the cliffs. They dominate this diminutive strand (it's only 600 feet long), sweeping round the sandy cove and framing the sea. Indeed, with the tide in, the bluffs make Botany Bay feel safe and sheltered. But as the water recedes, the beach opens up and the horizons broaden. Time it right and you can walk along the shore to Broadstairs in an hour, clambering over rocks along the way.

Bleak House Hotel, above Broadstairs. See p73.

Cycle the Viking Coastal Trail

Botany Bay

The Viking Coastal Trail is a 27-mile cycle route around the Thanet coastline. It covers beaches galore, plus smugglers' haunts, dramatic clifftops, historic churches, nature reserves and Dickens' memorabilia.

As well as taking in the towns of Broadstairs, Margate and Ramsgate, the trail leads through seven other pretty villages and plenty of wide open space. It forms part of the National Cycle Network Regional Route 15 that extends from Reculver, famous for the much-photographed twin towers of St Mary's Church, across the north coast, through Birchington-on-Sea, Westgate-on-Sea, Margate and Broadstairs to Ramsgate. From Cliffs End, just outside Ramsgate, it heads inland to Minster, then past Monkton and finishes at St Nicholas-at-Wade – and there are plans to extend the final section back to Reculver.

If the full ride seems a little daunting, the official Viking Coastal Trail map (www.visitthanet.co.uk/viking) breaks the route into six mini rides. The first, called the Six Churches (9.5 miles), travels through the inland section from Ramsgate, stopping at St Nicholas-at-Wade and Minster Abbey (see p67), as well as four other ancient buildings. The second, History, Art and Architecture (4.5 miles), is based around Ramsgate and visits the Hugin Viking Ship, St Augustine's Abbey Church and the Royal Harbour. The third section travels though Historic Broadstairs (3.25 miles) from the King George VI Memorial Park in Ramsgate, past the Dickens House Museum and up to the North Foreland Lighthouse. The Path of St Augustine (4.5 miles) route follows that of the saint who brought Christianity to England after landing at Ebbsfleet in 597; the ride effectively follows the same route as the Six Churches. Children may be more interested in the Smugglers' Haunts trail (3.5 miles) from Joss Bay, named after the smuggler Joss Snelling, to Margate Harbour, once rife with contraband. The final section is the Beaches and Bays route (5.3 miles), which travels from Margate Harbour to Minnis Bar, or to Reculver, another 4 miles away.

Seventy per cent of the trail is traffic-free and the route is well-signposted. There are seven railway stations along the way (Minster, Ramsgate, Dumpton Park, Broadstairs, Margate, Westgate and Birchington-on-Sea) as well as plenty of pubs and tearooms for refreshments.

Bikes can be hired at: Bike Shed (71 Canterbury Road, 01843 228866, closed Sun), St Peter's Cycles (98-100 Albion Road, 01843 865769, closed Sun winter), Ken's Bike Shop (26 Eaton Road, 01843 221422, www.kensbikes.co.uk) and Caitlins Beach Cruisers (07956 395896, www.caitlinsbeachcruisers.com).

For a more cerebral look at the environment, it's the chalk cliffs that provide the main attraction. Indeed, rocks are a distinguishing feature of the landscape here. When the tide goes out, the sea reveals an extensive chalk reef – deemed the best in Britain – that makes geologists weak at the knees. 'Rock Doc' walks are organised by the Thanet Coast Project (www.thanetcoast.org.uk), along with Summer Seashore Safaris, where even amateur rock-poolers can turn up starfish, crabs and cuttlefish eggs.

Botany Bay's rocky terrain and cliffs endeared it to smugglers, who plied a lucrative trade in the area during the 18th century. Establishments such as popular chain pub the Captain Digby Inn (above Joss Bay) revel in this unscrupulous past. The landscape also reveals signs: hidden around the chalk stacks and headland in nearby Kingsgate Bay, smugglers' holes are carved in the cliffs. Natural caves, eroded by the waves, were useful for stashing booty too.

Kent may not be synonymous with surfing, but Joss Bay (two bays round from Botany) is the choice of South-east boarders thanks to its decent groundswell. Surfing is at its best here from September to April (for lessons, see p70). Sheltered by white cliffs, the bay was named after 18th-century smuggler Joss Snelling, a local legend who managed to evade the noose and live till the age of 96; he was even presented to the future Queen Victoria as 'the famous Broadstairs smuggler'. Overlooking the beach, the North Foreland Lighthouse marks the southern entrance to the Thames. Nearby, Minnis Bay is great for rock-pooling, sailing and windsurfing; seal trips are also available.

Where to eat & drink

Away from the beaches there are any number of welcoming cafés. One of the best is Beaches on Albion Street (no.49, 01843 600065, closed Christmas to Easter), a poster-covered haven that plies families with coffee, cakes and milkshakes. Restaurant 54 (54 Albion Street, 01843 867150, www.restaurant54.co.uk) serves contemporary dishes such as potted local brown shrimps followed by spiced roast monkfish fillet. The Brown Jug (204 Ramsgate Road, 01843 862788) is a much-loved pub, known for its well-kept ales, some directly from the cask. Built using local flint, the pub dates back to 1795. The Continental Corner Delicatessen & Café (11-13 Charlotte Street, 01843 865805, closed Sun) can provide a beach picnic.

Broadstairs Pavilion
Harbour Street, CT10 1EU (01843 600999, www.pavilion-broadstairs.co.uk). Food served Summer 9-11.30am, noon-5pm daily. Winter 10-11.30am, noon-2.30pm Mon-Fri; 9.30am-4pm Sat, Sun.
This spacious pub offers beautiful views over the bay and serves baguettes, pastries, ice-cream and snacks – just right for a midday beach break. There is outdoor seating and a large garden.

Chiappini's
1 The Parade, CT10 1NB (01843 865051). Open Summer 9am-5.30pm daily. Winter 9am-4pm daily.
Serving cappuccino long before the Starbucks generation was born, this vintage Italian coffee bar is a delicious slice of 1960s nostalgia. Grab a table on the promenade, and watch the world go by, or serve yourself some lunch: freshly made pasta or salads. Top it off with an ice-cream served in a tall glass with a long spoon and a cherry on top.

Morelli's
14 Victoria Parade, CT10 1QS (01843 862500, www.morellisgelato.com). Open Summer 8am-10pm daily. Winter 8am-5pm Mon-Fri; 8am-5.30pm Sat, Sun. No credit cards.
Few places can match the character of this popular seaside caff and ice-cream parlour (established in 1932, and hardly changed since refurbishment in the 1950s). The ice-cream (also available at Harrods and Selfridges) is top-notch; flavours run from classic vanilla to wilder tastes such as bubblegum or turkish delight. Sundaes are wafer- and cherry-studded affairs.

Neptune's Hall
1-5 Harbour Street, CT10 1ET (01843 861400). Open noon-11pm Mon-Thur, Sun; noon-midnight Fri, Sat.
The friendly Neptune's Hall offers a good selection of beers from Shepherd Neame, the county's biggest brewer, complemented by seasonal guest ales, bar food and tapas. The pub also has a beer garden. The place really comes alive during Broadstairs Folk Week in August.

Osteria Pizzeria Posillipo
14 Albion Street, CT10 1LU (01843 601133, www.posillipo.co.uk). Food served noon-11pm daily.
A big, bustling and much-lauded pizzeria. You'll find pizza cooked in a traditional stone oven, plus fish and seafood specials. Next door to the Royal Albion Hotel, the restaurant offers wonderful sea views from its garden terrace, as well as plenty of seating in the dark wood interior. Booking is recommended.

Peens Gastro Bar ★
8 Victoria Parade, CT10 1QS (01843 861289, www. peensgastrobar.co.uk). Open 10am-10pm Mon-Thur,

Sun; 10am-midnight Fri, Sat. Food served 10am-9.30pm Mon-Thur, Sun; 10am-10pm Fri, Sat.
Peens serves the best food in Broadstairs. The interior is clean and modern, and small enough to feel intimate. Owner and chef Matt Peen sources most of the produce locally and makes everything from the mayonnaise to the biscuits that come with the coffee. Whether tapas-style snacks, light bites or a full menu, Peens has all options covered. The breakfasts are exceptional (especially when accompanied by a bloody mary). Main courses include dishes such as slow-braised rabbit with chorizo, ciabatta and fries, and renowned burgers. Bar snacks feature the likes of wild mushroom and poached egg on toast, and whitebait with aïoli. The long bar makes it a pleasant place for an evening drink.

Where to stay

Belvidere Place ★
Belvedere Road, CT10 1PF (01843 579850, www.belvidereplace.co.uk). Rates £115-£140 double incl breakfast.
Belvidere Place offers excellent boutique-style B&B accommodation. Each of the five double rooms is originally and individually furnished, with contemporary art on the walls and an emphasis on classic design items, such as lamps and upholstered furniture. Breakfasts feature locally sourced products. It's a highly popular weekend bolt-hole, so you'll need to book well in advance.

Bleak House Hotel
Broadstairs Harbour (01843 865338, www.bleakhouse holidays.co.uk). Rates phone for details.
Once a museum, the house where Dickens wrote *David Copperfield* and *The Old Curiosity Shop* has been converted into a hotel-cum-self-catering apartment. Grandly perched

Peens Gastro Bar

KENT

DICKENS LOCATIONS IN KENT

For Charles Dickens, Kent provided a rich source of characters and locations. *Great Expectations* and *The Pickwick Papers*, in particular, draw upon the landscape of the north Kent coast. As a consequence, there are dozens of places of pilgrimage across the county and two festivals dedicated to the author, one in each of the towns with the strongest connections: Broadstairs and Rochester.

BROADSTAIRS

Dickens loved Broadstairs, calling it 'our English watering place'. The Broadstairs Dickens Festival (www.broadstairsdickens festival.co.uk) in June has been held here since 1937.

Bleak House Hotel

Dickens visited Broadstairs regularly, staying at Fort House (now the Bleak House Hotel and used for holiday accommodation, *see p73*). He wrote *David Copperfield* here.

Dickens House Museum

In all likelihood Dickens based the character of Miss Betsey Trotwood in *David Copperfield* on Miss Mary Pearson Strong, who owned this lovely ramshackle house overlooking the bay in Broadstairs. Dickens visited the house regularly. It now contains Dickens memorabilia and explores his relationship with the town. *See p67.*

CHATHAM

Dickens' father worked as a clerk in the Admiralty based in Chatham. During the time they spent there, Dickens attended William Giles' School.

Fort Amherst

Several places in Chatham are name-checked in Dickens' novels. Pickwick and his entourage visit Fort Amherst to watch a training exercise, in the funniest chapter in the book.

Ordnance Terrace

The Dickens family lived at what is now 11 Ordnance Terrace (it was no.2 then) between 1817 and 1822 when Charles was aged five to ten.

on the top of a cliff, it overlooks Viking Bay. There are four bedrooms and one suite, including the Dickens room (featuring a bed slept in by Queen Victoria). The music room has a grand piano and a drum kit, but there's karaoke equipment for the less musical. The choice of a catered stay or self-catering is up to you.

Fishermen's Cottages

12 St Peters Road, CT10 2AQ (01843 601996, www.fishermenscottages.co.uk). Rates £180-£680 per week. No credit cards.
Built in 1614, Barnaby's Lodge is a quirky and charming flint and brick cottage, dotted with beams and ships' timbers and boasting a secret door. It offers one double bedroom, another with pine bunk beds, a separate lounge, a kitchen and a courtyard garden. Four other similarly rustic cottages are available, and there's a luxury apartment too. All the accommodation is self-catering, and all the cottages are a minute's walk from the beach and amenities.

North Foreland Lighthouse

North Foreland Road, CT10 3NW (01386 701177, www.ruralretreats.co.uk). Rates £593-£1,022 per week.
Set in rolling countryside just outside Broadstairs, the old lighthouse provides self-catering accommodation in two lightkeepers' cottages. The earliest reference to a light on North Foreland was made in a deed dated 1499, when it was a simple beacon; the first lighthouse was built in 1636. Although the original structure burned down in 1683, a manned lighthouse remained on the site until 1998. Each cottage, named Khina and Lodesman, has two bedrooms (sleeping four), a kitchen, a sitting room and a dining room. They are surrounded by a large, pleasant garden with decking and a patio, and ample space to sit out. The sands of Joss Bay are three minutes away. A minimum seven-night stay is required in July and August; five nights at Easter. Phone for details of other times of year. They're popular, so book well ahead.

Royal Albion Hotel

6-12 Albion Street, CT10 1AN (01843 868071, www.albionbroadstairs.co.uk). Rates £80-£140.
A handsome, old-fashioned seaside hotel and pub with marvellous views of Viking Bay and just steps from the sea. Built in 1760, its most illustrious guest (needless to say) was Charles Dickens. All 21 bedrooms have en suite facilities, satellite TV, radios, hairdryers and tea- and coffee-making facilities. The spacious outdoor patio area is popular with families who like to sit out after breakfast or before the beach. Anything from snacks to full meals are available, and it's a good drinking spot (the place is owned by Kent brewer Shepherd Neame).

RAMSGATE & MINSTER

Ramsgate is the liveliest, in the evenings at least, of the three Thanet towns, and the location for some of the best dining on the Island (Eddie Gilbert's and Age & Sons, for example) – largely as a result of its still busy fishing industry. Ramsgate is the only Royal Harbour in the country, a distinction awarded because of its proximity to Europe during the Napoleonic Wars. It was also a pivotal destination during the Dunkirk evacuation in 1940. Today the Port of Ramsgate, which developed between 1750 and 1850, still protects ferries (heading to Ostend) from the Channel. The harbour is busy all year round with the comings and goings of fishing boats, yachts and ferries, but it's especially hectic during the annual Power Boat Grand Prix and Ramsgate Regatta Week, both in July.

High on the cliffs above the bay, at the end of Victoria Parade, is King George VI Memorial Park, which houses the elegant 19th-century Italianate Greenhouse (Montefiore Avenue, open Apr-Sept Mon-Fri; park open all year). It's an attractive place for a walk whatever the season.

Ramsgate is also known for its connection with the architect Augustus Pugin who helped design the Palace of Westminster. He came to Ramsgate to find 'the delight of the sea with Catholic architecture & a Library'. He built the Grange house on St Augustine's Road, in his signature neo-Gothic style, and described it as one of the few buildings he designed without financial restraint. It's now let as holiday accommodation by the Landmark Trust (01628 825925, www.landmarktrust.org.uk). Tours take place on Wednesdays (2-4pm) and must be booked in advance (01843 596401). Pugin also designed St Edwards on the same road, while Granville House, along Victoria Parade, was built by his son, Edward.

For children, the best fun in Ramsgate is either the beach or Adventure Submarine (110-114 Harbour Parade, 01843 590591, www.adventuresubmarine.co.uk) – an indoor play area with a disco room, climbing wall, soccer net, toddler area, slide and crawl tunnel and ball pool complex.

For grown-up kids, the Pinball Parlour (2 Addington Street, www.pinballparlour.co.uk, open 1-6pm weekends) showcases more than 30 vintage pinball machines dating from 1958, most of which can be played. Evening entertainment can be found at the Granville Theatre (Victoria Parade, 01843 591750, www.granvilletheatre.com). It has a cinema, and a theatre with a programme of amateur and professional productions, as well as concerts. There's also a wide range of classes and workshops for children and adults.

Much of Ramsgate's economy depends on tourism and the Blue Flag Main Sands is the reason people still flock here during the summer. There's a promenade, deckchairs and lifeguards. When the beach gets boring or too cold, take a short walk along the coast to Cliff's End and St Augustine's Cross (Cottington Road, www.english-heritage.org.uk) – a 19th-century, Saxon-style stone cross placed on the site where St Augustine is said to have held Mass after reaching the coast in 597. He went on to became the first Archbishop of Canterbury. A little further on is Pegwell Bay and its nature reserve.

Just inland of Ramsgate is Minster – full name Minster-in-Thanet. This is the oldest settlement in Thanet, inhabited when Jutish Vikings Hengist and Horsa landed in 49 AD. Minster Abbey (see p67) was founded in 670 and gave the village its name. The parish church of St Mary the Virgin is of Norman origin, built around 1150, and worth a look for its delightful misericords, elaborately carved wooden leaning stands for monks, dating from 1400.

ROCHESTER & AROUND

The Kent town that crops up most regularly in his writing, in *The Pickwick Papers*, *David Copperfield* and *Great Expectations*. Rochester holds a two-part Dickens festival, in June and December (www.rochesterdickensfestival.org.uk).

Bull Inn

Dickens regularly stayed in this coaching house (the bed in which he slept is now in the Dickens House Museum in Broadstairs). It's mentioned at the beginning of *The Pickwick Papers* and in *Great Expectations* as the Blue Boar Inn.

Cooling

The bleak marshes around this little village north of Rochester were the setting for the grim opening chapters of *Great Expectations*. In the book, Dickens refers to the real graves of a young family buried in the churchyard of St James, and it is here that Pip first encounters the fearsome Magwitch.

Gads Hill Place

Gads Hill Place in the village of Higham, just outside Rochester, was bought by the author in 1856. When young, Dickens used to walk to the house he one day hoped to buy – and he did. It's now a school.

Rochester Cathedral

In *The Pickwick Papers*, Mr Jingle succinctly described it thus: 'Old cathedral too – earthy smell – pilgrims' feet worn away the old steps – little Saxon doors'.

Six Poor Travellers House

This house was created in 1579 after Rochester's MP, Richard Watts, left money in his will for a house for six poor travellers 'who not being ROGUES, or PROCTORS, May receive gratis for one Night, Lodging, Entertainment, and Fourpence each'. It was the inspiration for the story *The Seven Poor Travellers* – the seventh being the narrator.

Where to eat & drink

Ramsgate offers plenty of scope for eating out. The Royal Marina has encouraged a flotilla of smart restaurants (particularly along Harbour Parade), though none is particularly noteworthy.

The Jazz Rooms (88 Harbour Parade, Royal Harbour, 01843 595459) is the best bar in Ramsgate, with quality modern jazz on Tuesdays and occasionally other days.

Age & Sons

Charlotte Court, CT11 8HE (01843 851515, www.ageandsons.co.uk). Open Café 9am-5pm Tue-Sun. Bar 7pm-midnight Tue-Thur; 7pm-2am Fri, Sat. Restaurant Lunch served noon-3.30pm Tue-Sun. Dinner served 7-9.30pm Tue-Sat.

Age & Sons, run by the Leigh family, is a good-looking restaurant, café and bar with a growing reputation for imaginative British food. Head chef Toby Leigh's menu might feature faggots with savoy cabbage and red wine jus or fish cake with aïoli. Ingredients are carefully sourced, many from only a few miles away. The basement houses a moody bar with an excellent list of spirits and cocktails. The name, incidentally, comes from the building's former life as a warehouse for wine merchants Page & Sons. The P has since dropped off.

Eddie Gilbert's ★

32 King Street, CT11 8NT (01843 852123, www.eddiegilberts.com). Lunch served noon-2.30pm Mon-Sun. Dinner served 5.30-9.30pm Mon-Sat.

This is where to come for the best seafood in Thanet, served in the relaxed surroundings of a bustling dining room, above the respected fishmonger of the same name (the owner, Johnny Dunhill, has his own fishing fleet). The fish and chips are cooked in beef dripping, and come in mighty portions. Fancier offerings include grilled Ramsgate lobster with chips, saffron and tarragon aïoli and beetroot salad, or the amazing crispy smoked eel soldiers and soft boiled duck egg.

Surin

30 Harbour Street, CT11 8HA (01843 592001, www.surinrestaurant.co.uk). Lunch served noon-2.30pm Tue-Sat. Dinner served 6-11pm Mon-Thur; 6pm-midnight Fri, Sat.

This friendly harbourside restaurant has added to its charms by offering blond and dark Surin beers, both made in local microbreweries, which compliment the flavours of Thai cuisine. The menu offers an enormous variety of meat, fish and vegetarian dishes, along with soups, starters and weekly specials. Thai dishes run from green and red curry to beef with basil and chilli or seafood salad.

Where to stay

Eighteenth-century Durlock Lodge (01843 821219, www.durlocklodge.co.uk) in Minster has a choice of B&B accommodation with a continental breakfast in the Lodge or self-catering accommodation in a couple of adjacent cottages.

Wayside Caravan Park (Way Hill, 01843 821272, www.waysidecaravanpark.co.uk), near Ramsgate, about a mile from Minster village, offers roomy static caravans in lovely grounds, with a café-bar, play area, barbecue and outdoor seating area.

Augustus Pugin's house, the Grange (*see p75*), is available as self-catering accommodation for eight and is managed by the Landmark Trust (www.landmarktrust.org.uk).

Pegwell Bay Hotel

81 Pegwell Road, CT11 0NJ (01843 599590, www.pegwellbayhotel.co.uk). Rates £77.50 double incl breakfast.

With 42 en suite rooms (singles, doubles and twins) and free parking, the Pegwell Bay Hotel offers value-for-money accommodation. Bedrooms have been refurbished to a good standard and have LCD TVs with Freeview, free internet connection, and tea- and coffee-making facilities. Superior doubles also have sea views.

Royal Harbour Hotel

10-11 Nelson Crescent, CT11 9JF (01843 591514, www.royalharbourhotel.co.uk). Rates £98-£238 double incl breakfast.

In winter, there are open fires in the dining and sitting rooms of this delightful Georgian townhouse hotel. It's a cosy place at any time of year, with delightful decor that's emphatically not 'boutique'. There's a record player with a stack of old vinyl, toys, a tray of sweets for the children and a courtesy bar for the grown-ups. All 19 rooms have en suite showers and a television and video, with a complimentary video library. Rooms have wireless internet, and the snuggery has a computer with broadband access that guests can use for free. There's a garden and a new 20-seater DVD screening area in the basement for rainy days. Perhaps best of all, breakfast runs until 11.30am.

Dickens House Museum. See p67.

Canterbury & Around

The venerable city of Canterbury has been attracting tourists for the past 900 years. After Thomas Becket was murdered in the Cathedral in 1170, as all good English literature students know, pilgrims came from all over Christendom to visit his shrine, 'the hooly blisful martir for to seke' – as Chaucer described. Aside from the Cathedral, which is Kent's most-visited attraction, the city's historic buildings run from the ruins of its Norman castle and medieval city walls to its enchantingly crooked 16th- and 17th-century timber-framed houses. Despite its rich historical legacy, Canterbury doesn't wallow in the past. Today, it's a compact, thriving city, with a large student population and busy arts community. Jewellers, art galleries, craft shops and second-hand bookstores have brought new life to the ancient buildings around the King's Mile, and there are plenty of traditional pubs to enjoy.

The villages dotted around the area have their own appeal – not least Chilham, where Tudor cottages and a superb pub cluster round a remarkable market square. There's also an excellent wildlife park. Alternatively, you can walk or cycle from here to Whitstable Harbour on the Crab & Winkle Way, following a disused railway line and peaceful woodland trails.

CANTERBURY

Strategically positioned between London and the major seaports, Canterbury has serious tourist appeal. Top of the cathedral city premiership, it also has ludicrously picturesque streets and a winning position on the eastern bank of the River Stour. Canterbury's compact nature and antique charms make it irresistible to city breakers and overseas visitors, so it's elbows out on the High Street in high season (and far from quiet in low).

West Gate, the High Street & around

Standing guard over the river, the West Gate is an imposing medieval gatehouse, built from sturdy Kentish ragstone. It was used as a prison for centuries; these days, it houses the muskets and armour of the West Gate Towers Museum (see p81). By the riverside are the beautiful West Gate Gardens, presided over by a 200-year-old oriental plane tree with an implausibly enormous trunk – legend has it a circular iron seat once bounded it, but was swallowed up by the tree as it grew. While you're at this end of town, it's also worth taking a detour along Station Road West to the excellent farmers' market and restaurant at the Goods Shed (see p82), a converted engine shed beside Canterbury West station.

Back at the West Gate, attractive St Peter's Street runs to the High Street; amid its little shops, look out for the carved gables and demons on the 17th-century building at no.13. Where St Peter's Street crosses the river and turns into the High Street, you'll see the Eastbridge Hospital of St Thomas the Martyr (see p80), parts of which span the water. For 800 years it has given shelter to those in need, and now houses a Christian community. You can visit at set times to admire its chapels, refectory and remarkable arched undercroft, where pilgrims once slept on beds of straw.

Turn right down Stour Street to visit Greyfriars Chapel (see p81) and its small, tranquil walled gardens – all that remain of a 13th-century friary. A little further along Stour Street, the Museum of Canterbury (see p81) occupies the medieval Poor Priests' Hospital. Rather unexpectedly, its specialist subject is Rupert Bear; Mary Tourtel, the creator of the scarf-wearing bear, grew up in Canterbury and attended art school here. Continue along Stour Street, then turn left into any street to reach Castle Street, which runs down to the ruined, roofless remains of the city's Norman castle (see p80).

Back on the High Street, you'll find a happy marriage of middle-of-the-road fashion chains (Kew, Accessorize, Hobbs) and decent, vaguely hippyish independents, along with various second-hand bookshops and some excellent food shops, delis and cafés. Here too are the grand Victorian premises of the Royal Museum & Art Gallery (01227 452747, www.canterbury.gov.uk/museums). Its permanent works include the national collection of the art of Thomas Sidney Cooper, famed for his paintings of cattle, as well as pieces by Van Dyck, Gainsborough, Sickert and Epstein. There's also a large ceramics collection and the museum of the regiment of the Buffs (Royal East Kent Regiment), or the 3rd Regiment of Foot, one of the oldest regiments of the British army. It is, however, undergoing a massive refurbishment project, and will be closed until spring 2012.

Take a right turn off the High Street on to St Margaret's Street to visit the Canterbury Tales attraction (see p80). It's a colourful romp through the tales told by five of Chaucer's more characterful pilgrims, brought to life with mechanised waxworks;

KENT

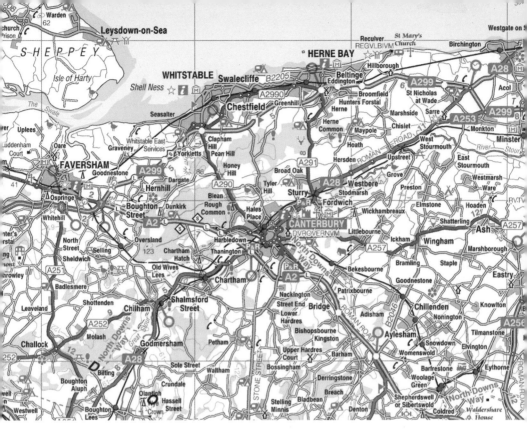

the bum-out-of-the-window episode in the Miller's Tale is particularly popular with younger visitors.

The somewhat more sedate Roman Museum (see p80) lies north of the High Street on Butchery Lane. The Roman settlement of Durovernum Cantiacorum, built at a crossing point on the Stour on the long march inland from the east Kent coast, flourished for 400 years, and the subterranean museum explores what remains beneath the modern-day city.

Christianity was practised here towards the end of the Roman period, but it was the arrival of St Augustine that gave the town its Mother Church status. The rather reluctant Augustine had been sent from Rome by the Pope to convert the pagans, and started at the top with the Saxon King Ethelbert. Augustine had a willing ally in the form of the king's wife, Bertha, a French Christian who'd been given a Roman building in which to practise her faith as part of a pre-nuptial agreement. The mass conversion to Christianity was a triumph for Augustine and his fellow missionaries, and he established an abbey, St Augustine's, just outside the city walls. He also became the first archbishop of Canterbury Cathedral (see p80) – founded in 602, though much rebuilt over the centuries that followed.

The Cathedral

Canterbury really became a place to flaunt your piety after Archbishop Thomas Becket's horrific murder in the Cathedral in 1172, at the hands of four of Henry

II's knights. Pilgrims flocked to the unfortunate archbishop's shrine – especially after Becket was canonised by Pope Alexander III in 1173 – and the guilt-ridden and remorseful king came to Canterbury to be scourged by monks at the martyr's tomb.

There was a lull in the traffic to Canterbury when Henry VIII accused the long-dead Becket of treason and threatened dire consequences if the ghost did not come out to explain himself. Oddly enough, Becket stayed in his grave and Henry destroyed the shrine and desecrated the Cathedral. It suffered further indignities from fanatical Puritans during the Civil War, and was the target for Hitler's bombers in the 'Baedeker Raids' of 1942 – an attempt to destroy England's heritage sites. The Cathedral escaped the worst of the raids, Deo gratia.

The Cathedral remains the city's centrepiece, and is top of most tourists' 'to do' list. From the splendour of the 16th-century Christ Church Gate to the Bell Harry tower soaring heavenwards, it is a magical place. It's at its loveliest just before dusk, especially if there is music going on within and the coach parties are long gone. The nave dates from around 1400, while must-sees include the lierne vaulting, stained glass, 15th-century quire screen and those spookily indented Pilgrims' Steps.

To delve deeper into Canterbury's ancient history, stroll eastwards to the ruins of St Augustine's Abbey (see p81), now in the capable hands of English Heritage. Still further east, past the

West Gate Gardens. See p77.

West Gate Towers Museum. See p81.

Cathedral Gate

Places to visit

Canterbury Tales

CANTERBURY

Opposite the Cathedral, Canterbury's Visitor Centre (The Butter Market, 12-13 Sun Street, 01227 378100, www.canterbury.co.uk) sells an Attractions Passport that gives entry into Canterbury Cathedral, St Augustine's Abbey, the Canterbury Tales and one of the city's museums (£20, £15.50 concessions).

Canterbury Castle
Castle Street (01227 378100, www.canterbury. co.uk). Open 8am-dusk daily. Admission free.
Now a hollow, roofless shell of its former self, Canterbury Castle stands on the south-west edge of the old town. The Norman successor of an earlier motte-and-bailey castle situated on the nearby Dane John Mount, it was one of three Kent castles built soon after the Battle of Hastings, on the route William the Conqueror took between Dover and London. The weighty flint and sandstone keep – one of the first keeps to be made from stone – was built in the early 12th century, and was later used as the county jail.

Canterbury Cathedral ★
The Precincts, CT1 2EH (01227 762862, www.canterbury-cathedral.org). Open Cathedral Summer 9am-5.30pm Mon-Sat; 12.30-2.30pm Sun. Winter 9am-5pm Mon-Sat; 12.30-2.30pm Sun. Crypt 10am-5.30pm Mon-Sat; 12.30pm-2.30pm Sun. Admission £8; £7 reductions.
Canterbury Cathedral is the centrepiece of the city – and, as the seat of the Archbishop of Canterbury, the heart of the Church of England. Thousands flock each day to admire its towering, intricate architecture

and contemplate the tombs of the great and good. As light pours through the magnificent stained glass windows, the oldest of which date from the early 12th century, it is wonderfully atmospheric, despite the hordes of visitors.

From the depths of the 11th-century crypt (the oldest part of the building) to the soaring arches of the 14th-century Perpendicular Gothic nave, the Cathedral reverberates with history. A modern memorial marks the spot where Thomas Becket was murdered in 1170; made of jagged steel swords, it casts a sinister shadow on the bare stone wall. In Trinity Chapel, meanwhile, a single candle burns at the former site of the martyr's shrine, which was ransacked and destroyed in 1538 on the orders of Henry VIII.

Canterbury Roman Museum
Longmarket, Butchery Lane, CT1 2JR (01227 785575, www.canterbury-museums.co.uk). Open June-Sept 10am-4pm Mon-Sat; 1.30-4pm Sun. Oct-May 10am-4pm Mon-Sat. Admission £3.10; £2.10 reductions; £8 family.
Canterbury's Roman heritage is brought to life at this acclaimed museum, located underground at the level of the old Roman town. Its collections include silver and glassware, as well as an impressive mosaic that was only discovered after wartime bombing. There are also reconstructions of a Roman marketplace and kitchen, and a 'touch the past' area where you can handle excavated artefacts.

Canterbury Tales
St Margaret's Church, St Margaret's Street, CT1 2TG (01227 454888, www.canterburytales. org.uk). Open July, Aug 9.30am-5pm daily. Mar-June, Sept, Oct 10am-5pm daily. Jan, Feb, Nov, Dec 10am-4.30pm daily. Admission £7.95; £5.90 reductions.
Chaucer's colourful characters are alive and well at the city's Canterbury Tales attraction – in animatronic form, at least. We first meet the pilgrims at the Tabard Inn, where, clad in the requisite wimples and cloaks, they prepare for their journey to the tomb of the 'hooly blisful martir' Thomas Becket, in Canterbury Cathedral. On the road we hear several of their lively tales, accompanied by suitable sounds, smells and special effects, before finally reaching our destination: a reconstruction of the shrine of St Thomas.

Eastbridge Hospital
25 High Street, CT1 2BD (01227 471688, www.eastbridgehospital.org.uk). Open 10am-5pm Mon-Sat. Admission £1; free-75p reductions. No credit cards.
If you break your arm or chop your finger off, don't expect these folk to do much more than make you a consolatory cup of tea. Eastbridge Hospital – or, to give it its full title, Eastbridge Hospital of St Thomas the Martyr – is a place of hospitality, founded in the 12th century to provide shelter for the pilgrims who flocked here following Thomas Becket's murder. True to its original remit, the Eastbridge has spent the last 800 years helping people from all walks of society, from soldiers to schoolchildren, and still provides a permanent home to several elderly people. Visitors are welcome during daytime opening hours, and can see the undercroft where pilgrims once slept,

and two chapels on the upper floors, where services are held by the resident Christian community.

Greyfriars Chapel
Stour Street, CT1 2NQ (01227 471688, www.eastbridgehospital.org.uk). Open Easter-Sept 2-4pm Mon-Sat. Admission free.
Spanning the River Stour, amid pretty English greenery, Greyfriars Chapel is all that remains of the first Franciscan friary in the country, built in the 1220s. The tranquil gardens make for a very pleasant stroll; inside the chapel, there's a modest exhibition on the building's history.

Museum of Canterbury
& Rupert Bear Museum
Stour Street, CT1 1NR (01227 475202, www.canterbury-museums.co.uk). Open June-Sept 11am-4pm Mon-Sat; 1.30-4pm Sun. Oct-May 11am-4pm Mon-Sat. Admission £3.60; £2.30 reductions; £9.20 family. No credit cards.
This comprehensive and engagingly eclectic museum offers a wealth of browsing, with displays ranging from pre-Roman times to the present. Arranged in chronological order, its exhibitions include a medieval discovery gallery, a wartime Blitz experience, and a gallery focusing on the novelist Joseph Conrad, who lived in the nearby village of Bishopsbourne in the 1920s and is buried in the city cemetery. The Saxon gallery houses some of the museum's treasures, the Canterbury Cross – a bronze and silver Saxon brooch, unearthed from below St George's Street in 1867.

Of more interest to children is the gallery devoted to Rupert Bear, whose creator, Mary Tourtel, lived in Canterbury. Nostalgia-hungry grown-ups will also enjoy the Clangers and Bagpuss display, where the original pink and white 'Old fat furry catpuss' now resides.

St Augustine's Abbey
Monastery Street, CT1 1PF (01227 378100, www.english-heritage.org.uk). Open July, Aug 10am-6pm daily. Apr-June 10am-5pm Wed-Sun. Sept, Oct 10am-5pm Sat, Sun. Jan-Mar, Nov, Dec 10am-4pm Sat, Sun. Admission £4.50; £2.30-£3.80 reductions; £11.30 family.
Part of the World Heritage Site in Canterbury (along with the Cathedral and St Martin's Church), this Benedictine abbey was founded by Augustine himself shortly after arriving in Kent in 597. It lies just outside the city walls, so is often overlooked by visitors – unfortunately, Henry VIII didn't miss it and it was gradually taken apart during the Dissolution. There are substantial remains and some formal gardens, first planted in the 17th century. A museum and audio tour are included in the entrance fee.

West Gate Towers Museum
St Peter's Street, CT1 2BQ (01227 789576, www.canterbury-museums.co.uk). Open 11am-12.30pm, 1.30-3.30pm Sat. Admission £1.30; 80p reductions; £3 family.
Looming over a stream of very 21st-century traffic, this 60-foot medieval gatehouse is a prominent feature on Canterbury's skyline. The only surviving example of the seven imposing gates that once defended the city, it now houses a weaponry museum, with guns and armaments dating from the Civil War to World War II. The gatehouse was used as a prison for centuries, and you can still visit the old cells; younger visitors of a bloodthirsty bent will also enjoy trying on the museum's replica armour.

AROUND CANTERBURY

Goodnestone Park Gardens
Goodnestone, CT3 1PL (01304 840107, www.goodnestoneparkgardens.co.uk). Open Mar-Oct 11am-5pm Tue-Fri; noon-5pm Sun. Feb-Mar noon-4pm Sun. Admission £5.50; £1-£5 reductions; £12 family. No credit cards.
Spread over 14 acres, the gardens at Goodnestone Park are wonderfully varied. The walled garden is perhaps the loveliest of all, entwined with clematis, jasmine and wisteria and encompassing a fragrant rose garden. Beyond it lies the mossy woodland garden, where spring snowdrops give way to foxgloves and magnolias in summer, then vivid blue hydrangeas come September. The main house overlooks a stunning box-hedge parterre, designed in celebration of the millennium; behind it is the village cricket ground, where matches take place on summer afternoons. There's also a plant nursery and tearoom.

Howletts Wild Animal Park ★
Bekesbourne, CT4 5EL (0844 842 4647, www.aspinallfoundation.org). Open Summer 10am-6pm daily. Winter 10am-5pm daily. Admission £17.95; £11.95-£15.95 reductions.
This first-rate animal park has an impressive array of furry, leathery and feathered inmates, from snow leopards and Bengal tigers to Red River hogs and Iberian wolves. If that wasn't enough, it's also home to the UK's largest herd of African elephants, and all sorts of primates; look out for the stunning apricot and white-coloured banded leaf monkeys. What sets Howletts apart, though, is the space afforded to the animals, with generously proportioned enclosures designed to replicate their inhabitants' natural habitats. Along with its sister establishment at Port Lympne (see p94), ten miles west of Folkestone, the park also runs a successful breeding programme for the endangered black rhino.

Wingham Wildlife Park
Wingham, CT3 1JL (01227 720836, www.winghamwildlifepark.co.uk). Open Summer 10am-6pm daily. Winter 10am-dusk daily. Admission £8.50; £7 reductions; £27 family.
Tucked away in the green Kentish countryside, this child-friendly zoo features a selection of walkthrough enclosures, allowing face-to-face encounters with deer, wallabies, prairie dogs and ring-tailed lemurs. The regular 'meet the animals' sessions are even more hands-on, giving you the chance to hold snakes, stroke iguanas, and generally get close and personal with some of the smaller inhabitants. The various birds that roam the park respond well to being fed with seed, and the new pool complex is the home to Kent's only humboldt penguin colony. Once the animals have been duly admired, the sizeable playground will occupy the children while adults can enjoy coffee and a slab of cake from the kiosk or main café.

KENT

forebidding walls of HM Prison Canterbury, St Martin's Church (North Holmes Road, 01227 768072, www.martinpaul.org) is the oldest parish church in England still in active use, and is part of the Canterbury World Heritage Site.

The King's Mile ★
For a scenic shopping experience, stroll down the historic streets of Canterbury's 'King's Mile' (www.thekingsmile.com), to the north-west of the Cathedral. Comprising Northgate, the Borough and Palace Street, it takes in all manner of independent shops, where you can find everything from a dolls' house to a vintage camera.

Chris and Les Harper's Siesta (1 Palace Street, 01227 464614, www.siestacrafts.co.uk) started in 1983 as a market stall selling handicrafts from Mexico and Guatemala. It now imports stock, especially musical instruments, from all over the world. Old-fashioned sweets are the speciality at Sugar Boy (31 Palace Street, 01227 769374, www.sugarboy.co.uk), where coconut mushrooms, toffee crumble, aniseed balls and other confections are dispensed in little stripey bags. Just around the corner on Burgate is Hawkin's Bazaar (no.34, 0844 573 4508, www.hawkin.com), filled to the rafters with great toys such as Make-your-own-Morph sets and spud guns.

Where to eat & drink
You'll find plenty of Shepherd Neame on the pumps in Canterbury's pubs; after all, it's brewed just up the road in Faversham. Two of the finest places for a pint are on St Dunstan's Street, near the West Gate. The Unicorn (no.61, 01227 463187, www.unicorninn.com) has four real ales, bar billiards and a beer garden, while the Bishop's Finger (no.13, 01227 768915) is a 16th-century pub with a penchant for cask ales and big-screen sport.

Deeson's
25-27 Sun Street, CT1 2HX (01227 767854, www. deesonsrestaurant.co.uk). Lunch served noon-4pm, dinner served 6-10pm daily.
With its white-tiled walls and pared-down decor, Deeson's puts the focus firmly on its food: Modern British grub, constructed with considerable panache. Dedicated carnivores will fare well here, with a menu that might include deep-fried pig's head served with egg and caper dressing and crispy pig's ear, alongside the less challenging likes of trio of lamb or slow-cooked duck leg with lentils and savoy cabbage. There are some fine fish dishes too, although vegetarians may find their options limited. Puddings are satisfyingly old-school: rhubarb trifle, perhaps, or spiced apple cake and custard.

Goods Shed ★
Station Road West, CT2 8AN (01227 459153, www. thegoodsshed.net). Breakfast served 8-10.30am Tue-Sat; 9-10.30am Sun. Lunch served noon-2.30pm Tue-Fri; noon-3pm Sat, Sun. Dinner served 6-9.30pm Tue-Sat.
A old railway freight store turned foodie emporium, this lofty Victorian building buzzes with activity. At the heart of the operation is the farmers' market, featuring traders

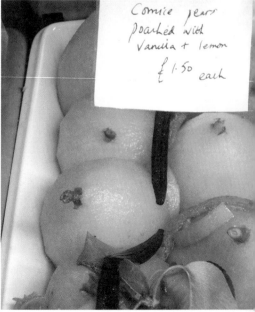

Comice pears poached with Vanilla + lemon £ 1.50 each

KENT

from local organic fruit and vegetable farms, apple juice squeezers, a butcher, a baker and a sandwich-maker, craftspeople, cheese and olive sellers and many more. Above the market, diners sit at scrubbed wooden tables and choose from the chalkboard specials. Impressively, every dish is made from ingredients sourced from the stallholders below, whether it be yellow courgette, mint and lemon soup, braised ox cheeks with creamed shallots or hake wrapped in ham with pea and tarragon broth.

Hutch

13 Palace Street, CT1 2DZ (01227 766700, www.the hutchcanterbury.co.uk). Lunch served noon-4pm Tue-Sun. Dinner served 6-10pm Tue-Sat.
This dapper little vegetarian restaurant is a relatively recent addition to Kent's foodie scene – and has got off to a flying start. The lunch menu runs from fresh soup and tapas platters to more substantial vegetable crumbles and stews, while the equally eclectic dinner menu might take in tagines, risottos and stir-fries. The wine list includes a couple of local offerings, including Chapel Down's delicious, aptly named Flint Dry.

Michael Caines ★

ABode Hotel, 30-33 High Street, CT1 2RX (01227 766266, www.michaelcaines.com). Lunch served noon-2.30pm daily. Dinner served 6-9.30pm Mon-Sat.
Soothingly lit and decorated in understated chocolate brown tones, this is one of Canterbury's smartest eateries. Like other ABode hotel restaurants, it bears the name of two-Michelin-starred chef Michael Caines, whose influence is evident in the ambitious, polished menu. Expect elaborate fine dining: roasted saddle of Godmersham rabbit with hazelnut and green bean salad and roasted almond purée, perhaps, followed by monkfish wrapped in parma ham with creamed leeks, tomato fondue, mussels and saffron velouté. If you're on a budget, the set lunch and early dinner menus are affordable alternatives to the evening à la carte.

Millers Arms

2 Mill Lane, CT1 2AW (01227 456057, www.millers canterbury.co.uk). Open 11am-11am Mon-Thur, Sun; 11am-midnight Fri, Sat. Lunch served noon-2.30pm Mon-Sat; noon-3pm Sun. Dinner served 6-9pm Mon-Sat.
Built to serve the mill workers in 1826, this riverside pub remains a firm local favourite – although the menu and drinks selection have definitely evolved for the better over the years. The seasonal dishes are well executed, and best accompanied by Shepherd Neame's traditional Kentish ales. After lunch, you can stroll along the river or head to the Cathedral. The pub also has 11 en suite rooms (£75 double incl breakfast).

Old Brewery Tavern

High Street, CT1 2RX (01227 826682, www. michaelcaines.com). Open 11am-11pm Mon-Thur; 11am-2am Fri, Sat; 11am-10.30pm Sun. Lunch served noon-2.30pm Mon-Thur; noon-3pm Fri-Sun. Dinner served 6-9.15pm Mon-Thur; 6-9.30pm Fri; 6-9pm Sat, Sun.
Huge black and white prints of coopers rolling barrels hang on the walls at the Old Brewery Tavern – another outpost of chef Michael Caines' growing empire. Its doesn't look like a traditional boozer (the decor is too self-consciously

Goods Shed

Things to do

CANTERBURY

Canterbury Ghost Tour
Alberry's Wine Bar, 38 St Margaret's Street,
CT1 2TY (0845 519 0267, www.canterburyghost
tour.com). Tours 8pm Fri, Sat. Admission £9;
£7-£8 reductions.
Discover the dark secrets of Canterbury's past
on this entertaining ghost tour, which investigates
spooky sightings around historic buildings. Those
of a nervous disposition may prefer the daytime tour
of the city centre.

Canterbury Golf Club
Scotland Hills, Littlebourne Road, CT1 1TW (01227
453532, www.canterburygolfclub.co.uk). Open
9.15am- dusk Mon-Fri; 11.30am-dusk Sat, Sun.
Half a mile outside the city, this wooded, 18-hole golf
course was created by Harry Colt in 1927. Although
overshadowed by the Open course in Sandwich, it's
well worth a visit, and the green fees are reasonable.

Canterbury Historic River Tours
Kings Bridge, CT1 2AT (07790 534744, www.
canterburyrivertours.co.uk). Open Mar-Nov 10am-5pm.
Tours £7.50; £4.50-£6.50 reductions; £21 family.
Escape the traffic and see Canterbury's historic
charms from a rowboat on the River Stour. With a
highly knowledgeable guide reeling off the facts and
doing all the arm work, all you have to do is sit back
and take in the scenery. Call in at the company's
office on Kings Bridge and staff will fix you up on
the next available departure. Each boat holds 12
passengers, and in high season tours run every
20 minutes.

Kent County Cricket Club
St Lawrence Ground, Old Dover Road, CT1 3NZ
(01227 456886, www.kent-ccc.co.uk). Open 9am-
5pm daily. Tickets £15-£22.
You'd be hard pressed to find a lovelier venue for
county cricket than Canterbury's St Lawrence
Ground. A 200-year-old lime tree famously stood
inside the boundary rope, necessitating special
scoring rules, until it was blown down in a gale in
2005. However, this was merely the end of an era,
not of a tradition: a replacement tree has since
been planted.

modern), but it shies away from gastropub pretensions with
solid, homely grub: think rump steak, simple lunchtime
baguettes and beer-battered fish or scampi and chips.

Parrot
1-9 Church Lane, St Radigunds, CT1 2AG (01227
762355, www.theparrotcanterbury.com). Open noon-
11.30pm Mon-Thur; noon-midnight Fri, Sat; noon-
11am Sun. Lunch served noon-3pm Mon-Fri; noon-4pm
Sat. Dinner served 6-9pm Mon-Sat; noon-6pm Sun.
Set in charming Grade II-listed premises built on Roman
foundations, the pub formerly known as Simple Simon's is
now the Parrot. There's a sterling line-up of draught beers,
some interesting wines and a good bar menu. For more
polished food (chargrilled organic salmon, say, or herb-
crusted lamb), book a table in the Tapestry Restaurant. The

flagstone-floored courtyard comes into its own in summer,
with smart wooden seating and a barbecue.

Where to stay
Accommodation in Canterbury can be rather chintzy
(net curtains, heavily floral walls and carpets), so
choose carefully. There are options to suit more
modern tastes, however, from the city's sleek
ABode outpost to the utterly charming Number 7
Longport (though with only one room, you'll need
to book ahead). If travelling by car, be aware that
parking is at a premium in the old city centre, and
not every hotel or B&B has a car park.
   If you don't mind a short walk into the centre,
the Ebury (65-67 New Dover Road, 01227 768433,
www.ebury-hotel.co.uk) has spacious rooms,
attentive staff and free parking. Although the New
Dover Road is rather dreary, rooms at the back
overlook the lovely walled gardens. The city's
youth hostel, resplendent in Victorian Gothic,
is on the same road (no.54, 0845 371 9010,
www.yha.org.uk). For self-catering options, consult
the Tourist Information Centre's website at
www.canterbury.co.uk.
   More characterful accommodation can be found
in Whitstable (*see p57*), 20 minutes' drive away,
where there are any number of old fishermen and
sailmakers' huts and seaside cottages to rent.

ABode ★
High Street, CT1 2RX (01227 766266, www.abode
hotels.co.uk). Rates £105-£165 double incl breakfast.
The third outpost in a small chain of smart hotels, ABode
has a prime city-centre location, close to the Cathedral. It's
glamorous but markedly unstuffy, with a lavish champagne
bar and an upmarket Modern British restaurant overseen
by Michael Caines (*see p83*). The 72 rooms feature
comfortable, handcrafted beds with cashmere throws, pale
wood floors and furniture, enamel baths, wet rooms,
enormous LCD TVs, DVD players and Wi-Fi. Rooms are
graded by price and size, from 'comfortable', through
'desirable' and 'enviable' to 'fabulous'; book the latter and
you'll find yourself in a swish penthouse with a private
rooftop terrace and a bed the size of a tennis court.

Canterbury Cathedral Lodge
The Precincts, CT1 2EH (01227 865350, www.
canterburycathedrallodge.org). Rates £75-£119 double
incl breakfast.
This modern, purpose-built hotel and conference centre
might lack historic charm, but its location inside the
Cathedral precincts is pretty unbeatable. (Residents get free
entry to the Cathedral, as well as magnificent views of it
from most of the 35 guest rooms.) The lodge is a bright and
comfortable place to stay, although the decor is quite plain;
there's no on-site restaurant, but a continental breakfast is
served in the refectory, or out on the terrace in summer.

Cathedral Gate Hotel
36 Burgate, CT1 2HA (01227 464381, www.cathgate.
co.uk). Rates £62-£145 double incl breakfast.
This characterful old hotel was built in 1438, predating the
adjoining Christ Church Gate. It's an atmospheric place,
with dark, narrow corridors and low doorways leading to

KENT

Canterbury Cathedral

25 simply furnished guest rooms. Don't expect sleek sophistication: sloping walls, floors and ceilings are par for the course, and some rooms share corridor bathrooms. The Daybreak, Cathedral and Joy rooms have Cathedral views, and there's a roof terrace under the shadows of the Cathedral tower where you can take a sunny breakfast.

Ebury Hotel
65-67 New Dover Road, CT1 3DX (01227 768433, www.ebury-hotel.co.uk). Rates £75-£155 double incl breakfast; £390-£650 per wk.
A ten-minute walk from the town centre, this privately owned 15-room hotel has a grandly Gothic exterior, a sweeping drive and an acre of grounds. The heated indoor swimming pool and spa are added attractions, and there's an elegantly old-fashioned restaurant – a bonus if you don't fancy the walk into town. The rooms, some of which have views over the garden, are large, light and comfortable; alternatively, there are self-catering flats on the lower ground floor and cottages in the grounds.

Greyfriars
6 Stour Street, CT1 2NR (01227 456255, www.greyfriars-house.co.uk). Rates £65-£75 double incl breakfast.
Greyfriars House dates back to the 12th century, when the first Franciscan monks built it as the gatehouse to their monastery. There isn't much inside to point to its great antiquity, apart from the creaky wonkiness of the stairs and floors, but it's a welcoming place. Guest rooms are clean and simply decorated, with en suite facilities and a full English to anticipate in the morning.

Magnolia House
36 St Dunstan's Terrace, CT2 8AX (01227 765121, www.magnoliahousecanterbury.co.uk). Rates £95-£125 double incl breakfast.
Compact, but highly recommended, Magnolia House treats its guests very well. Most of the rooms are small (with the exception of the grand Garden room, with its four-poster bed), but are clean and well equipped; little extras include a

ABode. See p84.

small fridge containing a complimentary half bottle of wine, mineral water and fresh milk for hot drinks. There's also a guests' sitting room. Breakfasts are beautifully presented, with plenty of choice, and served in a room overlooking the small walled garden. Although limited parking is available, it's nicer to come without your car and walk into town through peaceful West Gate Gardens.

Number 7 Longport

7 Longport, CT1 1PE (01227 455367, www.7longport. co.uk). Rates B&B from £90 double incl breakfast. Cottage from £500 per wk.
On the edge of the town centre, this tiny 15th-century cottage has been beautifully renovated to become a chic, one-bedroom B&B. There's a private sitting room, decorated in cool creams and heated by a cosy wood-burning stove, and a modern, mosaic-tiled wetroom; up the steep staircase is an equally stylish bedroom. The attention to detail is what marks this place out: the king-size bed has a hand-sprung mattress and plump down pillows, for example, and there's an iPod dock in the living room and Wi-Fi access throughout. Breakfast brings all manner of good things, from home-made yoghurt with fruit coulis to top-notch cooked breakfasts. If you'd rather self-cater, the owner also rents out a three-bedroom Victorian cottage, 14 Love Lane, which is just next door.

AROUND CANTERBURY

Around six miles south-west of Canterbury, in the River Stour Valley, is the beautifully preserved Tudor settlement of Chilham. Although its thriving market is long gone, the village still centres on the market square, lined with half-timbered houses. Here too is the 15th-century White Horse (*see p88*) – everything a village pub should be, with its whitewashed frontage, log fire and handsome beams. Behind the inn rises the impressive flint and stone tower of St Mary's Church, which has some fine stained glass.

From the square, you can look through the gates of Chilham Castle (www.chilham-castle.co.uk), a glorious 17th-century country pile that was built on the site of an enormous medieval castle; today, only the octagonal castle keep remains. The house is privately owned, but the landscaped gardens, notable for their splendid terraces, are occasionally open to the public; check the website for details.

The delightfully named village of Old Wives Lees is around a mile from Chilham, and considered part of the parish. Although it is far less picturesque than Chilham, it is set in an Area of Outstanding Natural Beauty on the North Downs, and affords expansive views over the Weald and Swale Estuary.

Three miles south-east of Canterbury, just off the A2, the small village of Bekesbourne is best known as the home of Howletts Wild Animal Park (*see p81*), which occupies a 90-acre swathe of ancient parkland. The Grade I-listed parish church, St Peter's, is also worth a look for its Norman north doorway and 13th-century stained glass, which survived a zealous 19th-century restoration. While you're in these parts, call by Mama Feelgoods (Chalkpit Farm, School Lane, 01227 830830, www.mamafeelgoods.co.uk) – an excellent deli

and café serving hearty hot food, doorstop sandwiches and own-made cakes.

North-east of Bekesbourne, Wingham is home to Wingham Wildlife Park (*see p81*); from here, it's just over a mile and a half to Ickham, where the Duke William pub (*see p88*) makes a fine lunchtime stop-off. A few miles further north, the Red Lion (*see p88*) in Stodmarsh is also known for its food.

Follow the Crab & Winkle way

When the track from Canterbury to Whitstable was laid, it was the third railway line ever to be built in Britain. In May 1930, the first trainload of passengers climbed aboard ten wooden, open-box carriages pulled by Stephenson's *Invicta* – a coal-powered locomotive that predated his more famous *Rocket*. To the onlookers lining the route, cheering and waving their hats, it must have seemed little short of a miracle.

Affectionately dubbed the Crab & Winkle Line, in honour of Whitstable's famous shellfish beds, the new railway line became the world's first regular passenger line, and the first railway to issue season tickets. It carried passengers until the early 1930s, when it was demoted to transporting goods; then, in December 1952, the line was closed for good.

It wasn't until 2000 that it was resurrected, thanks to the efforts of the Crab & Winkle Line Trust – this time as part of a seven-mile cycling and walking trail from Canterbury to Whitstable. The signposted, mostly traffic-free route takes in stints along some lovely woodland tracks, and forms part of the National Cycle Network Route 1. It's a relatively easy ride, though be prepared for a few climbs. If you need to hire bikes, try Downland Cycles (The Malthouse, St Stephens Road, 01227 479643, ww.downlandcycles.co.uk, open Apr-Oct, closed Sun).

You can pick the trail up at the Goods Shed (*see p82*) by Canterbury's West Station. From here, it leads through suburban residential streets and across meadows bordering the city to the campus of the University of Kent, then onwards to the railway line and the woods. Although walkers and cyclists follow different routes in parts, their paths rejoin at the Winding Pond: the first engines weren't powerful enough to make it up the hill unaided, which accounts for the Winding Station. These days it's a lovely spot for a picnic, with tables fashioned from old railway sleepers. The gradient is gentle down through beautiful Blean Woods (look out for woodpeckers, willow warblers and rare heath fritillary butterflies), across the roaring A299, past Tesco and on to Invicta Way, which covers the last mile of the route past back gardens to Whitstable harbour.

For detailed information on the route, visit www.sustrans.org.uk or www.kent.gov.uk/cycling.

Beyond Stodmarsh are the beautiful gardens at Goodnestone (*see p81*), created by the FitzWalter family: the village pub, the FitzWalter Arms (*see below*), was renamed in their honour in the 1920s.

Where to eat & drink

Duke William ★

The Street, Ickham, CT3 1QP (01227 721308, www.dukewilliam.biz). Open 11am-11pm daily. Lunch served noon-3pm, dinner served 6-10pm Mon-Sat. Food served noon-8pm Sun.

With its real ales, sociable buzz and excellent food, the Duke is everything a local pub should be. Bar snacks (chicken liver pâté on toast, filled baguettes) provide swift sustenance, while more substantial mains might include steak and ale pie, slow-roasted pork belly with cider and piled-high Sunday roasts. A log fire keeps guests well-toasted in winter, and there's a beer garden with a children's swing and slide for summer. Upstairs are four simple rooms (£65 double incl breakfast).

FitzWalter Arms

The Street, Goodnestone, CT3 1PJ (01304 840303, www.thefitzwalterarms.co.uk). Open noon-3pm, 6-11pm Mon, Wed-Fri; 6-11pm Tue; noon-11pm Sat, Sun. Lunch served noon-2pm Mon, Wed-Sat; noon-2.30pm Sun. Dinner served 7-9pm Mon-Sat.

This delightful Shepherd Neame pub has an impressive reputation for its food. Head chef David Hart has worked in several Michelin-starred kitchens, and his talent shines through in the short, seasonal menu. Mains might feature leek gratin with poached egg and mustard sauce, or thyme-spiked braised beef shin. To finish, sample a beautifully silky crème caramel with prunes in armagnac. Prices are higher than at your average pub, but so is the quality.

Granville

Faussett Hill, Street End, CT4 7AL (01227 700402, www.thegranvillecanterbury.com). Open noon-3pm, 5.30-11pm Mon-Sat; noon-10.30pm Sun. Lunch served noon-2pm Tue-Sat; noon-2.30pm Sun. Dinner served 7-9pm Tue-Sat.

Another restaurant flying the flag for Kentish produce is the Granville, some ten minutes' drive south of Canterbury. With the cheery air of a large farmhouse kitchen, it delivers an accomplished, daily-changing menu, best considered over a hunk of the chef's delicious own-made bread. It's simple but accomplished stuff: Monkshill leg of lamb with potato gratin and fresh mint sauce, perhaps, or braised brill fillet with mussels and saffron.

Red Lion

The Street, Stodmarsh, CT3 4BA (01227 721339). Open 10am-3am Mon-Sat, 10am-7pm Sun. Lunch served 12.15-2.30pm, dinner served 7.15-9.30pm daily.

The Red Lion's unassuming white exterior gives way to an enjoyably eccentric pub, where sheet music substitutes for wallpaper, mantelpieces are lined with wine bottles and cosy corners are filled with an eclectic mix of clutter. The kitchen whips up some seriously satisfying grub, and excels when it comes to meat dishes; rack of lamb is always a highlight. Puddings are resolutely traditional, with the likes of apple crumble and treacle sponge, and the cheeseboard will satisfy even the most ravenous diner. There are four rooms (£70 double incl breakfast).

White Horse ★

The Square, Chilham, CT4 8BY (01227 730355, www.thewhitehorsechilham.co.uk). Open noon-11pm daily. Lunch served noon-3.30pm Mon-Sat; noon-4pm Sun. Dinner served 6.30-9pm Mon-Sat.

Occupying pride of place on Chilham's market square, the White Horse is a splendid spot for a slap-up pub lunch. Most of the ingredients are organic, and come from named local farms, and the kitchen's attention to detail is impressive: the bread is own-made, for example, as are the chicken nuggets and fish fingers on the children's menu. Bar food is solid and satisfying (a cheddar ploughman's, say, or local beef and horseradish sandwich), while highlights of the dinner menu include own-made pâté with fig relish to start, and a main of free-range chicken with truffle cream sauce. Top things off with a devilishly rich chocolate pot.

Chilham Castle. See p87.

Sandwich to Hythe

The east Kent coastline offers secluded bays, rolling hills, fishing towns and the magnificent White Cliffs of Dover. Dover's iconic cliff faces are the striking centrepoint of the coastal strip that runs between the former medieval port of Sandwich, via the peaceful seaside resort of Deal, to the small market town of Hythe. Facing France, at the narrowest part of the English Channel, this vast chalk wall flecked with black flint is often a visitor's first glimpse of England; ferries still nip across the Dover strait to and from the French ports of Calais and Dunkirk. Together with Hastings, New Romney, Hythe and Sandwich, Dover is one of the Cinque Ports. This once meant considerable military and trade responsibilities (but no national tax), but today the Cinque Ports banner is wholly symbolic.

Further west sits a culturally resurgent Folkestone, followed by quaint Hythe. Folkestone is a town on the brink of change, currently benefiting from recent investment, and with a growing artistic community creating a real buzz.

SANDWICH

The once bustling medieval port of Sandwich now lies inland on the River Stour, and is surrounded by nature reserves. Between Ramsgate and Sandwich lies the Sandwich & Pegwell Bay Nature Reserve (see p92); with its eroding chalk cliffs, mudflats, dunes and saltmarsh, it's birding paradise. Closer to town, Gazen Salts Nature Reserve (01304 617197, www.visitkent.co.uk) is a network of woodland paths around a lake.

Sandwich was once on a bank of the Wantsum estuary, long since silted up, and served as one of the major seaports linking England to continental Europe. As a result it was heavily fortified – the Fisher Gate, built in 1384, is one of the only medieval gates in Britain to survive. It has seen various notable figures pass through, including Thomas Becket on the run from Henry II, and Richard the Lionheart returning from the Crusades. Sandwich is also said to have greeted the first elephant to arrive in England, when Louis IX of France gifted the beast to Henry III in 1255. The Guildhall Museum (see p92) inside the Elizabethan town hall (still used by the council) sets out the history of Sandwich and has tours of the mayor's parlour and the ancient courtroom. There's also a handsome toll bridge; no toll is payable nowadays, but the bridge is raised periodically to allow river traffic through.

Near the Quay are the Secret Gardens of Sandwich (see p93). Continue along Knightrider Street to St Clements, which has a 12th-century nave, a 13th-century chancel and a 14th-century chapel. The Norman tower, with its grotesque gargoyles, is one of the best preserved in the country. The principal shopping area in Sandwich is Market Street and around.

Festival week in late August sees Sandwich at its busiest (www.sandwichfestival.org.uk), with a long programme of events – from motorcycle meets to music in churches and a boat parade. There's also a food festival in April; contact the Tourist Information Office (Guildhall, 01304 613565, open closed Nov-Mar) for details. Golfers set their caps at the 18-hole course at Royal St George's (see p104), which is two miles from town, and opens to visitors on Tuesdays.

Where to eat & drink

The Bell Hotel (see below) is a popular spot, and a decent meal can also be had at a couple of old world pubs. The George & Dragon (24 Fisher Street, 01304 613106, www.georgeanddragon-sandwich. co.uk) matches an attractive modern menu (roast pork chop with chorizo, mixed bean and vegetable broth) with an extensive wine list. The Kings Arms Hotel (Strand Street, 01304 617330, www.kings arms-sandwich.co.uk) is equally ancient; pub grub includes own-made pies and a signature curry. Both pubs offer accommodation. The Salutation tearoom in the Secret Gardens of Sandwich (see p93) is worth investigating too.

Where to stay

Mulberry Cottages (www.mulberrycottages.com) administers a remarkable Tudor manor house in Ash, directly west of Sandwich. It has original oak beams, leaded windows and inglenook fireplaces, and sleeps up to eight adults and two children.

Bell Hotel

The Quay, CT13 9EF (01304 613388, www.bellhotel sandwich.co.uk). Rates £95-£215 double.
Pleasantly located by the River Stour, the old Bell Hotel is a labyrinth of stairways and corridors. There are 37 individually decorated en suite bedrooms, all with Wi-Fi, gleaming bathrooms and complimentary chocolates. Diners can choose between the likes of roast Kentish marsh lamb with parsnip, spinach and rosemary jus in the restaurant, or own-made beef burger with fat chips, tomato and chilli relish in the more intimate bar.

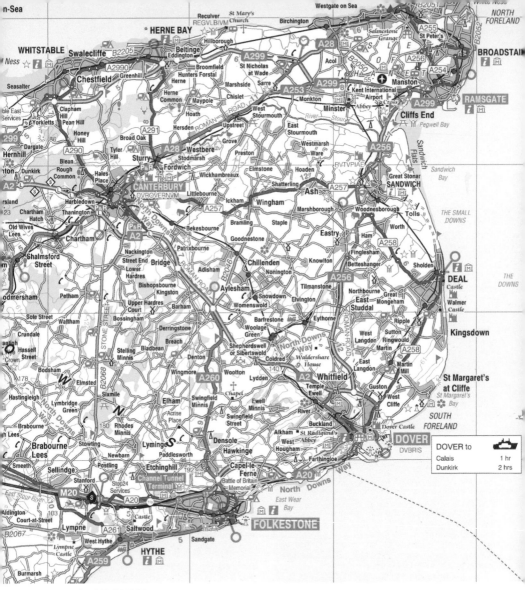

DEAL & AROUND

Deal & Walmer

Twenty-first century Deal has a sleepy air, but in the heyday of sail power, the town was a major port. In Tudor times, the economic and strategic importance of this little piece of coastline prompted Henry VIII to build a series of defensive fortifications against the threat of a French invasion. These became known as the Castles in the Downs, and include Walmer Castle and Deal Castle (for both, see p93).

The centre of Deal is a pleasant place, with alleyways and twittens off cobbled streets and winding roads. The place has been discovered by second-home owners, and you'll find vintage clothes and interiors shops, and bakeries and cafés, as well as the usual high-street chains.

On the way to the seafront, you pass by the Timeball as it rises and falls every hour (Victoria Parade, 01304 360897, http://dealtimeball. tripod.com). A museum is situated below, and explains the building's former use as a tower for signalling to ships at sea. Find out more on Deal's smuggling and sailing history in the Deal Maritime Museum (22 St Georges Road, 01303 381344, http://home.freeuk.net/deal-museum).

The long seaside promenade (part of the Saxon Shore Way) takes you past Deal Castle into Walmer, a predominantly residential area with some distinctive houses, and to Walmer Castle and its

Deal

gardens (and beyond to Kingdown and St Margaret's at Cliffe). Since 1708, Walmer Castle has been the official residence of the Lord Warden of the Cinque Ports – at one time a position of some power, with the holder controlling the five greatest ports of medieval England. Two famous wardens – the Duke of Wellington, victor of Waterloo, and WH Smith (yes, that WH Smith) – died here. The simply furnished room in which the Iron Duke expired (in his armchair at 3.25pm on 14 September 1852) has been left much as it looked then.

Kingsdown

Just a little south of Walmer is a secluded coastal village, Kingsdown. The pebbled beach here is bookended by National Trust-owned Kingsdown Wood on one side, and the foot of the White Cliffs (also looked after by the National Trust) on the other. From here there are panoramic views of the Channel, and of South Foreland Lighthouse (*see p93*) and Dover Castle (*see p93*). The Walmer & Kingsdown golf course (*see p103*) commands a fine clifftop position.

The village runs from fishermen's cottages on the beach up through lanes that climb a small hill peppered with interesting houses. An uncultivated stretch – Hawkshill Freedown – runs from Walmer Castle through to Kingsdown. En route there's a memorial to honour 16 pilots who lost their lives during World War I, flying from the airfield that once stood here.

Dover Castle

SANDWICH

Guildhall Museum
*Cattle Market, CT13 9AH (01304 617197,
www.sandwichtowncouncil.gov.uk). Open Apr-Oct
10.30am-12.30pm, 2-4pm Tue, Wed, Fri, Sat;
2-4pm Thur, Sun. Admission £1; 50p reductions.
No credit cards.*
This museum in the Elizabethan-era Town Hall
charts the history of Sandwich from its days as
a major seaport to the present time.

Pfizer Monks' Wall Nature Reserve
*Sandwich, CT13 9AH (01304 617197).
Admission free.*
Run jointly by Pfizer, the pharmaceutical company
that has a huge presence in the town, and the
Sandwich Bay Observatory Trust, this 69-acre site
attracts a large number of migratory wetland birds,
such as long-billed waders and the red-rumped
swallow. Access is by permit (free from the Tourism
Information Centre inside the Guildhall).

Rare Species Conservation Centre
*Bellar's Bush, Dover Road, CT13 0DG (01304
611578, www.rarespeciesconservationcentre.org).
Open school hols only; check website for details.
Admission £10.*

The Rare Species Conservation Centre is home to
endangered creatures often overlooked by mainstream
zoos, such as the bearded saki monkey, palawan
bearcats and Philippine cloud rats. Two black-footed
cat kittens – among the smallest species in the world
– were born in summer 2010.

Richborough Roman Fort
*Off Richborough Road, CT13 9JW (01304 612013,
www.english-heritage.org.uk). Open Apr-Sept 10am-
6pm daily. Admission £4.80; £2.90-£4.30 reductions;
£12.50 family.*
This fort is described by English Heritage as 'perhaps
the most symbolically important of all Roman sites in
Britain'. The walls of the fort and amphitheatre can be
seen; access is across grazed land, or you can arrive
by boat along the River Stour.

Sandwich & Pegwell Bay Nature Reserve
*Cliffsend, Ramsgate, CT11 5DR (01622 662012,
www.visitthanet.co.uk). Open 24hrs daily. Admission
free.*
The reserve is divided by the River Stour, and is an
important haven for waders and wildfowl, including
dunlin, curlew, oystercatcher and redshank. There's
a hide (with wheelchair access) and three nature trails
with information panels. The car park (open 8.30am-
dusk daily; £1.50) is on the Pegwell Bay side.

KENT

Secret Gardens of Sandwich
*The Salutation, Knightrider Street, CT13 9EW
(01304 619919, www.the-secretgardens.co.uk).
Open Apr-Sept 10am-5pm daily. Jan-Mar, Oct-Dec
10am-4pm daily. Tearoom Apr-Sept 10am-5pm daily.
Jan-Mar, Oct-Dec 11am-4pm Mon-Wed, Sat, Sun.
Admission £6.50; £3-£6 reductions; £16 family.*
The ornamental Secret Gardens surround a Grade
I-listed manor house designed by Sir Edwin Lutyens.
After years of neglect, the Secret Gardens were
reopened in 2007. Although they retain some of
their original character, there are new additions such
as the wollemi pine. There's a little island reached by
a small bridge, and an audio tour narrated by head
gardener Steve Edney. The Salutation tearoom
offers cream teas, cakes, soups and quiches.

DEAL & AROUND

Deal Castle
*Deal, CT14 7BA (01304 372762, www.english-
heritage.org.uk). Open Apr-Sept 10am-6pm daily.
Admission £4.50; £2.30-£3.80 reductions;
£11.30 family.*
On the seafront at Deal, this 16th-century castle
can be seen from far around and was one of the
last to be built for military purposes in England. Its
shape is based on the Tudor rose; visitors are able
to explore throughout, including storerooms and the
captain's residence.

Fowl Mead Country Park
*Sholden, Deal, CT14 0BF (01304 615390,
www.fowlmead.co.uk). Open 8am-4.30pm daily.
Admission free.*
This 200-acre park attracts everyone from cyclists
to ornithologists. Carefully created wildlife habitats
co-exist happily with a tarmac cycle path. The area
was also once home to the Betteshanger coal mine –
the largest in Kent and the last to close, in 1989.

Walmer Castle
*Kingsdown Road, Walmer, CT14 7LJ (01304 364288,
www.english-heritage.org.uk). Open Apr-Sept 10am-
6pm daily. Oct 10am-6pm Wed-Sun. Admission £7;
£3.50-£6 reductions; £17.50 family.*
Walmer Castle is similar in design to Deal Castle,
both of which were built by Henry VIII. The visitor
will find more of interest here, as it was a private
residence (of the Lord Warden of the Cinque Ports)
as well as an historic building. The gardens are
attractive, and the tearoom is excellent.

DOVER & AROUND

Dover Castle & Dover's Secret Tunnels ★
*Castle Hill, Dover, CT16 1HU (01304 211067,
www.english-heritage.org.uk). Open Mar-Oct 10am-
6pm daily. Nov-Feb 10am-4pm Thur-Sun. Admission
£13.90; £7-£11.80 reductions; £34.80 family.*
Dover has always been an important defensive point
and Dover Castle is one of the most impressive
castles in England. Beneath the castle lies a network
of tunnels, parts of which date from the Middle Ages.
Expanded to form subterranean barracks during the
Napoleonic War, they became the nerve centre for

secret military operations during World War II and
the Cold War. See the dimly lit underground hospital,
and peer into the atmospheric command centre,
telephone exchange and anti-aircraft operations
room. In addition, English Heritage has refashioned
the Great Tower to appear as it would have for the
arrival of Philip of Flanders in 1184, together with
an absorbing exhibition. The castle grounds also
house the oldest Roman lighthouse in Europe.

Dover Museum & the Bronze Age Boat Gallery
*Market Square, Dover, CT16 1PH (01304 201066,
www.doverdc.co.uk/museum). Open Apr-Aug 10am-
5.30pm Mon-Sat; noon-5pm Sun. Jan-Mar, Sept-
Dec 10am-5.30pm Mon-Sat. Admission £3; £2
reductions; £9.*
The history of Dover, in a permanent collection
(including several striking scale models of the town)
and a programme of changing exhibitions. The most
recent addition to the museum is a Bronze Age boat
that was discovered during the building of a new
road in Bench Street.

Pines Garden & the Pines Calyx
*St Margaret's Bay, CT15 6DZ (01304 851737,
www.pinesgardens.co.uk) Open 10am-5pm daily.
Admission £3; 50p-£2.50 reductions. No credit cards.*
Six acres of idyllic parkland, with wheelchair- and
buggy-friendly pathways. There's a waterfall and lake,
and a kitchen garden with more than 40 species of
fruit and veg. The eco-friendly conference centre, the
Pines Calyx (www.pinescalyx.co.uk), is made from
chalk and has a grass roof.

Roman Painted House
*New Street, Dover, CT17 9AJ (01304 203279,
www.theromanpaintedhouse.co.uk). Open Apr, June-
mid Sept 10am-4.30pm Tue-Sun. May 10am-4.30pm
Tue, Sat. Other times by appointment. Admission £3;
£2 reductions.*
Built around 200 AD, this is the finest Roman house
on show in Britain. Among other features, 26 painted
panels, devoted to Bacchus, can be clearly seen.

South Foreland Lighthouse
*The Front, St Margaret's Bay, CT15 6HP (01304
852463. www.nationaltrust.org.uk/main/w-
southforelandlighthouse). Open times vary; check
website for details. Admission Guided tour only
£4.20; £2.10 reductions; £10.50 family.*
This Victorian building was the first lighthouse to use
electricity and also received the world's first ship-to-
shore transmission on Christmas Eve, 1898.

FOLKESTONE & HYTHE

Battle of Britain Memorial
*New Dover Road, Capel-le-Ferne, CT18 7JL
(01303 249292, www.battleofbritainmemorial.org).
Open Visitor Centre Apr-Sept 11am-5pm daily.
Admission free.*
Just off the B2011 stands a permanent monument
to the RAF pilots who died during the Battle of Britain
in 1940. The memorial is in the shape of propeller
blades, with a seated statue of an RAF pilot in the
centre looking out to sea. The large site also features

KENT

Port Lympne Wild Animal Park

full-size replicas of a Hawker Hurricane and a Supermarine Spitfire, and the Foxley-Norris Memorial Wall, listing those who took part in the Battle. A visitor centre sells souvenirs and refreshments.

Kent Battle of Britain Museum
Aerodrome Road, Hawkinge, CT18 7AG (01303 893140, www.kbobm.org). Open June-Sept 10am-5pm daily. Apr, May, Oct 10am-4pm daily. Admission £6; £3-£5.50 reductions. No credit cards.
This museum holds some of the most important artefacts from the Battle of Britain. See weapons, vehicles, equipment and relics recovered from more than 600 aircraft. The museum building is based in what was a vital RAF station during the conflict in 1940, the nearest to occupied France.

Lower Leas Coastal Park
Lower Leas, Folkestone, CT20 1QN (01303 853000, www.shepway.gov.uk). Open 24 hrs daily. Admission free.
Set the kids loose in the South-east's biggest free adventure playground. There's a pirate ship half buried in the sand, a helterskelter, a climbing wall and an aerial runway. The playground is suitable for two- to 16-year-olds; there's also a separate play area for children with disabilities, and a sandpit for toddlers. The adjacent amphitheatre seats 300, and provides family entertainment throughout the summer.

Port Lympne Wild Animal Park
Lympne, nr Hythe, CT21 4PD (0844 842 4647, www.aspinallfoundation.org/portlympne). Open Apr-Oct 10am-6pm daily. Jan-Mar, Nov, Dec 10am-5pm daily. Admission £21.95; £15.95-£19.95 reductions.
Home to more than 650 animals, including the largest breeding herd of black rhino outside Africa. The park's latest offering is an overnight safari package: have dinner around the communal campfire, spend a cosy night under canvas in commodious tents with proper beds, and then accompany the rangers on a dawn safari, with close-up views of the park's free-range zebra, giraffe, antelope and wildebeest.

St Leonard's Church
Oak Walk, Hythe, CT21 5DN (01303 263739, www.stleonardschurchhythekent.org). Open Crypt May-Sept 10.30am-noon, 2.30-4pm Mon-Sat; 2.30-4pm Sun. Admission free.
Below the 11th-century church is Britain's largest ossuary (a resting place for human bones); this underground crypt holds around 2,000 ancient human skulls and some 8,000 thighbones. (It was thought, centuries ago, that a skull and thigh was enough to ensure resurrection.)

Where to eat & drink

Deal has a number of inviting cafés and traditional English pubs. The Clockhouse (15 South Court, 01304 367757, www.theclockhousecafe.co.uk, closed Sun) serves a good full English – tables in this small café are in high demand.

For a historical setting, drop by the Ship Inn (Middle Street, 01304 372222) for a well-kept ale. The best fish is found at the Middle Street Fish Bar (78 Middle Street, 01304 364738, closed Sun summer; Mon, Sun winter) and Court Yard Oyster Bar & Restaurant (Old Coach House, 01304 366661, www.thecourtyarddeal.com, closed Mon). For an inexpensive simple meal, Bistro Oregano (1-3 St George's Passage, 01304 372319, www.deal-bistro.co.uk, closed dinner Sun) is just off the middle of the high street.

In Kingsdown, the King's Head (Upper Street, 01304 373915), offers real ales, 350-year-old architecture and a warm welcome.

Bohemian

47 Beach Street, Deal, CT14 6HY (01304 374843, www.bohemianbythesea.com). Open noon-11pm Tue-Thur; 11pm-midnight Fri-Sat; 9am-7pm Sun. Food served noon-2.30pm Tue; noon-2.30pm, 7-9pm Tue-Sat; 9am-3pm Sun.

A simply decorated 'specialist beer bar and kitchen', where the menu covers hearty plates of roast cod and hand-cut chips, as well as elegant dishes such as seared scallops with truffled pea purée and alfalfa shoots. The selection of ales, ciders and lagers includes Weston's Old Rosie cider from Hertfordshire, Caledonian Deuchers IPA from Edinburgh, four ales from Cornwall and a Portuguese pilsner on tap.

Chequers

Golf Road, nr Deal, CT14 6RG (01304 362288, www.chequers-restaurant-kent.co.uk). Lunch served 11.30am-3pm Mon-Sat; 12.30-3pm Sun. Dinner served 6-11pm Mon-Sat.

Chequers is halfway between Sandwich and Deal, near the Cinque Ports Golf Course. It's a relaxed place, where both the wine list and menu have a South African accent. Lunchtime baguettes and omelettes give way to a dinner menu featuring such family recipes as bobotie (minced beef, flavoured with mild Cape Malay curry spices, apricots and almonds), alongside wild sea bass roasted with lime, ginger and chilli.

81 Beach Street

81 Beach Street, Deal, CT14 6JB (01304 368136, www.81beachstreet.co.uk). Lunch served noon-4pm daily. Dinner served 6-10pm Mon-Sat.

Directly on the seafront, and unremarkable from the outside, this intimate bistro is just the place in which to escape the coastal chill. The menu is fairly traditional: Sunday roasts come with all the trimmings, while during the week dishes include steak and chips or pan-fried skate with mustard mash and dill and caper sauce.

Where to stay

Several of the pubs in the area have rooms (*see above*), but otherwise the choice is between B&Bs or self-catering accommodation. Notably, the Garden Cottage and Greenhouse Apartment (*see below*) in the grounds of Walmer Castle can be hired. Otherwise, Hector's Apartments (Deal Castle Road, 01323 226107, www.luxuryholidayrentalskent.com) are undoubtedly one of the more chic self-catering options in Deal; think bold wallpaper and retro leather chairs in 1970s-style one- and two-bedroom apartments. They are next to the beach.

Garden Cottage & Greenhouse Apartment

Walmer Castle Grounds, Kingsdown Road, Walmer, CT14 7LJ (0870 333 1187, www.english-heritage. org.uk). Rates Garden Cottage £699-£1,060 per week. Greenhouse Apartment £871-£1,264 per week.

In the past few years, English Heritage has opened up a number of listed buildings for holidaymakers to rent; these two are located in the beautiful grounds of Walmer's Tudor castle. The Greenhouse Apartment and the neighbouring Garden Cottage share a view of the 300-year-old kitchen gardens. They have been extensively refurbished, and have a kitchen/dining area, two bedrooms (one twin, one double), a sitting room and a bathroom. They both comfortably accommodate four, with parking for two cars. Guests have access to most the castle grounds out of hours.

Gardener's Rest

Queensdown Road, Kingsdown, CT14 8EF (01304 371449, www.gardenersrest.me.uk). Rates £85-£95 double. No credit cards.

The Gardener's Rest has two well-decorated en suite rooms, each with its own balcony, and an acre of beautifully tended gardens (which are occasionally open to the public). Breakfast options include kippers, hash browns and eggs benedict. The owners also run two self-catering cottages, Gulls and Sea Watch (51 The Strand, 01304 371449) on the seafront in Walmer.

Number One B&B

1 Ranelagh Road, Deal, CT14 7BG (01304 364459, www.numberonebandb.co.uk). Rates £75-£90 double incl breakfast.

This four-bedroomed B&B mixes a Victorian exterior with a modern interior and such neccessities as high-speed Wi-Fi, flatscreen TVs and iPod docking stations. The owners have created a place with all the style and attention to detail of a hotel, and yet the comfort and familiarity of a B&B, all in a central Deal location.

DOVER & AROUND

St Margaret's at Cliffe

This charming village has a few shops for daily necessities and an inviting real ale pub, the Smugglers (01304 853404, www.thesmugglers-inn.co.uk), located on the High Street. Picturesque walks stretch out in all directions and it only takes 15 minutes to stroll from the village centre to secluded St Margaret's Bay. The best views are from the Roman-built lighthouses (only accessible on foot). South Foreland Lighthouse (*see p93*) is open to the public. The bay is also home to the Coastguard (*see p99*), a restaurant and bar with a good reputation.

White Cliffs (and above right)

South Foreland Lighthouse. See p93.

Marquis at Alkham

Dover

Dover is not an attractive town and is in need of regeneration, but it remains an important transport hub. Most people pass through it on the way to somewhere else, but there are a few attractions worth investigating. One very recent addition to the market square is a big screen, a gift from the London 2012 Organising Committee. On this, shows, short films, operas and ballets will be projected. Historical sites and places of interest include Dover Museum & the Bronze Age Boat Gallery, the Roman Painted House and magnificent Dover Castle (for all, see p93), behind which there is a monument marking the crash-landing of Louis Bleriot who, in 1909, was the first man to fly across the Channel.

On the outskirts of Dover are the remaining foundations of the medieval Knights Templar Church (Western Heights, 01304 211067, www.english-heritage.org.uk) and the accessible part of the Western Heights military redoubt (www.doverwesternheights.org; closed Nov-Mar). The most complete working Georgian mill in England can be seen at Crabble Corn Mill (Lower Road, River, 01304 823292, www.ccmt.org.uk, closed Oct-Easter Mon-Fri).

On the A20 to Folkestone from Dover, turn off for Samphire Hoe (www.samphirehoe.com), newly created out of Channel Tunnel spoil, to admire stunning views of the White Cliffs. Much of the site is accessible to wheelchair users, and the mile-long sea wall provides good fishing for anglers. Also off the A20, at Capel-le-Ferne, is the Battle of Britain Memorial (see p93).

Where to eat & drink

Family-run La Scala (19 High Street, 01304 208044, closed Sun) is a good choice for Italian food in the centre of Dover.

The Bay Restaurant (High Street, St Margaret's at Cliffe, 01304 852229, www.thewhitecliffs.com), attached to the White Cliffs Hotel (see right), is a reliable place for everything from afternoon tea to Sunday lunch. The same owners run Wallett's Court hotel (see right), which also has a smart restaurant covering most bases.

Allotment ★
9 High Street, Dover, CT16 1DP (01304 214467, www.theallotmentdover.co.uk). Open 8.30am-11pm Tue-Sat.
A pretty, light-filled bistro, which uses produce from nearby allotments in its quality dishes. Sit inside amid shabby-chic decor or in the courtyard garden for a menu that runs from breakfast (sourdough pancakes with syrup, eggs benedict with own-baked ham) to dinner. The main menu changes daily, but typical dishes are braised pork in cider and pannacotta with roast rhubarb.

Coastguard
The Bay, St Margaret's Bay, CT15 6DY (01304 851019, www.thecoastguard.co.uk). Open 10.30am-11pm daily. Lunch served 12.30-2.45pm, dinner served 6.30-8.45pm daily.
Coastguard is only separated from the beach by a small car park, and the view, from the foot of the cliffs, is stunning all year round. The restaurant specialises in locally caught seafood, but there are dishes such as gratin of Kentish

broccoli with cider, mushrooms and leeks too; it's a popular place, so book. It's possible to walk from St Margaret's at Cliffe in around 15 minutes, although the return journey is a steep one.

Marquis at Alkham ★
Alkham Valley Road, Alkham, CT15 7DF (01304 873410, www.themarquisatalkham.co.uk). Lunch served noon-2.30pm Tue-Sat. Dinner served 6.30-9.30pm Mon-Sat. Food served noon-6pm Sun.

Charles Lakin heads the kitchen at this contemporary restaurant with rooms. Lunch (£22.50 for three courses) might be rillette of Alkham Valley rabbit and prunes with pickled red cabbage, followed by butternut squash and sage risotto with white truffle oil and shavings of Twineham Grange cheese, topped by apple soufflé with caramel ice-cream. There's also a six-course tasting menu for £50. There are seven spacious luxury rooms (£95-£235 double incl breakfast), all equipped with LCD flat screens and Wi-Fi. Also for hire are two recently refurbished cottages next to Chalksole Estate Vineyard (about 20 minutes' walk from the restaurant).

Wallett's Court

Where to stay
The Marquis at Alkham (*see above*), a 15-minute drive west of Dover, is a stylish place to stay. If you need to stay in central Dover, Loddington House (14 East Cliff, 01304 201947, www.loddington househotel.co.uk) and Beulah House (94 Crabble Hill, 01304 824615, www.beulahguesthouse.co.uk) are classic, smart B&Bs.

Wallett's Court
Westcliffe, St Margaret's at Cliffe, CT15 6EW (01304 852424, www.wallettscourthotelspa.com). Rates £120-£190 double.

The 17 en suite rooms at Wallet's Court include three elegant four-posters and 14 light-filled bedrooms in the converted hay barn. There are also two well-equipped tipis. The REN spa has a wide selection of beauty therapies, an indoor pool, a sauna and a fitness studio. The restaurant is open all day; Sunday lunch is a highlight, with a choice of Chandler & Dunn beef with yorkshire pudding, Brogdale Farm pork with crackling or Romney Marsh lamb with mint. The bar opens late, and is heated by an impressive open fire.

White Cliffs Hotel
High Street, St. Margaret's at Cliffe, CT15 6AT (01304 852229, www.thewhitecliffs.com) Rates £99-£109 double.

This hotel is run by the same people as Wallet's Court; it's less grand, though just as comfortable. All 17 bedrooms are decorated in a light, modern style, with plenty of mod cons. Two family suites (sleeping up to five) are a few steps from the main building. The Bay Restaurant is open all day – among the many options is a Kentish cream tea.

FOLKESTONE & HYTHE

Folkestone
The town has had a chequered history, and by the end of the 19th century, it was tourism, rather than its maritime heritage (and smuggling) that kept the

KENT

town afloat. During World War II, the entire population was evacuated, and the town became a prohibited zone. The Luftwaffe then destroyed much of Folkestone and the place has struggled to regain prosperity since then, though the sandy beaches (rare in this area) are perenially popular.

However, Folkestone is emerging as a focus for artistic endeavour, most notably with the Triennial Art Festival. This flourish of creativity has been spurred by the efforts of local organisations, the Roger De Haan Charitable Trust (www.rdhct.org.uk) and the Creative Foundation (www.creative foundation.org.uk). Together they have refurbished and let shop and office spaces at low rates to artistic and distinctive businesses.

One of the legacies of the last Folkestone Triennial (in 2008) is a series of eight permanent public artworks: Tracey Emin's 'Baby Things' has life-size bronze casts of baby clothes around the town; Nathan Coley's piece along Tontine Street is an illuminated sculpture 'Heaven is a Place Where Nothing Happens'; Mark Wallinger's 'Folk Stones' contains 19,240 numbered beach pebbles, each representing a life lost on 1 July 1916, the first day of the Battle of the Somme. (The work is inspired by the one million soldiers who left from Folkestone harbour to fight in World War I.) Download an audio guide and a map at http://folkestonetriennial.org.uk, or pick up the map from the Visitor Centre in the Old High Street.

Along with Tontine Street, it's the cobbled Old High Street that is the heart of the Creative Quarter, and home to an interesting trail of shops, cafés, bars and restaurants. Distinctive galleries include Jo Letchford Mosaics (43 Old High Street, 01303 250717, www.joletchfordmosaics.co.uk, closed

'Folkestone' by Patrick Tuttofuoco

'Baby Things' by Tracey Emin

Folkestone harbour

Old High Street, Folkestone

Mon, Tue, Sun) and Chimaera Gallery (42 Tontine Street, 01303 211621, www.chimaeragallery.co.uk, closed Mon, Tue), a contemporary space showing many art forms. Both streets lead down to the harbour: it's rather murky at low tide, and you won't find any family-friendly pubs or sticks of rock here, just two small watering holes and a few shacks selling the latest catch (one shack, Chummy's, has been here for 50 years).

The Leas and Lower Leas

Head away from the centre of Folkestone towards Sandgate and there is a dramatic change in feel and architecture; witness the Grand (see p103) and the currently empty but just as magnificent Metropole hotels. Stroll along the promenade and take in the panoramic views, then walk down to the Lower Leas, or perhaps use the Leas Lift (see p104) to visit the 300-seat free amphitheatre and Lower Leas Coastal Park (see p94) – amazing fun for the kids. Spend some time exploring the woody and rocky cliffside paths – sea views appear in between the trees.

Hythe

Just south of Folkestone on the A259, Hythe is an attractive but modest seaside town with one main high street and a wide pebble beach, bisected by the Royal Military Canal (01797 367934, www.royalmilitarycanal.com), and surrounded by a network of villages. The High Street has plenty of independent cafés and shops. The beach offers many diversions; the vast open space is excellent for windsurfing, and watersports in general are popular. In summer, rowing boats can be hired on the Royal Military Canal, from near Ladies Walk Bridge. The canal stretches for 28 miles from Seabrook to Pett Level, near Hastings, and the route can be easily walked in two days.

The strong of stomach should investigate the crypt at St Leonard's Church (see p94). To return the colour to your cheeks take a ride on the Romney, Hythe & Dymchurch Railway (see p116). There are

KENT GOLF COURSES

Chart Hills

Weeks Lane, Biddenden, TN27 8JX (01580 292222, www.charthills.co.uk). Open times vary; check website for details. Green fees vary; check website for details.

This spectacular course was designed by Nick Faldo, who opened it in 1993. There are plenty of hazards: water, fast greens and a whopping 130 bunkers – it's a difficult course. There's a pleasant clubhouse and professional staff.

Knole Park

Seal Hollow Road, Sevenoaks, TN15 0HJ (01732 452150, www.knolepark golfclub.co.uk). Open 9am-5pm Mon-Fri. Green fees £45; £15 reductions.

Deer are often seen roaming the 1,000 acres of this parkland course. It's near Knole House, just outside Sevenoaks. The club was opened in 1924, a time when Ryder Cup player Sam King was a caddie here. The clubhouse has a snooker room and friendly bar. Visiting players must provide current handicap certificates.

Lamberhurst

Church Road, Lamberhurst, TN3 8DT (01892 890591, www.lamberhurst golfclub.com). Open times vary; phone for details. Green fees £31.

This beautiful course, dating from 1890, sits on the Kent and Sussex border. It's a challenging course, especially the 12th, which is shot over water. It's also heavily wooded. This is a busy club, with lots of competitions, so check availability before arriving.

Littlestone

St Andrews Road, Littlestone, N28 8RB (01797 363355, www.littlestone golfclub.org.uk). Open 9.30am-dusk daily. Green fees £65; £40 reductions.

An unassuming and friendly club that's rated among the top 100 golf courses in the country. The links course has hosted many championships since opening in 1899. The course is generally pretty dry, but the wind can be fierce.

Allotment. See p98.

several castles nearby, including Westenhanger Castle (Stone Street, 01303 261068, www.westenhangercastle.co.uk), off the A261; it's only open on Tuesdays, but it makes a stunning backdrop to Folkestone Racecourse (01303 266407, www.folkestone-racecourse.co.uk). Saltwood Castle (Castle Road, www.saltwood castle.com), once home of the late MP and diarist Alan Clark, is by far the most attractive; regrettably it isn't open to the public. In Lympne is Lympne Castle, (01303 261666, www.lympnecastle.co.uk): this Grade I-listed building opens its doors infrequently, but it does have some holiday cottages (*see p104*). An impressive number of exotic beasts can be seen at Port Lympne Wild Animal Park (*see p94*).

Where to eat & drink

In Folkestone, real ales and ciders from local breweries are served at Chambers (Cheriton Place, 01303 223333, www.pubfolkestone.co.uk, closed Sun), alongside good coffee and bistro food. The bar and restaurant at the Quarterhouse (*see p104*) is another possibility.

Paul's

2A Bouverie Road West, Folkestone, CT20 2RX (01303 259697, www.pauls-restaurant.com). Lunch served noon-2.30pm daily. Dinner served 6.30-9.30pm Mon-Sat.

Long-established Paul's serves the likes of local sausages on bubble and squeak with onion gravy at lunch, and pan-seared partridge breasts with celeriac mash and port jus at dinner. On Sundays there's a carvery – booking essential.

Where to stay

Folkestone is full of B&Bs, but has very little in the way of stylish accommodation, apart from Relish (*see p104*). The Grand Hotel (The Leas, 01303 222222, www.grand-uk.com) is a classic seaside hotel on the promenade.

London Golf Club

Stansted Lane, Ash, nr Brands Hatch, TN15 7EH (01474 879899, www.london golf.co.uk). Open 7.30am-dusk daily. Green fees £70-£110.

Opened by Denis Thatcher and designed by Jack Nicklaus, the London Golf Club has two courses – the Heritage and International. Only the latter is open to visitors, but it's a superb and tricky course in gorgeous surroundings. Its proximity to London makes it very popular, and there are regular national and international events, so you'll need to book well in advance.

Royal Cinque Ports

Golf Road, Deal, CT14 6RF (01304 374007, www.royalcinqueports.com). Open Summer 8am-8pm daily. Winter 8am-6pm daily. Green fees £60-£150; £30-£45 reductions.

Another good links course on the east Kent coast. Golf writer Bernard Darwin, grandson of Charles, wrote of it: 'a truly great course, most testing and severe of all championship courses'. It's on a narrow stretch of land, open to the elements and with plenty of sand dunes.

Walmer & Kingsdown

The Leas, Kingsdown, CT14 8EP (01304 373256, www.kingsdowngolf.co.uk). Open times vary; check website for details. Green fees £33.

Atop the cliffs between Dover and Deal, this course was designed by James Braid and opened in 1909. It's a community-minded place, and green fees are reasonable. Beware: it can get pretty windy up there.

Weald of Kent

Maidstone Road, Headcorn, TN27 9PT (01622 891671, www.weald-of-kent. co.uk). Open dawn-dusk daily. Green fees £23-£30; £15 reductions.

Though part of a hotel and conference centre, the Weald of Kent course is also frequented by pay-and-play visitors (check for offers on the website).

Wrotham Heath

Seven Mile Lane, Borough Green, TN15 8QZ (01732 884800, www.wrothamheathgolfclub.co.uk). Open 8am-dusk daily. Green fees £30; £15 reductions.

The setting, on the heavily undulating hills of west Kent, is beautiful. And in true Kent style, the clubhouse is a former oast house. It's a friendly club, close to Tonbridge, Sevenoaks and Maidstone. Visitors should book.

In Hythe, the 80-room Mercure Hythe Imperial Hotel & Spa (Princes Parade, 01303 267441, www.mercure.com) is part of an international chain, in an old seafront building; it's currently undergoing extensive refurbishment.

There are two holiday cottages in the grounds of Lympne Castle (www.lympnecastlecottages.com). Pineapple sleeps four and Lambourne six.

Relish ★

4 Augusta Gardens, Folkestone, CT20 2RR (01303 850952, www.hotelrelish.co.uk). Rates £69-£145 double incl breakfast.

This ten-room guesthouse is by far the most modern in town: simple decor is accompanied by Aveda products and crisp white linen. It is situated on the edge of a small public park, near both the Leas and the centre of Folkestone.

Things to do

Quarterhouse

SANDWICH

Royal St George's Golf Club
Sandwich, CT13 9PB (01304 613090, www.royalstgeorges.com). Open 8am-3pm Mon-Fri. Green fees Apr-Oct £150. Jan-Mar, Nov, Dec £70-90.
One of the country's best golf courses, the Royal St George hosts the Open Championship in 2011. The Open was first played here in 1894 – it was also the first time the competition had been held south of the Scottish border – so you're paying for a long and illustrious past, as well as faultless facilities. For other golf courses in Kent, see p102.

Sandwich River Bus
The Quay, Sandwich, CT13 9EN (07958 376183, www.sandwichriverbus.co.uk). Open Easter-mid July daily. Mid July-mid Sept Thur-Sun. Mid Sept-Easter by appointment only. Timetable varies; phone for details. No credit cards.
One of the best ways to see the local sites is by Sandwich River Bus, a traditional wooden vessel that cruises along the River Stour (spring 2011 should see the 1903 Dutch sailing barge *Dolphin*, currently being restored, in use). Trips runs daily in summer from the Quay by the Old Toll Bridge to Richborough Roman Fort (*see p92*) – it takes about an hour. Weekly seal-watching trips can be booked in advance.

FOLKESTONE & HYTHE

Leas Cliff Hall
The Leas, Folkestone, CT20 2DZ (01303 228600, www.leascliffhall.org.uk). Box office 9am-5pm Mon-Sat.
All you'd expect from a seaside theatre: Abba tribute bands, the Chippendales, the latest boy band and enough psychics to have a major seance.

Leas Lift
Lower Sandgate Road, Folkestone, CT20 1PR (www.leasliftfolkestone.co.uk). Open Summer 10am-5pm Tue-Sun. Winter 10am-4pm Thur-Sun. Admission 90p; 50p reductions. No credit cards.
The Leas Lift has been transporting passengers down to the Lower Leas for more than 125 years, and still has its original looks and design (using water and gravity). It's still running for visitors' enjoyment, thanks to the passion and determination of a local group of volunteers.

Quarterhouse
Quarterhouse, Tontine Street, Folkestone, CT20 1JT (01303 858500, www.quarterhouse.co.uk). Box office 10am-5pm Mon-Fri; 11am-4pm Sat, Sun.
An essential part of Folkestone's artistic resurgence, Quarterhouse runs a busy arts programme that encompasses film, dance, theatre, comedy and music. There's a decent bar and restaurant on the premises (open 11am-late Tue-Sun).

KENT

Romney Marsh & Low Weald

Reclaimed from the sea over centuries, the windswept wetlands of Romney Marsh stretch from the coast out to beyond the crescent of the Royal Military Canal, dotted with Romney Marsh sheep and crosshatched with ditches. It has a bleak beauty, but is an unsettling place, and nowhere is this more true than at Dungeness. Here, a roughly made road separates the shingle beach from a barren hinterland, where clapboard cottages lean into the breeze. With its treacherous tides, vast expanse of shingle and nuclear power station, Dungeness can seem like a hostile place to holidaying humans. For birds, it's heavenly: fish and sealife flourish in the power station's warm waters. At Dungeness RSPB reserve you can spot warblers, waders and widgeons; in June, there are fluffy cygnets and goslings.

Directly north the terrain barely rises above sea level, the flatness pierced only by a Norman church or a wooded hillock. The biggest town in the larger area is Ashford, from where the Eurostar ducks under the English Channel to France and Belgium. To the west is *Darling Buds of May* country, with cosy pubs in the villages of Pluckley and Biddenden appearing out of the wooded land.

North-west of Romney Marsh is the Low Weald. This is the Kent of oast houses and white weatherboard-clad buildings. At its heart is the county's prettiest town, Tenterden, known for its fine shopping and beautifully preserved High Street. Beyond that, Cranbrook is another quaint town with a hop sack full of charm. The Low Weald is also vineyard territory, and home to two of Britain's best wineries: Biddenden Vineyards and Chapel Down.

ROMNEY MARSH & DUNGENESS

Dymchurch to Greatstone-on-Sea
Along the A259 between Hythe and New Romney are the settlements of Dymchurch, St Mary's Bay, Littlestone-on-Sea and Greatstone-on-Sea, all with sandy beaches – rare for Kent and Sussex. The Romney, Hythe & Dymchurch Light Railway (*see p116*) puffs along the coastline, calling at seven stops, and each of the beaches has cafés and places to pick up an ice-cream. There's plenty of avian life too, as oystercatchers, turnstones and sanderlings hunt for shirmps and sandhoppers.

St Mary's Bay has the best beach. Long and flat, its pale sands seem endless when the tide is out. Military historians should look out for the squat, bleak-looking Martello towers, built as defensive forts in the 19th century. Closer to Dungeness is Romney Sands – another beach with a military flavour, thanks to the concrete 'listening ears' found nearby. These aeroplane-detecting sound mirrors were constructed for World War II, but their usefulness was eclipsed by the arrival of radar. Still, the massive concrete structures have an eerie beauty that suits the landscape, and could double as modern art installations.

Dungeness ★
Dungeness isn't your typical setting for a day at the beach. A picnic on the sand? A paddle in the shallows? Not here. The entire promontory barely looks like England at all. The sky stretches wide over flat marshland; a scattering of fishing shacks looks small and vulnerable against the unearthly, light-filled expanse; and the steep shingle banks are constantly reshaped by the relentless sea.

All this isolation and strangeness has its advantages, though: on fine days, when the English Channel turns a rich, deep blue, the beach remains sparsely populated. And when the weather is not so clement, Dungeness comes into its own, allowing you to believe that you're the only person left on this cramped island, with just the roiling grey water and the hum of the power station for company.

In a landscape where there are many unusual features, the imposing hulk of a nuclear power plant is the most unexpected. There are two reactors: one built in the 1950s and decommissioned in 2007, the other built in the 1980s and still generating electricity. But the biggest danger to day-trippers is not a nuclear explosion – touch wood – but the treacherous waters. Where the shingle meets the sea, there's no gentle lapping and no possibility of

cooling off up to the knee. Waves rise to the edge of the banks, smash down and then suck the shingle mercilessly. If paddling is hazardous, swimming would be suicide. After all, this beach was created by the power of longshore drift, which pushed shingle into banks up to 60 feet deep. The tide's strength has the opposite effect too, and a fleet of lorries is routinely deployed to shore up the stony piles and prevent their reclamation by the sea.

No wonder anglers are a more common sight here than families. Apart from solitary walkers, Dungeness's bread and butter consists of those hoping to ensnare a fish. In fact, the same conditions that make for lousy swimming ensure wonderful fishing: thanks to the steep shelving, the water is so deep that it's possible to fish off the edge of the beach, just as you might from the banks of a deep reservoir. Local diehards eat the fish caught here, despite any possible deleterious effect from the power station's warm, chlorinated wastewaters.

If dangerous to swimmers, the currents are no more forgiving to boats; there is still an RNLI station here, and the coast is littered with wrecks. Maps framed in the Old Lighthouse (see p110) pinpoint the lost vessels. Built in 1904, this lighthouse is now defunct; there's a new, black-and-white striped one, built in 1961. The Old Lighthouse is still open to the public, and you can even get married there. Squeeze on to the viewing platform to fully understand the lie of this odd land. From the highest vantage point, dark railway tracks slash through the sparse and scrubby earth below; Dungeness is the end of the line – physically and spiritually – for the Romney, Hythe & Dymchurch Railway. From above, the bleakness of this landscape is magnified; featureless to the average eye, it soon becomes apparent why Dungeness has been deemed Britain's only desert. Yet it's teeming with life.

Bizarrely, the natural environment seems to have benefited from the industrial detritus (gravel pits, nuclear power station). Dungeness is a breeding ground for unusual and rare forms of flora and fauna. There are around 600 plant species, and the old gravel pits harbour the protected great crested newt and the medicinal leech. The rare Sussex emerald moth appears in July, and spiders are in their element. Birdwatchers will have a field day: there's an RSPB reserve with hides for viewing the Slavonian grebe, the smew and the bittern. Instead of driving away the birds, the power station seems to have done the opposite – the warm wastewater has enriched the sea's biology and thus lured seabirds.

Not exactly Blue Flag material, then, but this moody corner of Kent has never been short of fans, who have found a singular charm in its bleak ambience. Film director Derek Jarman lived here, in Prospect Cottage (see p110), where his garden of beach-combings, driftwood and weirdly sculptural plants still draws curious visitors, years after his death.

The experimental style of Jarman's home and garden have set a trend. Just as visually unique is the RIBA award-winning Vista house, built by architect Simon Conder: here, the bones of a 1930s wooden fishing hut have been shrink-wrapped in matt black

rubber. By contrast, the silver curves of a vintage Airstream caravan parked outside reflect the pale light above. Nearby, other buildings have been improvised out of old railway coaches. The wonderfully twisted result looks something akin to a frontier community; a far cry from the neatly turned out bungalows of nearby Lydd. Dungeness, even in this already unconventional outpost of Kent, is a defiantly alien place, and one that seems proud to be flouting the normal rules of the British seaside.

Dungeness is most easily reached by car along the A259 towards New Romney, followed by the B2075 towards Lydd. Otherwise, the nearest train station is Rye (see p138), then hop on the 711 bus to nearby Lydd from where it's a short taxi ride.

Where to eat & drink
The restaurant at Romney Bay House Hotel (see p112) is the classiest option in the area.

Britannia
Dungeness Road, TN29 9ND (01797 321959). Open Summer 11am-11pm daily. Winter 11am-2.30pm, 6-9pm daily. Summer Lunch served noon-2.30pm, dinner served 6-8.30pm Mon-Fri. Food served noon-8.30pm Sat, Sun. Winter Lunch served noon-2.30pm, dinner served 6-8.30pm daily.
Fish and chips are the star of the show at the Britannia. This is a basic but comfortable pub only a short walk from the pebbles. Punters come for the location, the Shepherd Neame beers and the freshly caught fish rather than the decor.

Light Railway Café
Dungeness Station, Dungeness Road, TN29 9NB (01797 320221). Open Summer 10am-5.30pm daily. Winter 10am-3pm Sat, Sun.
The café is open only when the miniature railway is running, and at weekends during the winter. Fish and chips with cups of tea are very popular, as is the £8 Sunday roast plus dessert deal.

Pilot
Battery Road, Dungeness, TN29 9NJ (01797 320314, www.thepilot.uk.com). Open Summer 11am-10pm daily. Winter 11am-9pm daily. Food served Summer noon-9pm daily. Winter noon-8pm daily.
The atmosphere is jovial at this friendly pub and the food decent enough. The most satisfying of the pub grub options are fish and chips and the meat pies, while lighter dishes include a half pint of prawns or a classic ploughman's. Between 5pm and 6pm there's a special deal for families: one free child's meal with every adult main.

Where to stay
White Horses Cottage (01797 366626, www. white-horses-cottage.co.uk), in nearby Greatstone, is a budget option. It was once part of a Sussex farmhouse (witness the oak beams and leaded windows), but was moved to its current site in 1928. All three of the double rooms enjoy a sea view and share one balcony (great for a large group).

Mulberry Cottages (01233 813087, www. mulberrycottages.com) has two cottages for rent

KENT

Dungeness National Nature Reserve. See p110.

Prospect Cottage. See p110.

Old Lighthouse. See p110.

Light Railway Café. See p107.

Places to visit

Chapel Down

KENT

ROMNEY MARSH & DUNGENESS

Dungeness National Nature Reserve ★
Dungeness Road, Dungeness, TN29 9NB (01797 367934, www.dungeness-nnr.co.uk). Open 24hrs daily.
The strange landscape at Dungeness is as alluring to birds as it is to humans. Through a picture window at the visitor centre you can watch an avian spectacular unfold in the large gravel pit, and hides are dotted around the nature trail. The National Nature Reserve also harbours 600 species of plants, moths and newts. The RSPB manages various parts of the site, including its hides and nature trails, and has a visitor centre here (01797 320588, www.rspb.org.uk).

Horne's Place Chapel
Appledore, TN26 2BS (01304 211067, www.english-heritage.org.uk/daysout/properties/hornes-place-chapel). Open by appointment. Admission free.
Built for William Horne in 1366, adjacent to his timber-framed manor house, this rare domestic chapel survived an attack during the Peasants Revolt (1381); today, it's a peaceful spot. The house and chapel are privately owned, so you must arrange a visit in advance.

New Hall
New Hall Close, Dymchurch, TN29 0LF (01303 873897). Open by appointment. Admission free.
Opposite St Peter & St Paul's Church in Dymchurch, this old courtroom was where the so-called 'scot tax' was introduced – a levy on residents to fund the maintenance of the sea wall. It inherited its name from the fact that those living outside a certain boundary didn't have to pay, and so got off 'scot free'. It was rebuilt in 1575, after the original wooden premises were destroyed in a storm.

Old Lighthouse
Dungeness Road, Dungeness, TN29 9NB (01797 321300, www.dungenesslighthouse.com). Open July, Aug 10.30am-4.30pm daily. May, June, Sept 10am-4.30pm Tue-Thur, Sat, Sun. Mar, Apr, Oct 10.30am-4.30pm Sat, Sun. Admission £3; £2-£2.50 reductions; £9 family.
Opened in 1904, the Dungeness lighthouse was a guiding light for sailors in the Channel for 56 years.

It's no longer operational, but you can climb the 169 steps and soak in the stellar view. There's an exhibition on how the lighthouse works and maps of wrecks lying off the coast.

Prospect Cottage Garden
Dungeness Road, Dungeness, TN29 9NB.
The garden that film-maker and artist Derek Jarman designed and created in the eight years he lived at Dungeness should be obligatory viewing for anyone interested in the history or practice of art. Nowadays, it doesn't look that different to many of the other gardens around it, but that's because Jarman pioneered a trend, with a design that looks effortless. Shells, bits of broken tools, fishing kit and unrecognisable shards of corroded metal decorate sticks of driftwood, and standing stones sit alongside plants chosen for their ability to withstand strong winds, salt spray and inhospitable terrain, such as bonsai aloes, lavenders and poppies. Seen as a whole, it's a piece of conceptual art that's absolutely in tune with its surroundings. The garden featured in many of Jarman's later films, including *War Requiem* and *The Garden*, where it was both the Garden of Eden and the garden at Gethsemane. The little black and yellow cottage that was a haven for Jarman until his death in 1994 is privately owned, so you'll have to admire the garden from the road.

ASHFORD & AROUND

Godinton House & Gardens
Godinton Lane, Ashford, TN23 3BP (01233 620773, www.godinton-house-gardens.co.uk). Open Garden Mar-Oct 2-5.30pm daily. House & tearoom Apr-Oct 2-5.30pm Fri-Sun. Admission House & garden £8; free reductions. Garden only £5; free reductions.
Take a guided tour through this magnificent Jacobean house, full of antique furniture and fascinating family heirlooms. The 12-acre gardens are another draw, with ancient trees, pond features and statues, all encased by a yew hedge. There's a tearoom too.

King's Wood
White Hill, Challock (01420 520212, www.forestry.gov.uk).

Wander this beautiful slice of woodland and admire the sweet chestnuts, corsican pines and douglas firs. The area is well populated with animals – you might even spot a snuffling wild boar or see adders sunning themselves on a rock. There are places for picnics and a children's play area.

Rare Breeds Centre
Woodchurch, TN26 3RJ (01233 861493, www.rare breeds.org.uk). Open Apr-Nov 10.30am-5.30pm daily. Jan-Mar, Nov, Dec 10.30am-4pm Tue-Sun. Admission £8.50; £7.50-£8 reductions; £28 family.
Stroll through a butterfly tunnel, pet a giant spider, or dabble in a spot of pig racing at the Rare Breeds Centre. It's home to creatures of all shapes and sizes, and offers 'encounter paddocks' and meet the animals sessions for children, along with various play areas.

TENTERDEN & AROUND

Chapel Down ★
Tenterden Vineyard, Small Hythe Road, Smallhythe, TN30 7NG (01580 763033, www.englishwinesgroup. com). Open Tours June-Sept 11.30am, 1.30pm, 3pm daily. May, Oct 11.30am, 1.30pm, 3pm Sat, Sun. Shop 10am-5pm daily. Rates Guided tours and tasting £9; £2-£8 reductions.
Chapel Down vineyard is a slick, modern operation. The on-site restaurant (see p117) is a class act, while the wine and food shop offers tastings and sells local produce alongside Chapel Down wine. Guided tours – book ahead – last just over an hour and include a tasting. The vineyard produces some superb wines, notably the award-winning sparkling whites. Ales are also being produced.

CM Booth Collection of Historic Vehicles.
Falstaff Antiques, 63-67 High Street, Rolvenden, TN17 4LP (01580 241234, www.morganmuseum.org.uk). Open 10am-5.30pm Mon-Sat. Admission £3; £1 reductions.
A small and well-preserved private collection of motor vehicles; pride of places goes to the selection of three-wheel Morgans. Other vehicles include a 1929 Morris light van, a 1904 Humber Tri-car and a 1936 Brampton caravan, plus motorcycles, bikes and tricycles.

Hole Park
Rolvenden, TN17 4JB (01580 241344, www.hole park.com). Open Apr, May 11am-6pm daily. June-Sept 11am-6pm Wed, Thur; Oct 11am-6pm Sun. Admission £6; £1 reductions. No credit cards.
Edward Gibbon, author of *The Decline and Fall of the Roman Empire*, lived at Hole Park. The enchanting 15-acre garden was originally planted by Colonel Barham, the great-grandfather of the current owner, in the 1930s. It's spectacular in the spring, the carpet of bluebells being particularly beautiful.

Sandhurst Vineyard
Hoads Farm, Sandhurst, TN18 5PA (01580 850296, www.sandhurstvineyards.co.uk). Open times vary; phone for details. No credit cards.
Visitors are welcome to explore the 250-acre vineyard and visit the farm shop; pre-book for group tours and tastings (£2.50 per person). There's a B&B on site.

Smallhythe Place
Smallhythe, TN30 7NG (01580 762334, www.nationaltrust.org.uk/main/w-smallhytheplace). Open House Mar-Oct 11am-5pm Mon-Wed, Sat, Sun. Dec noon-3pm Sat, Sun. Tearoom Mar-Oct noon-4pm Mon-Wed, Sat, Sun. Admission £5.80; £3.15 reductions; £16 family.
This early 16th-century half-timbered house just south of Tenterden was home to Victorian actress Ellen Terry for around 30 years. Browse her elaborate costume collection, wander in her cherished rose garden, orchard and nuttery, or visit the working Barn Theatre. Catch the Smallhythe Music & Beer Festival in September for a toe-tapping time with real ales.

Tenterden & District Museum
Station Road, Tenterden, TN30 6HN (01580 764310, www.tenterdenmuseum.co.uk). Open July-Sept 11am-4.30pm Tue-Sun. Easter-June, Oct 1.30-4.30pm Tue-Sun. Admission £1.50; free-£1 reductions. No credit cards.
Local history is on show in a two-storey weatherboarded building. Read the history of the Cinque Ports in the entrance room; head to the Victorian room for a glance back to the 1800s; or look into the tapestry room where 14 woven panels depict the area's history.

CRANBROOK & AROUND

Biddenden Vineyards
Gribble Bridge Lane, Biddenden, TN27 8DF (01580 291726, www.biddendenvineyards.com). Open 10am-5pm Mon-Sat; 11am-5pm Sun.
Biddenden is more earthy than the Chapel Down experience (see left), but makes for an interesting comparison: both can easily be combined in one day. Biddenden is Kent's oldest commercial vineyard, established in 1969, and today it produces a range of white wines, including the award-winning Gribble Bridge Ortega dry white. There are usually two guided tours (free) a month; check the website for dates. The shop is open every day, and sells local produce.

Sissinghurst Castle ★
Biddenden Road, Sissinghurst, TN17 2AB (01580 710701, www.nationaltrust.org.uk/main/w-sissinghurst-castle). Open Estate dawn-dusk daily. Garden, shop & restaurant Mar-Oct 10.30am-5pm Mon, Tue, Fri-Sun. Vegetable garden May-Sept 10.30am-5pm Mon, Tue, Fri-Sun. Admission £10; £5 reductions; £25 family.
Vita Sackville-West and Harold Nicolson came to live at Sissinghurst in the 1930s, and planted a series of extraordinary gardens around the remains of the Elizabethan manor house. In the hands of the National Trust since the late 1960s, it remains a wonderfully evocative spot. The only part of the house open to visitors is the pink-brick tower that stands guard over the gardens; halfway up, you can peep into Vita's comfortably cluttered, book-filled study, preserved exactly as she left it. The gardens, meanwhile, are among the loveliest in England: a series of lushly planted, intimate spaces that are themed by season, making them worth visiting at almost any time of year.

KENT VINEYARDS

Barnsole Vineyard
Fleming Road, Staple, Canterbury, CT3 1LG (01304 812530, www.barnsole. co.uk). Open Apr-Oct 10.30am-5pm daily. Jan-Mar, Nov, Dec 10.30am-4pm daily.
A family-run vineyard with just three acres of vine, which specialises in small quantities of high-quality grapes. The grapes varieties grown here are reichensteiner and huxelrebe, both common in Kent, and they help to produce 15,000 bottles a year. A red wine has just been developed. Mini tours are free, full vineyard tours cost £2.50, while bottles are very reasonably priced at £5.80-£6.50.

Biddenden Vineyards
Set in a sheltered valley, this 22-acre winery grows ten varieties of grape suited to the Kent climate (mostly German and Austrian varieties, including schönburger, reichensteiner, müller-thurgau and huxelrebe). There's a well-stocked shop open daily and two guided tours a month. *See p111.*

Chapel Down
The granddaddy of the Kent vineyards, Chapel Down has by far the most developed visitor centre, with an irresistible shop and an excellent restaurant. Chapel Down is one of the biggest English producers, filling more than half-a-million bottles a year, and with several award-winning wines to its name. *See p111.*

Kent Vineyard
Colliers Green Road, Colliers Green, TN17 (www.kentvineyards.co.uk).
Kent Vineyard is one of the newer vineyards in the area, brought back into life in 2009. First harvests are expected in late 2011, with wines landing on dinner tables in 2012. In the meantime, visitors can enjoy wine tastings at events such as the Kent Vineyard May Fair, plus there is the opportunity to rent and tend your own vine – check the website for details.

Sandhurst Vineyard
Small-scale Sandhurst makes wine from a limited selection of grape varieties (bacchus, reichensteiner and schonberger for white; rondo and dornfelder for red), with a range that includes sparkling and dessert wines. Beers are also brewed. *See p111.*

in Dungeness. Fulmar is a bright green cottage on the marshland (sleeping four) that is ideal for artists or those looking for absolute solitude, with uninterrupted views out to sea. Helvitia, also with two double bedrooms, is on the seafront near the Old Lighthouse.

Shingle House ★ (www.living-architecture.co.uk) is another sensational property, right by the beach in Dungeness. Sleeping eight, the striking, tarred-timber house is part of Living Architecture's expanding portfolio of affordable, architect designed accommodation – a project spearheaded by philosopher Alain de Botton. Inside it's bright and airy, with timber-panelled walls, sleekly modern fittings and spectacular views.

Broadacre Hotel
North Street, New Romney, TN28 8DR (01797 362381, www.broadacrehotel.co.uk). Rates £65-£80 incl breakfast.
This family-run hotel consists of six rooms in a 17th-century farmhouse and three in a converted cottage built in the 1860s. The traditionally decorated rooms have flatscreen TVs and Wi-Fi internet; one has a four-poster bed. There's a bar (open to non-residents) too.

Romney Bay House Hotel
Coast Road, Littlestone, TN28 8QY (01797 364747, www.romneybayhousehotel.co.uk). Rates £95-£164 incl breakfast.
This small hotel has a glamorous past. Designed and built in the 1920s for the doyenne of gossip columnists, Hedda Hopper, it was the creation of Sir Clough Williams-Ellis, who built Portmeirion, the Welsh village made famous by 1960s TV series *The Prisoner*. There are ten rooms with views over the nearby golf course or the sea. Today, it's noted for its quietly classy restaurant. Expect modern Anglo-French food prepared with fresh, local ingredients and matched by an excellent wine list. Cream teas hit the spot, rain or shine.

ASHFORD & AROUND
Ashford is the largest town in the area, and one of the fastest growing in the country. The train station at Ashford International (www.ashford-international. co.uk) serves Eurostar (0843 218 6186, www. eurostar.com), operating direct trains to France and Belgium. It is this position, directly en route between London and the nearest crossing to the continent, that has always defined the town.

Traditionally, the town has been under the rule of Canterbury, 23 miles away. When the Domesday Book was completed in 1086, records show Ashford as having two churches and a mill. By the 17th century, though, it was a busy market town, thanks to its central location at the crossroads of the north and south Kent coast, and Romney Marsh and the Weald.

Today, it's an important hub for cross-channel commerce, and as a consequence much of the architecture around the town is functional rather than beautiful. In the centre itself, new post-war buildings dominate, housing the usual stores, especially along the pedestrianised High Street. However, there are some interesting buildings.

KENT

Shingle House.

The largely 15th-century parish church of St Mary the Virgin dominates the town centre; inside, there's an excellent collection of medieval brasses and the tomb of Sir John Fogge (1417-1490), a survivor of the War of the Roses who held offices under five kings. Have a look at the Clergy House, and the vicarage with its Tudor doorway. Also of historical interest is Ashford Museum (St Mary's Churchyard, www.ashfordmuseum.co.uk, closed Sun and Nov-Mar); housed in a 17th-century schoolhouse, it exhibits local geological and archaeological artefacts, old photos and other displays relating to the town's past.

Directly to the west of Ashford are low-lying villages, connected by a series of winding roads and boasting some splendid village pubs. Of particular note is the Dering Arms (*see below*) in Pluckley. Game shooting is a common sport in these parts, and rural pubs are often set up for shooting parties on Saturday afternoons, who'll bring in their pheasants to cook.

Pluckley

Pluckley was owned for almost 900 years by the Dering family, who sold it only in 1928. They left their mark on the village, though: all the older houses feature distinctive double-arched 'Dering' windows, as decreed by the 19th-century head of the family, Sir Edward Cholmeley Dering, who had a penchant for round-arched windows. The Dering family crest of a black horse is also visible on the cowls of the oast houses, and in the south chapel of St Nicholas church, as well as on the sign of the Black Horse pub.

Pluckley has two claims to fame. One is as the setting for the TV adaptation of HE Bates' *The Darling Buds of May*, which captivated a nation and launched the career of Catherine Zeta-Jones. Bates, who lived in nearby Little Chart Forstal, wrote the novel in 1958, while the TV version aired in the early 1990s.

'The most haunted village in England' is Pluckley's other boast. It's claimed that there are around 12 resident spectres, including a discerning poltergeist that haunts the Black Horse (The Street, 01233 841948) and is supposed to prey on teetotallers, and a Red Lady who frequents nearby St Nicholas churchyard, sobbing as she searches for the unmarked grave of her stillborn baby. It's difficult to find a local who will admit to ever having seen one of the many ghosts, though this could have much to do with weariness at the unending procession of ghost hunters who troop through.

Where to eat & drink

Dering Arms

The Grove, Pluckley, TN27 0RR (01233 840371, www.deringarms.com). Open 11.30am-3.30pm, 6-11pm Mon-Sat; 11.30am-4pm Sun. Lunch served noon-2pm, dinner served 6.30-9pm daily.

The Dering Arms is an atmospheric former hunting lodge, complete with flagstones, wooden floors, high ceilings and the requisite Dering windows. Fish and seafood are the mainstays of the menu; try the soft herring roes and Sussex smokies (flaked smoked mackerel and cheese sauce). It's a popular place, so booking is advisable. The bar serves regional ales and ciders, as well as a good selection of wines. The inn also has three smart B&B rooms (£65-£85 double).

Wife of Bath

4 Upper Bridge Street, Wye, TN25 5AF (01233 812232, www.thewifeofbath.com). Lunch served noon-2.30pm Wed-Sat; noon-5.30pm Sun. Dinner served 6-10pm Tue-Sat.
A 'restaurant with rooms' that does both exceedingly well, based in a old house in the pretty village of Wye, north-east of Ashford. The menu's colourful dishes pack a flavourful punch; tuck into rack of lamb with crushed new potatoes, broad beans and pea salsa, followed by caramelised rice pudding with apple brandy and cinnamon tuile. Sunday lunch is very popular, especially with groups who can order a whole roast joint to be carved at the table. There are five classy en suite B&B rooms (£95 double incl breakfast).

Where to stay

Thanks to Ashford's international train station and connections to the M20, there are plenty of functional hotel chains: Holiday Inn (0871 423 4896, www.holidayinn.com), Premier Inn (0871 527 8000, www.premierinn.com), Travelodge (www.travelodge.co.uk). For more individual accommodation, try the Dering Arms (*see p113*) or the Wife of Bath (*see above*).

Eastwell Manor

Eastwell Park, Boughton Lees, TN25 4HR (01233 213000, www.eastwellmanor.co.uk). Rates £140-£295 double incl breakfast.
Eastwell Manor, just north of Ashford, has a helipad, a spa with a 20-metre heated pool, a golf course and two restaurants, and is inevitably popular for weddings and conferences. The Manor House has 23 rooms, some of which are huge, and each decorated in a classic style. Set in converted Victorian stables, Eastwell Mews contains 39 more modern rooms, a couple of which have private terraces with views across the North Downs.

Elvey Farm

Elvey Lane, Pluckley, TN27 0SU (01233 840442, www.elveyfarm.co.uk). Rates £100-£225 double incl breakfast.
Nine rooms are spread across an oast house, a stableblock and a farmhouse. There are four suites in the stableblock, three with a living room and one with two extra family beds. The most intriguing rooms are the two in the oast house; the Appledore room is in the roundel. The Canterbury Suite has a four-poster bed and a private outdoor hot tub. The restaurant (in the 16th-century barn) is open every evening and for Sunday lunch, and has a wholly seasonal Kentish menu, accompanied by local wines.

TENTERDEN & AROUND

Tenterden

Tenterden is easily one of the prettiest places in Kent. Spread along the tree-lined High Street is a splendid hodgepodge of architectural styles from the last 700 years. Most emblematic of the town are its white weatherboarded houses. They are popular throughout Kent, but mention Tenterden and it's this characteristic people mention. The town's population of around 8,000 rockets in summer with tourists, many enjoying its excellent shopping – in particular, upmarket homewares and antiques. It's the kind of place where the Shire Clothing Company (3-5 High Street, 01580 766719, www.shirecountryclothing. co.uk, closed Sun) can thrive across the road from the Tackle & Gun Shop (3 East Well, High Street, 01580 764851).

The oldest building in Tenterden is St Mildred's Church, which contains two 13th-century windows in its chancel. At this time, Tenterden was a Cinque Port on the busy River Rother. The river silted up in the 15th century, and Tenterden lost its link to the sea – there are now ten dry miles between the town and the sea. However, it remained the centre of the Wealden wool trade, as it had done since Edward III banned imported wool in 1331. The buildings along the High Street, added to over the centuries, have remained remarkably untouched; only the shops inhabiting them have changed.

At 24 High Street is Tenterden Town Hall (01580 762271, www.tenterdentown.co.uk), built in 1790. If it's open – and it often is for craft fairs and the like – walk up to the Mayor's Parlour to see a roll call of all the mayors and a selection of portraits. Next door, the 15th-century Woolpack Hotel is thronged during the Tenterden Folk Festival (www.tenterdenfolkfestival.org.uk) in late September. Through the alleyway by the pub is St Mildred's Church. The Reverend Philip Ward, the husband of Admiral Nelson's daughter, Horatia, was appointed vicar of the church in 1830 and lived in the vicarage until his death in 1859.

Back along the High Street, heading west, are various buildings using the trick of mathematical tiles to give the impression of brick. Just over Church Road are a couple of antiques shops. Tenterden Antique & Silver Vaults (66A High Street, 01580 765885) specialises in jewellery and porcelain china, with curios and cheaper antiques next door. The Vine Inn (*see p117*) is at no.76. From here the street widens and the shops are more sporadic. But do visit Truffles at Coco at no.128 (01580 763501), a small shop with stunning chocolates. At no.122 is Peggottys Tea Shoppe (01580 764393).

Across the road, the buildings are largely residential, set well back from the High Street. If you walk back towards the centre on this side, you'll pass the White Lion pub (*see p117*), a pleasant place for a coffee or a pint. Shoppers will need sustenance before entering one of the Webbs of Tenterden outlets (www.webbsoftenterden.com). Webbs began life as a hardware store set up by William Webb in 1910. As well as a shop in Battle, there are now three premises, almost next door to one another on the High Street. No.45 is Webbs Kitchen (01580 762132, closed Sun), selling such lines as Emma Bridgewater, Henkel Knives and Le Creuset. Next is the ironmongers, opened in 1917, followed by the latest addition to the empire, a linen and gift shop. Finally, there's Thumbelina, the Enchanted Toy Shop (no.17A, 01580 763303, closed Sun). It is truly enchanting, with a range of high-quality wooden and traditional toys.

Tenterden

Things to do

ROMNEY MARSH & DUNGENESS

Action Watersports
Lake 1, Dengemarsh Road, Lydd, TN29 9JH (01797 321885, www.actionwatersports.co.uk).
Whether you fancy waterskiing, wakeboarding or making some noise on a jet ski, Action Watersports can set you up. As well as all the on-the-water action, they have a huge selection of watersports gear, lakeside play and picnic areas, barbecues and a repairs workshop.

Littlestone Golf Club
St Andrews Road, Littlestone, TN28 8RB (01797 363355, www.littlestonegolfclub.org.uk). Open 9.30am-dusk Mon-Fri; 11am-dusk Sat, Sun. Green fees £40-£80; £15-£25 reductions.
Green fees are very reasonable at this pleasant golf course, which was established in 1899. Nearby Littlestone Warren (www.romneywarrengolfclub.org.uk) offers a cheaper pay-and-play experience over 18 holes.

Lydd International Raceway
Dengemarsh Road, Lydd, TN29 9JH (0845 644 5501, www.daytona.co.uk/venues/lydd/index.html). Open Feb-Dec 9am-dusk daily. Rates £30 per 30mins.
A high-octane day out can be had at this Daytona karting venue, where all abilities are welcome.

Marsh Maize Maze
Haguelands Village, Burmarsh, TN29 0JR (07515 932601, www.haguelandsfarm.co.uk). Open 10am-6pm Mon-Sat; 10am-4pm Sun. Admission £6; £4 reductions; £18 family.
Test your directional skills and explore three miles of paths winding through six acres of corn and maize crops in this walk-round maze. In addition, there's a farm shop and bistro (with a cooking school).

Romney, Hythe & Dymchurch Railway
New Romney Station, New Romney, TN28 8PL (01797 362353, www.rhdr.org.uk). Open check website for timetable. Fares Romney rover ticket £14; £7-£12.50 reductions; £38 family.
As the world's smallest public railway, this narrow-gauge train adds some fun to melancholy Dungeness. It chugs merrily for 13.5 miles from Dungeness Point to Hythe, stopping at the small beach towns along the coast. In addition to the flat, bleak scenery, it seems to sweep through several back gardens along the way. The line has been in operation since 1927, and the scale engines are only a third of the size of your average steam locomotive.

ASHFORD & AROUND

Kent Ballooning
Yew Trees Studio, Stanford North, TN25 6DH (0800 032 5060, www.kentballooning.com). Open Apr-Oct by appointment. Flights from £110 per person.
Of its seven launch sites across Kent (which are chosen by the pilot on the day, according to the wind), possibly the most coveted is in the centre of Canterbury, where you ascend over the cathedral and soar above the historical World Heritage Site. After the pilot finds a suitable landing spot, the flight is toasted with a glass of champagne – a tradition dating from the Montgolfier brothers' first balloon flight in the late 18th century. There are also launch sites at Headcorn and Ashford.

TENTERDEN & AROUND

Kent & East Sussex Railway
Tenterden Town Station, Station Road, Tenterden, TN30 6HE (01580 765155, www.kesr.org.uk). Open times vary; check website for details. Fares Day rover £13.50; £8.50-£12.50 reductions; £37 family.
Weave through the Rother Valley on a scenic 10.5 mile train ride from Tenterden Town station to Bodiam. The classic vintage railway coaches are sympathetically restored, and the trains are mainly powered by steam.

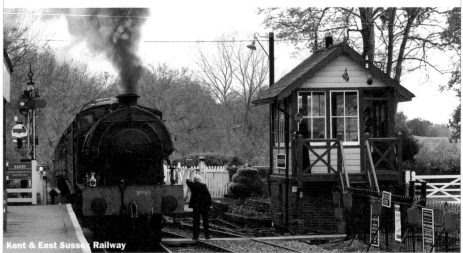
Kent & East Sussex Railway

There's no mainline rail service to Tenterden, although the Kent & East Sussex Railway (*see left*) puffs its way here. The nearest stations are Headcorn (nine miles) and Ashford (12 miles). There are regular buses from Ashford, Hastings, Rye and Tunbridge Wells.

Rolvenden & Benenden

A few miles south-east of Tenterden, on the A28, is the little village of Rolvenden. The weatherboard houses were almost all built after the Great Plague in 1665, when the first settlement, then called Riolvinden, was burned to the ground. Villagers moved to the nearby common where the village now stands. The town saw more turmoil during the Swing Riots of 1830. Labourers rioted against the lowering of wages, destroying threshing machines, and the vandalism swiftly swept across the country. What they would have made of the profusion of Land Rovers and BMWs hereabouts is anyone's guess; this is no longer a poor part of the country.

The parish church, St Mary the Virgin, was built in 1220, while the war memorial in the churchyard was designed by Edwin Lutyens. A well-attended farmers' market is held here every Thursday morning, but the most notable attraction is the CM Booth Collection of Historic Vehicles (*see p111*).

From Rolvenden, turn on to the B2086 to reach Hole Park (*see p111*) and Benenden. This is as near a quintessential English village as you'll find: village green used by the local cricket club? Tick. Great pub? Tick. Norman church with a good bit of history? Tick. On summer Saturdays, the whole town seems to line the green to watch the cricket before descending on the old coaching inn, the Bull (*see right*). The cricket fixtures can be found at www.benendenvillage.org.uk.

At one end of the green is St George's Church (www.benendenchurch.org). It's mentioned in the Domesday Book, although much of the original building burned down in 1672. According to church records, 'a storm of lightening, thunder, a hard gale of wind and some rains' set fire to the steeple, and the church was 'consumed in four or five howers time; the five large bells melted'. It was rebuilt in 1677. The churchyard is the last resting place of Kitty Fisher who expressed a wish to be buried in her best ballgown. A hugely famous high-class prostitute, Fisher was painted by many of the artistic greats of the day: Joshua Reynolds' *Cleopatra Dissolving the Pearl*, completed in 1759, is the most enduring image of her. She was also immortalised in the nursery rhyme Lucy Locket: 'Lucy Locket lost her pocket, Kitty Fisher found it/But ne'er a penny was there in't, Except the binding round it.' Benenden's final claim to fame is as the home of Benenden public school.

Where to eat & drink

There are plenty of places in Tenterden for a meal or snack. The Lemon Tree (29-33 High Street, 01580 763381, www.lemontreetenterden.co.uk), which occupies a 14th-century timber-framed house, serves classic English dishes such as steak and ale pie

(using Shepherd Neame, of course) and local bangers with mash. It's also a good place for tea, with buttered teacakes and crumpets. The White Lion (57 High Street, 01580 765077, www.white lionpubtenterden.co.uk), run by Marston Taverns, offers an extensive menu of good pub food. The Nutmeg Deli (01580 764125) on Sayers Lane, off the High Street, has a a relaxing little café with interesting snacks and great coffee. Shepherd Neame's Vine Inn (76 High Street, 01580 762718, www.shepherdneame.co.uk) is fittingly located in a former 18th-century brewery, with a Victorian façade and a spacious, modern interior and conservatory.

Just outside Tenterden, the Raja of Kent (Biddenden Road, St Michaels, 01233 851191, www.therajaofkent.com) serves excellent Indian and Bangladeshi cuisine.

Bull Inn ★

The Street, Benenden, TN17 4DE (01580 240054, www.thebullatbenenden.co.uk). Open noon-midnight daily. Lunch served noon-2.15pm Mon-Sat; 12.15-3pm Sun. Dinner served noon-9.15pm Mon-Sat.
This fine old pub, built in 1601, is a focal point for the local community. The cricket club drinks here after Saturday games, and shooting parties come for food in winter. The Bull takes its commitment to local produce further than most pubs – not only in dishes such as wild rabbit and bacon casserole or dressed Rye Bay crab, but with wines, ales and, uncommonly, lagers all coming from the locality. Two large fires keep drinkers warm in winter.

Richard Phillips at Chapel Down ★

Chapel Down, Tenterden Vineyard, Small Hythe, TN30 7NG (01580 761616, www.richardphillipsatchapeldown. co.uk). Lunch served noon-3pm Tue-Sat; noon-4pm Sun. Dinner served 6.30-10.30pm Thur-Sun.
In the gorgeous surroundings of the Chapel Down vineyard complex (*see p111*), this restaurant is part of chef Richard Phillips's portfolio (alongside Thackeray's in Tunbridge Wells and Hengist in Aylesford). Seasonal dishes might include duck and guinea fowl terrine with pickled vegetables and toasted sourdough to start, followed by pan-fried fillets of South Coast plaice, Tenterden new potatoes with chervil, broad beans, and pea and morel ragoût. The wine list is extensive, and of course includes plenty of options from Chapel Down. The modern space is nicely buzzy, and there's a jazz night every Thursday.

Where to stay

Good B&Bs and country house hotels are plentiful around Tenterden. The London Beach Country Hotel & Spa (Ashford Road, 01580 766279, www.londonbeach.com), on the outskirts of town, has 100 acres of grounds, including a pristine golf course and a swimming pool. In Tenterden itself, the Tower House (27 Ashford Road, 01580 761920, www.towerhouse.biz) is a charming B&B set in a Georgian mansion, while the White Lion (*see above*) has recently refurbished and reasonably priced rooms.

Three miles east of Tenterden, in Woodchurch, Brook Farm B&B (Brook Street, 01233 860444, www.brookfarmbandb.co.uk) provides a touch of luxury, including a heated outdoor pool.

Little Silver
Ashford Road, Tenterden, TN30 6SP (01233 850321, www.little-silver.co.uk). Rates £97-£199 double incl breakfast.
This well-established hotel is a leafy haven with 16 rooms. There are four-poster beds and spa baths in the high-end rooms; the standard doubles are much more basic. The restaurant has views over landscaped greenery, and serves straightforward but accomplished dishes such as roast duck breast with sticky raspberry syrup or seared tuna steaks with coriander and lime butter.

CRANBROOK & AROUND

Cranbrook
'Cranbrook is a village giving the impression of trying to remember what once made it important,' observed HE Bates in *The Darling Buds of May*. Although the popular television series was filmed in nearby Pluckley (*see p113*), the 'perfick' story of family life in the Garden of England was written with this area in mind.

The village was the centre of the Wealden cloth industry in the 14th and 15th centuries – the proceeds of which paid for the construction of St Dunstan's Church. Known as the 'Cathedral of the Weald', it is one of the largest churches in Kent; in the evening sunlight, its sandstone walls take on a rich, golden hue. The church tower was completed around 1425, but the clock, a prototype for Big Ben, was added in 1855. On the wall under the tower are the Green Men: four intricately carved oak shields, pagan in origin and dating from the 13th or 14th century. Beside the entrance to the churchyard is the Old Fire Station, now the Weald Information Centre (01580 715686, closed Sat, Sun), where you can pick up a walking heritage tour of the town and a guide to St Dunstan's.

The beautifully preserved High Street is lined with buildings dating from the Tudor to Georgian ages, some with weatherboard cladding. Opposite Caiston Road is the Old Studio, originally a cloth hall, where artists from the 19th-century Cranbrook Colony group, known for their romantic images of rural Kent life, once worked. Fab Jules (no.49A, 01580 714036, www.fabjules.co.uk, closed Mon & Sun) sells hand-made jewellery.

Cranbrook Museum (Carriers Road, 01580 712475, www.cranbrookmuseum.org, open Apr-Oct 2-4.30pm Tue-Sat) is set in a fine, 15th-century timber-framed building and contains a collection of historic local tools and artefacts. Stone Street has some reliable independent shops and delis; Gastronomia Campo Vecchio (no.16, 01580 720555, closed Sun) is one of the best, with a wide range of Italian comestibles. Also along here is Apicius (*see p119*), a well-regarded restaurant. Continue down Stone Street and on to The Hill to visit Union Mill (01580 712984, www.unionmill. org.uk), the largest smock-mill (only the cap rotates) in England. In use from 1814 until 1958, it has now been restored and turned into a museum; check the website for opening times.

Sissinghurst & Biddenden
A couple of miles north-east of Cranbrook is the hamlet of Sissinghurst. It's best known for Sissinghurst Castle – actually an Elizabethan mansion – and its magnificent gardens (*see p111*).

East on the A262 from Sissinghurst is the village of Biddenden, a small slice of untouched antiquity. The first striking aspect of this tiny place is its adopted symbol: a pair of conjoined twins. Born in the village in 1100, Mary and Eliza Chulkhurst were known as the Biddenden Maids. They were joined at the shoulder and hip, and lived until the age of 34 – a reasonable innings in the 12th century. It's said that when they died, they left five plots of land to the church to pay for bread, cheese and beer to be given to the poor every Easter. Whether or not the story is true, an Easter tradition of giving food to the poor has existed here for centuries and continues to

Three Chimneys

this day; 'Biddenden cakes' bearing the twins' image are still distributed at Easter.

The prettiest part of the village is around the thatched Flemish weavers' cottages. Built in 1689, the timber-framed buildings are now private residences, a shop and Ye Maydes restaurant (01580 291306, www.yemaydes.co.uk, closed Mon, Tue, Sun). Opposite is the Red Lion pub (12-14 High Street, 01580 291347), and further down is the Michelin-starred West House (*see right*). The best pub in the area, just west of town on the A262, is the Three Chimneys (*see below*).

Where to eat & drink

Five miles north of Biddenden, the village of Headcorn is home to the George & Dragon (01622 890239), a characterful pub with good beers and ciders. It also serves food, although you might be lured in by the Headcorn Teashop (01622 890682) instead, with its enticing array of own-made cakes.

Apicius ★

23 Stone Street, Cranbrook, TN17 3HF (01580 714666, www.restaurant-apicius.co.uk). Lunch served noon-2pm Wed-Fri, Sun. Dinner served 7-9pm Wed-Sat.
The kitchen at this thimble-sized eaterie produces the sophisticated likes of pan-fried sea bream with roast leeks, sweetcorn and vanilla purée and chanterelle mushrooms, and a selection of tempting desserts such as iced fig mousse and passion fruit rice pudding. The presentation is beautiful, and prices are surprisingly affordable given that the chef has a Michelin star.

George Hotel & Brasserie

Stone Street, Cranbrook, TN17 3HE (01580 713348, www.thegeorgehotelkent.co.uk). Open 11am-11pm daily. Breakfast served 8.30-10.30am, lunch served noon-3pm, dinner served 6-9.30pm daily.
There has been a pub called the George on this spot since at least 1300. The current building has changed somewhat since Queen Elizabeth I visited in 1573, especially in the contemporary brasserie, which serves upmarket pub food. For a bit of tradition, eat in the dining room with its antique furniture and 16th-century inglenook fireplace. Good accommodation comes in the shape of 12 individually designed rooms (£75-£140 double incl breakfast); four are contemporary, while others play on the history of the hotel.

Great House

Gills Green, Hawkhurst, TN18 5EJ (01580 753119, www.elitepubs.com/the_greathouse). Open 11.30am-11pm daily. Food served noon-9.30pm daily.
This charming 16th-century inn serves British and French brasserie-style dishes in a rustic setting. The sharing boards – charcuterie, fish or cheese – are particularly popular, and there's game in season. Alternatively, pop in for a dessert and a coffee: the Kentish apple and berry crumble with honeycomb ice-cream is very moreish.

Three Chimneys ★

Hareplain Road, Biddenden, TN27 8LW (01580 291472, www.thethreechimneys.co.uk). Open 11.30am-3pm, 5.30-11pm Mon-Fri; 11am-3.30pm, 5.30-11.30pm Sat; noon-3.30pm, 6-10.30pm Sun. Lunch served noon-2pm

Mon-Fri; noon-2.30pm Sat, Sun. Dinner served 6.30-9pm Mon-Thur, Sun; 6.30-9.30pm Fri, Sat.
A tiny old pub with incredibly low ceilings and open fires in winter – find yourself a corner tucked beneath the beams and soak up the atmosphere. There's a fantastic terrace for alfresco drinking, beautiful gardens packed with herbs and lavender, and a conservatory if it's a little nippy. Top-notch pub food uses locally sourced ingredients (from herbs to meat) where possible, and there's a fine choice of ales.

West House ★

28 High Street, Biddenden, TN27 8AH (01580 291341, www.thewesthouserestaurant.co.uk). Lunch served noon-2pm Tue-Fri; noon-3pm Sun. Dinner served 7-9.30pm Tue-Sat.
Chef Graham Garrett's cooking is worthy of its Michelin star, but his restaurant, housed in a 15th-century weaver's cottage, is without airs and graces. The decor mixes old and new to pleasing effect, while the short menu is both inspiring and comforting. Dishes might include warm haddock carpaccio with bacon dressing or pickled rock samphire and pea shoots to start, followed by roast partridge with honeyed quince, potato pancake and rosemary butter. With 24 hours' notice, the kitchen can create bespoke vegetarian dishes.

Woodcock

Iden Green, TN17 4HT (01580 240009, www.the woodcockinn.com). Open noon-11pm Tue-Sun. Lunch served noon-2.15pm Tue-Sat; noon-2.30pm Sun. Dinner served 6-8.45pm Tue-Sat.
This country pub serves great food, much of it hearty fare – try chunky pheasant pâté or wild mushroom fricassée. Gather around one of the dining tables, curl up on a leather sofa near the inglenook fireplace, or sit at the picnic benches in the garden. Various ales and a decent wine list complete the picture.

Where to stay

In Cranbrook, the location of Church Gates (Stone Street, 01580 713521, www.churchgates.com) couldn't be better. One of the two rooms has a rolltop bath and looks over the churchyard, while the other has an inglenook fireplace and views over the centre of the village.

A mile south of Cranbrook, Hallwood Farm Oast (Hawkhurst Road, 01580 712416, www.hallwood farm.co.uk) has two large beamed bedrooms, very much in the country farmhouse style. It's still a working farm, with apple orchards, blackcurrant bushes and sheep, and there's some excellent walking to be had; Bedgebury Forest is adjacent.

Sissinghurst Castle Farmhouse

Sissinghurst, TN17 2AB (01580 720992, www. sissinghurstcastlefarmhouse.com). Rates £125-£170 double incl breakfast.
This gorgeous house on the Sissinghurst Castle estate is now run as a B&B. The Victorian red-brick mansion has been thoroughly refurbished, but has retained much of its character. There are seven elegantly appointed en suite rooms with views over the estate; Sissinghurst is one of the most appealing, with its oak sleigh bed, velvety armchairs and original fireplace.

KENT

Tunbridge Wells & Around

On the upper end of the Weald – a Saxon name for wood – is the elegant spa town of Tunbridge Wells. Its grand architecture and tranquil parkland are the legacy of its Regency heyday, when the rich and royal flocked to sample its healing waters and giddy social scene. Today, it is the area's principal town, and still exudes a quietly prosperous air.

Until the discovery of the celebrated spring, Tunbridge Wells was just forest and fields. By contrast, Tonbridge (now overshadowed by its famous sister town) has existed since medieval times, and has the craggy remains of a motte-and-bailey castle to prove it. In much better shape is the Tudor Hever Castle, near Edenbridge. With its moat, portcullis and crenellated towers, it's the sort of castle that children draw – and as the childhood home of Anne Boleyn, is steeped in history.

To the east of Tunbridge Wells, the Weald rises up to Goudhurst, offering sweeping views of the Kent countryside, dotted with oast houses and Norman church towers. West of Tonbridge, tiny villages such as Penshurst and Chiddingstone are timelessly lovely, with their crooked Tudor cottages and cosy village pubs.

The green valleys, dense forests and rocky outcrops of this part of Kent also attract increasing numbers of adventure sport aficionados. Mountain-bikers hurl themselves around the tracks at Bedgebury Forest, while climbers scale Harrison's Rocks and High Rocks. More genteel activities include a ride on the Spa Valley Railway steam train, or a walk around the Pinetum at Bedgebury.

GOUDHURST & LAMBERHURST

Goudhurst

Sitting atop a high plain, with sweeping views across the surrounding countryside, Goudhurst is a quintessential village of the High Weald. Oast houses? Tick. Hop fields? Tick. Orchards? Tick. Its name is thought to derive from the Old English for Battle Hill, guo hyrst – although when the supposed battle took place no one knows.

The oldest building in the village is St Mary's Church (01580 211739, www.goudhurst.deanery intheweald.org.uk) – a handsome, predominantly 13th-century construction, built from mellow Kentish ragstone. Although a lightning strike destroyed its spire in 1637, there are splendid views from the tower. On a clear day, it's said you can spot 51 other churches and see as far as Canary Wharf, some 40 miles away. Inside the chapel, an early 15th-century brass commemorates local landowner John de Bedgebury, who fought at Agincourt with Henry V; he is depicted in his armour, with his feet resting on a lion. Other imposing tombs and monuments remember the Culpepers, a powerful family with a large interest in the once-significant Kentish iron industry.

One of the most exciting episodes in the village's otherwise sleepy history took place in 1747, when locals formed the Goudhurst Band of Militia and made a stand against the Hawkhurst Gang, a violent band of smugglers. The villagers killed three of the malefactors during the 'Battle of Goudhurst', although the gang's reign of terror only came to an end two years later, when their leader was hanged.

When they weren't stealing and smuggling, the Hawkhurst Gang would drink in the timbered Star & Eagle (see 122), by the the churchyard. Heading down into the village from here, look out for the well-preserved weavers' cottages on the left. A little further down, the High Street is lined with traditional weatherboard houses and tile-hung façades; at no.12, Weeks Bakery & Tearoom (01580 211380, closed Sun) serves cream teas and light lunches in quaint 16th-century premises. Across the road, Sizzlers Family Butchers (01580 211247, closed Sun) is a good place to pick up some game or buy supplies for a picnic. The High Street comes to an end at the tranquil village pond, which completes its bucolic good looks.

Lamberhurst

Continuing west on the A262 through Goudhurst, drive over the roundabout and along the B2162 to Lamberhurst (signposted). A left turn on to the A21 will take you to Scotney Castle (see p128), while

Chequers. See p122.

Bedgebury Forest. See p124.

Bedgebury National Pinetum. See p128.

Bayham Old Abbey (*see p128*), Bewl Water (*see p124*) and Finchcocks (*see p128*) are also nearby.

Sitting on the River Teise, a tributary of the Medway, Lamberhurst is smaller than Goudhurst but no less lovely. It was once the centre of the Kent iron industry, and the railings of St Paul's Cathedral were cast here. Today, it's a very quiet village that was home to Denis and Margaret Thatcher in the 1970s. Although a wander won't take long, the Chequers (*see below*) is good for accommodation and food, and the community website, www.lamberhurstvillage.co.uk, has details of local events.

Where to eat & drink

Chequers
The Broadway, Lamberhurst, TN3 8DB (01892 890260, www.thechequersinnlamberhurst.co.uk). Open Apr-Oct 11am-11pm daily. Nov-Mar 11am-11pm Tue-Sun. Food served Apr-Oct noon-3pm, 6-9pm Mon-Sat; noon-4.30pm Sun. Nov-Mar noon-3pm, 6-9pm Tue-Sat; noon-4.30pm Sun.
This venerable riverside inn started life as a 12th-century manor house. A pub since 1414, it later became a coaching inn, and claims a Jane Austen connection. Today, it's a Shepherd Neame pub with a reputation for good food and a focus on local produce. Soup, ciabattas and home-made pies are served in the bar, while the restaurant menu might include potted shrimps or pork belly with cider and Kentish apple sauce. The five guest rooms (£85-£95 double incl breakfast) are small but reasonably appointed.

Star & Eagle
High Street, Goudhurst, TN17 1AL (01580 211512, www.starandeagle.com). Open 9am-11pm Mon-Sat; 9am-3pm, 6.30-10pm Sun. Lunch served noon-2.30pm Mon-Sat; noon-3pm Sun. Dinner served 6.30-9.30pm Mon-Sat; 6.30-9pm Sun.
Once the headquarters of the notorious Hawkhurst Gang, the Star & Eagle is a hospitable, old-fashioned affair. Behind its timbered façade lies a cosy bar with hefty beams, an inglenook fireplace and log fires in winter. British classics such as sautéed calf's liver or beef wellington are menu mainstays, although owner and chef Enrique Martinez has also introduced some Spanish flourishes: Basque-style hake with salsa verde might feature among the mains, while tapas include calamari and gambas al ajillo (garlicky, chilli-spiked prawns). There are ten comfortable rooms (£90-£140 double incl breakfast), including two with four-poster beds; ask for a room with views over the Weald.

Where to stay
Both the Chequers and the Star & Eagle (for both, *see above*) offer B&B accommodation; for more choice, head to Tunbridge Wells (*see pp126-127*).

TUNBRIDGE WELLS
'Dear Tunbridge Wells, I am so very fond of it,' wrote a young Princess Victoria – and she wasn't the first royal to fall for the town's charms. Queen Henrietta Maria, wife of Charles I, set the

Dunorlan Park, near Tunbridge Wells

The Pantiles

precedent, after arriving with her entourage in 1630 to 'take the waters' and convalesce after the birth of the future Charles II.

The story of how Dudley, Lord North first stumbled upon the spring in 1606 may be apocryphal, but is inextricably tied to the fate of Tunbridge Wells. Advised by doctors to take a six-month sabbatical from society, the young nobleman packed himself off to the countryside. A month later, finding it intolerably dull, he set off back to London. Riding through the vast forest that covered the Weald he came across a chalybeate spring, whose iron-rich waters seemed to have an invigorating effect on his health. His physician agreed, and doctors were soon touting the springwater as a remedy from anything from indigestion to insomnia.

In the early days there wasn't much provision for visitors: when Queen Henrietta visited, her party had to camp in tents on the common. By the end of the century, though, all manner of new developments had sprung up around the spring – not least the elegant, colonnaded promenade known as the Pantiles. A typical day for a wealthy visitor would consist of two hours 'taking' the water (14 pints were advised, and there was a 'pissing house' nearby) before an afternoon of long luncheons, leisurely strolls and perhaps a visit to the church of King Charles the Martyr (see p129). Evenings were spent dancing, socialising and gambling. The town certainly attracted a colourful crowd, as Daniel Defoe drily attested: 'As for Gaming, Sharping, Intriguing; as also Fops, Fools, Beaus and the like, Tunbridge is as full of these, as can be desired.'

The Pantiles ★ remain one of the town's biggest draws – and from Easter to September, you can take a swig of the famous water, served by a costume-clad 'dipper'. Upmarket jewellers, antique shops, boutiques and cafés cluster along the pedestrianised walkway, while a Tourist Information Centre occupies the Old Fish Market (01892 515675, www.visittunbridgewells.com). A farmers' market is held here on the first and third Saturday of the month.

On the other side of London Road from the Pantiles, Tunbridge Wells Forum (Fonthill, the

Things to do

Go Ape!

GOUDHURST & LAMBERHURST

Bewl Water
Bewlbridge Lane, Lamberhurst, TN3 8JH (01892 890000, www.bewlwater.co.uk). Open 9am-dusk daily. Admission £4; £3 reductions.
Set at the bottom of the beautiful Bewl river valley, on the Kent and Sussex border, this man-made reservoir is the largest inland body of water in the south east. A 12-mile track runs along the shore and into the surrounding meadows and woodland, and is open to cyclists and horseriders from May to October. Bewl also offers an abundance of waterbourne activities, from rowing and sailing to windsurfing, boat trips and fishing. Adrenalin junkies will enjoy the hydroballing or zip wire, and a playground is tucked amid the trees by the visitor centre. Bring a picnic, or lunch on the terrace at the Waterside Bistro & Bar.

Bedgebury Forest Trails
Bedgebury Visitors Centre, nr Flimwell, TN17 2SJ (01580 879842, www.forestry.gov.uk). Open times vary; call for details. Admission free (parking £8).
Eight miles of single-track mountain biking trails weave through the trees at Bedgebury Forest; most is graded as red, but there are some fiendishly tricky black runs for experienced riders. Those looking for a more gentle ride amid unspoilt scenery can peddle the six-mile family trail. Bikes can be hired from Quench Cycles (01580 879694, www.quenchuk. co.uk), by the car park. If you prefer horse power, the Bedgebury Park Equestrian Centre (01580 211602, www.bedgeburypark.com/equestrian) offers hacks and lessons.

Go Ape! ★
Bedgebury Road, Goudhurst, Cranbrook, TN17 2SJ (0845 643 9215, www.goape.co.uk). Open times vary; phone for details. Admission £30; £20 reductions.
Not for suffers of vertigo, this Go Ape! outpost offers a high-wire forest adventure. Between the tree trunks of Bedgebury Forest is a network of ladders, walkways, bridges and zip-lines. Once you're safely harnessed

and hooked on, and have been given a half-hour safety briefing, you're free to clamber, swing and swoop through the trees.

TUNBRIDGE WELLS

Harrison's Rocks
Groombridge, near Eridge. Classes are run by Nuts 4 Climbing (01892 860670, www.rock climbingclasses.co.uk). Open by appointment. Rates £90/day. No credit cards.
One of the finest places to rock-climb in the south east, this sandstone crag is maintained by the British Mountaineering Council for the sole use of climbers. Despite not being particularly high, the rocks offer climbs to suit all levels, from a simple 1a scramble up to a frankly terrifying 6c, with overhangs and sheer walls (in the UK, climbs are graded between one and nine, with nine being the hardest). As a result, it's hugely popular with the climbing fraternity. The Huntsman (Eridge Road, 01892 864258) is a good bet for a sustaining, locally sourced pub lunch.

Heritage Walking Trail
www.visittunbridgewells.com/microsite/home.
In 2006 a Heritage Walking Trail was devised, marking the 400th anniversary of the discovery of the chalybeate spring that sparked the town's development. Maps are available from the Tourist Information Centre in the Pantiles, close to the start of the walk; after the spring, the route takes in the Corn Exchange, Calverley Park, Holy Trinity Church, Tunbridge Well Museum and the Common, finishing at the Church of King Charles the Martyr. Guided tours are also offered; ask at the Tourist Information Centre for details.

High Rocks
High Rocks Lane, TN3 9JJ (01892 515532, www.highrocks.co.uk). Open 10am-dusk daily. Admission Climbers £10. Non-climbers £2; £1 reductions.
Unlike Harrison's Rocks (*see above*), High Rocks is privately owned. The sheer scale and heft of the rocky outcrops are undeniably impressive, bisected by mossy ravines and clefts, and linked by little bridges: together with the surrounding woodland, it makes for a dramatic walk. Children will relish exploring the nooks and crannies – though keep a watchful eye on them near the edge. Climbers, meanwhile, stick to the serious business of scaling the dauntingly steep, flat walls.

Spa Valley Railway
West Station, TN2 5QY (01892 537715, www.spa valleyrailway.co.uk). Open timetable varies; see website for details. Fares £9; £4.50 reductions.
The Spa Valley steam engine runs between Tunbridge Wells and Groombridge, some three-and-a-half miles away, with a stop at High Rocks; an extension to Eridge is also on the cards. Chugging through the Kent and Sussex Weald, with the soothing smell of stream train in the breeze, is a soothingly timeless experience, and there are themed events for families, involving Thomas, Santa and other special guests.

TONBRIDGE

Cycle Ops
Bank Street, Tonbridge, TN9 1BL (01732 500533, www.cycle-ops.co.uk). Open Oct-Easter 9am-5.30pm Mon-Wed; 9am-7pm Thur; 9am-6pm Fri; 9am-5pm Sat; 10am-4pm Sun. Easter-Sept 9am-5.30pm Mon-Thur; 9am-6pm Fri, Sat; 10am-4pm Sun. Cycle hire £15/2hrs, £19/day; £6/2hrs, £9/day reductions.
The most famous cycle route in the area is from Tonbridge to Penshurst (*see p127*) – well signposted with blue Regional Cycle Route 12. As well as hiring out cycles (book ahead if you can), this place is also home to a well-respected bike shop and repair centre.

Poult Wood Golf Centre
Higham Lane, Tonbridge, TN11 9QR (01732 364039, www.poultwoodgolf.co.uk). Open times vary; check website for details. Weekday round £17, weekend round £24.
Three miles north of Tonbridge, this pay and play golf course is in a lovely setting. There are 18- and nine-hole courses, and a pleasant clubhouse and bar. Lessons are offered by PGA professional David Copsey and his team.

Harrison's Rocks

Common, 0871 277 7101, www.twforum.co.uk) is a little independent music venue with an impressive track record at talent-spotting: Green Day, Oasis and Radiohead all played here before they hit the big time. Behind it is Tunbridge Wells Common (www.twcommons.org) which, combined with Rusthall Common, extends for some 250 acres. Within its boundaries are Toad Rock and Wellington Rock, two famous sandstone outcrops along Mount Ephraim on the northern border. It's a lovely place for a ramble at any time of year.

Pedestrianised Chapel Place climbs from the Pantiles to the High Street. Off to the right is Bedford Terrace, a beautifully preserved row of Georgian buildings. On Chapel Place itself, Peter Speaight (no.15, 01892 616668) is the best butcher's in the area, famed for its own-made pies. Opposite, Le Petit Jardin (nos.14-16, 01892 541152, www.le-petit-jardin.com, closed Sun) stocks upmarket gear for gardeners, running from ash-handled trowels to ornate garden furniture.

The High Street itself is lined with independent retailers rather than generic high street names – although Cath Kidston and Farrow & Ball do make an appearance. At nos.76-78 are the delightfully old-fashioned premises of G Collins & Sons (01892 534018, www.gcollinsandsons.com, closed Sun), with a window full of contemporary jeweller and vintage sparklers: Harry Collins is the official jeweller to the Queen, and keeps the Crown Jewels looking their sparkling best.

To the right, up Frog Lane or Little Mount Sion, is the area known as Mount Sion, named by 17th-century Puritans. It's worth a wander, with a glorious mish-mash of architectural styles; the houses were once lodging houses for the rich and well-connected, who would descend for six-week periods during 'the season'. Royalty were regulars – Victoria often stayed at Mount Pleasant House and delighted in its parkland, the Calverley Grounds. The house is now the Hotel du Vin (*see p131*); to stroll in the grounds, walk back along the High Street to the BBC South-East Centre and turn right. In summer, when the ornamental gardens are in full bloom, it's a popular picnic spot, while children slide down its steep slopes on snowy days. Climb up to Calverley Crescent and the gate that marks the entrance to the Calverley Estate. The grounds and crescent were all designed by Decimus Burton, an influential Victorian architect who also had a hand in Kew and St Leonards-on-Sea.

Walking out of the gate, and past the Hotel du Vin, is to approach Tunbridge Wells' commercial centre. The northern end of Mount Pleasant Road is largely occupied by chain stores, banks and coffee shops. Look in the old Opera House at no.88, though. Built in 1902, this grand old landmark building is now a Wetherspoons pub (01892 511770). Ignore the fruit machines and take in the opulent surrounds.

On the corner of Mount Pleasant Road and the pedestrianised Newton Road is the Royal Victoria Place shopping centre (01892 514141, http://uk.westfield.com), which offers a concentrated blast of retail therapy.

KENT

Where to eat & drink

By and large, the dimly lit restaurant at the Hotel du Vin (*see p127*) plays it safe with classic bistro grub; Devon crab with walnut bread, say, or steak with fat chips and peppercorn sauce. After dinner, retire to the bar for cocktails.

Close to Royal Victoria Place, Sankey's Seafood Brasserie & Oyster Bar (39 Mount Ephraim, 01892 511422, www.sankeys.co.uk, closed Sun) is supplied by a fishmonger's run by the same owners.

On the Pantiles, the Ragged Trousers (01892 542715, www.raggedtrousers.co.uk) is a music-loving pub with above-average food and real ales on tap. It's set in the former Assembly Rooms, where 18th-century smart society danced, drank and played cards. The revelries were officiated by the dandyish Master of Ceremonies, Beau Nash, from whom the pub at 62 Mount Ephraim (01892 539350, www.royalwells.co.uk) takes its name.

Thackeray's ★

85 London Road, TN1 1EA (01892 511921, www.thackerays-restaurant.co.uk). Lunch served noon-3pm Sun. Food served noon-midnight Tue-Sat.

This smart little restaurant serves as a suitably polished showcase for the talents of chef Richard Phillips, whose CV includes stints as head chef at the Criterion and Mirabelle. Built in around 1660, Thackeray's Grade II-listed premises retain plenty of character: the restaurant takes its name from the author of *Vanity Fair*, who lived here in the 19th century. Lavish decor and a low-lit ambience make for an intimate meal, while the modern French menu makes excellent use of seasonal ingredients, from wild mushrooms to game. If you can't afford to go à la carte, the lunchtime menu du jour is a steal.

Woods Restaurant ★

62 Pantiles, TN2 5TN (01892 614411, www.woods restaurant.co.uk). Open/food served 9am-5pm Mon, Sun; 9am-9pm Tue-Sat.

Set on the Pantiles, this restaurant, café, bar and food shop (open 9am-6pm daily) has a strong focus on Kentish produce. Almost everything on the menu, from the sausages to the wine, is sourced locally. There's an extensive breakfast menu (the bacon sandwich is recommended), and assorted sandwiches and lunchtime snacks: the rarebit, made with local cheddar and Larkins beer, is always a sound bet. Main courses are solid and satisfying, with some excellent vegetarian options.

Where to stay

Perched on Mount Ephraim, the Royal Wells Hotel (59 Mount Ephraim, 01892 511188, www.royal wells.co.uk) has an illustrious history: the young Victoria stayed here, and her coat of arms still grandly crowns the building. Its 23 en suite rooms are individually decorated, mixing antiques with tasteful modern touches. Nearby, the 70-room Spa Hotel (Mount Ephraim, 01892 520331, www.spahotel.co.uk) occupies a stately, 18th-century mansion, set in 14 acres of grounds; unsurprisingly, it's popular with weekend wedding parties.

A couple of miles outside Tunbridge Wells, in Pembury, the Camden Arms Hotel (1 High Street, 01892 822012, www.camdenarms.co.uk) is a friendly pub and restaurant with comfortable rooms for around £100.

Brew House Hotel

1 Warwick Park, TN2 5TA (01892 520587, www.thebrewhousehotel.net). Rates £109-£195 double incl breakfast.

Within easy reach of the Pantiles, the Brew House is a modern boutique hotel. Its 15 rooms are sleekly contemporary, with a palette of black, white and cream and little luxuries such as free Wi-Fi; for more space, opt for a superior or deluxe. In some rooms, the flick of a switch changes the bathroom's glass walls from opaque to clear, while REN toiletries and cosy underfloor heating are standard. In the ONE Bar & Lounge, stark white tables and chairs are offset by bold pink and purple walls, and the menu runs from club sarnies to slow-roasted shoulder of Lamberhurst lamb.

Hotel du Vin

KENT

Hotel du Vin

*Crescent Road, TN1 2LY (01892 526455, www.hotel
duvin.com). Rates £105-£300 double incl breakfast.*
The Tunbridge Wells outpost of the Hotel du Vin chain
occupies a fine sandstone mansion, built in 1762; back when
it was Calverley House, the young Queen Victoria often
stayed here. There are 34 large, well-appointed bedrooms
(hand-sprung mattresses, Egyptian cotton linen and
freestanding baths), each with its own character. The best
are at the back, with views over Calverley Park. The snug
Burgundy Bar has an impressive collection of whiskies, and
there's also a bistro (*see p126*).

Swan Cottage

*17 Warwick Road, TN1 1YL (01892 525910,
www.swancottage.co.uk). Rates £85 double incl breakfast.*
Built in 1810 and set on a cobbled road just off the High
Street, this quietly dignified red-brick house is a lovely place
to stay. The double room is en suite, while the single has its
own private bathroom; both are nicely decorated, and have
free Wi-Fi access. The artist owner cooks up superb
breakfasts, while a friendly resident cat adds to the home-
from-home feel.

TONBRIDGE

Poor Tonbridge. It was once called Tunbridge
(the pronunciation is the same), until its upstart
younger sister filched its name. It was also the
most important town in the area until its namesake
stole all the glory. Whereas Tunbridge Wells was
all fields until the mid-1600s, Tonbridge scored a
mention in the Domesday Book, and has had a
weekly market since 1259.

These days it is a modest provincial town, strung
out along its mile-long High Street. Overlooking
the River Medway stand the remains of Tonbridge
Castle (*see p130*), with its twin-towered, 13th-
century gatehouse. Open-air concerts are held
in the grounds in August, and there's a three-day
Festival of Music and Fireworks in late July. The
Tourist Information Office (01732 770929) is
in a converted mansion next to the Gatehouse,
and has details of walking tours of the town.

Down below is the river, overhung with weeping
willows. It was made navigable in 1740, linking
Tonbridge to Maidstone, Rochester and the North
Sea; today, only swans, canoes and rowing boats
take to the water. The latter can be hired from
Tonbridge Castle Rowing Boats (01732 360630),
by the 19th-century Big Bridge, at weekends and
during the summer holidays.

A little further on from the bridge, on the left of the
High Street, is Ye Olde Chequers (122 High Street,
01732 358957), a beamed pub that has stood
here for 500 years. The noose that dangles outside
is a throwback to the days when the upper storey of
the pub housed the Justices' room; some say Wat
Tyler's brother was hanged here after the Peasants'
Revolt in 1381. Further up the High Street, the
18th-century Rose & Crown (*see p131*) is another
historic spot for a pint.

Turn right down Church Lane to reach St Peter
& St Paul Parish Church (01732 770962, www.
tonbridgeparishchurch.org.uk), most of which dates

from the 14th century. After walking around the
peaceful churchyard, head on to Bordyke. Various
buildings along here, including the red-brick Ferox
Hall, are now boarding houses for Tonbridge
School – an imposing presence at the northern end
of the High Street. Founded in 1553, the school has
a long and illustrious history, counting EM Forster
among its former pupils. The boar's heads guarding
its entrance are a symbol of the school's governors,
the Skinners' Company of the City of London.

Around half a mile south of Tonbridge on the
A21, the RSPB reserve at Tudeley Woods (01273
775333, www.rspb.org.uk) is open daily from 9am
until 6pm or dusk if earlier. As well as birds such as
nightjars and tree pipits, over 1,000 types of fungus
have been recorded here (autumn is the best time
to see them), and delicate orchids mingle with the
bluebells in spring.

One of the most important tourist attractions
in the area is the Hop Farm (*see p130*). It's well-
signposted all over the area, but out of Tonbridge
take the B2017 to Paddock Wood. Once in Paddock
Wood, follow Maidstone Road (B2160) north for half
a mile and you'll see the entrance.

Cycle to Penshurst Place

Taking in fairytale castles, forests and lakes, this
glorious five-mile ride runs from Tonbridge Castle to
Penshurst Place. Created by Sustrans, the route is
well signposted with blue Regional Cycle Route 12
signs, and follows designated cycle paths and tracks
for most of the way.

It starts at Tonbridge Castle (*see p130*), on
Castle Road. You can take an hour or so to
explore this medieval motte-and-bailey castle,
or press onwards. At the outer reaches of town
the ride starts to blossom into countryside as
you pass playing fields and head into the Haysden
Country Park. This expansive nature reserve takes
in two lakes and a section of the River Medway,
and is dotted with wildflowers. The best is yet to
come, though. Once you've passed beneath the
A12, you turn right then left to cycle into a magical
wood filled with coppiced trees, butterflies and
birdlife; in springtime, there's a carpet of pink
and yellow stitchwort, clover and buttercups.

Cycling on, following the Medway's broad flank,
you reach the ride's only real climb, which comes
between the bridge over the river and Well Place
Farm. Adult cyclists will conquer this with ease, while
younger ones might want to get off and walk. Pause
at the summit to admire the surrounding countryside
before freewheeling down past two lakes to arrive
at Penshurst Place (*see p130*). There's £1 off the
entrance fee for anyone arriving by bike to this rather
splendid medieval mansion and grounds.

You can picnic here or head a couple of minutes
up the road into Penshurst for a well-earned pint
at the Leicester Arms (*see p132*). Those up for
more pedaling can press on to the Penshurst Off
Road Cycling Centre (01892 870136) in nearby
Viceroys Wood; otherwise, Penshurst station is
nearby. See www.sustrans.org.uk for further
information and maps.

KENT

Places to visit

GOUDHURST & LAMBERHURST

Bayham Old Abbey

Clay Hill Road, Lamberhurst, TN3 8DE (01892 890381, www.english-heritage.org.uk/daysout/ properties/bayham-old-abbey). Open Apr-Sept 11am-5pm daily. Admission £4; £2 reductions.
Although little is left of Bayham Old Abbey, the ruins are still impressive, as are the grounds (designed by landscape gardener Humphry Repton, who took the mantle from 'Capability' Brown). The abbey was founded in around 1207, but fell into ruin after the Dissolution of the Monasteries; today, its tumbledown walls, ornate stonework and finely carved pillars exude their own peaceful charm.

Bedgebury National Pinetum ★

Flimwell (01580 879842, www.bedgeburypinetum. org.uk). Open 8am-dusk daily (see website for monthly details). Admission free (car park £8).
With more than 10,000 trees planted over 350 acres, the Pinetum at Bedgebury has the most complete collection of conifers in the world. Bats, woodpeckers, fallow dear and wild boar are among the residents, and spring brings swathes of bluebells and daffodils. Aside from its flora and fauna, Bedgebury has other strings to its bow: an expansive network of mountain biking routes, and the Go Ape! high-wire course (for both, *see p124*).

Broadview Gardens

Hadlow College, Tonbridge Road, Hadlow, TN11 0AL (01732 853211, www.broadviewgardens.co.uk). Open 9am-5pm Mon-Sat; 10am-4pm Sun. Admission free. Guided tours £3.
Run by Hadlow College, these ten-acre gardens take in sensory and water gardens, a Japanese garden and a dry garden: not bad going, considering this was a sheep grazing field until 1992. There's also a tea room and a shop selling Kentish produce.

Finchcocks Musical Museum

Goudhurst, TN17 1HH. (01580 211702, www. finchcocks.co.uk). Open Apr-Sept 2-6pm Sun & bank hols. Aug 2-6pm Wed, Thur, Sun. Garden Apr-Sept 12.30-6pm Sun & bank hols. Aug 12.30-6pm Wed, Thur, Sun. Admission £10; £5 reductions; £22 family. Garden only £3. No credit cards.
Occupying a stunning Georgian manor house, the museum's collection comprises over 100 keyboard instruments, including harpsichords, clavichords, organs and a piano that belonged to Prince Albert. Around 40 are in working order, and the key to the museum's success is the fact it allows visitors to play the instruments, under supervision. In addition, professional musicians often give recitals and concerts; check the website for details.

Scotney Castle

Lamberhurst, TN3 8JN (01892 893820, www.national trust.org.uk/main/w-scotneycastlegarden). Open House Late Feb-Oct 11am-5.30pm Wed-Sun. Nov, Dec 11am-5pm Sat, Sun. Old castle Late Feb-Oct 11am-3pm Wed-Sun. Garden Late Feb-Oct 11am-5.30pm Wed-Sun. Nov, Dec 11am-5pm Sat, Sun. Admission House & garden £10; £5 reductions; £25.50 family. Garden only £7.75; £4.25 reductions; £21.50 family.
At the bottom of the valley, the 14th-century Scotney Castle is now in ruins – though you can still see the

KENT

priest-hole, built by Nicholas Owen in the 16th century. In the 1590s, Father Richard Blount twice hid here to evade capture by the Protestant Elizabeth I's priest-hunters, enduring the hole's squalid conditions for over a week. The 'new' house on the hill, meanwhile, was built in 1837 for Edward Hussey III. However, it's the displays of rhododendrons and azaleas and romantic gardens that attract most visitors.

TUNBRIDGE WELLS

King Charles the Martyr ★
London Road, TN1 1YX (01892 511745, www.kcmtw. org). Open 11am-3pm Mon-Sat. Admission free.
Although the church's unassuming red-brick façade is easily missed, it is the oldest building in Tunbridge Wells. It dates back to 1676, when there were no other permanent structures in the area, and was funded by wealthy visitors to the famous spring: a list of the great, good and just plain rich can still be seen in a roll call by the stairs. Princess Victoria was among the worshippers, sitting demurely with her mother in the North Gallery. The church's spectacular plasterwork ceiling was the work of Henry Doogood, chief plasterer for Sir Christopher Wren.

Tunbridge Wells Museum & Art Gallery
Civic Centre, Mount Pleasant Road, TN1 1JN (01892 554171, www.tunbridgewellsmuseum.org). Open 9.30am-5pm Mon-Sat; 10am-4pm Sun. Admission free.
The museum's collections run from old-fashioned vintage toys to costume, textiles and intricately-worked Tunbridge ware, a local style of marquetry that was particularly prized by 19th-century visitors to the town. Natural history specimens round off the collection, taking in rocks, fossils, insects and a whole menagerie of glassy-eyed stuffed animals, and there are various art exhibitions, special events, talks and workshops.

Groombridge Place Gardens & Enchanted Forest
Groombridge, Tunbridge Wells, TN3 9QG (01892 861444, www.groombridge.co.uk). Open Apr-Oct 10am-5.30pm daily. Nov-Mar 10am-4pm Sat, Sun. Admission £9.95; £8.45 reductions; £33.95 family.
The 17th-century formal gardens at Groombridge are a delight, presided over by the magnificent resident peacocks. Once the grown-ups have finished swooning over the shady, romantic secret garden and fragrant white rose garden, make a beeline for the Enchanted Forest. In place of prim and proper flowerbeds and perfectly manicured lawns there are giant swings, tree houses and aerial boardwalks – not to mention some mysterious footprints, which look suspiciously like dinosaur tracks. Deep in the woods, small children can enjoy the sandpit and swings in the Groms' Village – and fall for the gorgeous giant rabbits.

TONBRIDGE & AROUND

All Saints Church
Tudeley, near Tonbridge, TN11 0NZ (01732 357648, www.tudeley.org). Open Summer 9am-6pm Mon-Sat; noon-6pm Sun. Winter 9am-dusk Mon-Sat; noon-dusk Sun. Admission (voluntary) £2. No credit cards.
In a battle of artistic merit between Chichester Cathedral and Tudeley's small, 12th-century parish church, you might expect the former to win hands

KENT

Hever Castle. See p130. ▶

down. But while the cathedral does boast one window by Russian émigré artist Marc Chagall, Tudeley has 12. Glowing with jewel-like colours, the windows were commissioned as a memorial to Sarah d'Avigdor-Goldsmid, who died in a sailing accident at the age of 21. The first was installed in 1967; the rest were added over the next 18 years, until Chagall's death in 1985. Each year, the church hosts a dozen or so chamber concerts for the annual Tudeley Festival; see www.tudeleyfestival.org.uk for details.

Hop Farm
Maidstone Road, Paddock Wood, TN12 6PY (01622 872068, www.thehopfarm.co.uk). Open Feb-Oct 10am-5pm daily. Nov-Dec 10am-5pm Sat, Sun. Admission £12.50; £8.50-£10.50 reductions; £46.50 family.
Once a working hop farm, this 400-acre site is now a vast family park, with a huge array of activities. One of the most popular places for youngsters to let loose (and adults to fall over in amusing ways) is among the Giant Jumping Pillows, while Driving School lets smaller children take to the road on a scaled-down circuit, complete with zebra crossings and roundabouts. More sedate pursuits include the Victorian carousel and farm – home to llamas and reindeer, along with the more standard rabbit, pigs and chickens. Special events include July's Hop Farm Music Festival, which saw Bob Dylan grace the stage in 2010.

Tonbridge Castle
Castle Street, Tonbridge, TN9 1BG (01732 770929, www.tonbridgecastle.org). Open Castle 8.30am-5pm Mon-Fri; 9am-5pm Sat; 10.30am-4.30pm Sun. Grounds 8am-dusk daily. Admission Gatehouse Tour £6.50; £3.90 reductions; £19 family. Grounds free.
Within the castle walls, all Tonbridge once lived and traded. Its first incarnation was as a simple motte-and-bailey castle, built in 1068 by Richard de Clare after William the Conqueror gifted him the land; you can still climb the 20m-high motte (a circular mound of earth) and look out across Tonbridge and the Weald. The castle was much-altered over the centuries, becoming a formidable stronghold; today, the only part still standing is the three-storey gatehouse, which dates from the 13th century. The audio tour of the gatehouse uses special effects and interactive displays to explore the castle's tumultuous history, and takes about an hour.

PENSHURST TO EDENBRIDGE

Chiddingstone Castle
Hill Hoath Road, Chiddingstone, TN8 7AD (01892 870347, www.chiddingstonecastle.org.uk). Open Apr-Oct 11am-5pm Mon-Wed, Sun. Admission House & grounds £7.00; £4 reductions; £19.50 family. Grounds only £1; free reductions.
Although it has existed on this spot in one form or another since the 16th century, the castle has never been more than a grand country house, despite its name. In 1955 it was bought by Denys Eyre Bower, who amassed a remarkable collection of Buddhist, Egyptian and Japanese art and artefacts. The Stuarts and the Jacobite cause were another of his passions, and a small piece of James II's heart was one of his more unusual acquisitions. Displays in the study

recount some of the more sensational episides from Bower's own life, including a conviction for attempted murder that was later overturned. The mummified cat and Japanese armour and swords should appeal to macabre-minded children, and there are arty activities to keep them busy: making a pyramid, perhaps, or creating an origami samurai helmet.

Haxted Watermill Museum & Restaurant
Haxted Road, Edenbridge, TN8 6PU (01732 862914, www.hammerwood.mistral.co.uk/haxtmill.htm). Open Apr-Oct 10am-3.30pm Tue-Sun. Admission £2; £1 reductions. No credit cards.
Built in around 1580, and expanded two centuries later, Haxted's waterwheels still turn today, albeit for visitors. Inside, a gallery looks at the history of the mill and related local industry, while the brasserie is open for lunch and dinner year round. It is currently on the market, so call before visiting.

Hever Castle
Hever, near Edenbridge, TN8 7NG (01732 865224, www.hevercastle.co.uk). Open Castle Apr-Oct noon-6pm daily. Nov, Dec, Mar noon-4pm Wed-Sun. Garden Apr-Oct 10.30am-6pm daily. Nov, Dec, Mar 10.30am-4pm Wed-Sun. Admission Castle & Garden £14; £8-£12 reductions; £36 family. Garden only £11.50; £7.50-£10 reductions; £30.50 family.
Hever's fairytale good looks belie a sordid history. If these walls could talk, what tawdry tales they'd tell: randy royals, extramarital affairs, incest, sibling rivalry, social climbing and restless ghosts. For such a tiny castle, it has plenty of talking points. First and foremost, this was the family home of Anne Boleyn, born here in 1501 – a connection it has been trading on ever since. Anne's father, Sir Thomas Boleyn, had married into royal circles, and was determined that his daughters would do the same; Henry VIII was a frequent visitor. Displays recount the story of the ill-fated match, which would culminate in Anne's execution at the Tower of London. The superb Tudor portrait collection includes depictions of all six of Henry VIII's unfortunate wives. The gatehouse contains some alarming instruments of torture.

Outside, the sculpture-dotted Italian gardens, walled rose garden and stately walks offer some respite, while the mazes will please the children. Along with the baffling yew maze there's a thrilling water maze, comprising a series of walkways across the lake; step on the wrong stone and you're in for a soaking.

Penshurst Place
Penshurst, TN11 8DG (01892 870307, www.penshurstplace.com). Open Mar-Oct House noon-4pm daily. Gardens 10.30am-6pm daily. Admission £9.80; £6.20 reductions; £26 family .
This splendid medieval mansion and estate has been the seat of the Sidney family since 1552, when Edward VI gifted it to his loyal steward and tutor, Sir William Sidney. Its centrepiece is the Baron's Hall, with its soaring, chestnut-beamed roof and central octagonal hearth, while dignified-looking family forebears line the Elizabethan Long Gallery. Two walking trails meander through the lovely gardens (ablaze with colour in autumn), and there's a small adventure playground.

KENT

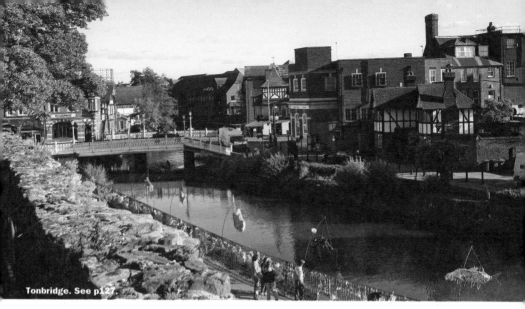
Tonbridge. See p127.

Where to eat & drink

Several pubs and restaurants are listed in the Penshurst to Edenbridge section, *see pp132-133*.

Chaser Inn

Stumble Hill, Shipbourne, TN11 9PE (01732 810360, www.thechaser.co.uk). Open 11am-11pm Mon-Thur; 11am-midnight Fri, Sat; noon-11pm Sun. Food served noon-9.30pm Mon-Sat; noon-9pm Sun.

The Chaser overlooks the village green in Shipbourne, some four miles from Tonbridge. Its sign depicts a horse and rider in Fairlawne colours, a prestigious local stables – now closed – that used to train steeplechasers for the Queen Mother. This is a proper country pub, with log fires, well-kept ales and a pleasant beer garden. The menu mixes time-honoured classics (ploughman's lunches, home-made burgers, confit of pork belly) with more modish dishes: goat's cheese panna cotta with spiced tomato compôte, say.

Ivy House

199 High Street, Tonbridge, TN9 1BW (01732 771249, www.ivyhousetonbridge.com). Open noon-3pm, 6-11pm Mon-Thur; noon-11pm Fri-Sun. Lunch served noon-3pm, dinner served 6-11pm Mon-Thur. Food served noon-11pm Fri-Sun.

Restored in 2009, the once run-down Ivy House is now a lovely little spot for a drink or a meal. The tile-clad Grade II-listed premises look appealingly old-fashioned; inside are a small bar and a spruced-up dining room, serving salads, chunky sandwiches and gastropub-style grub.

Where to stay

Places to stay are limited around Tonbridge, though there is a Premier Inn (109 London Road, 0870 850 6344, www.premierinn.com) just north of town.

Rose & Crown

125 High Street, Tonbridge, TN9 1DD (01732 357966, www.bw-roseandcrown.co.uk). Rates £64-£120 double incl breakfast.

Built in the 16th century, this was one of the most important coaching inns between London and Hastings or Rye. Today, it's owned by Best Western and has 56 functional, en suite rooms at good rates. There's free parking, a small bar and a reasonable restaurant.

PENSHURST TO EDENBRIDGE

Penshurst

The village of Penshurst owes its existence to Penshurst Place (*see p130*), the ancestral home of the Sidney family. Now open to the public, it's an imposing, wonderfully preserved slice of history.

The village itself is a quaint little place, dotted with Tudor and Victorian mock-Tudor buildings. At its heart is Leicester Square, named after the second Earl of Leicester and lined with timber-framed Tudor cottages. By the Old Guild House, an archway leads to the venerable church of St John the Baptist ★; its first priest, Wilhelmus, was installed in 1170 by the ill-fated Thomas à Becket, Archbishop of Canterbury, who was murdered two days later. The Friends of Penshurst Church (01892 871596, www.friendsof penshurstchurch.co.uk) provide tours of the church by appointment.

At the eastern end of the church, the Sidney family's 19th-century private chapel features an intricately-painted ceiling and some fine memorials. The churchyard is equally atmospheric, with its weathered, gently leaning gravestones; as you enter the churchyard, look for the grave of Richard Sax, who was murdered by a farmhand in 1813.

Opposite the church is the Leicester Arms (*see p132*). Once part of the Penshurst Estate, it's now a traditional pub with well-kept real ales and an all-day menu. Another option is Quaintways Tea Rooms (*see p132*), set in a 16th-century cottage opposite the village hall.

As well as being a popular destination for walkers, Penshurst is at the end of the five-mile Tonbridge to

KENT

Penshurst cycle path (*see p127*) – and those on two wheels get a discount at Penshurst Palace. It's also worth noting that Penshurst train station is actually two miles away in Chiddingstone Causeway (*see below*).

Heading east, back towards Tonbridge and the A26, is Speldhurst and the George & Dragon (*see below*), known for its superb seasonal menu.

Chiddingstone

Set between Tonbridge and Edenbridge, Chiddingstone is impossibly quaint and unspoiled – partly due to the fact that the village is owned by the National Trust, which describes it as 'one of the prettiest villages in Kent, and perhaps England'.

Among the half-timbered Tudor cottages are a post office, village shop and the little Burghesh Court Tea Room (*see below*), while the tile-hung Castle Inn (*see below*) was built in 1420. The sandstone St Mary's Church (01892 871651) was largely destroyed by fire in 1624, when it was struck by lightning; after a massive fundraising effort that raised the modern equivalent of a quarter of a million pounds, it was rebuilt. A brass from 1584 remains in the nave, commemorating Richard Streatfeild, and there is some fine stained glass.

The Streatfeilds, whose vault can be seen in the churchyard, built their fortune on the local iron industry. The family home was Chiddingstone Castle (*see p130*) – a medieval manor house that was remodelled in Victorian times, set in glorious grounds.

A footpath from the village leads to the Chiding Stone, a massy sandstone boulder at the edge of a field that bears marks from the last half millennium. Some say it was a place where wrongdoers were scolded or 'chided', hence the name, while others believe it was a druid altar. Which came first, Chiddingstone Village or the Chiding Stone, no one knows.

From Chiddingstone it's a short signposted drive to Hever Castle; on the way, drop by the singular Wheatsheaf pub (*see p133*) at Bough Beech.

Hever

Surrounded by fields and woodland, the tiny village of Hever is most famous for its castle (*see p130*), home to the powerful Boleyn family. The tomb of Sir Thomas Bullen, father of the ill-fated Anne Boleyn and grandfather to Queen Elizabeth I is in the 13th-century village church, St Peter's. A magnificent brass depicts him in the flowing robes of the Knights of the Garter, while another lovely brass in the chancel depicts Margaret Cheyne, wife of a local landowner, with angels hovering around her head and a lapdog at her feet.

At the centre of the village, opposite the entrance to the castle, is the staunchly traditional King Henry VIII Inn (01732 862457, www.kinghenryviiiinn. co.uk), with its beamed bar, grassy beer garden and four simple rooms.

Edenbridge

From Hever it's a short drive to Edenbridge – a centre of the Wealden iron industry in the 16th century, and still the largest settlement in the area. For more on the town's history, and the Eden valley's industrial heritage, check out the Eden Valley Museum, set in a medieval farmhouse on the High Street (01732 868102, www.evmt.org.uk). While you're here, pick up a Town Trail map for a tour of some of the town's historic buildings.

There's no missing the 14th-century Old Crown Inn (High Street, 01732 867896) next door, thanks to a 'bridging sign' that spans the High Street – one of two in the country. Although much of the High Street is unremarkable, there are some appealing shops along Church Street, including Farringtons Jewellers (01732 863934, closed Mon, Sun), Edenbridge Bookshop (01732 862180, closed Sun) and Edenbridge Galleries (01732 864163, www. edenbridgegalleries.com), which specialises in fine art, antiques and interior design.

The oldest surviving building in Edenbridge is the 13th-century Church of Sts Peter and Paul, approached via little wooden lych gate: don't miss the beautiful stained glass window on the east wall, designed by Edward Burne-Jones.

Where to eat & drink

In Penshurst, the Quaintways Tea Room (High Street, 01892 870272, closed Mon) fortifies hungry walkers with snacks and cream teas, while the Leicester Arms (High Street, 01892 870551, www.leicesterarmspenshurst.co.uk) has a lengthy menu and cosy chesterfields to sink into.

In Chiddingstone, Burghesh Court Tea Room (01892 870700, open weekends only) serves sandwiches, full English breakfasts, cakes and cream teas, and the 15th-century Castle Inn (01892 870247, www.castleinn-kent.co.uk) is in fine fettle after a change of ownership. Bar snacks run from own-made chicken pie to a half pint of prawns, while more substantial mains might include braised Kentish lamb or local sausages and mash.

George & Dragon ★

Speldhurst Hill, Speldhurst, TN3 0NN (01892 863125, www.speldhurst.com). Open 11am-11pm Mon-Sat; 11am-10.30pm Sun. Lunch served noon-2.30pm Mon-Sat; noon-3pm Sun. Dinner served 7-9.30pm Mon-Sat.
The George & Dragon has been dispensing ale to thirsty locals since the 13th century. The current building is a few centuries younger, but the beams, flagstones and fireplace are original, and add to the snug atmosphere. There's Harveys and Larkin's on tap and exceptional food, made from locally sourced and mostly organic ingredients. Your options might include risotto verde with Kentish spinach and broad beans, seared Speldhurst pigeon breast salad with smoked bacon and puy lentils, or hake with home-made linguini. The desserts list is a pleasure to behold: Valhrona chocolate brownie with vanilla ice-cream, perhaps, or sumptuous eton mess, made with locally grown raspberries.

Little Brown Jug

Chiddingstone Causeway, TN11 8JJ (01892 870318, www.thelittlebrownjug.co.uk). Open 11am-11pm Mon-Thur; 11am-midnight Fri, Sat; noon-11pm Sun. Food served noon-9.30pm Mon-Sat; noon-9pm Sun.

This solid, red-brick pub does a good line in reasonably priced food, and is very popular at weekend lunchtimes. In winter, roast pheasant and traditional Irish stew keep the cold at bay, and an open fire burns in the grate; come summer, nab a table in the garden.

Spotted Dog
Smarts Hill, Penshurst, TN11 8EP (01892 870253, www.spotteddogpub.co.uk). Open Apr-Sept 11am-11pm Mon-Sat; noon-10.30pm Sun. Oct-Mar 11am-11pm Mon-Sat; noon-7pm Sun. Lunch served noon-2.30pm Mon-Fri; noon-6pm Sun. Dinner served 6-9pm Mon-Fri. Food served noon-9pm Sat.

Known for its one-of-a-kind sign, which dates back to Victorian days and possibly beyond, the Spotted Dog has changed hands a fair few times in recent years. The current family have turned it around, offering a friendly welcome and a sturdy, simple pub menu. It's a freehouse, so there's a decent selection of ales. The premises are gorgeous: a converted row of 15th-century, white-painted clapboard cottages, decked with flowers in summer. The real reason to come here, though, has to be the views over the valley from its beer garden.

Wheatsheaf ★
Hever Road, Bough Beech, TN8 7NU (01732 700254, www.wheatsheafatboughbeech.co.uk). Open 11am-11pm Mon-Thur, Sun; 11am-midnight Fri, Sun. Food served noon-10pm daily.

Filled with a glorious jumble of colonial artefacts, stuffed stag heads and inexplicable odds and ends (including a shark's jawbone), the Wheatsheaf is a fantastic sight. It was built at the end of the 14th century (a rare crown post was uncovered during alterations a few years back), and has an exposed section of wattle and daub wall that reads '1607 Foxy Holanby' – thought to be the name of a local squire. The meat on the menu is sourced locally, mostly from within a few miles, and all the game is shot hereabouts too.

Where to stay

In Penshurst, the Leicester Arms Hotel (see p132) has seven bedrooms, decorated in keeping with the style of the pub. Three miles south of Edenbridge, Beckett's B&B (Pylegate Farm, Hartfield Road, Cowden, 01342 850514, www.becketts-bandb.co.uk) offers three rooms in a 300-year-old listed barn with splendid flagstone floors; the pick of the bunch has a four-poster.

The hotels and B&Bs of Tunbridge Wells (see pp126-127) are also within easy reach.

Starborough Manor
Marsh Green, Edenbridge, TN8 5QY (01732 862152, www.starboroughmanor.co.uk). Rates £130 double incl breakfast.

Set at the end of an impressive, tree-lined drive and overlooking the ruins of Starborough Castle, this is a decidedly upmarket B&B. The 18th-century country house, remodelled in the 19th century, looks like the setting for a period drama, while the pristine grounds include a summer-only outdoor pool and a tennis court; bring your own rackets and balls. Three guest rooms are prettily and thoughtfully appointed (free Wi-Fi, White Company toiletries), and guests have access to a shared sitting room.

SIX KENT CASTLES

Deal Castle
This fantastically preserved Tudor artillery castle (see p93) is one of a chain built along the Kent coast at the behest of Henry VII. Its study bastions and low, circular keep are a formidable sight; inside, you can explore dark underground passageways or check out an interactive exhibition on the castle's history.

Dover Castle
Described as the 'Key to England', thanks to its strategic importance, Dover Castle (see p93) has stood guard over the realm for centuries; as recently as World War II, its subterranean tunnels were used as a command centre for secret military operations.

Hever Castle
Along with Leeds Castle, Hever (see p130) is one of England's finest fortresses. The childhood home of Anne Boleyn, it also has a gruesome collection of torture devices. Children will enjoy getting lost behind the high yew hedges of the maze, and trying to reach the centre of the water maze without getting drenched.

Leeds Castle
Set on two interconnected islands on the River Len, Leeds Castle (see p30) is impossibly lovely. Its lavish interiors are the legacy of Lady Baillie, who bought the castle in the 1920s, while the Dog Collar Museum is delightfully quirky: leave time to wander the formal gardens and sprawling parkland, though.

Rochester Castle
Built from Kentish ragstone, this early 12th-century castle (see pxxx) stands guard over the crossing where the Medway meets the Thames estuary. In 1215 it was occupied by rebel nobles and besieged by King John; after bombarding it with rocks and mining under its walls, his men set light to the fat of 40 pigs, burning the great tower down.

Walmer Castle
Walmer Castle (see p93), like Deal, was built in the 16th century to defend the English coastline. In 1708 it became the official residence of the Lord Warden of the Cinque Ports, and gradually evolved into a comfortable country house. The Duke of Wellington, who held the post for over 20 years, wasn't one for luxury, though: you can still see the army camp bed on which he slept in his room overlooking the ramparts.

KENT

Sussex

Ditchling Beacon. See p211.

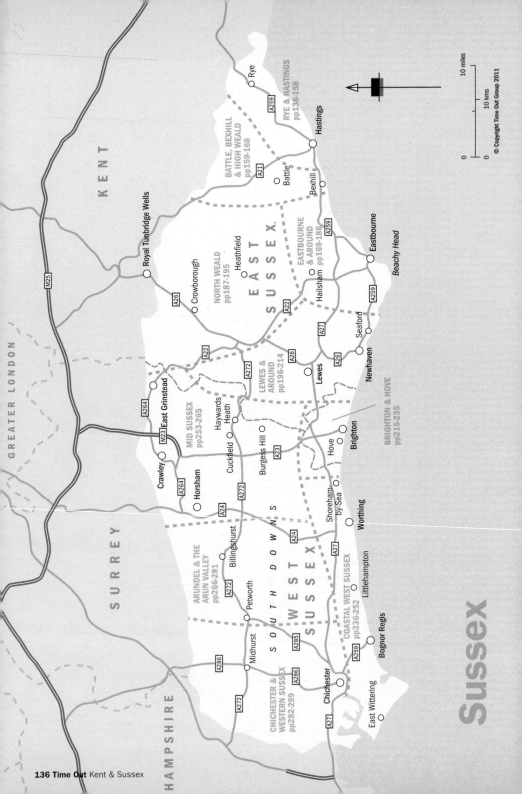

Sussex

Rye

RYE & HASTINGS
pp138-158

A259

Hastings

BATTLE, BEXHILL
& HIGH WEALD
pp159-168

A21

Battle

Bexhill

EAST SUSSEX

KENT

Royal Tunbridge Wells

A26

Crowborough

Heathfield

NORTH WEALD
pp187-195

EASTBOURNE
& AROUND
pp169-186

A259

Eastbourne

Beachy Head

Hailsham

A22

A27

Seaford

A26

A26

Newhaven

Lewes

LEWES &
AROUND
pp196-214

A272

A22

East Grinstead

A264

M23

MID SUSSEX
pp253-265

Haywards
Heath

Cuckfield

Burgess Hill

A23

BRIGHTON & HOVE
pp215-235

Brighton

Hove

Crawley

A264

Horsham

A272

Shoreham-
by-Sea

Worthing

A24

A27

SOUTH DOWNS

ARUNDEL & THE
ARUN VALLEY
pp266-281

Billingshurst

A272

A24

Petworth

A27

Littlehampton

COASTAL WEST SUSSEX
pp236-252

A259

Bognor Regis

WEST SUSSEX

Midhurst

A285

A286

CHICHESTER &
WESTERN SUSSEX
pp282-299

A286

Chichester

A27

A272

East Wittering

SURREY

GREATER LONDON

M25

HAMPSHIRE

10 miles

10 kms

© Copyright Time Out Group 2011

West Wittering. See p247.

Sussex

Rye & Hastings

There's astonishing variety contained within the 15 miles between Camber and Rye on the Kent border and St Leonards-on-Sea, just west of Hastings. Camber Sands is a glorious beach, while Rye is picturesque in the extreme, with cobbled streets leading to ancient pubs, fine restaurants and quirky galleries and ateliers. Heading west, Winchelsea, once one of England's principal ports, is today a relic of maritime history and a reminder of a wine industry 500 years before the current resurgence – the vast cellars can still be seen. From here, it's a steep rise over the clifftop to Hastings Country Park, before a descent to the old town of Hastings itself.

Even within Hastings, there are huge differences: upmarket antiques shops and rundown amusement arcades lie within a few paces of one another. But this is part of its charm. Although the pier is destroyed, Hastings is on the rise. The refined Old Town, full of atmospheric pubs, fish restaurants, curio dealers and wet fish markets, often surprises visitors expecting kiss-me-quick hats and candy floss (which certainly still exist). Skipping through the identikit town centre, you emerge in the America Ground area, home to trendy cafés and businesses such as Collared, a shop selling fashionable accessories for chic canines; proof that Hastings is moving beyond its dog-on-a-string demographic.

Past the sad sight of the pier, burned down (deliberately?) in October 2010, is St Leonards-on-Sea – seamlessly joined to Hastings, but very independent-minded. Although it was formerly down-at-heel (and some parts still are), gentrification is moving quickly here – it even has its own Banksy. Along the upper end of Norman Road, dealers in mid-century furniture, independent coffee shops, farmers' markets and one of the best restaurants in the area, St Clement's, can all be found. Just don't call it Hastings.

CAMBER SANDS

Situated west of Dungeness and east of Rye, Camber lacks the character of the former and the classiness of the latter, but in terms of pure, unadulterated beach, this is the best strand on the south coast. The majestic beach ★ remains hidden behind high dunes, rewarding you at the last minute with surprising views; sometimes slate-grey sky and black sea, sometimes crashing waves, sometimes the sea so far out that it's barely there and the sky stretches on forever. On perfect summer days, the bright blue water, glorious blue sky and golden sand are idyllic.

Camber Sands' immensity also breeds versatility. Families hunker down in their sturdy windbreak bunkers (you'll need them, and they're available for hire) and build huge sandcastles, or paddle and swim in the clean sea. At the water's edge are couples walking dogs and horse riders gently cantering through the surf (there are restrictions in place for dogs and horses – see www.rother.gov.uk for details). Kiteboarders and windsurfers, for whom Camber is a huge destination, career across the sand and through the waves.

The Kit Kat Café, fenced off from the sands with driftwood posts, is a characterful spot. While away an hour on the deck, eating ice-cream, watching the world at play or listening to the wind whistle. Against a constant sea breeze, the grass on the dunes looks as if it's being brushed by an invisible hand.

Back in the dunes, nature lovers watch the wildlife. The sand dunes are an anomaly along the pebbly Sussex coast. No piddly little mounds these, they have stood in for deserts in a number of film shoots – notably as the Sahara in the 1967 film *Carry On... Follow that Camel*. To act out your Lawrence of Arabia fantasies, walk away from the village to the west end of the beach. Here, the dunes are at their biggest and the sands are secluded.

Not only are the dunes rare for these parts, they're also a Site of Special Scientific Interest. They host wildlife (hen harriers, short-eared owls and snow bunting all winter here) and have an interesting geological story to tell: they have formed over the last 350 years and are growing by about 300,000 square feet every year. The mounds take shape when sand blows inland and builds up around plants and fences – in Camber's case, pretty, traditional chestnut fences, erected to help stabilise the dunes. Mother nature contributes too: marram grass, which fringes the beach, has a deep root system that holds the sand in place. If not for these defences, both natural

Camber Sands

and man-made, the village of Camber would be swallowed by the sea or buried under the sand.

Camber village is nowhere near as appealing as its beach, with a sprawl of undistinguished housing and holiday camps, though the area is subtly changing, with the occasional designer house appearing between the seaside bungalows. The opening of a boutique hotel (*see p144*) here in 2003 also helped to kick-start the renaissance. Camber is easy to reach by bus from Rye; catch the 711 or 100 near the railway station.

Where to eat & drink

If you haven't stocked up on picnic fare in Rye, the Gallivant (*see p144*) is by far the best bet for food. The Green Owl (11 Old Lydd Road, 01797 225284, www.thegreenowl.co.uk) has a great location, a short distance from the beach. It serves the usual pub grub and has six simple bedrooms.

Where to stay

As well as the Gallivant, there are some good self-catering residences. Try www.camberbeach.co.uk for properties such as Seascape (The Suttons, 01797 224754). For £140-£180 a night, you get a large bedroom, with incredible views over the beach and sea, and a bed made out of driftwood. The

SUSSEX

Camber Sands

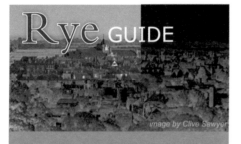

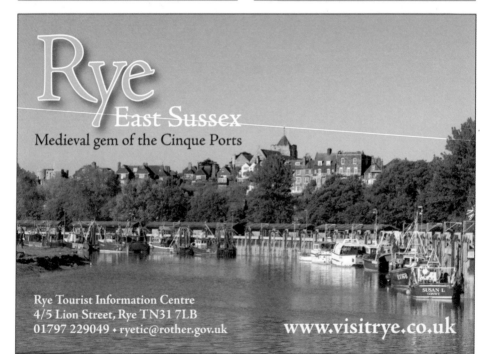

Things to do

CAMBER SANDS

Action Watersports
*Lake 1, Dengemarsh Road, Lydd, TN29 9JH
(01797 321885, www.actionwatersports.co.uk).
Open times vary; phone for details. Waterski starter
package £79.99.*
Whether you fancy learning to waterski, wake board
or strut your stuff on a jet ski, Action Watersports
have the equipment and instructors to help.

Gallivant Hotel Cookery School
*New Lydd Road, Camber, TN31 7RB (01797 225057,
www.thegallivanthotel.com). Courses £95 per day.*
Experience a day in the life of a chef, from meeting
local suppliers to whipping up an impressive feast.
Start off with a trip to meet fishermen and farmers,
discovering where the produce comes from and how
it is prepared before it reaches the restaurant. In the
kitchen, hone your culinary skills before enjoying a
well-deserved feast.

RYE, WINCHELSEA & AROUND

Rye Watersports
*Northpoint Water, New Lydd Road, Camber,
TN31 7QS (01797 225238, www.ryewatersports.
co.uk). Open Apr-Oct 9.30am-5pm daily. Beginner
windsurfing two-day course £149.*
Windsurfing and sailing lessons are offered on this
coastal lake. A range of kids' activities are available,
and kite surfing lessons are run on the nearby
beaches of Camber Sands and Greatstone.

Webbe's Cookery School
*Fish Café, 17 Tower Street, Rye, TN31 7AT
(01797 222226, www.webbesrestaurants.co.uk).
Courses £95 per day.*
Whether you have a few hours one morning, or a few
weeks to spare, the programme at Webbe's Cookery
School caters for all abilities and availabilities. Based
at the Fish Café in Rye, the day course focuses on
making lunch with co-founder Paul Webbe in the
commercial kitchen.

HASTINGS & ST LEONARDS

Crypt
*53-57 Robertson Street, Hastings, TN34 1HY
(01424 444675, ww.myspace.com/thecrypt
hastings). Open varies; phone for details.*
Championing new and alternative music, the Crypt
is one of the area's key music venues. The low-
ceilinged, atmospheric space sees all kinds of acts
take to the stage, from acclaimed breakthrough
talent to local bands. Its affordable, upbeat club
nights are another plus.

Electric Palace Cinema
*39A High Street, Hastings, TN34 3ER (01424
720393, www.electricpalacecinema.com).
Open varies; phone or check website for details.*
Set up in 2002, this not-for-profit venture is now
a much-loved independent cinema. Showing a
comprehensive selection of films – from classic hits
to world cinema – the Electric Palace is a charming
addition to the town's cultural landscape. A licensed

Action Watersports

bar offers organic wine and pre-film snacks; tickets can
be booked online or bought at the door.

White Rock Theatre
*White Rock, Hastings, TN34 1JX (01424 462280,
www.whiterocktheatre.org.uk). Box office 10am-6pm
Mon-Sat. Tickets £12-£18.*
The White Rock (capacity 1,000) puts on a varied
programme of shows, from ballets and acclaimed
comedians to the odd psychic medium and a spirited
Christmas panto. A bite to eat, accompanied by
splendid sea views, can be had in the refurbished
Pavilion Café (which opens one hour and 45 minutes
before curtain-up). For a theatrical evening with a twist,
the Murder Mystery soirées and Comedy Curry nights
go down a treat.

BEST SUSSEX BEACHES

Birling Gap
Set between Beachy Head and the Seven Sisters near Eastbourne, this little visited pebble beach is a popular spot for summer barbecues and picnics. When the tide is out, the rock pools can be investigated with a net; when the tide is in, surfers take to the waves here. *See p180.*

Black Rock Beach
Part of the larger Brighton beach, Britain's first nudist beach is still going strong. It's shielded from voyeurs and the idly curious by a bank of pebbles. *See p223.*

Brighton beach
It may be made up of unyielding pebbles, but the number of activities possible here makes this one of the best. On summer evenings, visitors and locals drift down to the beach to watch the sun setting over the bare frame of the West Pier. *See p215.*

Camber Sands
Camber Sands is one of the most famous beaches in Sussex, being one of the few that is actually sandy. Backed with windswept, ever-shifting dunes, its huge swathes of golden sand are beautiful in any weather. *See p138.*

Littlehampton
The East Beach and West Beach Cafés kickstarted something of a revival for this stretch of coast. It's now becoming popular with windsurfers, kitesurfers and even regular surfers. *See p238.*

West Wittering
This long, sandy beach is perfect for families. The gently shelving sand and shallow, sun-warmed tidal pools are great for splashing around in. Windsurfers and wind-pulled sand buggies weave around on blustery days. *See p247.*

Winchelsea Beach
Shingle beaches, groynes and rock pools make this a beautiful, and sometimes lonely, stretch. There's a promenade if the shingle is too rough. *See p148.*

---

living room has an open fire and a pull-out sofa bed. Seabreezes, part of the same property group, has two bedrooms in an open-plan, modern house.

Gallivant
New Lydd Road, TN31 7RB (01797 225057, www.the gallivanthotel.com). Rates £95-£125 double incl breakfast. What was the Place (2003-2010) has become the Gallivant. It remains a minimalist boutique hotel built around a courtyard, minutes from the best part of the beach. The 18 rooms are well appointed and modern, with a blue and white nautical vibe. The brasserie serves locally sourced produce (including wines) and seafood from sustainably fished sources in dishes such as Rye Bay fish and chips. There's even a cookery school.

RYE, WINCHELSEA & AROUND

Rye ★
Rye has it all: an attractive, well-preserved centre that's a joy to walk around, lots of independent shops, pubs and cafés, plus a fetching harbour area – and, of course, just along the coast at Camber, the best beach for miles. Although much of the place is given over to genteel tourism, it remains a working town, with enough real stores and down-to-earth pubs – and a commercial fishing fleet – to prevent a theme park atmosphere. It's easy to reach by rail (the walk from the station to the heart of town takes about a minute) and by road; the A259 between Folkestone and Hastings is routed directly through the town.

The town has a long history. It became a Cinque Port in the 13th century (the others were Winchelsea, Romney, Hythe and Dover) and held trading privileges in return for providing maritime protection in the Channel in the days before a national navy. In effect, it was given a royal licence for piracy. By the 18th century, smuggling played a big role in the town's economy. Contraband (including wool) was rife and criminal gangs, notably the Hawkhurst Gang, used to drink in the Mermaid Inn. Like Winchelsea, Rye declined in importance as access to the sea changed over the years.

Soak up the atmosphere and architecture by investigating the cobbled streets around West Street, Mermaid Street and Church Square, an ancient part of the town known as the citadel. There are wonderful views, especially if you climb to the top of 900-year-old St Mary's church.

From the church, walk up Church Square and right on to Market Street. Round the bend is the entrance to the Rye Castle Museum & Ypres Tower (*see p146*). Along with St Mary's, it's one of the oldest buildings in Rye. Built in 1249 to defend the town from the French, it is named after one of the owners, John de Ypres. Around the corner on Lion Street is the Tourist Information Centre (01797 229049, www.visitsoutheastengland.com). Visitors can buy an excellent audio tour for an MP3 player, or download it from www.ryesussex.co.uk/audio for £2.99.

One of the places the tour will direct you to is Lamb House on West Street (01580 762334,

SUSSEX

Rye High Street

Rye Castle

RYE, WINCHELSEA & AROUND

Rye Castle Museum & Ypres Tower

3 East Street, Rye, TN31 7JY (01797 226728, www.ryemuseum.co.uk). Open Museum Apr-Oct 10.30am-5pm Sat, Sun. Tower Apr-Oct 10.30am-5pm daily. Nov-Mar 10.30am-3.30pm daily. Admission Museum £2.50; £2 reductions. Tower £3; £2.50 reductions. Joint ticket £5; £4 reductions.

The Ypres Tower, built in 1249, is one of the oldest buildings in Rye. Often called Rye Castle, it now houses part of the Rye Castle Museum. Displays examine the tower's roles over the years, from a fortress to a mortuary, while a recent addition is the Millennium Embroidery, showing the life and history of Rye. There are plenty of hands-on exhibits for children, alongside games and puzzles. The museum's main exhibition space is just along East Street, in a former bottling factory. Its attractions include a fire engine built in 1745, and a display charting Rye's naval history. For children there's a Captain Pugwash treasure hunt, curated by creator John Ryan's wife and daughter.

HASTINGS & ST LEONARDS

Blue Reef Aquarium

Rock-A-Nore Road, Hastings, TN34 3DW (01424 718776, www.bluereefaquarium.co.uk). Open Mar-Oct 10am-5pm daily. Nov-Feb 10am-4pm daily. Admission £7.95; free-£5.95 reductions; £25.80-£30.75 family.

Tropical reef fish as well as British coastline species offer a chance to see what life is like under the sea. The 30 or so displays are very well kept, and include sharks, giant lobsters and delicate seahorses. There's an underwater tunnel too.

Hastings Castle

East Hill, Hastings (01424 444412, www.discover hastings.co.uk). Open Easter-Oct 10am-4pm daily. Admission £4.25; £3.50-£3.95 reductions; £13.25 family.

The weathered stone walls of Hastings Castle have had a fair old battering since William of Normandy ordered their construction, shortly after the Battle of Hastings. But the structure has survived – even after King John ordered its destruction, and the violent storms of 1287 attacked the south coast with such rage that part of the cliff face tumbled into the sea, taking pieces of the castle with it. Although the castle isn't much more than a shell these days, its history is fascinating; watch 'the 1066 Story', a video presentation on the castle and the famous battle.

Hastings Country Park

West Hill, Hastings, TN35 4AD (01424 451050, www.hastings.gov.uk/hcp). Open 24hrs daily.

A 660-acre slice of natural beauty, Hastings Country Park comprises a collage of ancient woodland, rugged heath, sandstone cliffs and choppy coastline. It's also an archaeological hotspot, with finds dating from Palaeolithic times to World War II. Located in the High Weald Area of Outstanding Natural Beauty, much of the park is a Special Area of Conservation, and a Site of Special Scientific Interest, thanks to its wildlife and geological importance. Black redstarts (generally found in urban areas) breed on the cliffs in summer, and the autumn migrations can be spectacular. Visitors are well catered for, with ample parking, designated picnic spots and a visitor centre (closed on Thursdays and in particularly inclement weather). The park is also right next to the town, and can be accessed via the East Hill Lift funicular (see p151).

Hastings Fishermen's Museum

Rock-a-Nore Road, Hastings, TN34 3DW (01424 461446, www.hastingsfish.co.uk). Open Apr-Oct 10am-5pm daily. Nov-Mar 11am-4pm daily. Admission free.
The Fishermen's Museum is set within a church built in 1852 in the heart of the fishing industry to 'rescue' the fishermen from a life of sin, but fell out of use after World War II. In 1956, it opened as this museum, with one of the last luggers as its centrepiece. Artefacts, photos and paintings offer a small but intriguing look at the industry.

Hastings Museum & Art Gallery

John's Place, Bohemia Road, Hastings, TN34 1ET (01424 451052, www.hmag.org.uk). Open Apr-Sept 10am-5pm Mon-Sat; 11am-5pm Sun. Oct-Mar 10am-4pm Mon-Fri; 11am-4pm Sat. Admission free.
This well-established museum's crowning glory is the great Durbar Hall, which features collections of Asian and Pacific artefacts, as well as an Indian and Colonial exhibit, originally held in South Kensington, for which the hall was built back in 1886. Other items relate to local celebrities, such as inventor of television John Logie Baird, writer Robert Tressell and architect James Burton; there are also fascinating insights into how local wildlife would have looked over a million years ago. Five or six temporary art exhibitions are put on each year, which have ranged from large-scale wall drawings and mixed media images to coastal paintings by JMW Turner.

Shipwreck Museum

Rock-a-Nore Road, Hastings, TN34 3DW (01424 437452, www.shipwreck-heritage.org.uk). Open Apr-Oct 10am-5pm daily. Nov-Mar 11am-4pm Sat, Sun. Tours by appointment only. Admission £1 donation; free reductions.
This part of the coast has claimed many ships, as this multi-faceted museum shows. The most significant wreck is the Dutch East Indiaman *Amsterdam*, once part of Samuel Pepys' Restoration Navy, which was wrecked in 1749 in suspicious circumstances. Guided walks to the remains, still visible at low tide, are offered. Part of the museum explores more ancient history, through items such as dinosaur footprints, fossils and the finely preserved head of a 138-million-year-old fish.

Smugglers Adventure

West Hill, Hastings, TN34 3HY (01424 444412, www.smugglersadventure.co.uk). Open Easter-Sept 10am-5pm daily. Oct-Easter 10am-4pm daily. Admission £7.20; £5.20-£6.20 reductions; £22.80 family.
A themed tour of the 200-year-old sandstone caves and subterranean passages hidden in the chalk cliffs of Hastings that once stored smugglers' booty. Interactive activities and lots of ghoulish characters feature along the way.

www.nationaltrust.org.uk), where Henry James lived for years; later residents include novelists EF Benson and Rumer Godden. It's owned by the National Trust and has limited opening times – Thursday and Saturday afternoons, from late March to late October.

Pottering round the shops is a favourite pastime in Rye. Food shops in general punch above their weight: there's Ashbee & Son (100 High Street, 01797 223303, www.ashbeeandsonbutcher.co.uk), a butcher with especially good sausages, and Rye Delicatessen (28B High Street, 01797 226521, www.battledeli.co.uk), an excellent source of picnic fare. For fish sold fresh off the boat, try Market Fisheries (Unit 1, Simmons Quay, Rock Channel East, 01797 225175, closed Saturday). There's a farmers' market every Wednesday morning at Strand Quay, but regrettably nothing at weekends. Britchers & Rivers (109 High Street, 01797 227152) is an old-fashioned sweetshop that often has a queue coming out the door on Saturdays – try its hardcore sour sweets. There are plenty of antiques and bric-a-brac shops too, including specialists such as Glass etc (18-22 Rope Walk, 01797 226600, www.decanterman.com). This unpompous antiques and 20th-century glass shop is run by Andy McConnell, one of Britain's leading authorities on glassware. There's also Jane Wicks Kitchenalia (Strand Quay, 01424 713635) for vintage kitchen equipment and crockery, along with retro treasure trove New 2 You (Cinque Ports Street, 01797 226379, www.new2youretrorye.vpweb.co.uk).

Also of interest to day-trippers who like to rummage are the second-hand bookshops and charity shops dotted around town, and for vinyl junkies, Grammar School Records (Old Grammar School, High Street, 01797 222752, www.grammarschoolrecords.com), which has more than 20,000 discs in stock. Metropolitan tastes are catered to at Bird (113 High Street, 01797 229927, www.boutiquebird.co.uk), which stocks its own-label womenswear alongside Eley Kishimoto pieces, gorgeous cashmere from Queene & Belle, and covetable homewear.

Rye has a vibrant cultural scene too. In September, the Rye Arts Festival (www.ryefestival.co.uk) has a fine programme of events from music to literature, and has been steadily growing in stature since launching in 1972. Local artists also take part in the open studios strand of Coastal Currents (www.coastalcurrents.org.uk). Then there's the Rye Bay Scallop Festival (www.ryebayscallops.co.uk) in February, which involves cookery displays, scallop-opening lessons and molluscs on every menu in town.

Winchelsea & Icklesham

Just outside Rye, in the direction of Hastings, is Winchelsea – a tiny, blink-and-you-miss-it sort of place. Visiting Winchelsea today, with the sea more than a mile and a quarter away, it's curious to think that 700 years ago it was one of England's leading ports. But this is not the first Winchelsea: that was sited on a massive shingle bank and was

St Thomas, Winchelsea

devastated by the great storm of 1287, which changed the topography of the south coast forever. At the time, the loss of Winchelsea was as great a blow as losing Portsmouth would be today. King Edward I ordered the construction of a new port and work started in the 1280s, from the Strand to the New Gate (where you can see the deepest section of the town's defensive ditch), with the streets being laid out on a grid system.

The wealth of new Winchelsea was largely based on the wine trade. (There are 47 known cellars in the town.) Other prominent industries included wool, timber, iron, and shipbuilding and repair. Along with Rye, Winchelsea emerged as one of the key ports in south-east England.

However, new Winchelsea's heyday only lasted for a few generations, and by the mid 14th century the town was in terminal decline. In the 1340s it started to suffer from shingle drifts, and when ships were no longer able to reach the town its livelihood, quite literally, dried up. In the village today there are a couple of worthwhile stops, in particular the church of St Thomas, where stained-glass windows commemorate the dead of World War I.

Most people stop in Winchelsea, however, for the beach (www.winchelseabeach.org.uk). It's a typical south coast shingle beach whose dilapidated groynes and mirror-like rock pools give it an ethereal beauty – great for long walks and atmospheric photographs, particularly at low tide. If the shingle proves too tricky, there is a promenade.

Further towards Hastings, along the A259, is the hamlet of Icklesham. Inside the part-Norman All Saints church, a legacy notice of 1592 leaves more than £3 a year 'for ever' for highway maintenance. Paul McCartney, who has a house nearby, funded the restoration of the Hog Hill windmill on Wickham Rock Lane (it's privately owned, and not open to visitors). Icklesham is also known for its excellent real ale pub, the Queens Head (see right).

Pett & Fairlight

South of Icklesham are Pett, Pett Level and Fairlight. While they are little more than hamlets, the drama of their coast is worth exploring. Pett Level comes to an abrupt halt at Cliff End, under which is a shingle beach. At low tide, you can see the stumps of fossilised trees dating from the last Ice Age. Pett is also the end of the 28-mile Royal Military Canal: running from Seabrooke, near Folkestone, to Cliff End, it was built in the early 19th century to defend Romney Marsh should Napoleon attack. How effective it would have proved is a moot point; as journalist William Cobbett wrote in 1823, 'Here is a canal – I crossed it at Appledore – made for the length of thirty miles, from Hythe in Kent to Rye in Sussex, to keep out the French; for those armies who had so often crossed the Rhine and the Danube were to be kept back by a canal, made by Pitt, thirty feet wide at the most!' However, it has proved handy as an overflow channel for the marsh's drainage ditches.

A little further west is Fairlight, and Fairlight Cove, two adjoining wind-swept little villages on top of cliffs. The sea has battered Fairlight Cove and some of the coastguard houses are now precariously close to being consumed by the Channel. There are, nevertheless, expansive views across the Channel and Hastings Country Park. On a clear day, it's said you can see more than 50 churches and Beachy Head by Eastbourne.

Where to eat & drink

Finding somewhere to eat in Rye is easy. The streets are lined with decent options, from cheap and cheerful eateries such as Simply Italian (The Strand, 01797 226024) to destination restaurants such as Webbe's (*see below*), the George (*see p150*) or the Landgate Bistro (*see below*) – and you're never far from a teashop.

There's a good array of pubs too: have a drink in the Mermaid Inn (*see below*) for its olde worlde charm and signed photographs, or soak up the view in the beer garden at the Ypres Castle Inn (*see p150*); we also like the Standard Inn (High Street, 01797 225996, www.standardinn.co.uk), a friendly pub with an open fire and local cider.

In Winchelsea, the Winchelsea Farm Kitchen (High Street, 01797 226287, www.winchelsea farmkitchen.co.uk) is a popular deli and coffee shop. A great range of English cheeses, cured meats and terrines is matched in the café by fabulous cakes and coffee, plus own-made quiche and fish pie.

Landgate Bistro

5-6 Landgate, Rye, TN31 7LH (01797 222829, www.landgatebistro.co.uk). Lunch served noon-2.15pm Sat, Sun. Dinner served 7-11pm Wed-Sat.
This small restaurant occupies two interconnecting Georgian cottages, and places its emphasis firmly on local produce such as potted wild rabbit or Romney Marsh lamb with gratin potatoes. The chef describes his approach as British with a modern slant, while the fish menu is decided by what looks tempting in the morning catch. The set lunch menus are excellent value.

Mermaid Inn

Mermaid Street, Rye, TN31 7EY (01797 223065, www.mermaidinn.com). Open noon-11pm daily. Lunch served noon-2.30pm, dinner served 7-9.30pm daily.

With cellars dating from 1156, and the main building from 1420, the Mermaid oozes history. The Giant's Fireplace Bar has a large inglenook fireplace supported by a beam that crosses the entire room. There are ghost stories attached to the place, and a priest's hole in the chimney dating from the reign of 'Bloody' Mary; added to that, it was once a smugglers' haunt. These days the Mermaid is much more genteel, with only the odd Morris dancer breaking the quiet. As much a hotel as it is a pub, it has 31 rooms (£160-£210 double incl breakfast), eight of which have four-poster beds, and a slightly old-fashioned restaurant.

Queens Head

Parsonage Lane, Icklesham, TN36 4BL (01424 814552, www.queenshead.com). Open 11am-11pm Mon-Sat; noon-10.30pm Sun. Lunch served noon-2.30pm, dinner served 6.15-9.45pm Mon-Fri. Food served noon-9.30pm Sat, Sun.
Lauded by CAMRA for its excellent range of real ales, the Queens Head was built in 1632 as two farmhouses and became a pub in 1831. With a huge inglenook fireplace, beamed walls and hops hanging from the ceiling, it's a cosy spot. The large beer garden has fine views, and the kitchen serves good pub grub (steak and kidney pie, pint of prawns). There's live music every Sunday afternoon.

Webbe's at the Fish Café ★

17 Tower Street, Rye, TN31 7AT (01797 222226, www.webbesrestaurants.co.uk). Lunch served noon-2.30pm daily. Dinner served 6-8.30pm Mon-Fri; 6-9.30pm Sat, Sun.
Owned by Paul Webbe, who also runs the Wild Mushroom in Westfield and Webbe's Rock-a-Nore in Hastings, this is one of the best seafood restaurants in the area. Pan-fried Rye Bay scallops with roast button onions, pancetta and creamed potato would tempt most diners, but there are also decent steaks and the odd veggie option; the fish-based, tapas-style tasting dishes are popular too. Locally sourced produce is used where possible, and it's all served in a sleek, smart setting.

SUSSEX

Queens Head

Ypres Castle Inn

Gun Gardens, Rye, TN31 7HH (01797 223248, www. yprescastleinn.co.uk). Open 11am-10pm Mon-Thur; 11am-1am Fri; 11am-11pm Sat; 11am-6pm Sun. Lunch served noon-3pm daily. Dinner served 6-9pm Mon-Sat.

The 'Wipers' is a lively little inn with a whitewashed weatherboard façade. Rare for a pub in Rye, it has a beer garden with views over Ypres Tower and across the Romney Marshes. Pub food includes plenty of fish specials, and bands play every Friday.

Where to stay

Luxury guesthouses reign supreme in Rye, and visitors will find plenty of well-run establishments in fascinating buildings. The Rye Guide (www.ryeguide. co.uk) has a large selection of local accommodation. For self-catering options, Mulberry Cottages (01233 813087, www.mulberrycottages.com) has a range of characterful properties, including rooms in an ancient farmhouse and a flat above an art gallery.

In Winchelsea there are two good places to stay. The Strand House (Tanyards Lane, 01797 226276, www.thestrandhouse.co.uk) is a Tudor house with ten comfortable bedrooms and a dining room. The Lodge (Hastings Road, 01797 226211, www.the lodgeatwinchelsea.co.uk) is a modern hotel with 28 simple, good-value rooms.

The George ★

98 High Street, Rye, TN31 7JT (01797 222114, www.thegeorgeinnrye.com). Rates £135-£195 double incl breakfast.

Rye's premier hotel since it reopened after a major revamp in 2006, the George is a handsome coaching inn dating from 1575. It has 24 bedrooms, a Georgian ballroom and a restaurant. Rooms are all modishly designed, and each is different, though all have beautiful bathrooms stocked with Ren products and beds covered with Frette linen. The restaurant serves the likes of wild sea bass with fennel, roast red pepper and pickled mushrooms or smoked Romney Marsh lamb neck with mini lamb pie and devilled kidneys, while the tap room is a welcoming nook with a crackling fire and real ales.

Jeake's House

Mermaid Street, Rye, TN31 7ET (01797 222828, www.jeakeshouse.com). Rates £90-£138 double incl breakfast.

This popular 17th-century guesthouse is full of character, from the honesty bar on the ground floor to the king-size four-poster beds in the luxury suites. The 11 rooms take their names from literary and artistic figures who have visited the area, Radclyffe Hall and Malcolm Lowry among them. The breakfast menu is a marvellous spread: feast on buttered kipper fillets, devilled kidneys on toast, or an almighty traditional English breakfast.

Rye Windmill

Off Ferry Road, Rye, TN31 7DW (01797 224027, www.ryewindmill.co.uk). Rates £70-£145 double incl breakfast (two-night min stay over a Sat night).

For a unique stay, try kipping in a windmill. This one is a Grade II-listed building, with en suite bathrooms, high-quality furnishings, and picture-postcard views of the adjacent River Tillingham. There are ten rooms, though only two are inside the windmill itself. The Windmill Suite is spread over two floors, and features a super-king sleigh bed, a freestanding roll-top bath and a balcony, while downstairs in the mill's brick base is the Four Poster Room (complete with a period bed).

Simmons of Rye

68-69 The Mint, Rye, TN31 7EW (01797 226032, www.simmonsofrye.co.uk). Rates £135-£165 double incl breakfast.

Each of the four bedrooms at this charming, immaculately presented B&B has period features, but also contemporary touches such as an MP3-enabled digital radio and luxury toiletries. The Watchbell Suite is the star room, accessed by a private stairwell and featuring an oak-beamed dressing and shower room.

White Vine House

24 High Street, Rye, TN31 7JF (01797 224748, www.whitevinehouse.co.uk). Rates £130-£190 double incl breakfast.

This restaurant with rooms offers a winning combination of good food and beautifully appointed rooms. Softly lit, dotted with antiques and impeccably tasteful, the guest rooms are perfect for romantic weekends away; up in the eaves, meanwhile, is a light, airy family room. Free Wi-Fi, DVD players, hairdryers and all-natural toiletries add to the boutique hotel vibe. Downstairs, the Vine restaurant serves polished-up comfort food and bistro classics: think thick-cut chips with gourmet burgers, stone-baked pizzas or scallop and prawn tagliatelle.

Willow Tree House

113 Winchelsea Road, Rye, TN31 7EL (01797 227820, www.willow-tree-house.com). Rates £90-£130 double incl breakfast.

Unwind in one of the six luxury rooms at this laid-back retreat, each of which is named after a local village (Appledore, Bodiam, Iden, Fairlight, Playden and Winchelsea). All are en suite, and well stocked (they even have hair straighteners); Playden, with its sloping walls and beamed ceiling, is particularly nice. Breakfast features smoked salmon with poached eggs, or home-made hash browns with creamed horseradish.

HASTINGS & ST LEONARDS

Hastings

'Each day poured in new coach-fulls of new cits, Flying from London Smoke and dust annoying, Unmarried Misses hoping to make hits, And new-wed couples fresh from Tunbridge Toying.' So wrote the poet Thomas Hood in *A Storm at Hastings* in 1825. Just as in Brighton and Eastbourne, further along the coast, the late 1700s and early 1800s saw the fashion for sea-bathing reach dizzy heights. Dignified Georgian terraces such as Pelham Crescent and Wellington Square were built, and the shift from a small fishing enclave and smugglers' haven to seaside town was complete.

Despite the lack of a natural harbour, Hastings' proximity to the sea has always provided its income, whether through smuggling or fishing. For the last

Hastings Country Park. See p146.

SUSSEX

1,000 years, the boats here have landed their catch on the shore, and it's the biggest beach-launched fishing fleet in the country.

Although the name Hastings is filed in every schoolchild's mind under the title 1066 and all that, the Battle of Hastings in fact took place near Battle (see p159), eight miles north.

Old Town

The Old Town is the most atmospheric part of Hastings. Starting by the distinctive, black-painted fishermen's net shops, the Stade, meaning 'landing place', is still the centre of the Hastings fishing industry. The boats land in the morning, while carts of fresh fish are shunted around through the day and sold in the handful of wet fish shops along the Stade. Hastings Fishermen's Museum (see p147) charts the history of the industry. Just outside, among the net shops, are a couple of fishing boats and the sweet Half Sovereign Cottage, purportedly built from half a boat, and with a small exhibit inside.

At the end of Rock-a-Nore parade is the Shipwreck Museum (see p147), which has good audio-visual displays about the many shipwrecks off the coast. It also offers guided tours to the wreck of the Amsterdam, which sank in 1749 and can still be seen at low tide. Next door is the Blue Reef Aquarium (see p146).

Along this stretch is one of the town's two funicular railways, East Hill Lift (01424 451111, open Mar-Sept daily, Oct-Mar weekends only). Opened in 1903, it was originally powered by an ingenious water-balancing system, but was converted to electricity in the 1970s. It valiantly rises 267 feet up Hastings Country Park (see p146) at a perilously steep-seeming gradient.

The most talked-about (and in some parts, controversional) development in Hastings is the Jerwood Gallery on the Stade (www.jerwood gallery.org). Due to open in 2011, this sensitively designed building, clad in dark tiles, will provide a permanent home for the Jerwood Collection, which focuses on British art between World War I and the 1960s, and includes works by LS Lowry, Stanley Spencer, Walter Sickert and Augustus John. It's also the southern home of the Jerwood Visual Arts programme which will organise exhibitions, events and awards in the space.

Walking back up Rock-a-Nore, towards the old town, there are several stalls selling wet fish. On the right-hand side, after the Dolphin pub, Rock-a-Nore Fisheries (01424 445425, www.rockanorefisheries.co.uk, closed Mon) smokes its own fish and sells jars of own-made fish soup. After the excellent fish restaurant, Webbe's Rock-a-Nore (see p157), turn right up All Saints Street. Although largely residential, there are some fabulous old buildings along this little-visited stretch. After passing the Fisherman's Institute, call in at the 16th-century Stag Inn at no.14 (see p157). It's known for the two cats found in the chimney and now displayed in a glass cabinet in the bar.

At the end of All Saints Street stands its namesake church. Built in 1436, it is notable for the Doom, an ancient painting of the Last Judgment over the chancel arch that was rediscovered in the late 1800s. Next door is the Old Rectory (see p158), now a splendid four-room boutique hotel.

Cross Harold Road, past the Stables Theatre (The Bourne, 01424 423221, www.stables-theatre.co.uk), which puts on ten or so quality amateur productions a year, and on to High Street, which takes you directly back to the seafront and along the most interesting row of shops in Hastings. On the right is St Clements's church, rebuilt in 1380 after being ransacked by the French in 1339. It has lovely stained-glass windows by Philip Cole, and two fabulous antique chandeliers.

There are few more welcoming pubs in Hastings than the First In Last Out, known locally as the FILO (*see p156*). It has its own microbrewery, turning out superb ales, along with a central open fire and snug booths. A couple of doors down is another excellent small hotel, the Laindons (*see p158*); next door, Scooter & Jinx (23 High Street, 01424 719401, www.scooterandjinx.com, closed Mon) is an independent shop specialising in the latest Japanese collectors' toys. Continuing along High Street are contemporary galleries such as Weekend Gallery (86 High Street, 01424 719296, www.weekendgallery.co.uk, closed Mon-Wed) and First Sight (34 High Street, 01797 344655, closed Mon-Thur). Made in Hastings (82 High Street, 01424 719110, www.madeinhastings.co.uk) sells a range of local crafts, from delicate ceramics to playful hand-printed tea towels.

On the right are the Hastings Old Town Tourist Information Centre (01424 451166, www.hmag. org.uk) and the Old Town Hall Museum (01424 451166, www.hmag.org.uk). Its displays recount the area's history, from its days as a Cinque Port and thriving Victorian resort to the clearances of the 1930s. The Electric Palace Cinema (*see p143*) at no.39A is the town's only independent cinema, screening contemporary arthouse releases, classic films and world cinema. Nearby is the almost implausibly wholesome Judges Bakery (51 High Street, 01424 722588, www.judges bakery.com). Every product on its shelves is made from organically certified ingredients, from the jam doughnuts to the deliciously dense rye bread. Artificial additives are a no-no: even the pink meringue pigs are dyed with raspberry and beetroot juice.

At Swan Terrace, either take a right and climb through the maze-like streets to West Hill for fabulous views over the town and across the channel, or continue down to George Street.

To reach the castle, follow the signpost marked 'Caves & Castle' on the corner of Swan Terrace and Croft Road. Follow the steep twittens (Sussex alleyways) up past the Smugglers Adventure (*see p147*) and on to the wide open stretch of ground known as Cliff Rly. Heading towards the sea is Hastings Castle (*see p146*), but Cliff Rly is worth a detour for the views, and is a great picnic spot.

Back at High Street, take a right down pedestrianised George Street, the most significant shopping street in the town. Dozens of independent boutiques, restaurants and pubs throng this stretch. At no.68A is Warp & Weft (07947 225424), a small shop of carefully sourced, beautifully made clothes and other wares. There's a small sculpture garden on the right. At no.45B, Soak (01424 422267, www.soakhastings.com) is an aromatic cavern full of bathroom treats, including a rainbow palette of bath bombs.

Also along George Street are three good restaurants: Black Pearl (*see p156*), Pomegranate (*see p157*) and Dragon (*see p156*). Another interesting stop-off is the Boulevard Bookshop & Thai Café (no.32, 01424 436521, www.thaicafe andbookshop.com, closed Mon, Sun), which serves excellent Thai food amid shelves of books. There are a couple of other good second-hand bookshops along here too. The lower station of the town's second funicular, the West Hill Cliff Railway, is also on George Street. Built in 1889, it ascends through a tunnel to Hastings Castle – always an option if you don't want to walk up.

Town Centre & America Ground

From the Old Town, the main route to the town centre is through an underpass which spits you out in a pedestrian centre lined with chain stores. Directly south, along the seafront, is the Hastings of slot machines, garish sweet stalls and boating lakes. A hellish row of tat for parents, perhaps – but for kids, it's non-stop excitement. The amusement arcades house rows and rows of flashing, noisy machines. Head to the Rock Shop and Old Fashioned Candy Shop for sticky piles of rock, humbugs, cola cubes and rhubarb and custards.

America Ground (www.americaground.co.uk) is a small enclave of shops and cafés along Robertson, Claremont and Trinity Streets, with the Victorian Holy Trinity Church in the middle. The area has a fascinating history. In the mid 13th century, a series of brutal storms battered towns all along the coastline, shifting the contours of the landscape and all but destroying Hastings. One of the consequences of the storms was a vast build-up of shingle at this spot. Because no one owned the land (after all, it was previously underwater), canny locals realised they could live there without paying taxes or rent.

By the 1800s, over 1,000 people were living on the land, while the wrangle over who owned it continued. As local novelist Sheila Kaye-Smith observed, it was 'free to any beggars, gypsies or other undesirables... a mock city of shacks, huts and tents'. When Hastings Borough decided to impose its authority, however, the residents raised the American flag and declared their independence and intention to become the 24th state of America. It didn't work, of course, and the land was claimed for King George IV in 1827. Today, it's still known as the America Ground and in a moment of shrewd marketing, the White Rock & America Ground Business Group celebrated American Independence Day here for the first time in 2010, with bands, an art event and a street market.

On the corner of Trinity Street and Robertson Street, an enormous mural of the America Ground is followed by a run of good shops. At 45 Robertson Street is the F-ISH gallery (01424 205400, www. f-ish.co.uk, closed Mon, Tue), which is the most cutting-edge gallery in Hastings, with an eclectic programme of multimedia arts. At no.40 is the unmistakable façade of Substance (01424 438089, www.substance666.com, closed Sun), the spiritual home of Hastings goths and clubbers.

The George. See p150.

Hastings. See p150.

Directly opposite is Inspire Artwork (01424 422588, www.inspirehastings.com), an urban art gallery that runs highly popular courses for all ages, on graffiti as well as oil painting and life drawing.

At the end of Robertson Street is Collared (no.37E, 01424 719918, www.collareddog.co.uk), a new dog boutique (with some cat items) with clothes and accessories for fashionable pooches. The Bullet Coffee House (01424 717477, www.bullethastings.co.uk) opposite is a popular place to relax with a latte and a paper. Turning right up Claremont, Knit Connections (01424 444038, closed Mon, Sun) is a trendy textile shop that also runs workshops and sewing classes. Finally, B&T Music (9 Claremont, 01424 434480, www.bandt music.co.uk, closed Sun) is beloved by the town's music scenesters.

St Leonards-on-Sea

St Leonards, like Hove, has been swallowed up by its larger neighbour. Some residents feel fiercely independent from Hastings, but in reality, there's no noticeable difference between the two towns. It wasn't always thus. Until the 1870s a huge white chalk outcrop extended into the sea, defining Hastings and St Leonards. Traffic was forced to travel two miles inland. It was finally blown up – the rough cliff can now be seen directly behind the White Rock Theatre – and a pier was built in its place, marking the boundary between the two towns.

Hastings pier opened in 1872, at a time when both Hastings and St Leonards were hugely popular seaside destinations. The 1970s saw Jimi Hendrix, Pink Floyd and the Who play in its pavilion. After being declared unsafe in 2006, the pier was closed. It opened again for a year in 2007, but a storm put the structure at risk again, and on 5 October 2010 the pier burned down.

Founded before the fire, the Hastings Pier & White Rock Trust (01424 435587, www.hpwrt.co.uk, closed Tue, Wed) was set up to save the pier; they now really have their work cut out. At 34 White Rock, former tailor's Arthur Green's is now a shop that aims to raise funds for the pier. It sells T-shirts, cushions and posters designed by local artists, as well as some antiques. The original shop fittings remain, and plaques offer information about the pier and the history of St Leonards.

The White Rock Theatre (see p143) remains the town's pre-eminent venue for music concerts, shows and pantos. The White Rock Hotel (see p158) next door has a pleasant lounge and serves real ales. The expansive seafront is spectacular: Eastbourne and Beachy Head can usually be seen clearly to the west. Banksy has sprayed a fabulous piece of work on a west-facing staircase below St Leonards Parish Church, near Marine Court.

St Leonards came into existence in 1833, when it was commissioned as a new town. The architect James Burton and his more famous son, Decimus,

who helped with the Royal Botanic Gardens at Kew and London Zoo, built it on a grand scale, with a wealthy target market in mind.

Walk further west along the seafront to Warrior Square Gardens, opened in 1852. This large garden, surrounded by Victorian townhouses, has been spruced up in recent years. With her back to the garden, facing the sea, is a statue of a surly-looking Queen Victoria; the bullet hole in her royal person (near her knee) is thought to have been caused by a stray bullet from a World War II plane. Pranksters often like to dress her up.

Next comes the unmistakeable Marine Court, an art deco tower block built to resemble an ocean liner and completed in 1937. Writer Iain Sinclair, no stranger to the town, described it thus: 'burdened with a forest of radio masts and photovoltaic scanners, this prewar monster looms over the remnants of James Burton's 1820s colonnades, at a slight angle, like a stack of dirty plates from a wedding breakfast in the Royal Victoria hotel'. After a long period of neglect, it is once again becoming a desirable residence; one of the apartments is available for holiday lets (see p158).

Under Marine Court, in keeping with the 1930s theme, is the excellent Marina Post Office Tearooms (see p156). The Burton Gallery (5 Marine Court, 01424 719817, www.theburtongallery.co.uk closed Mon-Thur Apr-Dec, Mon-Fri Jan-Mar) has a good range of art in a variety of disciplines, and is influenced by the building it sits under. A little further along is the Hastings Arts Forum (36 Marina, 01424 201636, www.hastingsartsforum.co.uk), founded to raise the profile of art in Hastings and one of the most important galleries in the area.

After a row of shops to the west of Marine Court, head inland and climb East Ascent and left on to Mercatoria. Past one of Hastings' finest restaurants, St Clement's (see p157), and the civilised Horse & Groom pub (01424 420612, www.horseandgroom stleonards.co.uk) is St Leonards Gardens on Stanhope Place, a lovely quiet park.

Directly opposite St Clement's is Norman Road (www.thenormanroad.co.uk), an unassuming street whose fortunes are on the rise. Once home to boarded-up shops and the occasional antiques storage space, it's now packed with shops and galleries. Among them are photography specialist the Lucy Bell Gallery ★ (no.46, 01424 434828, www.lucy-bell.com); McCarron's of Mercatoria (no.68, 01424 428929, www.mccarrons.co.uk, closed Mon, Sun), which has a charming range of furnishings and gifts, much of it from local artists; and retro shop Skylon (no.64, 01424 445691, www.skyloninteriors.co.uk). The Double Elephant art gallery (no.42, 07710 198825) is worth a visit too. Opposite is the Little Larder café (see p156).

At the end of the road is a vast mural by Ben Eine. A pixelated depiction of a young Prince Charles, it has become a major attraction – especially since

David Cameron gave Barack Obama one of Eine's pieces. Under the mural, on Friday to Sunday, is the Love Market, a handful of stalls selling artisan bread and cheese as well as vintage clothing; there's also the good Love Café (*see below*). Close by, on Grand Parade, is delicatessen Plenty (no.16, 01424 439736, www.plentyprovisions.co.uk), which sells bread from the Lighthouse Bakery at Bodiam.

Where to eat & drink

Compared with Bexhill and Eastbourne along the coast, there are plenty of decent places to eat in Hastings. Webbe's and Pomegranate (for both, *see right*) are respected seafood restaurants, but for traditional fish and chips head for the Blue Dolphin (61B High Street, 01424 425778), which has a small restaurant as well as a takeaway counter. Or try the ever busy Maggies (01424 430205, closed Sun winter), above the fish market and among the net shops of Rock-a-Nore Road. A more upmarket seafood choice is Black Pearl (9 George Street, 01424 719919, www.blackpearlrestaurant.co.uk) which also offers some meat dishes.

St Leonards, in particular, is embracing café culture, with at least three great little coffee houses. Norman Road is home to the Little Larder (no.39, 01424 424364, closed Sun), a pleasant café with good coffee and even better own-made cakes, plus lunch items such as pumpkin soup. Across the road is the quirky Love Café (http://thelovestudio.co.uk, closed Mon, Tue). Coffees, cakes and sandwiches are served, among bookshelves and long sofas. Under Marine Court is the Marina Post Office Tea Rooms (40a Marina, 01424 426885, closed Mon, Tue). There's art for sale and it's built up quite a community, especially when the *Archers* Sunday omnibus comes on the radio. All the food is seasonal and traceable, some of it back to its own farm.

Dragon

71 George Street, Hastings, TN34 3EE (01424 423688). Open noon-11pm daily. Food served noon-10pm daily.
Somewhere between a bar, restaurant and gastropub, Dragon is a relatively recent addition to Hastings' George Street. It's dark any time of the day, and the bare wood floors and panelled walls add to the feeling of a trendy basement bar in Shoreditch. There's alternative art on the walls and a set of decks on the bar. The menu, scribbled daily on chalkboards, lists the likes of french onion soup or braised fennel and wild mushroom stuffed trout; there's also pizza. The beers and wines go beyond the usual suspects.

First In Last Out (FILO) ★

14-15 High Street, Hastings, TN34 3EY (01424 425079, www.thefilo.co.uk). Open noon-midnight daily. Lunch served noon-2.30pm Mon-Sat. Dinner served 6-8.30pm Mon.
The FILO is one of the best pubs in Hastings. It's an unassuming but friendly place: during the winter, a fire burns, and booth seating makes it even cosier. Warmer weather sees the covered beer garden at the rear come into its own. Pub grub includes dishes such as fish cakes or liver and bacon, and Monday night is tapas night. The main

SUSSEX FOOD FESTIVALS

Apple Festival

Held at Middle Farm's National Collection of Cider & Perry (*see p201*) in Firle in October, this two-day festival celebrates the apple season. Morris dancers, produce stalls, a puppet theatre and bands all feature, alongside apple pressing and cider making.

Arundel Food Festival

www.arundelfoodfestival.org.uk.
Most pubs, restaurants and food shops in Arundel do something to mark the town's October food festival, from stocking a wider range of beers to offering foraging walks, butchery demonstrations or cupcake classes.

Brighton & Hove Food Festival

www.brightonfoodfestival.com.
Held every September, this is one of the biggest food festivals in the South-east, and attracts top chefs and restaurants. There are market stalls, cooking lessons and talks; 2010 saw 110 events.

Chilli Fiesta

www.westdean.org.uk.
This chilli festival is held over three days in August in the lovely West Dean Gardens. There are more than 300 types of chilli on show, including the fiery naga jolokia, or California Death Pepper, the hottest in the world.

Glynde Food & Drink Festival

www.glynde.co.uk.
Although it missed a year in 2010, organisers promise the two-day Glynde Food & Drink Festival, usually held in September, will return. Set in the sumptuous grounds of Glynde Place, near Lewes, it is a showcase for the best food producers and wine makers in Sussex. There are demonstrations, talks and entertainment.

reason for a trip here, however, is the selection of ales from their own brewery. Crofters is their best bitter and always available, but also look out for Ginger Tom, a light ale infused with a hint of ginger, or the Sussex porter, Cardinal. An all-round delight.

Pomegranate
50 George Street, St Leonards, TN34 3EA (01424 429221, www.pomegranatehastings.co.uk). Open/food served 6pm-midnight Wed-Fri; 11am-4pm, 6pm-midnight Sat; 11am-4pm Sun.
An old picture frame hung in the window of Pomegranate announces the 'food & drink house' to visitors along pedestrianised George Street. A bright pink façade helps it stand out too. The restaurant gives off a distinctly bohemian – and welcoming – vibe. Seafood dominates the seasonal menu, alongside a handful of vegetarian and meat dishes. Options might include spiced gurnard with tomato, spring onion and herb gnocchi or local fish hotpot with garlic bread and rouille. There's also a wholesome Pirate's menu for children.

St Clement's ★
3 Mercatoria, St Leonards, TN38 0EB (01424 200355, www.stclementsrestaurant.co.uk). Lunch served noon-3pm Tue-Sun. Dinner served 6-10.30pm Tue-Fri; 7pm, 9pm Sat.
Situated at the end of up-and-coming Norman Road, St Clement's has gained a stellar reputation locally, as well as a Michelin Bib Gourmand. Dishes such as roast saddle of venison with wild mushroom sauce or fish stew with chorizo, chickpeas and tomato are served in a relaxed, unpretentious dining room. There are excellent-value set menus Tuesday to Thursday evenings, and the decent wine list has some interesting bottles. St Clement's is run by head chef/owner Nick Hales, previously of London's Le Caprice.

Stag Inn
14 All Saints Street, Hastings, TN34 3BJ (01424 425734). Open noon-midnight daily. Lunch served noon-3pm Mon-Sat; noon-5pm Sun. Dinner served 6-8pm Mon-Sat. No credit cards.
This down-to-earth Hastings pub dates from at least 1547. It has largely retained its old-time feel and is a true drinkers' pub, with a roaring fire and nice open bar. Tunnels, probably used by smugglers, run beneath the pub, and two mummified cats in a glass case preside over the bar. They were found in the chimney during restoration work. One theory is that they merely got stuck there when a fire was lit; we prefer the story that they belonged to a witch, said to haunt the pub to this day.

Webbe's Rock-a-Nore ★
1 Rock-a-Nore Road, Hastings, TN34 3DW (01424 721650, www.webbesrestaurants.co.uk). Lunch served 10.30am-2.30pm, dinner served 5.30-11pm Mon-Fri. Food served 10.30am-9.30pm Sat, Sun.
The latest addition to Paul and Rebecca Webbe's portfolio is this relaxed, family-friendly restaurant, serving fish that has made a very short boat-to-plate journey. The modern decor is inviting, and there's some outdoor seating for summer. The extensive menu features seafood platters and tapas-style tasting dishes alongside starters and mains. The tasting dishes include crispy squid fritters with chilli jam and succulent smoked haddock risotto balls. The spectacular

Hastings Seafood & Wine Festival
www.visit1066country.com.
Stalls piled high with fresh seafood cluster around the Stade landing beach in Hastings at this well-attended September festival. It also has displays from Sussex and Kent vineyards.

Lewes Octoberfeast
www.lewesoctoberfeast.com.
There's a great ten days' worth of events at the Octoberfeast in Lewes. Food markets, Polish feasts, apple pressing workshops, a fungi and foraging cook-up, talks from chefs and authors and tours around Harvey's Brewery have all featured in past years.

Rye Scallop Festival
www.ryebayscallops.co.uk.
Plump, juicy Rye scallops are the focus of a week's worth of events and demonstrations at this February event. Most local restaurants have scallop dishes on the menu.

Spring Harvest Food & Drink Festival
Little sister to the Brighton & Hove Food Festival, this smaller April event celebrates the coming of spring and coincides with the Brighton Whisky Festival and the British Beer Festival. Events include a chefs' race, food awards and specialist food and drink markets.

Sussex Food Festival
Held at the Bluebell Railway (*see p205*), this one-day event promotes Sussex food and wine producers, including those from the Bluebell Vineyard. It's held on a Sunday in August.

seafood platter boasts oysters, winkles, whelks, prawns and crab, nearly all landed just across the road. There are some meat dishes too, such as wild boar sausages.

Where to stay

Although it would have been hard to imagine ten years ago, Hastings and St Leonards now have some of the best accommodation in East Sussex (though plenty of dodgy B&Bs remain). There are a handful of high-end boutique hotels: in Hastings, Zanzibar (9 Eversfield Place, 01424 460109, www.zanzibarhotel.co.uk) was one of the first. Its nine rooms are lightly themed around different destinations.

Much of the other accommodation is in B&Bs and guesthouses. Lavender Lace 1066 (106 All Saints Street, 01424 716290, www.lavenderlace 1066.co.uk), set in a Grade II-listed building in Hastings Old Town, is traditional and utterly charming, with breakfasts that occasionally include ingredients from the owners' allotment. Senlac House (47 Cambridge Gardens, 01424 435767, www.senlacguesthouse.co.uk) is a contemporary guesthouse with eight rooms and two apartments.

In St Leonards, Tower House 1066 (28 Tower Road West, 01424 427217, www.towerhouse 1066.co.uk) offers upmarket B&B accommodation at reasonable rates. Another option is the self-catering studio apartment for rent in Marine Court (www.marinecourtapartment.co.uk).

Black Rock House

10 Stanley Road, Hastings, TN34 1UE (01424 438448, www.black-rock-hastings.co.uk). Rates £100-£125 double incl breakfast.
High up in the Braybrooke residential area of Hastings, this Victorian villa has been beautifully converted into a luxurious little hotel. The five rooms come with either wet rooms or baths, and demonstrate a real flair for design: downstairs, the lounge area is equally charming. The two-course gourmet breakfast features own-made muesli and plenty of Sussex-sourced goodies, from sausages and bacon to Oakwood Farm apple juice; there are some great vegetarian options too.

Hastings House

9 Warrior Square, St Leonards, TN37 6BA (01424 422709, www.hastingshouse.co.uk). Rates £99-£140 double incl breakfast.
Leading the St Leonards style revival, Hastings House is aimed squarely at the boutique city break market, and run by the convivial Seng and Elisabeth Loy. There are eight rooms in this converted Victorian townhouse, and rooms three, five and seven (our favourite) have fine views over the square and the sea. The bathrooms are as thoughtfully designed as the rooms. There's a lounge with a small bar and a terrace out the back, and the breakfasts feature plenty of locally sourced produce.

Laindons

23 High Street, Hastings, TN34 3EY (01424 437710, www.thelaindons.com). Rates £110-£125 double incl breakfast.

A former coaching house, the Laindons is now a handsome three-bedroom residence. Each of the rooms mixes original elements of the Grade II-listed Georgian building, such as the fireplaces, with modern design touches. The linen is top quality, toiletries are by the White Company, and room three has a striking contemporary four-poster bed. The guest lounge continues the modern aesthetic, as does the sun-trap breakfast room with views over the Old Town and East Hill.

Old Rectory ★

Harold Road, Hastings, TN35 5ND (01424 422410, www.theoldrectoryhastings.co.uk). Rates £130-£150 double incl breakfast.
The Old Rectory used to serve the 13th-century All Saints church next door. It has since been converted to a hotel, in spectacular fashion, by the same owners as Swan House. Each of the five bedrooms is lavishly decorated in a different style, and named after local streets. The All Saints Suite is the most muted, while the Crown room, with a ball-and-claw standalone bath in the bedroom (concealed behind a false bookcase), the most singular. Tackleway is a more modern affair. Shared facilities include an extensive garden, and a lounge with a big fire.

Swan House ★

1 Hill Street, Hastings, TN34 3HU (01424 430014, www.swanhousehastings.co.uk). Rates £120-£150 double incl breakfast.
From the moment you enter Swan House (built in 1490), you know you're somewhere special. The beautiful wooden floors are covered in rugs, a fire burns in the grate, and the plump sofas are piled with cushions. The muted colours add to the ambience – it's all been very carefully designed. There are four rooms, including the two-bedroom Renaissance Suite. Breakfast (Hastings kippers with parsley butter, perhaps) is served in the small courtyard in summer.

White Rock Hotel

White Rock, Hastings, TN34 1JU (01424 422240, www.thewhiterockhotel.com). Rates £59-£99 double.
The White Rock is located directly in front of the pier, and most of the rooms have a sea view. The 40 rooms are light, airy and modern, and there are pieces of 1950s-style furniture dotted around. The lounge café/bar stocks Sussex ales and is a convenient spot for a drink before visiting the White Rock Theatre next door. Dogs are welcome; the owners also run dog accessory boutique Collared (*see p154*).

Hastings Fish Market. See p151.

Battle, Bexhill & High Weald

Battle, eight miles inland from Hastings, marks the place where the Battle of Hastings was actually fought. The spot where Harold the Saxon got one in the eye (although the only reference for this is the Bayeux Tapestry) is marked within the walls of Battle Abbey. Today, the town is stunningly preserved, with buildings dating back to the time of the Abbey, as well as rickety Tudor houses and Victorian coaching inns. Surviving primarily as a tourist destination, Battle's High Street has a fine selection of tearooms, restaurants and some quirky independent shops.

From Senlac Ridge, where the opposing armies clashed, there are views across the High Weald. This hilly, heavily wooded area may be little visited, but it lies within the fourth largest Area of Outstanding Natural Beauty in England, and along its winding roads are the handsome villages of Robertsbridge, Northiam, and Bodiam, home to one of Britain's most atmospheric castles.

Bexhill, on the coast, is even more ignored, but there's one very good reason to visit: the De La Warr Pavilion. A modernist masterpiece, the pavilion hosts an innovative programme of exhibitions and concerts.

BATTLE

Battle lies directly north of Hastings on the A2100. Driving from the coastal town, you rise up on the Senlac Ridge, and towards the location of the Battle of Hastings (or Battle of Senlac). Squint hard, and you can almost picture the scene in 1066 – despite a few modern anachronisms. The Battle is revisited every year on the weekend that falls nearest to 14 October, with a cast of 1,500 colourful archers, cavalrymen and footsoldiers, plus a ramshackle village of 'living history' extras. The clanking English army are defending the side of Senlac Hill (giving spectators a good view from the top), while King Harold is brought down right by the plaque that marks the historic spot. Once the battle has been fought, the Conqueror's hordes go on to pillage the craft tents and merry refreshment stalls.

But come here on a normal weekend and you can still immerse yourself in history with the 1066 Battle of Hastings, Abbey & Battlefield experience (*see p162*), run by English Heritage. It includes an exhibition and a monastic life tour, but by far the best part is the chance to spend a couple of hours wandering around the battlefield and abbey ruins.

Former battlegrounds can be intensely evocative, and this is an opportunity to tread the soil where a pivotal episode in English history took place. (Some say that Senlac Ridge – Senlac is Norman for Lake of Blood – still seeps blood after rain; the discoloration of the water is actually caused by iron in the ground.) The audio tour is packed with fascinating details and anecdotes that paint a vivid picture of the battle. Over 14,000 troops were involved in the brutal conflict between Saxon

King Harold and William of Normandy on 14 October 1066 – a battle for the English throne. You'll learn about the tactics used by each side, the advantages and disadvantages of their respective positions and, ultimately, the reasons for Harold's defeat. Standing on the spot where Harold was slain, and gazing up the hill at the abbey you'll find yourself drifting into another world – complete with spears, shields, clubs and armour.

Battle Abbey still dominates the High Street. Directly in front of the Abbey entrance is a small square lined on one side by a mostly Tudor terrace. A Taste of Battle (2 High Street, 01424 774204, www.atasteofbattle.co.uk) has delectable home-made cakes. On the opposite side of the street is Yesterday's World (*see p162*), which provides an opportunity to point and shriek 'I had that when I was a kid'. Almost next door is the Truffle Pig Deli (no.87, 07739 041930, www.trufflepigbattle.co.uk, closed Sun), good for a local ice-cream or a wholesome snack. Head down the High Street, and past the Battle Memorial Hall where local boys Keane played in the early days. On Friday mornings it holds the Battle Country Market. At no.14 is Steamer Trading (01424 772038, www.steamer.co.uk), a Sussex-based chain selling upmarket kitchenware. It's housed in what used to be the second oldest bootmakers in the country. A few doors down is Nobles restaurant (*see p161*), the best eatery in the town. It has a great value two-course lunch menu.

A little further along the High Street, next to an old pharmacy (whose sign remains), is the George Hotel (*see p161*), here since 1699. Downstairs

Battle Abbey. See p162

there is a branch of Simply Italian (no.23, 01424 772100, www.simplyitalian.co.uk), a Sussex- and Kent-based chain of five restaurants. The Bull Inn (see below), on the same side of the High Street, is another former coaching inn. Almost directly opposite is a twitten that leads to Old Ladies Court, a shopping arcade with a few independent stores, the most tempting of which is Bittersweet Chocolates (01424 777060, www.bittersweetofbattle.co.uk, closed Sun) at no.4. All the chocolates are hand-made on the premises. The arcade comes out on Mount Street by the Ye Olde Kings Head (see below), a cosy 15th-century pub with real ales and a regular music nights. Mount Street is also the location of the nearest car park to the High Street.

North-east of Battle, on Marley Lane towards Robertsbridge, is Battle Great Wood (www.forestry. gov.uk). It's an 186-acre coniferous wood, tended by the Forestry Commission, and an agreeable place to spend a couple of hours. Home to foxes and badgers, as well as nightjars and tree pipits, it also has trails used by horse riders and mountain bikers.

Where to eat & drink

Set beside Battle Abbey, Pilgrims (1 High Street, 01424 772314) is a popular spot for a cream tea. Traditional pub Ye Olde Kings Head (37 Mount Street, 01424 772317, www.yeoldekingshead.org) serves a choice of cask ales, while the Bull Inn (27 High Street, 01424 775171, www.bullinnbattle.eu) attracts visitors for tea and coffee and a younger crowd in the evening.

Battle Deli

57 High Street, TN33 0EN (www.battledeli.co.uk, 01424 777810). Open 8.30am-5pm Mon-Sat.
A delightful deli full of fresh treats: stuffed olives, roasted peppers, unusual cheeses and warm baked bites. The menu changes daily, but more substantial dishes include soups, stews, casseroles and curries. Staff can also put together a splendid hamper. There is a sister deli in Rye.

Nobles

17 High Street, TN33 0AE (01424 774422, www.noblesrestaurant.co.uk). Lunch served noon-3pm daily. Dinner served 6.30-10.30pm Mon-Sat.
Nobles is a modern, if slightly clinical space, serving well-executed modern British dishes. Mains cost around £15, but are worth it: saffron and tomato paella comes packed with tiger prawns, squid, mussels, chicken and pork belly, while steak is a forte. The £10.66 two-course lunch menu is a nice offer.

Where to stay

Within the town centre, the Bull Inn (see above) and the George Hotel (01424 775512, www. thegeorgehotelbattle.com) both offer decent accommodation from around £50 per night. There are also several B&Bs and self-catering options in the town. The tourist board website (www.visit1066country.com) lists a wide selection of B&Bs, including Abbey Cottage (01424 775258,

www.the-abbey-cottage.com), overlooking the Abbey itself. Prices are from £365 a week. For boutique hotel accommodation, you're better off staying in Hastings (see p158).

Bannatyne Spa Hotel

Battle Road, TN38 8EA (01424 851222, www.bannatyne.co.uk). Rates £95-£190 double incl breakfast.
Luxurious if a little bland, this spa hotel has 41 rooms. The spa offers plenty of pampering options, as well as outdoor hot tubs. The Conservatory Restaurant has garden views and dishes such as roast breast of Gressingham duck or pan-fried halibut. Lighter meals and snacks are served in the Terrace Bar. The hotel is situated roughly halfway between Battle and Hastings.

Crowhurst Park

Telham Lane, off Hastings Road, TN33 0SL (01424 773344, www.crowhurstpark.co.uk). Rates £295-£1,175 per week.
Forty-nine spacious pine lodges, all with leafy views, make up this village of holiday homes in the grounds of Crowhurst Park. The Manor House holds a clubhouse, where food, drink and a family lounge are offered. There's an indoor pool, which is complemented by a sauna, steam room, jacuzzi and children's paddling pool.

Things to do

HIGH WEALD

Carr Taylor Vineyard

Wheel Lane, Westfield, TN35 4SG (01424 752501, www.carr-taylor.co.uk). Open 10am-5pm daily. Tours £1.50; free-£1.25 reductions.
One of the largest English vineyards, with a wide range of wines and accompanying accolades. Tours (self-guided) can be taken at any time, although it's best to call ahead. The shop sells the full range of the vineyard's wine – its sparkling whites are excellent. Carr Taylor also recently introduced the first wine expressly blended to go with curry. Other cordials, brews and chutneys can be found in the shop.

Sedlescombe Vineyard

Hawkhurst Road, Cripps Corner, Robertsbridge, TN32 5SA (01580 830715, www.englishorganic wine.co.uk). Open Easter-Christmas 10.30am-5.30pm daily. Jan-Mar noon-dusk Sat, Sun. Guided tours by appointment.
The oldest vineyard in Britain offers a wine tasting and woodland nature trail tour. After a walk around the area, the tour moves to the winery to learn about organic wine and cider making. The self-guided trail and tasting costs £6.

Virgin Balloon Flights

01952 212750, www.virginballoonflights.co.uk. Prices from £99.
One of the most enduing images of Bodiam Castle is one with the sky above dotted with hot air balloons. Virgin Balloon Flights has a number of launch sites near Bodiam (plus three more in Kent and one each in East and West Sussex).

Places to visit

BATTLE

1066 Battle of Hastings, Abbey & Battlefield ★
Battle, TN33 0AD (01424 775705, www.english-heritage.org.uk/1066). Open Apr-Sept 10am-6pm daily. Oct-Mar 10am-4pm daily. Admission £7; £3.50-£6 reductions; £17.50 family.
William the Conqueror marked his victory by establishing the abbey, and despite Henry VIII's best efforts to destroy it during the Dissolution of the Monasteries, it remains a beautiful and spiritual experience. Set amid well-tended leafy grounds on Senlac Hill, the abbey looks out across the fields where the English and Norman armies fought the Battle of Hastings in 1066. The grassy battlefield comes to life with an informative audio tour. The longest walk around the site lasts under 40 minutes, and the audio accompaniment takes you step by step through the conflict. A visitor centre gives further information on the site; there's a discovery room for children.

Battle Museum
The Almonry, High Street, TN33 0EA (01424 775955, www.battlemuseum.org.uk). Open Apr-Oct 10am-4.30pm Mon-Sat. Admission £1; free reductions.
This small-scale museum focuses on local history, covers many centuries and touches on archaeology, industries (iron, leather and gunpowder), decorative art, costume and textiles.

Yesterday's World
89-90 High Street, TN33 0AQ (01424 777226, www.yesterdaysworld.co.uk). Open Apr-Sept 9.30am-5pm daily. Oct-Mar 10am-4pm daily. Admission £7; £5-£6 reductions.
This quaint attraction has around 20 reconstructions of shops and rooms from the past, including a Victorian playroom and a wartime kitchen. Nosy folk will enjoy a letter by Queen Elizabeth II about her first meeting with Prince Philip. The pretty garden is a plus, and the tearoom serves an excellent cream tea.

HIGH WEALD

Bodiam Castle ★
Bodiam, nr Robertsbridge, TN32 5UA (01580 830196, www.nationaltrust.org.uk/bodiamcastle). Open Feb-Oct 10.30am-5pm daily. Nov, Dec 11am-4pm Wed-Sun. Jan 11am-4pm Sat, Sun. Admission £6.40; £3.20 reductions; £17 family.
A castle fit for valiant knights and golden-haired princesses (from the outside anyway), Bodiam Castle rises majestically from its moat. Inside, the castle is a ruin, but visitors can nonetheless clamber up the stairs for views out across Sussex. The castle was built for Sir Edward Dalyngrygge in 1385 as a defence against the increasingly threatening French (who had sacked nearby Rye and Winchelsea in 1377). The only military action the castle saw was during the Civil War (1642-51), when the interior was gutted. It was then left to deteriorate until a local squire, John 'Mad Jack' Fuller, aquired it in 1828 for £3,000. However, it wasn't until Lord Curzon bought it in the early 1900s that extensive restoration was carried out. At certain

Bodiam Castle

days during school holidays children can try on armour, and there is also a Bodiam Bat Pack on sale featuring games and trails.

Giants of Brede
Waterworks Lane, Brede, TN31 6HG (01323 897310). Open 10am-4pm 1st Sat of the mth & bank hols. Admission free.
The water industry gets a historical going-over at this museum, which features lovingly restored, giant water pumping machinery dating back to the 1800s. The collection includes triple expansion and compound steam pumps – a 1940s Worthington Simpson engine is one of the highlights. Local water services have retained a selection of watery artefacts demonstrating the evolution of the industry. It's all located in a lovely part of the Brede Valley.

Great Dixter ★
Northiam, TN31 6PH (01797 252878, www.great dixter.co.uk). Open House Apr-Oct 2-5pm Tue-Sun & bank hols. Gardens Apr-Oct 11am-5pm Tue-Sun & bank hols. Admission House & gardens £8.70; £4.20 reductions. Gardens only £7.20; £3.70 reductions.
The family home of the late Christopher Lloyd, built in the 1400s and restored by Lutyens, has one of the largest timber framed halls in Britain. It is also home to a needlework collection of some note. Outside, however, is where the real glories lie: Lloyd and his head gardener Fergus Garret created an imaginative and diverse botanical wonderland. From the aptly

named Exotic Garden to the acclaimed Long Border, a dazzling array of plant life is on show, ranging from delicate meadow blooms and natural ponds to clipped topiary, subtropical plants and a formal pool. There's also a nursery, selling many of the plants on show in the garden.

King John's Garden
Sheepstreet Lane, Etchingham, TN19 7AZ (01580 819220, www.kingjohnsnursery.co.uk). Open Apr-Oct 10am-5pm Mon, Wed-Sun. Nov-Mar 10am-4pm Mon, Wed-Sun.
This romantic garden has ancient trees, water features, wild flowers, well-tended borders and scented roses. There's also a medieval barn to explore. In the centre of all the flowery goings-on is King John's Lodge – a listed Jacobean house (closed to the public).

Merriments Gardens
Hawkhurst Road, Hurst Green, TN19 7RA (01580 860666, www.merriments.co.uk). Open Apr-Sept 10am-5.30am Mon-Sat; 10.30am-5pm Sun. Admission £5; £2 reductions.
Colour takes centre stage here; from the vibrancy of the Hot Border and the Golden Border, to the cool tones of the Blue Gravel Garden, Merriments Gardens is a floral rainbow. Visit the Wild Area, designed specifically for wildlife – from birds and butterflies to bees and insects. There's a hide for bird-watching and, in the Wild Bird Care and Wildlife Centre, resident experts answer queries.

BEXHILL

Bexhill Museum
Egerton Road, TN39 3HL (01424 787950, www.bexhill museum.co.uk). Open Feb-mid Dec 10am-5pm Tue-Fri; 11am-5pm Sat, Sun. Admission £3; £2 reductions.
Get to grips with local history at this refurbished museum. From fossils and dinosaurs through to period costume and motor racing, the Bexhill Museum covers the events connected with this little seaside town. Key exhibits includes the original architectural model of the nearby modernist landmark, the De La Warr Pavilion. The museum also hosts temporary exhibitions, and runs a workshops and lectures programme.

De La Warr Pavilion ★
Marina, TN40 1DP (01424 229111, www.dlwp.co.uk). Open 10am-5pm Mon-Fri; 10am-6pm Sat, Sun.
Reopened in 2007 following an £8 million restoration project, Erich Mendelsohn and Serge Chermayeff's 1935 modernist masterpiece looks better than ever. This magnificent light-filled structure on the seafront came about thanks to the mayor, the 9th Earl De La Warr. He talked Bexhill Town Council into running an international competition for the design of a seaside pavilion that was to bring culture and entertainment to the region. The De La Warr Pavilion was the outcome.

It now houses a small but splendid permanent collection of classic design drawings, twin gallery spaces and a theatre, and runs a vibrant programme of exhibitions, music and comedy. The view from the first-floor balcony out to sea is wonderful.

Robertsbridge to Bodiam

'Nine years ago, as I was sitting in the George at Robertsbridge, drinking that port of theirs and staring at the fire, there arose in me a multitude of thoughts through which at last came floating a vision of the woods at home and of another place – the lake where the Arun rises.' So wrote Hilaire Belloc in *The Four Men: A Farrago* (1912), a fictional but still highly readable account of a four-day trek from Robertsbridge to South Harting in West Sussex.

The Robertsbridge and Salehurst that Belloc would have known at the beginning of the 20th century are little changed today – and you can still drink a glass of port by the George's large inglenook fireplace.

A settlement first sprung up in the area around a Cistercian abbey built in 1176 (the remains are on private land). In 1198, Richard I granted Robertsbridge a market charter and the town flourished. Many of the buildings on the High Street date back to the 14th and 15th centuries. The most notable example is the Seven Stars Inn (01580 880333, www.seven7stars.co.uk), built at the end of the 14th century and still standing strong, although the red brick base was added in the 19th century; it's said to be haunted. Beer comes from Harvey's, and food options run from toasties to Sunday roasts. At the end of the High Street, by the war memorial and some gorgeous Tudor Houses, is the George Inn (*see p167*). Built in 1714, it retains many original features and is the best place to eat in the village.

Take time to wander up and down the High Street, perhaps popping into the Old Saddlery Bookshop (56 High Street, 01580 880631, closed Wed and Sun), which specialises in second-hand and rare antique books. Heading downhill, just before the bridge that gives the town its name, is a traditional forge run by Mark Ripley (01580 880324, http://ripleyfireplaces.com), who produces fireplaces, wood burning stoves and even sculptures.

Just over the A21, coming out of Roberstbridge, is Salehurst, a tiny village mentioned in the Domesday Book. It's worth stopping to see the largest rural church in Sussex, the 13th-century St Mary the Virgin. Salehurst Halt (*see p167*) is a good local pub. (The parish records in Salehurst have a fine entry from 1610: 'Henry Turner, a profane drunkard, died excommunicate and was buried in ye highway to the terror of all drunkards').

There's a strong cricketing connection with Robertsbridge and Saleshurst (the word Salehurst is thought to mean 'willow wood' in Old Saxon). It's in this village that LJ Nicholls opened his cricket bat workshop in 1876, counting WG Grace among his customers. Nicholls later merged with Gray and Sons to become Gray-Nicholls, a leading manufacturer of cricket bats to this day. Another claim to fame is that the world's oldest music manuscript for the keyboard, written in 1360, was found in Robertsbridge. The Robertsbridge Codex, containing six pieces for organ, is now preserved in the British Library.

Great Dixter. See p162.

Curlew

The A21 continues to Hurst Green, Etchingham and the sumptuous Merriments Gardens (*see p163*) along the Kent border. Also worthy of note is the Assumption of Blessed Mary and St Nicholas church in Etchingham, thought to have the oldest brass weathervane in England. The church is also home to a large selection of misericords – small, carved shelves on which the monks leant when praying.

From Salehurst it's only three miles to the village of Bodiam. The village was built around its castle (*see p162*). It's a small place, but the Curlew restaurant (*see right*) has put the village on the culinary map. It's the evocative castle, however, that attracts most visitors.

Just south-east of Bodiam is Ewhurst Green, where it's worth stopping at the White Dog Inn (*see p167*) for a pint and the expansive views from the beer garden over the Rother Valley to Bodiam Castle.

Northiam to Westfield

Great Dixter (*see p162*) in Northiam, home to the late Christopher Lloyd, is a must for anyone interested in gardening. Surrounding the house (part 15th- and 16th-century, and part designed by Sir Edwin Lutyens) are wonderful gardens. There are meadow flowers, dazzlingly colourful mixed borders, yew topiary, natural ponds, a formal pool and beautiful exotic plants, all in perfect harmony.

Northiam is one of the larger villages in the area and has weatherboard houses characteristic of this area of the Weald. Elizabeth I dined on the village green during a tour of Sussex. The ancient oak under which she sheltered died recently, although the stump remains. Sir Winston Churchill visited the fields around Northiam in 1944, to give his final address to the troops of Southern Command before the D-Day invasion.

South again on the A28 and the Weald opens up, revealing stunning views all along the road down into the Brede Valley. The next village is Brede itself, home to the Giants of Brede (*see p162*) – huge Victorian pumping engines in an art deco building. Further along is the village of Westfield, and the excellent Wild Mushroom (*see p167*) restaurant. For a more down-to-earth drink, try the Old Courthouse (*see p167*). Also worth a look is the church of St John the Baptist. It passed into the care of Battle Abbey in 1100, along with a pit for the ordeal of trial by water (the innocent sank).

From here, Carr Taylor vineyard (*see p161*) lies west on Wheel Lane.

Where to eat & drink

Curlew ★
Junction Road, Bodiam, TN32 5UY (01580 861394, www.thecurlewrestaurant.co.uk). Lunch served noon-2.30pm, dinner served 6-9.30pm Wed-Sun.

De La Warr Pavilion. See p163.

Understated style greets visitors to the Curlew: muted browns, smoky slate walls and warm lighting make for a welcoming space. Roast haunch of venison with onion marmalade potato, brussels sprouts and butternut purée is typical of the modern British menu; the Earl Grey ice-cream is divine. Dishes arrive on an array of rustic boards, slates and metal dishes. In fine weather, diners have the option of a pristine fenced-in outdoor area. A Michelin star was awarded in 2011.

George Inn ★
High Street, Robertsbridge, TN32 5AW (01580 880315, www.thegeorgerobertsbridge.co.uk). Open 11am-11pm Tue-Sat; noon-8pm Sun. Lunch served noon-2.30pm Tue-Sat; noon-3pm Sun. Dinner served 6.30-9pm Tue-Sat.
This 18th-century coaching inn offers a friendly welcome and top-notch food, much of it sourced from within 30 miles of the pub. Regional wines and ales complement the inviting menu – favourites on which are tempura cod with chunky hand-cut chips, and the Sussex cream tea. Even the fruit juices are pressed from fruit grown in the area. There's a small bar by a large inglenook fireplace for drinkers. Have a look at the gallery dedicated to the pub's basset hound; he has pen pals around the world. The George also has four modern, luxuriously decorated rooms available for bed and breakfast (£90-£105 double incl breakfast).

Old Courthouse
Main Road, Westfield, TN35 4QE (01424 751603, www.oldcourthousepub.com). Open noon-11pm Mon-Sat, noon-10.30pm Sun. Food served noon-9pm daily.
This pub is known for its real ales and claims to have served more than 600 different ales since the current owners took over in 2004. It's also popular with walkers on the 1066 Country Walk path. With darts, shove ha'penny and billiards, it's a proper rural pub, with food to match (ham, eggs and chips, say, or sausage and mash).

Salehurst Halt
Church Lane, TN32 5PH (01580 880620, www.salehursthalt.co.uk). Open noon-3pm, 6-11pm Tue, Wed; noon-11pm Thur-Sun. Lunch served noon-2.30pm Tue-Sat; noon-3.30pm Sun. Dinner served 7-9.30pm Tue-Sat.
For a quiet pint or an appetising meal (steak and ale pie, roasts on Sundays) beside an open fire, this unpretentious country pub is lovely option. You'll find sofas, board games, real ales and friendly staff, plus the occasional music night to liven things up a little.

White Dog Inn
Village Street, Ewhurst Green, Robertsbridge, TN32 5TD (01580 830264, www.the-white-dog-inn.co.uk). Open 5.30-11pm Mon-Thur; 5.30pm-midnight Fri; noon-midnight Sat; noon-6pm Sun. Lunch served noon-2pm Sat; noon-3pm Sun. Dinner served 6.30-9pm Mon-Sat.
A cosy country pub, with real ales, a fire in winter, and a beer garden with flawless views over the Rother Valley up to Bodiam Castle. The food is good, with most of the produce sourced from the locality (Rye Bay cod in beer batter and chips, say, or braised lamb shank with mashed potatoes, carrots and a red wine jus). There are three neat double rooms at £75 a night.

Wild Mushroom ★
Woodgate House, Westfield Lane, Westfield, TN35 4SB (01424 751137, www.webbesrestaurants.co.uk). Lunch served noon-2.30pm Tue-Sun. Dinner served 7-9.30pm Tue-Sat.
This is the flagship restaurant of the small chain that includes the Fish Café in Rye and Webbe's at Rock-a-Nore in Hastings. Set in a converted farmhouse, the Wild Mushroom has a lovely interior and serves seasonal, contemporary dishes, such as pan-fried wood pigeon with bubble and squeak, beetroot, glazed onion and port jus. The gastronomic highlight of the immediate area.

Where to stay
The White Dog Inn and the George Inn (for both, *see left*) both have a few rooms. For more high-end accommodation, try nearby Hastings (*see p158*).

Slides Farm
Silverhill, Robertsbridge, TN32 5PA (01580 880106, www.slidesfarm.com). Rates £80-£90 double incl breakfast. No credit cards.
In a shiny new section of Slides Farm, guests can enjoy all mod cons in rural tranquillity. Two comfortable en suite rooms open on to beautiful gardens. Breakfast options include plenty of local produce (Salehurst bacon and sausages, Wealden smoked haddock), and if the weather is kind, you can eat on the terrace.

BEXHILL
Head west out of Hastings on the A259, and the next town of any size is Bexhill, just a few miles away. Quiet even by the standards of its neighbours (Eastbourne and Hastings), Bexhill is often derided as a retirement haven famous for nothing, and parts are indeed are rather shabby. But it does have modernist masterpiece the De La Warr Pavilion (*see p163*). It's a truly beautiful building that maximises its location on Bexhill's expansive, groyne-free seafront.

It was built at a time when wealthy visitors were coming to enjoy the resort, which was purpose-built in the mid 1800s by the 7th Earl De La Warr. He transformed Bexhill from a small village to a bustling resort, one which became even more popular after the railway arrived in 1847. The Sackville Hotel, completed in 1890, became the town's centrepiece accommodation (it's now serviced apartments). In 1902, Bexhill was granted a Royal Charter by Edward VII and for the first time, this was delivered in a new invention, the motor car. As part of the town's celebrations the 8th Earl of Bexhill planned car races along the seafront. It was the first car race in the country, and explains the signs on the way into the town: 'Bexhill: the Birthplace of British Motor Racing.' The Bexhill 100 Motoring Club (www.bexhill100.com) celebrates the fact with a classic and custom car show every August, and other events throughout the year.

Like many resorts along the south coast, Bexhill's appeal for holidaymakers declined

FOUR SEASIDE GALLERIES (AND A FESTIVAL)

De La Warr Pavilion

The De La Warr Pavilion in Bexhill was built in in 1935. It has always been dedicated to the arts, but since reopening in 2007, it has run a particularly fine programme of exhibitions. The building also has a versatile auditorium. *See p163.*

Jerwood Gallery

Opening in summer 2011, the Jerwood Gallery (www.jerwoodgallery.org) is planned to be the focal point for the vibrant arts community in Hastings and St Leonards-on-Sea. The building, by HAT Projects, is on the Stade and is in keeping with its surroundings. Funded by the Jerwood Foundation, this seaside gallery will become the permanent home of the Jerwood Art Collection. *See p151.*

Towner

Since moving in to its spectacular new home in 2009, Eastbourne's Towner has attracted a wide range of touring shows as well as commissioning some of its own. The striking building, by Rick Mather Architects, has won awards for its design and offers a flexible space. The permanent collection includes work by Eric Ravilious, Henry Moore and Tacita Dean. The view from the café over the South Downs is lovely, but the vast elevator is the talking point. *See p177.*

Turner Contemporary

As with the Jerwood in Hastings, it's hoped the arrival of a world-class art gallery will bolster the fortunes of Margate. Opening in April 2011, the Turner Contemporary is a landmark building on the seafront, designed by David Chipperfield Architects. The gallery will host all manner of workshops and classes for adults and children as well as high-profile exhibitions. *See p67.*

Folkestone Triennial

A lot of money has been invested in turning Folkestone into a creative centre, and it's almost there, with many public art pieces on show. Artists, attracted by low rents, are snapping up space around the town. The focal point is the Folkestone Triennial (next one in 2011), a festival that spans the whole town. In the 2008 Triennial, eight permanent art works were commissioned. Tracey Emin's *Baby Things* saw bronze baby clothes discarded around the town. The Folkestone Triennial Visitor Centre is open all year (56-58 Old High Street, 01303 854080, www.folkestone triennial.org.uk).

during the 1950s and '60s, and the De La Warr Pavilion lost its lustre too. But after a two-year closure, and £8 million pounds investment, the Pavilion reopened in 2007 as a contemporary art gallery and auditorium. Go regardless of the exhibition (although chances are it will be worthwhile) and enjoy the building and restaurant.

The seafront is the focal point for the Bexhill-on-Sea improvement scheme known as Next Wave. The idea is to regenerate the very beautiful – but very quiet – seafront with a new surface, shelters and play equipment. The town centre is pretty low-key, but good for bargain hunting in charity shops and antique dealers, especially along Sackville Road and Parkhurst Road.

Where to eat & drink

Bexhill has few pubs. Local haunt the Sportsman (15 Sackville Road, 01424 214214) will suffice for a pint, but most visitors will probably prefer a glass of wine or a Peroni at the De La Warr bar. Although pricey, it's the best place to eat in Bexhill. For ice-cream, go to Di Paolo's (5 Marina, 01424 210337) on the seafront.

De La Warr

Marina, TN40 1DP (01424 229111, www.dlwp.co.uk). Café Open 10am-5.30pm daily. Restaurant Lunch served noon-2.30pm Mon-Fri; noon-3pm Sat, Sun. Dinner served from 5.30pm before concerts; phone for details.
The first-floor restaurant at the De La Warr is light and airy. It has the feel of a café, but the food is a notch above. Dishes such as dressed Rye bay crab with toasted sourdough and mixed leaf salad are expertly assembled and professionally served. The café/bar (also on the first floor) serves coffee, cakes, sandwiches and light lunches and has free Wi-Fi. However inclement the weather, take a look at the sea view from the terrace.

Where to stay

If you're looking for a stylish hotel, try nearby Hastings (*see p158*).

Coast

58 Sea Road, TN40 1JP (01424 225260, www. coastbexhill.co.uk). Rates from £70-£90 double incl breakfast.
An Edwardian townhouse, with three smart en suite B&B rooms – Crimson, Teal and Sage. Crimson is the largest and suitable for a family stay. Affable owners, and the proximity of the beach (just a pebble's throw away), add to the appeal.

The Old Manse

18 Terminus Avenue, TN39 3LS (01424 216151, www.theoldmansebexhill.co.uk). Rates £75-£112 double incl breakfast.
The two rooms at this B&B are spacious and well-appointed. A first-rate breakfast – which runs from fruit salad to bacon and eggs – is served in the south-facing dining room, or, weather permitting, on the terrace outside.

Eastbourne & Around

Beachy Head, rising 530 feet out of the Channel with a candy-striped lighthouse at its foot, is one of the most iconic coastal views in Britain. As are the Seven Sisters, a series of chalk cliffs that eventually slump into the meandering Cuckmere River near Exceat. Inland from this formidable coastal frontier is Friston Forest – great for mountain biking – and the settlements of Litlington, Wilmington with its Long Man figure carved into the hillside, and Alfriston, surely one of England's loveliest villages.

Eastbourne is the largest town along this stretch. Once a fashionable Victorian resort, it's now a relaxed seaside town with a budding arts scene centred on the brand-new Towner art gallery. Eastbourne's location at the beginning, or end, of the 100-mile South Downs Way, also makes it a useful base for walkers. Just outside Eastbourne, Pevensey was the landing point for William the Conqueror and his army. Further inland is the historic village of Herstmonceux.

Homely and atmospheric country pubs can be found in hamlets and villages across the region, many serving top-quality Sussex produce; the county's lamb and fish enjoy particular renown.

PEVENSEY & HERSTMONCEUX

Pevensey

Pevensey is about seven miles west of Bexhill, via the A259. If arriving by train, the Eastbourne-Hastings line stops in the village.

Pevensey Castle (*see p176*) reigns over the town. The impressive walls and towers are Roman in origin; built in the third century on what was then a peninsula surrounded by salt marsh and sea (it's now a mile inland), this was one of the last Saxon Shore forts. Pevensey was where William the Conqueror's army landed in 1066, and a medieval castle was constructed within the Roman walls. The fortification was still being used up to World War II – Pevensey was earmarked by the Germans as a principal landing place in Operation Sealion. It's also frequented by ghost hunters. The paranormal, it seems, love Pevensey and there's at least enough wraiths for an interesting dinner party: the grey lady, the grey man, a little drummer boy, a hundred Roman soldiers, a black monk, a young girl and a dog – an enjoyable Saturday night ghost walk (*see p171*) can fill you in on details.

On the High Street, the 13th-century Pevensey Court House Museum (01323 733419, closed Oct-Apr) was used as the town hall and jail until 1886. The museum has recreated the courtroom and cells, and has a display of local history. Ghost nights are also held here. Even the Old Mint House antiques shop (01323 762337, www.minthouse.co.uk) has its own ghost. It's that of the mistress of Thomas Dight, who, upon finding her in bed with another man in 1586, cut out her tongue and let her bleed to death. The lover was roasted over a fire.

By the west entrance to the castle is the parish church of St Nicholas, one of the oldest Norman churches in the country, with the nave dating from

1205. It fell into disrepair as the port became marshland, and was even used as a cattle shed and smugglers' hideaway before being extensively restored in the late 19th century.

Pevensey Bay is a separate village by the beach, and popular with windsurfers and kitesurfers. The Pevensey Flats, north of the town, is fine walking territory.

Herstmonceux

The ancient village of Herstmonceux is about six miles inland from Pevensey. It's best known for its castle with attached science centre (*see p176*), but there are other places of interest, including some excellent pubs and restaurants. Its name is derived from the Anglo-Saxon word 'hyrst', meaning wooded hill, and the Monceux family, the 12th-century lords of the manor.

The village is known for its trugs (shallow baskets traditionally made from sweet chestnut). Trug making has been practised here for hundreds of years and is still very much alive. Stop off at the Truggery (Coopers Croft, www.truggery.co.uk, 01323 832314, closed Mon-Thur, Sun) to buy an example. The Sussex Trug is a sturdy little thing, useful for gardening or holding fruit.

Where to eat & drink

Of the three pubs in Pevensey, the most atmospheric is the Smugglers Inn (High Street, 01323 762112, www.smugglerspevensey.co.uk). It's been a pub since 1527 and has collected both trinkets and character over the years (and a ghost, of course). It gained its name in the 18th century, when it was a stopping point for the Groombridge Gang of tea smugglers. There's a piano should a singsong begin, plus jam sessions on Thursday nights and live bands

Pevensey Castle. See p169.

on Saturday nights. There's a large beer garden and playground, and appetising pub grub is served.

In Herstmonceux, Eastern Promise (Gardner Street, 01323 832533) Indian restaurants is well-regarded. The Brewers Arms (01323 832226) on the same street is a friendly locals' pub – a true community establishment. It's a Greene King pub, with two bars, open fires and a beer garden.

Lamb Inn
Wartling Road, Wartling, BN27 1RY (01323 832116, www.lambinnwartling.co.uk). Open 11am-3pm, 6-11pm Tue-Sat; noon-3pm Sun.

Lunch served noon-2.15pm Tue-Sun. Dinner served 7-9pm Tue-Sat.

With 500 years of experience, the Lamb Inn certainly knows a thing or two about serving weary travellers. Food is hearty, with dishes (lamb shank with rosemary mash; pie of the day) showcasing high-quality ingredients. Summer sees the patio and garden fill with those enjoying the view, while three open fires keep chilly evenings cosy. Wartling is about halfway between Pevensey and Herstmonceux.

Sundial
Gardner Street, Herstmonceux, BN27 4LA (01323 832217, www.sundialrestaurant.co.uk). Lunch served

Things to do

PEVENSEY & HERSTMONCEUX

Pevensey Ghost Walk
07740 828215, http://slaterjas.parks.officelive. com. Tours 7.30pm Sat. Rates £6; £3 reductions.
This 90-minute guided walk mixes the remarkable history of Pevensey with stories of paranormal activity. Honed over 17 years, it's great fun for both children and adults. Thre's no need to book, just turn up at the castle car park.

EASTBOURNE

Allchorn Pleasure Boats
Fishermans Green, Royal Parade, BN22 7AA (www. allchornpleasureboats.co.uk). Open Mar/Apr-Sept/ Oct; cruises usually hourly 10.30am-3.30pm daily. Tickets £9; £1-£6.50 reductions; £16-£31 family.
A 45-minute cruise around the coast is a great way to take in the area's top seaside attractions. You'll pass the Wish Tower, Holywell, Cow Gap and, finally, the soaring white cliffs of Beachy Head and its lighthouse. Allchorn Pleasure Boats has been zipping folk around on the water since 1861 – the live onboard commentary is packed with local knowledge.

Eastbourne Theatres
01323 412000, www.eastbournetheatres.co.uk.
Like seagulls and postcards, theatrical happenings are in good supply in Eastbourne. Eastbourne Theatres runs four venues: the Congress on Carlisle Road (a modern building with West End musicals, international ballets and large-scale productions); the Devonshire Park on Compton Street (an elegant Victorian theatre with dramas and comedy); the Winter Garden on Compton Street (also Victorian, with assorted events from music and comedy shows to tea dances; the Royal Hippodrome on Seaside Road (the oldest venue, dating from 1883, with a wholesome selection of music hall staples.

Spray Water Sports
Royal Parade, BN22 7LD (01323 417023, www.eastsussex.gov.uk/spray). Open all year; classes by appointment. Rates 2hr introductory sailing session £30.
Based on the beach at the eastern end of the seafront, opposite Princes Park, this is a great outfit that runs courses in all manner of watery activities, including sailing, powerboating, windsurfing and canoeing. All ages and levels of experience welcome.

Sussex Voyages
The Waterfront, Sovereign Harbour (0845 838 7114, www.sussexvoyages.co.uk). Open check website for sailing times. Rates £25 to Beachy Head & Seven Sisters.
Hop aboard an orange and black inflatable boat (capacity 12), and speed around the coast, past points of interest such as the Royal Sovereign Light Tower (six miles out at sea), and places of natural beauty such as Birling Gap and Beachy Head. Phone booking essential.

BEACHY HEAD, ALFRISTON & AROUND

Arlington Stadium
Arlington Road West, nr Hailsham, BN27 3RE (01323 841642, www.spedeworth.co.uk). Open varies; check website for fixtures. Admission £12; £6-£10 reductions.
Racing fanatics get thrills a-plenty at this motor sports stadium just west of Hailsham. Speedway motorbike racing and stock car racing are the mainstays, with fixtures throughout the year.

Discovering Fossils
www.discoveringfossils.co.uk. Public fossil hunts check website for dates. Rates £12; £6 reductions.
Discovering Fossils runs monthly hunts in various locations in Sussex, including Beachy Head and Peacehaven. They're great fun, especially for children. You might find fossilised plants, shells and seeds or – if you're really lucky – exotica such as turtle shells and sharks' teeth. Hard hats, eye protection, hammers and chisels are provided. Email events@ discoveringfossils.co.uk to book. You can also arrange a private fossil hunt (£150 for up to 20 people).

Seven Sisters Cycle Company
Granary Barn, Seven Sisters Country Park, Exceat, BN25 4AD (01323 870310, www.cuckmere-cycle. co.uk). Open Apr-Oct 10am-6pm daily. Nov-Mar 10am-4pm Tue-Sun. Rates £10/2hrs, £25/day.
Pick up sturdy cycles for some of the best mountain biking in the South-east. Although the roams aren't as developed as at Bedgebury (*see p124*) in Kent, this Forestry Commission site is more dramatic, with technical single-track for experts and wide-open fire roads for families. A popular ride is along the flat path beside the Cuckmere to the sea.

noon-2pm Tue-Sat; noon-2.30pm Sun. Dinner served
7-10pm Tue-Sat.
This smart but relaxed French restaurant, set in a timber-framed building, serves accomplished seasonal dishes: roast rack of lamb with basmati rice, glazed winter vegetables and a herb and beetroot jus, or pan-fried wild seabass fillet with lobster ravioli and lobster sauce. Desserts are equally extravagant. Three courses from the à la carte menu cost £40, but there's also a cheaper 'fine dining' menu for £22 (£25 Saturday night).

White Horse Inn

Bodle Street Green, BN27 4RE (01323 833243, www.whitehorsefolk.co.uk). Open 11am-3pm, 6-11pm Tue-Sat; noon-3pm, 7-11pm Sun. Lunch served noon-2pm Tue-Sun. Dinner served 7-9pm Tue-Sat.
This unassuming pub in Bodle Street Green, just north of Herstmonceux, is well known for its Monday night folk club, which has been running for almost 20 years. Although it's mostly open mic, the quality is high and touring acts are booked at least once a month. Food is reasonable, but the beer is better – as you'd expect from a folky pub.

Where to stay

Most people choose to stay in Eastbourne. But there are some B&Bs in the area, including 16th-century Butlers Farmhouse (Butlers Lane, 01323 833770, www.butlersfarmhouse.yolasite.com) with its three rooms, great views over the Downs and a swimming pool. The most upmarket hotel in the area is the five-star Wartling Place Country House (Wartling, 01323 832590, www.wartlingplace.co.uk) in a Georgian Grade II-listed building. There are three 'deluxe' rooms, and two 'premier' rooms with four-poster beds. The decor is traditional and makes use of old furniture, but the rooms are all light and airy. Each has a LCD TV, iPod dock, DAB radio and DVD players. There's also a cottage which sleeps four people.

EASTBOURNE

Eastbourne, genteel Eastbourne. With its Victorian hotels, immaculate flower beds, family-packed beaches and busy pier, Eastbourne viewed from the seafront looks like a town frozen in time. The Allchorn family still runs pleasure boats (*see p171*) from the promenade to Beachy Head lighthouse, as they have done for more than 150 years; military brass bands still play on the bandstand several nights a week throughout summer (when the number of concerts was cut, the local paper was inundated with complaints); Alan Ayckbourn farces still sell out in the theatres; and lawn tennis is still played at Devonshire Park, as it has been since 1841.

But behind the clichés is a town reinventing itself – albeit slowly. Towner (*see p177*), a new £8.5 million art gallery designed by Rick Mather, has wowed architecture critics with a contemporary space that makes as much of the view outside as the work within. Art critics have been equally impressed with its innovative, and occasionally risqué, exhibitions – Robert Mapplethorpe in Eastbourne? Shock! horror!

Another major development is Sovereign Harbour, two miles east of town. The building spree has slowed down to give time for the amenities to catch up, but yacht owners and second-homers have snapped up many of the new harbour apartments, and the Waterfront complex (www.eastbourneharbour.com) contains a handful of shops and eating places.

Eastbourne as we know it today owes its existence largely to the 7th Duke of Devonshire, William Cavendish, Earl of Burlington, who oversaw much of its development in the second half of the 19th century. If Brighton was the 'Queen of Watering Places', Eastbourne was to be the 'Empress of Watering Places' (a later dignitary called it 'Brighton without the chewing gum'). It grew from the amalgamation of the four villages of Bourne (now the Old Town), Southbourne (Town Hall area), Sea House (east of the pier) and Meads. The train arrived in 1849, and Eastbourne's reputation as an upmarket bathing place was assured.

The oldest area is around Motcombe, a ten-minute stroll inland (and uphill) from the train station, along Upperton Road. Fork left at the Goffs, which becomes High Street, where you'll find the fabulous Lamb Inn (*see p179*). The timber-framed building is of Tudor origin, although parts date from the 12th century – which is when St Mary's Church (01323 725722, www.stmaryseastbourne.com) next door was built. It was extended in the 14th and 19th centuries, and is said to have tunnels that lead to the pub. Across the road is large and pleasant Gildredge Park.

Little Chelsea

Most visitors arrive at the rail station on Terminus Road in the pedestrianised town centre. It could be anywhere in England, with its Arndale Centre, charity shops and high-street outlets. Gildredge Road leads towards the seafront, but a more interesting route heads past the library and along Grove Road into an area called, rather ambitiously, Little Chelsea.

Charity shops have taken over several premises – the British Red Cross shop at 20 Grove Road was named by *Vogue* as one of the best places in the country to find a designer bargain – but there remain some good independent shops. Camilla's Bookshop (no 57, 01323 736001, www.camillasbookshop. com, closed Sun) has an astonishing number of second-hand and antiquarian titles over three floors. You could, perhaps, pick up a biography of Antarctic explorer Ernest Shackleton. (He lived at 14 Milnthorpe Road in Meads. A blue plaque identifies this house – and also Cyril Connolly's at 48 St John's Road.) Or perhaps a copy of the *Communist Manifesto* – not ideal holiday reading, granted, but Karl Marx and Friedrich Engels both visited the town while writing it (Engels loved the South Downs so much, he had his ashes sprinkled over Beachy Head). Or maybe something by George Orwell, who wrote *Animal Farm* in Eastbourne and name-checked his local pub, the Red Lion in Willingdon, in the book.

At the Town Hall, a grand red-brick construction built in 1886 to mark the incorporation of

Eastbourne

Eastbourne, turn left down South Street. On the corner is Bibendum (*see p175*), a good evening pub with a restaurant area. Further down is the unassuming Dolphin (*see p175*), which, after a remarkable reinvention, has become one of Eastbourne's best pubs. At 27 South Street, Garnish Interiors (01323 738866, closed Mon, Sun) stocks classic and contemporary furniture and furnishings. Penelope's Portmanteau (no.47, 01323 649982, www.penelopesportmanteau.com) specialises in vintage jewellery, handbags and accessories. Henry Paddon (no.113, 01323 411887, www.henrypaddon.com, closed Mon, Sun) is a contemporary gallery with a wide selection of work by more than 60 artists.

Turn right into Cornfield Terrace to find the 'How We Lived Then' Museum of Shops (no.20, 01323 737143, closed Jan-mid Feb), which displays a vast collection of everyday items from the last 200 years in a high-street setting. The excellent Emma Mason Gallery (no.3, 01323 727545, www.emma mason.co.uk, closed Mon-Wed, Sun) specialises in original work by British printmakers, new and old.

At the junction with Compton Street is the Devonshire Park Theatre. It held its first performance on 4 June 1884 and has been running non-stop since – not even heavy bombing in World War II halted the show. Head right on Compton Street to the Winter Garden; designed as a miniature Crystal Palace in 1875, it's still used as a concert hall and ballroom. Most of Eastbourne's major events, such as the Beer Festival (www.eastbourne beerfestival.co.uk) in October, are held here, as well as notable monthly comedy nights, Screaming Blue Murder, and occasional rock gigs by the likes of Blur and Beirut. Next door is the rather ugly Congress Theatre, home to mainstream touring productions. There's something almost every evening – but it's

as likely to be a Queen tribute act as comedian Eddie Izzard (who went to school in Eastbourne). Adjacent is the brand-new Towner art gallery (*see p177*).

From here, it's a short hop down Carlisle Road to the bandstand and the sea, past Favoloso's ice-cream parlour, little changed from the 1950s, and the Cavalier, a contender for the Britain's quirkiest pub – say hello to Bilbo the giant fish in the tank.

The seafront

By any resort's standards, Eastbourne's seafront is glorious. The seafront promenade is three and a half miles long; you can walk from Sovereign Harbour in the east all the way to Holywell, the westernmost point in Meads village.

If you stand at the foot of Carlisle Road, you can see to the west (right) the Wish Tower, one of the Martello towers that were built all along the south coast to contain the threat from Napoleonic invasion. To the east is the blue-domed art deco bandstand, where brass bands still play *Those Magnificent Men in Their Flying Machines* most days throughout the summer, and the pier. On a clear day, Hastings, and occasionally Dungeness in Kent, are visible. The pier contains a large amusement arcade, chip shop, kiosks, a pub and a nightclub. At its tip, anglers cast for mackerel, and a speedboat offers soggy rides out to sea. The most notable attraction is the Camera Obscura, which opened with the pier in 1870. By the entrance to the pier are the extravagant floral displays of the Carpet Gardens (geraniums lined up with military precision).

Further east is the Redoubt Fortress & Military Museum (*see p177*) and Treasure Island adventure park (*see p177*). Just beyond the playground is a row of fishermen's net huts, many still used for their original purpose. There's also the lifeboat station and an excellent fishmonger, Southern Head (net shop 6, 01323 646366, www.southernhead fishing.com, closed Mon). The bizarre crennellated structure is a water treatment plant.

Back at the Wish Tower, you'll find the Lifeboat Museum (www.eastbournernli.org.uk, closed Mon-Fri Jan, Feb). It's an even more pleasant walk in this direction, with the promenade running on two levels. The long green expanse of the Western Lawns, once popular with parading Georgians, is now the focal point for Eastbourne's flagship event, the Airbourne air show in August. The huge white building facing the grass is Eastbourne's most sumptuous hotel, the Grand (see p179). Behind the hotel is a small parade of shops, including Cooden Cellars (14 Grand Hotel Buildings, 01323 649663, www. coodencellars.co.uk, closed Sun), an excellent independent wine merchant.

At the end of the promenade is Holywell, where there's a tearoom and the beginning of the chalk cliffs that work their way up to Beachy Head. Holywell Road leads into Meads, Eastbourne's upmarket residential district. On Meads Street, you'll find the superb Village Butcher (no.52, 01323 732591, www.villagebutcher.co.uk, closed Mon, Sun), the Black Cat Tea Rooms (no.50, 01323 646590, closed Sun) and the Ship Inn (see p179), a delightful pub with Eastbourne's best beer garden. From here, it's a 15-minute walk back to the town centre.

There's a pebble beach along the entire seafront, with a lifeguard station between the Wish Tower and the bandstand (the recommended place for bathing with children). Groynes provide useful windbreaks. At low tide, sand is revealed and you can walk out for some distance. Head towards Holywell to find some excellent rock pools where you can hunt for mussels, crabs and even lobsters. Barbecues are allowed east of the pier only. Beach huts can be hired by the week from Eastbourne Council, though the majority are long-term annual rentals.

Where to eat & drink

Eastbourne has a long way to go before it is considered a culinary leader. Don't be deterred by the bland and rather dismal chain pubs and soulless watering holes in the centre; it does have a smattering of jolly pubs that are more than acceptable for an evening meal. For fish and chips, Qualisea (189 Terminus Road, 01323 725203) is large and always busy.

Beachhouse ★

Lower promenade, between Wish Tower & bandstand (07526 930625, www.thegreenhousebar.com). Open 10am-dusk daily. Lunch served Summer noon-3pm daily. No credit cards.
When the council finally allowed a couple of bars to open along the seafront, many proprietors clamoured for the slots. The Beachhouse is under the same ownership as the Greenhouse (see right), and has a similarly relaxed and professional vibe. The prime location means the outside decking is packed in summer (to breaking point during the Airbourne festival), but it's also open in winter on all but

Eastbourne beach

the rainiest of days. Food (summer only) includes pastries baked on the premises daily, salads, sandwiches and hot dishes such as fish cakes.

Bibendum

1 Grange Road, BN21 4EU (01323 735363, www.bibendum-eastbourne.co.uk). Open 11am-11pm Mon-Thur; 11am-12.30am Fri, Sat; noon-10.30pm Sun. Lunch served noon-3pm Mon-Sat; noon-7pm Sun. Dinner served 6-9.45pm Mon-Sat.
This wine bar and restaurant is slightly outside the centre, opposite the Town Hall. It's upped its game in recent years, and is a good choice for a daytime coffee or an evening meal. Wraparound windows fill the restaurant with light, and the pavement seating area is packed in sunny weather. The straightforward menu is well executed; the Moroccan-spiced lamb shank with dates, herbs and spices is particularly tasty.

Dolphin

14 South Street, BN21 4XF (01323 746622). Open 11am-11pm Mon-Sat; noon-10pm Sun. Lunch served noon-2.30pm Mon-Fri; noon-3pm Sat. Dinner served 6-9pm Mon-Fri; 5-9pm Sat. Food served noon-9pm Sun.
The ever-popular Dolphin does what decent British pubs do best, with its open fire, slouchy sofas, hearty food and lots of beer. Arrive early to nab a seat in the lively front bar, or one of the sofas or dining tables in the spacious rear room. The burgers are rated highly by locals. The only shame is that outdoor space is limited to a little patio.

Greenhouse

10 Station Street, BN21 4RG (01323 738228, www.thegreenhousebar.com). Open 11am-11.30pm Mon-Thur; 11am-2am Fri, Sat; 6-11.30pm Sun. Lunch served noon-2.30pm Mon-Sat.
This well-established wine bar is the venue of choice for Eastbourne's middle-class punters. Set on a small

SUSSEX

Sharnfold Farm

PEVENSEY & HERSTMONCEUX

Herstmonceux Castle & Observatory Science Centre

Herstmonceux, BN27 1RN.
Castle (01323 834444, www.herstmonceux-castle.com). Open Mid Apr-Oct 10am-6pm daily.
Admission Gardens, grounds & Science Centre
£12.50; £8-£10 reductions; £37.70 family.
Gardens & grounds £6; £3-£4.95 reductions;
£14 family. Castle tour £2.50; free-£1 reductions.
Observatory Science Centre (01323 832731,
www.the-observatory.org). Open Apr-Sept 10am-6pm daily. Feb, Mar, Oct, Nov 10am-5pm daily
(and some wkds Jan, Dec). Admission £7.80;
free-£6.10; £24.10-£27.45 family.
Herstmonceux Castle isn't really a castle, but
it's certainly impressive with its crenellated brick
turrets, leaded windows and wide moat on one side.
Constructed in the mid 15th century, it had fallen into
ruin by the early 20th century when it was rebuilt by
Lt Col Claude Lowther. The surroundings are lovely,
with formal gardens that include an Elizabethan
garden and herb and rose beds, plus woodland trails,
peacocks and a lake. England's Medieval Festival
(www.mgel.com) is held here on the August bank
holiday weekend, should you fancy a spot of jousting
or bird of prey displays.
   The grounds also contain the Observatory Science
Centre, focusing on space and astronomy (the site
belonged to the Greenwich Royal Observatory from
the 1940s to the late '80s). Large-scale interactive
exhibits dotted about the Discovery Park explain
force, movement and water power, while the six
green domes house renovated telescopes; check
the website open evenings and star-gazing courses.

Pevensey Castle

Castle Road, Pevensey, BN24 5LE (01323 762604,
www.englishheritage.org.uk). Open Apr-Sept 10am-6pm daily. Oct 10am-4pm daily. Nov-Mar 10am-4pm
Sat, Sun. Admission £4.50; £2.30-£3.80 reductions;
£11.30 family.

Within the Roman walls of Pevensey Castle are the
ruins of a medieval castle, a major stronghold for
years after the Norman Conquest. It survived sieges
by William Rufus in the rebellion of 1088, during the
civil war known as the Anarchy between 1135 and
1141, and again in 1264 when Simon de Montfort
attacked Henry III's army, who were taking refuge in
the castle. You have to pay to enter the medieval part,
where there's an exhibition, but the grounds are free
and open all year around.

Sharnfold Farm

Hailsham Road, Stone Cross, Pevensey, BN24 5BU
(01323 768490, www.sharnfoldfarm.co.uk). Open
9.30am-5pm daily.
The PYO farm has a big range of soft fruit and veg
(including broad beans, sweetcorn and squashes)
available between April and October. There's also a
well-stocked farm shop, a café, a play area, a fishing
lake (£7 day ticket) and a farm animals trail.

EASTBOURNE

Eastbourne Miniature Steam Railway

Lottbridge Drove, BN23 6QJ (01323 520229,
www.emsr.co.uk). Open Mar-Sept 10am-5pm daily.
Oct 10am-5pm Sat, Sun. Fares £4.85; £4.35
reductions; £17.50 family.
Feel like Gulliver at this family attraction, where trains
shrunk to one-eighth of normal size wind their way for
almost a mile through a pretty country park, with
passengers perched atop the carriages.

Fort Fun

Royal Parade, BN22 7LQ (01323 642833, www.fortfun.
co.uk). Open June-Oct 11am-5pm Sat, Sun & school
hols. Admission prices vary; check website for details.
Fort Fun offers seafront entertainment for energetic
offspring, both indoors and out. The newest attraction
is the Aqua Splash water park (summer only) with
slides, tunnels and sprinklers. Rocky's Adventure
Land is a spacious indoor soft play zone, with a
smaller area for under-fives. There are also gentle
fairground rides such as a carousel and teacups.

SUSSEX

Redoubt Fortress & Military Museum
*Royal Parade, BN22 7AQ (01323 410300,
www.eastbournemuseums.co.uk). Open Apr-Nov
10am-5pm Tue-Sun. Admission £4; £2-£3 reductions.*
After standing guard over Eastbourne's pebbly strip of
coastline for nearly 200 years, the Redoubt Fortress
is now a museum of military paraphernalia, including
weaponry, uniforms and medals. Sections include the
Royal Sussex Regimental collection, and the Queen's
Royal Irish Hussars collection, featuring a Desert
Rat uniform worn at the Battle of El Alamein in 1942.
Opening times change from year to year, so it's
worth calling ahead to check.

Towner ★
*Devonshire Park, College Road, BN21 4JJ (01323
415470, www.townereastbourne.org.uk). Open
10am-5pm Tue-Sun. Admission free. Special
exhibition prices vary.*
The crowning glory of Eastbourne's cultural offerings,
this gleaming white building is a widely acclaimed
addition to the town. The gallery started life in the
1920s, when local alderman John Chisholm Towner
bequeathed 22 paintings to the town, to form the
basis of a public art collection. Originally displayed
in a Georgian building in the Old Town, the collection
grew steadily (it's now around 4,000 pieces) and a
new home was needed; Towner opened in spring
2009. The exterior is impressive enough, but the
huge interior is spectacular: high ceilings, white
walls and light pouring in through vast windows.
As well as displaying a rotating selection from the
original collection, the gallery hosts temporary
exhibitions, while the views of the South Downs
changing season by season from the main exhibition
floor and the café are a permanently stunning feature.
Look out for work by Eric Ravilious. Having studied
and taught at Eastbourne School of Art, the artist's
work is a key element of the collection, and includes
everything from woodcuts to London Transport posters
and Wedgewood ceramics.

Treasure Island
*Royal Parade, BN22 7AA (01323 411077, www.
treasure-island.info). Open Apr-Sept 10am-6pm daily.
Admission £5 children; £2.50 adults. No credit cards.*
A swashbuckling time is to be had at Treasure Island, a
pirate-themed seafront park ten-minutes' walk east of
the pier. Little ones run riot in the Little Buckaneers
indoor soft play area, while older kids climb the rigging
in Long John Silver's Shipwreck adventure playground.
The whole family can play on the crazy golf course, and
when the Sunshine Coast is living up to its nickname,
cool down at the Splash Lagoon, a grassy park with a
paddling pool.

BEACHY HEAD, ALFRISTON & AROUND

Alfriston Clergy House
*The Tye, Alfriston, BN26 5TL (01323 870001, www.
nationaltrust.org.uk/main/w-alfristonclergyhouse).
Open Aug 10.30am-5pm Mon-Wed, Fri-Sun.Mid Mar-
July, Sept, Oct 10.30am-5pm Mon-Wed, Sat, Sun.
Nov-mid Dec, end Feb-mid Mar 11am-4pm Mon-Wed,
Sat, Sun. Admission £4.50; £2.30 reductions;
£11.30 family.*
Before the National Trust started amassing vast
stately homes with manicured acres, its first ever
property, acquired in 1896, was this modest 14th-
century thatched house. Initially a farmer's home, the
building retains much of its original charms, including
a floor made from chalk. The small garden, designed
by horticulturist, artist and gardener Graham Stuart
Thomas, offers views across the Cuckmere River.

Drusillas Park
*Alfriston Road, Alfriston, BN26 5QS (01323 874100,
www.drusillas.co.uk). Open Summer 10am-5pm daily.
Winter 10am-4pm daily. Admission £11.30-£14.30;
£10-£13.80 reductions; £43.20-£55.20 family.*
This furry-themed fun park is home to entertaining
creatures including meerkats, otters, monkeys, lemurs,
penguins, prairie dogs, beavers, bats, crocodiles and
snakes, plus more familiar English farmyard animals.

Towner

Drusillas Park. See p177.

Those keen to get involved can spend a day shadowing a keeper (£130-£140). Drusillas also has numerous play areas, including Eden's Eye, a new interactive maze, and Amazon Adventure, a soft play jungle.

Filching Manor & Campbell Circuit
Jevington Road, nr Polegate, BN26 5QA (01323 487838, www.campbellcircuit.co.uk). Open 1.30pm-4pm Wed-Fri; 9am-4pm Sat, Sun. Rates £30/30mins.
The Campbell Circuit is a 650-metre go-kart track, with enough twists and turns to satisfy wannabe racing drivers and vehicles that can go up to 50mph. The track is named after Sir Malcolm Campbell, and the motor museum here includes his speed record-breaking boat, Bluebird 3, as well as a 1907 Corbin Racer, several Bugatti cars, and an 1898 Orient Express. The museum is open only to pre-arranged group bookings, with prices starting at £100.

Knockhatch Adventure Park
Off the A22, nr Hailsham, BN27 3PR (01323 442051, www.knockhatch.com). Open times vary; check website for details. Admission off-peak free-£5 children; £4 adults; £14 family.
Rides, animals, birds of prey, a climbing wall and a boating lake are some of the elements that make up this countryside adventure park. Activities are tailored for all ages, with go-karting for bigger kids and adults, and a new indoor soft play centre for youngsters. Knockhatch also has a ski and snowboard centre, with a 110-metre dry ski slope and two nursery slopes.

Long Man of Wilmington
Windover Hill, Wilmington (www.sussexpast.co.uk). The 235-foot high Long Man of Wilmington, perfectly proportioned and holding two staffs, has confused historians for hundreds of years. No one knows exactly why the giant outline, cut out of the South Downs turf, exists. One theory is that it was created by a monk at a nearby priory and dates from the 11th to 15th centuries, or perhaps even earlier – similar motifs have been found on fourth-century Saxon helmets. Or perhaps he's an 18th-century folly. Whatever the truth, the giant figure is certainly worth admiring: he's situated six miles north-west of Eastbourne, off the A27 (Lewes Road) – signposts mark the way.

Michelham Priory & Gardens
Upper Dicker, BN27 3QS (01323 844224, www. sussexpast.co.uk). Open Aug 10.30am-5.30pm daily. Apr-July, Sept 10.30am-5pm Tue-Sun. Mar, Oct 10.30am-4.30pm Tue-Sun. Admission £7; £3.80-£6 reductions; £18.40 family.
Both the function and looks of Michelham Priory have changed substantially over the years, and today it's a montage of the ages. Founded as an Augustinian priory in 1229 and boasting England's longest medieval water-filled moat, it was ripped from its ecclesiastical roots during the Dissolution and transformed into a substantial country home. The house contains a fascinating mix of tapestries and furnishings from throughout its history. Outside, there's a restored watermill (visitors can watch it operating and buy flour), a garden sculpture trail, a replica Iron Age roundhouse and a blacksmith's forge. On Saturday afternoons you might find longbowmen in medieval regalia practising on the lawn behind the house. The priory is about a 20-minute drive north of Eastbourne.

Seven Sisters Sheep Centre
Gilberts Drive, East Dean, BN20 0AA (01323 423302, www.sheepcentre.co.uk). Open Mar-early May, July-Sept 2-5pm Mon-Fri; 10am-5pm Sat, Sun & school hols. Admission £5; £4-£4.50 reductions; £17 family. No credit cards.
Lambing continues from March to early May here. If you're feeling broody, you can bottle-feed a newborn, albeit a woolly one. There's never a shortage of mouths to feed: the centre has 300 ewes and more than 40 breeds, including rare and traditional breeds that are no longer used in modern farming. From July to September, you can shear or milk a sheep, weave wool or make cheese. If you tire of following the flock, take a tractor ride or feed the chicks, pigs, goats and rabbits.

SUSSEX

backstreet (Printers, *see below*, is next door), it occupies a basement, with a covered patio at ground level – a pleasant spot in summer – that gives the bar its name. Seating is at booths and tall tables with stools, but it's standing room only on Friday and Saturday nights. There are good own-made burgers and upmarket snacks at lunchtime, and service is excellent. The owner also runs the Beachhouse (*see p175*).

Lamb Inn ★

36 High Street, BN21 1HH (01323 720545). Open 11am-11pm Mon-Thur, Sun; 11am-midnight Fri, Sat. Lunch served noon-3pm, dinner served 6-9pm daily.
Eastbourne's oldest inn (parts date from 1180) is a ten-minute walk from the train station, up in the old town next to similarly aged St Mary's church, with the Downs rolling off into the distance. Wooden tables, low ceilings and wine-red furnishings within the wonky, timber-framed building make for a snug evening. Food can be hit or miss, but the beers are good; it's a Harveys pub. The Lamb Folk Club (www.lambfolkclub.freeuk.com) meets upstairs on the first and third Wednesday of the month, and attracts some big names. The Lamb Theatre group (www.thelambtheatre.co.uk) is also based here.

Printers

12 Station Street, BN21 4RG (01323 430880, www.printersbarbrasserie.co.uk). Open 11am-11pm Mon-Sat; noon-6pm Sun. Food served noon-10pm Mon-Sat; noon-6pm Sun.
A former printing shop on narrow Station Street is now a rustic and relaxed bar-brasserie. The menu isn't ground-breaking – think fajitas, burgers, pizza and pasta dishes – but it's tasty, filling and fairly priced. Handy if you're doing some shopping too.

Ship Inn

33-35 Meads Street, BN20 7RH (01323 733815). Open 11am-11pm Mon-Sat; 11am-10.30pm Sun. Lunch served noon-2.30pm, dinner served 6-9.30pm Mon-Thur. Food served noon-9.30pm Fri, Sat; noon-8.30pm Sun.
The Ship's slightly out-of-the-way location in Meads means it's a proper locals' pub. Food is decent pub grub; what makes the Ship stand out from the rest is its fantastic beer garden. When the sun shines and the barbecue sizzles amid the greenery, there are few better places to be in Eastbourne. There's also a popular quiz night on Sunday.

Where to stay

For a modest-sized town, Eastbourne has plentiful accommodation. B&Bs line the seafront and adjoining roads, while Victorian gems such as the five-star Grand Hotel (*see right*) and the reliable Devonshire Park Hotel (*see right*) evoke the town's heyday. For a traditional B&B near the town centre, try the Manse (7 Dittons Road, 01323 737851, www.themansebandb.co.uk). An Arts and Crafts-style house built in 1906, it has three comfortable double bedrooms, all en suite. It's not just floral bedspreads and doilies, however – newer spots such as the Waterside (*see p180*) and the Big Sleep (*see right*) provide as contemporary a stay as you're likely to find anywhere.

The tourist office (0871 663 0031, www.visit eastbourne.com) on Cornfield Road, opposite Santander bank, has a hotel booking service.

Big Sleep Hotel

King Edward's Parade, BN21 4EB (01323 722676, www.thebigsleephotel.com). Rates £35-£79 double incl breakfast.
This affordable, high-style seafront stay is a compact bolthole for those who like their hotels awash with the contemporary – fittingly, it's located near the Towner (*see p177*). The 50 en suite rooms come in all sizes from singles to family rooms. Mixing white, muted tones and blocks of pink and blue, with boldly patterned wallpaper, they resemble a series of doodles from an Apple Mac sketchpad. All come with flatscreen TVs, and guests have access to a games rooms with pool, table tennis and darts. There are also branches in Cheltenham and Cardiff.

Devonshire Park Hotel

Carlisle Road, BN21 4JR (01323 728144, www. devonshire-park-hotel.co.uk). Rates £80-£140 double incl breakfast.
This Victorian building in Eastbourne's theatre district, offerers mid-priced accommodation in a convenient location. The 29 rooms and six suites are simple and functional, though they do have iPod docs, flatscreen TVs and DAB radios. Friendly service plus a bar and restaurant make this a thoroughly pleasant place to stay, but with seating on the front lawn and the beach a few minutes' stroll away, perhaps the real highlights are outside rather than within.

Eastbourne Youth Hostel

East Dean Road, BN20 8ES (0845 371 9316, www.yha.org.uk). Rates £14-£20 per person; £10.50-£15 reductions.
The new, improved Eastbourne YHA (the last one burned down) is a pleasant medley of en suite bedrooms and shiny self-catering facilities, in a leafy suburb a mile from the centre of town. There are seven rooms, sleeping 30 in total. It's at the beginning (or end) of the South Downs Way, so can get packed out in summer.

Grand Hotel

King Edward's Parade, BN21 4EQ (01323 412345, www.grandeastbourne.com). Rates £195-£540 double incl breakfast.
The Grand is the regal and monied grandmother of Eastbourne's hotels. The pristine white, ornate Victorian structure has stood proudly on the seafront since 1875, and has welcomed such personages as Charlie Chaplin, Winston Churchill and Edward Elgar. It retains its period elegance today, while offering five-star luxury across 152 traditionally styled rooms. There are two restaurants, including the acclaimed Mirabelle, and a sumptuous afternoon tea.

Guesthouse East

13 Hartington Place, BN21 3BS (01323 722774, www.theguesthouseeast.co.uk). Rates £74-£98 double.
There are some stylish self-catering suites in this Grade II-listed Regency property. Each suite is furnished to its own theme, from 'boutique hotel chic', to 'peaceful oasis'; some are suitable for families. Most of the suites have their own kitchens, but a cooked breakfast is also on offer. The

accommodation is more basic than you'd find in a boutique hotel in a larger city, but prices are very reasonable.

Waterside

11-12 Royal Parade, BN22 7AR (01323 646566, www.watersidehoteleastbourne.co.uk). Rates £80-£150 double incl breakfast.
Eastbourne's first boutique hotel, the Waterside has 20 rooms kitted out with plush furnishings, flamboyant wallpaper, mood lighting and contemporary art. At the top of the extravagance hierarchy are the suites, with special treats that range from a private jacuzzi to a sea-facing telescope. The on-site seafood restaurant is as good as anywhere in Eastbourne, and with the sea practically lapping at the door, you know the ingredients are salty-fresh. Guests have 24-hour access to the champagne and cocktail bar. Check the website for accommodation deals.

BEACHY HEAD, ALFRISTON & AROUND

Beachy Head & the Seven Sisters ★

The rolling cliffs of Beachy Head and the Seven Sisters, which stretch west from Eastbourne to the Cuckmere River, are the finest examples of chalk downland in Britain. Beachy Head is the tallest point, with a vertical drop of 530 feet to the sea (it's the highest chalk seacliff in Britain) and magnificent views from the top. Looking east, Eastbourne, Bexhill, Hastings and, on a clear day, Dungeness, are visible; looking west, you can see even further, up to 70 miles, beyond Brighton and Chichester.

You can drive to Beachy Head: a loop road runs between Eastbourne and the village of East Dean, via the A259, and there's a large pay-and-display car park at the top. Alternatively, catch a bus from Eastbourne seafront, or walk – the nicest way – from the end of the promenade; it's about two miles. This is also the start (or end) of the South Downs Way (*see p182*), which runs for 100 miles to Winchester. Climbing up the steep hill, notice that the ash and hawthorn trees and gorse bushes are permanently bent at right angles because of the prevailing south-westerly wind. Few trees are able to survive the storms that hit the coast, but there are plenty of plants below knee height, including round-headed rampion and rainbow-coloured milkwort, which attracts silver-spotted skipper and adonis blue butterflies. As autumn approaches, the blackberry and raspberry bushes are laden. More than 20 types of orchid have also been found in the area.

At the brow of the hill is a communications tower and the Beachy Head pub (01323 728060, www.vintageinn.co.uk/thebeachyheadeastbourne) – which serves food and is popular with families. Next door is the Beachy Head Countryside Centre (01323 737273, closed Mon-Fri winter, a modest volunteer-run place with displays on the history and flora and fauna of the South Downs.

In summer, the grassy foreland is often packed with holidaymakers flying kites and eating picnics, while hang-gliders fling themselves off the edge over the sea. The landmark has attracted such illustrious visitors as George Orwell, Claude Debussy, Karl Marx and Friedrich Engels; the latter loved the place so much that he requested his ashes be tipped over Beachy Head. It's also starred in films as varied as *Quadrophenia*, *Harry Potter and the Goblet of Fire*, and *Atonement*.

Beachy Head is also notorious as a suicide spot – hence the sombre sign for the Samaritans next to the phone box opposite the pub. Take extreme care here: every year several people are blown off the top or fall when a soft chalk overhang crumbles beneath their feet. The ledge is receding at about 16 inches a year (in the Bronze Age, the edge would have been more than a mile closer to France) and the council gave up replacing most fences years ago, so keep children and dogs close.

Continue west along the clifftop past the former lighthouse of Belle Tout, now a fabulous B&B (*see p186*), and then down to Birling Gap. The village has mostly been consumed by the ravaging sea – a few houses, a car park and an unremarkable pub and tearoom are all that remain. Coastal erosion means that the only way to reach the shingle beach is down a staircase. It's a good picnic spot, with rock pools and patches of sand, and is secluded enough to appeal to nudists.

Birling Gap is also the start of the Seven Sisters, seven chalk cliffs that are one of the most photographed places in the South-east. The peaks were first named in the Mariners Mirrour sea charts of 1588. From east to west, they are: Went Hill Brow, Baily's Hill, Flagstaff Point, Brass Point, Rough Brow, Short Brow and Haven Brow. Occasionally, the subtle Flat Hill is recognised – but the Eight Sisters obviously didn't have the same ring to it.

To walk across the Seven Sisters to Cuckmere Haven (just under three miles), take the path to the right of the Birling Gap Hotel. On the eastern slope of Baily's Hill is an obelisk built by WA Robertson, who donated the land to the National Trust in memory of his brothers who died on the Somme. A more ancient memorial can also be discerned: the unnatural mound at the top of Baily's Hill is one of the thousands of tumuli that dot the South Downs. The Downs have been inhabited for more than 6,000 years, but the burial sites came into use around 2,000 BC, when the first farmsteads were built. This was also when sheep farming (still the main form of agriculture in the area) led to the decimation of the forests, creating the scrub and chalkland we see today.

Continuing over the undulating grassland, kittiwakes and jackdaws can often be seen flitting around their cliffside nests, while skylarks, wheatears and meadow pipits choose to make their home among the shrubs. Kestrels hover gracefully before swooping on an unsuspecting field mouse, and sparrowhawks and peregrine falcons can often be seen hunting small birds. As you climb over the final hill – Haven Brow, with splendid 360-degree views of the Cuckmere Haven – the habitat changes dramatically.

Beachy Head

Cuckmere Haven. See p182.

Cuckmere Haven & Friston Forest

The Cuckmere Haven is a shallow tidal estuary that attracts all kinds of birdlife, including ringed plover, dunlin, oystercatchers, kingfishers and geese. A canal, cut in 1847, can be seen on the far side of the valley, while the meandering 'river' is actually a lake, preserved in its original shape. (There are plans to flood the valley again, returning it to its natural saltmarsh.)

From the top of Haven Brow, follow the gentle slope down and inland until you reach an easy-access trail (good for wheelchairs, pushchairs and bikes) that leads along the river to meet the A259. Housed in an 18th-century barn on the main road, in Exceat, is the Seven Sisters Country Park visitor centre (01323 870280, www.sevensisters.org.uk, closed Mon-Fri Nov-Mar). A café serves cream teas and, across the bridge, the Golden Galleon pub (01323 892 247, www.vintageinn.co.uk/thegoldengalleonseaford) is popular with coach parties in summer. Behind the visitor centre is Friston Forest, good for walking and cycling; you

You may imagine the South Downs Way is all about blisters, stinging nettles and traipsing through amusingly named villages (Cocking, Winding Bottom) and – well, it is. But it also crosses some of the most beautiful countryside in the South-east, with many opportunities to rest weary legs in the kind of pub that inspired Sir John Betjeman to write 'The village inn/the dear old inn/So ancient, clean and free from sin/True centre of our rural life'.

The South Downs Way national trail meanders for 100 miles between the ancient former capital of Winchester and the charming seaside town of Eastbourne, crossing Hampshire, West Sussex and East Sussex. Walking its length takes about seven days, and it's often best to start in Winchester because of the prevailing westerly wind – it can get breezy on the chalk ridges. The South Downs have been inhabited for more than 6,000 years; on Ordnance Survey maps it's Bronze Age tumuli (burial mounds) that provide many of the reference points, along with pubs, of course.

From Winchester, the path traverses Queen Elizabeth Country Park before entering West Sussex just south of Midhurst. It cuts through the village of Amberley and the Arun Valley, then rises again up the ridge of the now more pronounced

South Downs. Near Washington, be sure to spend time at Chanctonbury Ring, an Iron Age hill fort marked by a ring of trees. North of Brighton is Devil's Dyke and the highest part of the walk, Ditchling Beacon. Many prefer to break from the route at this point and stop in Lewes for its good pubs and comfortable accommodation before making the final two-day trek to Eastbourne. This is the most spectacular part of the walk, leading directly through Alfriston before following the coast path across the Seven Sisters to Beachy Head and the end of the trail in Eastbourne.

There are campsites en route, although some are a little distance from the path; most walkers opt for the YHA hostels that are conveniently spaced about a day's hike from one another. it's wise to plan your stops and to book accommodation in advance, especially in high summer. Cyclists and horseriders can also follow the South Downs Way, although the bridleway used by mountain bikes and horses takes a different route on the last stretch to Eastbourne.

All the tourist centres in the area will have information leaflets, and there are plenty of guidebooks. For online information, visit www.nationaltrail.co.uk/southdowns or the unofficial www.southdownsway.co.uk.

can hire bikes from the Seven Sisters Cycle Company (*see p171*) next to the visitor centre. Tucked into the forest is the attractive village of Westdean with its duckpond and Norman church. A mile and a half further north is Litlington village. You can drive there, or it's a pleasant walk along the South Downs Way. Beyond Charleston Manor, you'll see a white horse carved into the chalk of High and Over hill on the other side of the valley. Then it's straight through the door of the Plough & Harrow (*see p185*), where you can order a pint of Dark Star's delicious Hophead.

From Litlington, it's worth staying on the east side of the Cuckmere to see Ewe Dean (a geological crease, formed 60 million years ago), one of the loveliest valleys in the South Downs.

East Dean & Jevington

Numerous tiny villages dot the South Downs near Eastbourne, often containing little more than a pub, a church and a few houses. Two of the most beautiful are East Dean and Jevington.

East Dean is two miles west of town. You can walk there, catch the no.12 bus from Terminus Road or drive. The A259 goes straight though the village, but the more scenic route is via Beachy Head and Birling Gap, where you turn inland and go past the Seven Sisters Sheep Centre (*see p178*). After some flint cottages comes a classic Sussex scene. The whitewashed Tiger Inn (*see p186*) is a lovely pub any time of year, but in summer when hikers, day-trippers and locals sit on the village green with a pint and a ploughman's, it's glorious. Also beside the green is the Hiker's Rest café and gift shop (01323 423733, www.beachyhead.org.uk) and Frith & Little (01323 423631, www.frithandlittle.com, closed Mon), a wonderful deli stocking local chocolate, ice-cream and bread, as well as Spanish products from Brindisa and wines. A house on the green has a blue plaque claiming that Sherlock Holmes retired there to keep bees. From the Tiger Inn, you can climb the footpath parallel to the road up to St Mary's Church in Friston, from where you can cross diagonally to Friston Forest (*see p182*).

Jevington also has swag-bags of character. From Eastbourne, take the A259 towards Seaford and at the top of the steep hill, opposite Friston's church and pond, turn right. Across the folds of the South Down's, Jevington's church spire can be seen in the valley – a view that seems to have changed little for hundreds of years.

The first notable building in the village is the Hungry Monk restaurant (*see p185*) inside a 14th-century monk's house. It's lost some of its lustre since the days when people would travel from Brighton and London to eat there, but it still serves the best food around Eastbourne. Further along the High Street is the Eight Bells (*see p184*), a fine country pub with a colourful history.

In the 1780s, Jevington was notorious for smuggling, masterminded by local innkeeper James Pettit, known as 'Jevington Jigg', whose activities were well documented in newspaper reports of the time. His gang would unload contraband at Birling Gap and Crowlink, then store it in the inn and the

Long Man of Wilmington. See p178.

rectory cellar. In 1788, armed constables attempted to arrest Jigg as he played cards in the pub, but the resourceful smuggler escaped by donning women's clothes and feigning hysterics. Soon after, however, he was discovered hiding in the pub's loft. After various other adventures, he was convicted of horse stealing and sentenced to 14 years in Botany Bay.

Just beyond Jevington is Filching Manor (*see p178*), home to the Campbell Circuit kart track.

Alfriston ★

Alfriston is almost unbearably quaint, with three old pubs, a market cross, a village shop, a highly renowned bookshop, one superb restaurant, a National Trust-owned thatched clergy house and what must be the most beautiful church in Sussex, set in an idyllic village green. No wonder Eleanor Farjeon felt moved enough to write the hymn *Morning Has Broken* here in 1931. The village has led a quiet life, largely untouched by major historical events, and is still a peaceful haven. If you approach from the south along Alfriston Road, it could be a scene from 500 years ago: smoke rises from flint cottages, and the spire of the church (built in the 14th century and still the tallest building) pokes through the early morning mist, common in the Cuckmere valley.

You can also reach Alfriston from the other direction – the village is a mile of so below the A27. There are two car parks at the north end of the village, which fill up early in summer when Alfriston is packed with tourists.

Starting from the car parks, walk south down West Street. Your first stop should be Much Ado Books (no.8, 01323 871222, www.muchadobooks.com) – one of the best bookshops to be found anywhere. It moved into these lovely new premises at the end of 2010 (the opening was attended by the Dowager Duchess of Devonshire and Lynne Truss). Over two levels are carefully selected new releases and rare books on antique bookshelves. There's a special collection of works by the Bloomsbury Group, and some hard-to-find art editions. At the bottom of West Street is the Market Square, with the historic market cross. Next to Ye Olde Smugglers' Inne (*see right*) is Alfriston Village Stores & Post Office (Waterloo Square, 01323 870201), a delicatessen and sweet shop, useful for picnic supplies. Spot the early 20th-century till fittings that used to whizz above the clerk to the money changer. Also here are a couple of tearooms, an antiques shop and a sweet shop.

Continue south, along the High Street, to another pub, the Star Alfriston (*see p186*). The bright red lion outside is believed to be the figurehead from a Dutch warship that sank off the coast in the 1800s; the lion was stolen by Stanton Collins and his crew of smugglers. Collins was eventually sent to New South Wales for stealing sheep. Opposite is another historic watering hole, the George Inn (*see right*).

Next to the Star is Steamer Trading (01323 870055, www.steamer.co.uk), the original branch of an upmarket kitchenware shop that now has outlets across the South-east. It's named after the 14th-century building it occupies, the former Steamer Inn. Just before the excellent Moonrakers restaurant (*see p185*) – another reference to Alfriston's smuggling heritage – turn left down a twitten to the Tye, Alfriston's village green. There are few more beautiful sights in all Sussex than this view of St

Andrew's Church and thatched Afriston Clergy House (*see p177*) next door, especially in late afternoon sunlight. The handsome, flint-walled parish church was built in the 1370s; the Clergy House, also 14th-century, was the National Trust's first property.

To the left of the church, a footpath leads across the Cuckmere River and either up to the South Downs or to the village of Litlington and the Plough & Harrow pub (*see p185*) – an idyllic walk. There's another fine trek from the opposite end of the town, along the Old Coach Road bridleway to Firle (*see p207*). Bear left at the market cross and follow West Street uphill. Just after the church on the left, the sealed road ends; continue directly over the crossroads on to the trail. The route is centuries old (some say a black dog haunts it) and lovely at any time of year: it's open to cyclists and horseriders too. It's just over four miles to Firle.

Where to eat & drink

Alfriston has couple of tearooms. The best is Badgers @ The Old Village Bakery (30 North Street, 01323 871336, www.badgersteahouse.com) just off the Market Square, where you'll find bone china teacups, silver teapots and divine cakes. Ye Olde Smugglers Inne (Waterloo Square, 01323 870241), a former hideout of the Stanton Collins smuggling gang, is a friendly spot in with real ales on tap, a large inglenook fireplace and a garden. It's a maze of a place – one of the reasons it was favoured by the smugglers – so there's always somewhere quiet to sit.

Eight Bells

High Street, Jevington, BN26 5QB (01323 484442, www.8bellsonline.co.uk). Open 11am-11pm Mon-Sat;

Afriston

noon-10.30pm Sun. Lunch served noon-3pm, dinner served 6-9pm Mon-Sat. Food served noon-9pm Sun.
This delightful free house is an excellent destination for a walk over the Downs – the route from Butt's Brow car park in Willingdon is popular. It's a cosy spot, with two rooms linked by a single bar, but the beer garden is a lovely place on a summer evening and keeps expanding. Food includes Sussex smokies, steaks and hearty pies. The rotating selection of beers is excellent, but Harveys is always on.

George Inn ★
High Street, Alfriston, BN26 5SY (01323 870319, www.thegeorge-alfriston.com). Open 11am-11pm Mon-Thur, Sat; 11am-midnight Fri; 11am-10.30pm Sun. Food served noon-9pm daily.
This gorgeous, part flint, part timber-framed pub was one of the first inns in the country to licensed – way back in 1397. Mind your head on the low beams as you order a well-kept pint of ale or something from the chalkboard menu: perhaps steak, mushroom and Guinness suet pudding, monkfish wrapped in parma ham or a sharing platter of houmous, tsatsiki, anchovies, feta and other finger food.

Giant's Rest
The Street, Wilmington, BN26 5SQ (01323 870207, www.giantsrest.co.uk). Open 11am-3pm, 6-11pm Mon-Fri; 11am-11pm Sat; noon-10.30pm Sun. Lunch served noon-2pm, dinner served 6.30-9pm Mon-Fri. Food served noon-9pm Sat, Sun.
This homely pub just off the South Downs Way is a short walk from the Long Man of Wilmington (*see p178*). It's a friendly place, made even more so when groups of jolly Morris dancers descend. The beers are excellent (it's a free house), the food simple and reasonably priced; Sunday lunches are very busy. Dogs and children are welcome.

Hungry Monk
High Street, Jevington, BN26 5QF (01323 482178, www.hungrymonk.co.uk). Lunch served noon-2pm, dinner served 6.45-9.30pm Wed-Sun.
Located in the same village as the Eight Bells, the Hungry Monk has been rated one of the area's most reputable restaurants for more than 30 years. The beamed interior is old-fashioned and welcoming. Food tends to be traditional and hearty, featuring, in winter, the likes of guinea fowl breast stuffed with black pudding and apple, and served with cider sauce. It's also the home of that English culinary masterpiece, banoffee pie (invented here in 1972 – the recipe was held under lock and key for a long time afterwards). There's a set-price menu at lunch.

Moonrakers ★
High Street, Alfriston, BN26 5TD (01323 871199, www.moonrakersrestaurant.co.uk). Lunch served noon-3pm Fri, Sat; noon-5pm Sun. Dinner served 6pm-midnight Fri, Sat.
Relaunched in 2008, Moonrakers has attracted a strong local and celebrity fan base, including restaurant critic Jay Rayner. It offers a happy balance of fine (but not intimidating) dining in an upscale, but unstuffy setting inside a 500-year-old cottage. It's not cheap – dinner tasting menus are £35 and £55, while set lunch is £19.95 or £24.95, but it's top-quality fare. Head chef Ross Pavey sources all ingredients within 25 miles of the restaurant; dishes might include sea bass with buttered savoy cabbage, parsnip purée and a vanilla and saffron sauce, followed by white chocolate and jerusalem artichoke cheesecake with roasted cashew nut ice-cream.

Plough & Harrow ★
The Street, Litlington, BN26 5RE (01323 870632, www.ploughandharrowlitlington.co.uk). Open 11am-11pm Mon-Sat; noon-10.30pm Sun. Lunch served noon-2.30pm

SUSSEX

Mon-Fri; noon-3pm Sat, Sun. Dinner served 6-8.30pm
Mon-Fri; 6-9pm Sat, Sun.

This delightful, 17th-century flint pub is handy for walks
or bike rides in Friston Forest, and ideal for lunch if you're
spending the morning on the Cuckmere. It works well for
both diners and drinkers, with plenty of seating, well-kept
ales and food that is a cut above the usual fare; dishes
include slow-braised rabbit with vegetables, and Kentish
sausages on mustard grain mash.

Rose Cottage Inn
*Alciston, BN26 6UW (01323 870377, www.therose
cottageinn.co.uk). Open 11.30am-3pm, 6.30-11pm Mon-
Sat; noon-3pm, 7-10.30pm Sun. Lunch served noon-2pm,
dinner served 7-9pm daily.*

This is the kind of pub where ale is served directly out of
the barrel, a parrot squawks away and Good Friday's
annual Skipping Day is a serious event. Located in the tiny
cul-de-sac village of Alciston, just off the A27 west of
Wilmington, it's popular with weary walkers who come for
hefty ploughman's or local sausages, chips and onion rings.
Self-catering accommodation is available. Note that children
aren't allowed.

Star Alfriston
*High Street, Alfriston, BN26 5TA (01323 870495,
www.thestaralfriston.co.uk). Open 11am-11pm daily.
Bar Food served 6-9pm Mon-Thur; noon-9pm Fri-Sun.
Restaurant Dinner served 7-9pm daily.*

The Star occupies another of Alfriston's incredible old
buildings, first erected in the 13th century, though most of
the. half-timbered building dates from the 16th century.
Once called the Star of Bethlehem and run by the monks of
Battle Abbey, it offered shelter to pilgrims en route to
Chichester. Nowadays it's a pub, restaurant and country
hotel (with a modern annex at the back). Drop in for
afternoon tea or a pint or a full-blown meal in the Capella
Restaurant: Ashmore Farm loin of lamb with ratatouille,
perhaps, or sea bass with potatoes and oyster mushrooms.

Tiger Inn ★
*The Green, East Dean, BN20 0DA (01323 423209,
www.beachyhead.org.uk). Open 11am-11pm daily.
Lunch served noon-3pm, dinner served 6-9pm daily.*

There are few more picturesque locations for a pub than the
village green in East Dean. The Tiger dates from the 15th
century, and seems little changed inside, with its stone floor,
large fireplaces and low beams. The pub has been through
a few owners recently (losing some regulars in the process),
but seems to have found its feet now. The food has
improved too, and includes ambitious dishes such as honey-
and pepper-crusted duck breast with vanilla and lime mash,
alongside ploughman's and sandwiches. Draught beers
come from Harveys and the small Beachy Head Brewery,
based here. There are also five pleasant B&B rooms (£90
double incl breakfast).

Where to stay
There are five B&B rooms at the historic Tiger Inn
(*see above*) in East Dean, plus three fabulous self-
catering cottages (sleeping four, five and six),
run by the Beachy Head Estate (01323 423878,
www.beachyhead.org.uk), which also manages the
pub. The Star Alfriston (*see above*) doubles as a

hotel, with 37 traditionally furnished en suite rooms
(£115-£130 double incl breakfast). Also in Alfrison
the George Inn (*see p185*) has one suite, four
doubles and a single – all en suite and recently
refurbished. They're fairly basic, but keep the
characteristics of the ancient inn.

Alfriston Youth Hostel
*Frog Firle, Alfriston, BN26 5TT (0845 371 9101,
www.yha.org.uk). Rates £14.50-£20.40; £10.50-£14.50
reductions.*

The flint cottage housing Alfriston YHA is about half a mile
south of the village, in a beautiful setting overlooking the
Cuckmere Valley. It has 68 beds (including four double
rooms), a comfortable common room, facilities for cyclists
and a garden. It's not as modern as the Eastbourne hostel,
but the location is lovely and the building (parts of which
date from 1530) atmospheric.

Belle Tout Lighthouse ★
*Beachy Head, BN20 0AE (01323 423185,
www.belletout.co.uk). Rates £145-£195 double
incl breakfast.*

Belle Tout lighthouse sits at the edge of a cliff just beyond
Beachy Head. Built in 1832, it was decommissioned in 1902
and replaced by the famous red and white striped
lighthouse at the base of the cliff. It recently opened as a
B&B to rave reviews – and not just for the unique location.
The view over the Channel is vast, though the view inland,
over the waves of the South Downs, is possibly even more
beautiful. The six modern bedrooms are tastefully
decorated and well equipped. The Keepers Loft is a tiny,
circular space with brick walls and the original stepladder
to reach the double loft bed); the other rooms are more
spacious, if less idiosyncratic. The lantern room at the top
of the lighthouse is now a guest lounge with stunning 360-
degree views. There's a two-night minimum stay.

Deans Place
*Seaford Road, Alfriston, BN26 5TW (01323 870248,
www.deansplacehotel.co.uk). Rates £90-£150 double
incl breakfast.*

This former farming estate is an elegant getaway on the
edge of Alfriston beside the Cuckmere River. There are 36
traditionally furnished en suite rooms (some with four-
poster beds), a lovely walled swimming pool and an
impressive restaurant, open daily for lunch and dinner.
Typical dishes include pressed chicken and pistachio
terrine, local pheasant breast, with pears poached in local
cider for pudding.

Wingrove House
*High Street, Alfriston, BN26 5TD (01323 870276,
www.wingrovehousealfriston.com). Rates £95-£155
double incl breakfast.*

Extensively refurbished in 2010, this colonial-style
Victorian house overlooking Alfriston's village green and
church is a stunner. The five en suite bedrooms (two with
access to the lovely wooden verandah) are peaceful, with
pale walls, shutters and artfully distressed furniture. In
summer, relax on the sunny outdoor terrace or the lawn; in
winter, retreat to the leather sofas and log fire in the lounge.
The brassiere is a classy affair, with many ingredients
sourced locally (pheasant from the Firle Estate, fish
from Hastings).

North Weald

Open spaces, woodland and quiet rural communities make up most of the northern end of the Sussex Weald, between Eastbourne and Tunbridge Wells. It's this sense of remoteness and solitude that attracted Rudyard Kipling to buy Bateman's in Burwash and live there for more than 30 years. He wrote: 'It is a good and peaceable place... we have loved it ever since our first sight of it.' Further north, the landscape of wood and heath around Hartfield and Ashdown Forest inspired AA Milne to write *Winnie-the-Pooh*. Today, Pooh fans travel from all over the world to play Poohsticks and visit the real-life locations that inspired the classic book.

The villages, which local writer Ben Darby described as seeming 'to have grown there, like the trees', were, until the mid 20th century, largely isolated settlements. Remains of the once formidable Wealden iron industry are evident, especially in Wadhurst, but most villages are still pretty quiet today, with snug traditional pubs and good walking the main attractions. It has been called 'the place where London ends and England can begin'.

HEATHFIELD & AROUND

North of Eastbourne are a series of little villages and seemingly inconsequential towns. At the Boship Roundabout, just north of Hailsham, the road forks. The A22 heads north-west past the villages of Chiddingly and East Hoathly to Uckfield and then into Ashdown Forest. The A267 weaves north through Horam, Heathfield and Mayfield eventually to reach Tunbridge Wells.

Chiddingly to Uckfield

There's little to detain visitors on this stretch of the A22 unless pubs are high on the agenda – and they should be, given their quality. Just off the main road, Chiddingly is a tiny village, but very active in the arts. This is particularly evident in the ten-day Chiddingly Festival (www.chiddinglyfestival.co.uk) at the end of September, with its bell ringing, Morris dancing, jazz concerts, storytelling, theatre productions and a beer festival. Events are held in the village hall and the Six Bells pub (*see p189*), which has a prolific year-round musical programme. A sculpture garden next to the village car park contains four stand-alone figures representing the seasons, carved out of a single 150-year-old oak.

A little further along the A22 is the parish of East Hoathly & Halland. The former village is notable for the excellent King's Head pub (*see p189*) and attached microbrewery, while the latter is home to the family-friendly Bentley Wildfowl & Motor Museum (*see p190*). Just north of Halland is the acclaimed East Sussex National golf resort (*see p194*), with two championship golf courses, a posh hotel and a spa.

The rather dull town of Uckfield gained notoriety in the 20th century for its association with the Piltdown Man hoax. The fossilised remains of an early human skull were discovered in a gravel pit in the nearby village of Piltdown in 1912; it wasn't until 1953 that they were revealed as a forgery.

Uckfield was also the last place Lord Lucan was seen. On the outskirts are a number of nature reserves, including the 27-acre West Park reserve next to the West Park housing estate. It includes woodland, grassland and sandstone outcrops and is home to a rare marshland orchid.

Heathfield to Crowborough

Heathfield isn't large, but it's the largest town in this part of the Weald. It's also the northern end of the Cuckoo Trail, a popular 11-mile walking, cycling and horse riding route along a disused railway line to Polegate, with a three-mile extension to Hampden Park in Eastbourne. It's mainly flat and child-friendly. You can download a trail leaflet from the East Sussex County Council website (www.eastsussex.gov.uk). Every April, Heathfield holds the Heffle Cuckoo Fair (www.hefflecuckoo fair.org.uk), which is claimed to date from 1315 and celebrates a certain Dame Heffle, who released a cuckoo from a basket to mark the arrival of spring. Expect traditional food, country crafts, falconry displays and a poultry show. More country fun occurs at the Heathfield Show, an agricultural extravaganza on the Saturday of the second May bank holiday weekend.

A few miles further north, Mayfield is a delightful village of Saxon origin situated at the end of an almost detached ridge above the headwaters of the River Rother. Along with other settlements in the area such as Wadhurst, Mayfield prospered in the Middle Ages thanks to the thriving Wealden iron industry. The High Street, with its raised red-brick pavements, is lined by attractive old buildings. Set back from the street is the church of St Dunstan (www.stdunstansmayfield.org.uk), which was destroyed and rebuilt (along with most of the village) after a fire in 1389. The Dunstan in question served as Archbishop of Canterbury from 960 to 988, and founded Mayfield Palace,

one of the archbishopric's great residences and today a Roman Catholic boarding school.

However, St Dunstan is most famous locally for his part in an often-declaimed legend. The saint was formerly a blacksmith and was casting a horseshoe at his forge when a beautiful woman approached. The wily saint spotted a cloven hoof protruding from beneath her dress and realising this was the Devil in disguise, grabbed the evil one's nose with his red-hot pincers, causing him to make a mighty leap to Tunbridge Wells to bathe his nose in a stream. Thereafter, the Devil vowed never to enter any building with a horseshoe over the door.

Six miles north-west of Mayfield is the market town of Crowborough. Sir Arthur Conan Doyle spent his last 23 years here, often at the Crowborough

Beacon golf club (*see p194*) where he was captain. It's a reasonably sized place with the usual supermarkets and banks.

Where to eat & drink

Blackboys Inn ★

Lewes Road, Blackboys, TN22 5LG (01825 890283, www.theblackboysinn.com). Open noon-11pm Mon-Thur, Sun; noon-midnight Fri, Sat. Lunch served noon-2.30pm Mon-Thur. Dinner served 6-9pm Mon-Wed; 6-9.30pm Thur; 6-10pm Fri. Food served noon-9.30pm Sat; noon-9pm Sun.

Supposedly established in 1389, this historic pub is thought to have earned its name from the workers in the local charcoal industry. With a small green and pond at the front, and a covered patio with piano at the rear, it's tailor-made for summer drinking. The interior is homely. The restaurant menu offers the likes of pan-roasted partridge and dressed Cornish crab, while the bar menu features excellent own-made burgers. There are two B&B guestrooms (£75-£85 double incl breakfast).

Brewers Arms
Vines Cross, TN21 9EN (01435 812288, www.brewers armspub.co.uk). Open noon-3pm, 6-11pm Mon-Thur; noon-midnight Fri-Sun. Lunch served noon-2.30pm Mon-Fri; noon-3pm Sat, Sun. Dinner served 6.30-9.30pm Mon-Fri; 6-10pm Sat, Sun.

One for foodies, the Brewers Arms, located a couple of miles south of Heathfield, serves a classy British menu of seasonal flavours. In autumn and winter, enjoy dishes such as pumpkin ravioli with sage butter, beetroot tart tatin with blue cheese and rocket salad, or roast partridge with wilted spinach and rosti potato. The food draws quite a crowd, and the three rooms and bar area can fill up quickly. Decor includes an open fire, a wood-burning stove, flickering candles and stripped floorboards.

King's Head
Mill Lane, East Hoathly, BN8 6QB (01825 840830). Open 11am-11pm Mon-Sat; noon-11pm Sun. Lunch served noon-2pm daily. Dinner served 6.30-9pm Mon-Thur; 6.30-9.30pm Fri, Sat; 7-9pm Sun.

The jolly King's Head has a lot going for it. As well as being an attractive 16th-century inn, it produces its own beer at the excellent 1648 Brewing Co. The name refers to the year the warrant of execution was signed for Charles I, a copy of which can be seen in the pub.

Rose & Crown
Fletching Street, Mayfield, TN20 6TE (01435 872200, www.roseandcrownmayfield.co.uk). Open 11am-11pm Mon-Thur; 11am-midnight Fri, Sat; noon-10.30pm Sun. Food served noon-9pm Mon-Thur; noon-9.30pm Fri, Sat; noon-8pm Sun.

Tuck into wild mushrooms on toast, chicken and chorizo skewers or wild boar and apple sausages with red onion gravy at this 16th-century pub. The two intimate front rooms have pewter tankards hanging above the bar, bare floorboards and bench seating. There's more seating and a wood-burning stove in another larger room to the left, and also a sunny front terrace. Coffee is served from 11am daily.

Six Bells
The Street, Chiddingly, BN8 6HE (01825 872227). Open 11am-3pm, 6-11pm Mon-Thur; 11am-midnight Fri, Sat; noon-10.30pm Sun. Lunch served noon-2.15pm, dinner served 6-9.15pm Mon-Thur. Food served noon-9.15pm Fri-Sun.

This long-established music pub has bands at weekends and a well-regarded folk and blues club (www.6bellsfolk. co.uk) on alternate Tuesdays. There are half a dozen rooms, so there's always a cosy corner in which to tuck into the hearty pub grub or get rowdy over a boardgame. The walls are lined with vintage car memorabilia – a car rally meets here once a month.

Where to stay
In Chiddingly, Hale Farm House (01825 872619, www.halefarmhouse.co.uk) is a 14th-century hall that today makes for a very pleasant B&B stay. It has three rooms, one of which is en suite.

Blackboys Inn

Places to visit

Ashdown Forest Llama Park

HEATHFIELD & AROUND

Bentley Wildfowl & Motor Museum
Halland, BN8 5AF (01825 840573, www.bentley. org.uk). Open Mar-Oct 10.30am-5.30pm daily. Jan, Feb, Nov, Dec 10.30am-4pm Sat, Sun. Admission £8; £6-£7 reductions; £26 family.
It may seem a rather incongruous mix of motor vehicles and nature, but there are enough elements here to entertain the whole family. The museum houses a eye-dropping range of veteran, Edwardian and vintage cars (including assorted Bentleys), many still roadworthy. Outside, a 23-acre bird reserve and striking gardens create an enchanting haven. An impressive 125 species of wildfowl are at home here, including flamingos and Australian black swans. There are also winding pathways, willow tunnels, formal gardens frothing with old roses, an adventure playground and a miniature steam train. You can have lunch in the stableblock café or bring your own picnic.

Farley Farm House
Muddles Green, nr Chiddingly, BN8 6HW (01825 872691, www.farleyfarmhouse.co.uk). Open House (guided tours only) Apr-Oct 10.30am-3.30pm 1st & 3rd Sun of the mth. Garden Apr-Oct 10am-5pm 1st & 3rd Sun of the mth. Admission House tour & garden £9. Garden only £2.
Set in a particularly idyllic patch of Sussex hillside, the former house of photographer Lee Miller and Surrealist painter and art critic Roland Penrose is a fascinating place, set out for the most part just as they left it. As well as Miller and Penrose's possessions, there are works by some of the many famous artists who visited the family (including Man Ray, Picasso, Max Ernst and Joan Miró). There's no need to book for the regular 50-minute guided tour, but reservations are required for the occasional extended tours (three hours, £30) led by Antony

Penrose, Lee and Roland's son. Farley Farm House is open on extra weekends during local arts festivals in Brighton (May), Uckfield (July) and Chiddingly (Sept/Oct).

WADHURST & BURWASH

Bateman's ★
Bateman's Lane, Burwash, TN19 7DS (01435 882302, www.nationaltrust.org.uk/batemans). Open House mid Mar-Oct 11am-5pm Mon-Wed, Sat, Sun. Dec 11.30am-3.30pm Sat, Sun. Garden, shop & tearoom Mar-Oct 10am-5pm Mon-Wed, Sat, Sun. Nov, Dec 11am-4pm Mon-Wed, Sat, Sun. Late Feb-early Mar 11am-4pm Sat, Sun. Admission £7.80; £3.90 reductions; £19.50 family. Garden Nov, Dec free.
Built around 1634 using local sandstone and Sussex oak, this beautiful house set amid rolling countryside remains much the same as when Rudyard Kipling called it home. From the literary airs of the study to the oriental ornaments and the shiny 1928 Rolls-Royce Phantom I in the garage, the author's passions run through the imposing property that was his refuge for more than 30 years. A blanket of soft green sweeps around the house, with manicured lawns, rose beds and a wildflower garden, while riverside strolls and a working watermill are a few steps away. It's all remarkably atmospheric, if somewhat melancholy (witness the high yew hedges); the death of his six-year-old daughter in 1899 and his son in World War I affected Kipling greatly, and he found fame a burden.

Pashley Manor Gardens
Ticehurst, TN5 7HE (01580 200888, www.pashley manorgardens.com). Open Apr-Sept 11am-5pm Tue-Thur, Sat. Oct 10am-3pm Mon-Fri. Admission £8.50; free-£5 reductions. Tulip festival £9.
Surrounding Grade I-listed Pashley Manor, this quintessential English garden is a joy throughout the year. Spring visitors can enjoy wild daffodils, fruit tree blossoms, bluebells and wisteria, while summer guests are greeted by a fragrant concoction of roses, lavender and sweet peas. The tulip festival in late April/early May is spectacular and extremely popular. Produce from the kitchen garden is used in the café. Ticehurst is a few miles south-east of Wadhurst, on the B2099.

HARTFIELD & ASHDOWN FOREST

Ashdown Forest Llama Park
On the A22, Wych Cross, RH18 5JN (01825 712040, www.llamapark.co.uk). Open Feb-Oct 10am-5pm daily. Jan, Nov, Dec 10am-4.30pm daily. Admission £6.50; £5.50 reductions; £21.50 family. Llama walk £30 1 person; £50 2 people.
It may sound peculiar, but leading a llama is a wonderful way to chill out. Your pace becomes slower, so the walk is as much about taking in and enjoying your surroundings as appreciating the therapeutic qualities of being with an animal companion. And the spitting? Apparently, it's rarely at people. There are about 100 llamas and alpacas here, plus a few reindeer, as well as an adventure playground, farm trail, picnic area and coffee shop. The shop has alpaca knitwear and llama-themed merchandise.

Fair Oak Farm

Witherenden Road, Mayfield, TN20 6RS (01435 884122, www.fairoakfarm.co.uk). Rates £434-£1,186 per week.

Up to 15 people can stay in these three Grade II-listed farm buildings set in 12 acres of greenery; you can hire just one building or the whole shebang. The Barn & Cow Shed (sleeping up to seven), Stable Cottage and Grain Store (both sleeping up to four) have been lovingly refurbished to provide luxury self-catering facilities while retaining their original features and charm. Two circular tree houses, each sleeping two, should be available in summer 2011. Guests have sweeping lawns, gardens and an orchard to wander, plus a pond and striking views. The minimum rental period is one week.

Hidden Spring Vineyard

Vines Cross Road, Horam, TN21 0HG (01435 812640, www.hiddenspring.co.uk). Rates Camping £8 per person. Small yurt from £120 2 night weekend. No credit cards.

Cider, wine, honey and yurts: it's a good life to be found at Hidden Spring. Campers can pitch their own tents or, for a touch more luxury, book one of the two yurts or the geodesic dome (beds, stove and crockery provided). New for 2011 are a tipi and a showman's wagon. Campfires are encouraged, there are sheep and chickens, and you can try (and buy) farm produce, including apple and pear juices made from the orchard fruit.

Horsted Place

Little Horsted, TN22 5TS (01825 750581, www.horstedplace.co.uk). Rates £140-£360 double incl breakfast.

This very grand manor house was built in 1850 in the Gothic Revival style, with input by Augustus Pugin, architect of the Houses of Parliament. The Queen and Prince Philip were entertained here before it became a hotel and wedding venue. There are 20 bedrooms and suites, designed in classic country house style, but with flatscreen TVs and all mod cons. The large grounds include landscaped gardens, a tennis court and croquet lawn, and guests can play at the adjoining East Sussex National golf club (*see p194*).

Middle House

High Street, Mayfield, TN20 6AB (01435 872146, www.middlehousemayfield.co.uk). Rates £95-£120 double incl breakfast.

This intimate, five-room hotel inside a splendid Grade I-listed Elizabethan building is bursting with character, with blackened beams and four-poster beds and cracking views of the South Downs. The restaurant serves some big flavours; try corn fritter and harrisa-roasted vegetable stack with feta cheese, or quail filled with mushrooms, pancetta and pine nuts.

Old Whyly

London Road, East Hoathly, BN8 6EL (01825 840216, www.oldwhyly.co.uk). Rates £95-£135 double incl breakfast. No credit cards.

For a superior B&B stay, you can't do better than this gorgeous Grade II-listed Georgian manor house. As well as three double/twin bedrooms, charmingly decorated in a low-key country style, there's a dining room, plus a tennis court and swimming pool (summer use only). Food is a highlight,

with owner Sarah Burgoyne preparing delicious breakfasts – with her own eggs and honey – and classy dinners. Hampers are also available.

WADHURST & BURWASH

From Heathfield, it's a 20-minute drive north-east to delightful and historic Wadhurst, while Burwash – best-known for being Rudyard Kipling's home – is six miles to the east, along the A265.

Wadhurst

You'd never think to look at it now, but the attractive village of Wadhurst was once the heart of the thriving Wealden iron industry. From modest beginnings in the second century AD, the growth of iron-smelting slowly propelled Sussex to become England's foremost industrial county by the middle of the 16th century, and made Wadhurst a wealthy, handsome settlement. Competition from Swedish iron imports in the 17th century led to the industry's gradual decline, and in its extinction at the start of the 19th century.

Today, the ridgetop village with its many distinguished weatherboarded and tiled houses still has an air of prosperity. The main sight of interest is the church of St Peter & St Paul (www.wadhurstparishchurch.org). The tower was built in the early 12th century, and the floor reflects Wadhurst's industrial past, with its 31 iron tomb slabs (dating from 1617 to 1799) – more than can be found in any other church in England. The Norman tower has a pretty needle spire, and the west window in the south aisle was designed by Burne-Jones and made by William Morris. The parish records feature two intriguing entries, the first from 1691: 'Baptised Elizabeth, daughter of Francis and Ann Comber. This child was heard crying in the womb before it was born.' The second is from 1784: 'Baptised Harriet, base born daughter of Elizabeth Rogers a very noted strumpet of this parish.' From the back of the churchyard, there's a pleasant little walk along a path that opens out to spectacular views over Bewl Water on the Kent border.

Burwash

Burwash will be forever associated with Rudyard Kipling who lived in Bateman's (*see p190*) from 1902 until his death in 1936. It's easy to see why he fell in love with the village. The 17th- and 18th-century cottages along the High Street, many given facelifts by the Georgians and clad in weatherboard, would have been as quaint to him as they are to us today. He moved to the Jacobean house, hidden away down a narrow lane, to escape the pressure of his fame, though he continued to write prolifically, notably setting some of the stories in *Puck of Pook's Hill* (1906) in the area.

Antiques lovers will enjoy Chateaubriand Antiques (High Street, 01435 882535, www.chateaubriandantiques.co.uk, closed Mon, Tue), which deals in decorative antiques, historic maps and prints and Staffordshire pottery. It occupies the oldest house in the village, dating from 1375, and is also a B&B (*see p192*). Pick of the pubs is the Rose & Crown

Hartfield

(*see below*), a 15th-century inn with two large inglenook fireplaces and low beams. You might even see village residents Roger Daltrey or the Cure's Robert Smith having a drink.

Where to eat & drink

Greyhound
St James Square, Wadhurst, TN5 6AP (01892 783224, www.thegreyhoundwadhurst.co.uk). Open 11am-11pm Mon-Fri; 9.30am-11pm Sat; 9.30am-10.30pm Sun. Breakfast served 9.30-11am Sat, Sun. Lunch served noon-3pm Tue-Fri; noon-4pm Sat, Sun. Dinner served 6-9.30pm Tue-Sat.
The Greyhound is the best bet for a beer in Wadhurst. It's a relaxed, friendly spot – walkers, dogs and children are all welcome – with two bars, a large fireplace, a secluded beer garden and decent pub food. The building dates from 1502, when it was used as a coaching inn. The former stables now contain five bedrooms (£79 double incl breakfast).

Rose & Crown
Ham Lane, Burwash, TN19 7ER (01435 882600, www.roseandcrown-burwash.co.uk). Open noon-3pm, 6-11pm Mon-Fri; noon-11pm Sat; noon-10.30pm Sun. Lunch served noon-2.30pm daily. Dinner served 6-9pm Mon-Sat.
In the centre of Burwash, the 15th-century Rose & Crown is an archetypal country inn: inglenook fireplaces and low beams, real ales (it's a Harveys pub), and a sturdy menu. To start, try poached pear, stilton and walnut salad or baked goat's cheese wrapped in parma ham, or head straight for the hearty mains: ham, egg and chips, steak and kidney pudding, sausage and mash. There are also four neat

bedrooms providing basic B&B accommodation (£65 double incl breakfast).

Wealden Wholefoods Café
High Street, Wadhurst, TN5 6AA (01892 783065, www.wealdenwholefoods.co.uk). Open 9am-5.15pm Mon-Sat.
The shop is a wholesome haven, supplying organic veg, bread, dairy products and alcohol, as well as eco-friendly toiletries and household cleaners. At the back a glassed-in café serves basic breakfasts, snacks, cakes and a few vegetarian hot dishes. A glass of wine in the pretty garden is a delight in summer; in winter you can feast on thick soups and hearty bakes.

Where to stay
In Wadhurst, the Best Beech Inn (Mayfield Lane, Best Beech Hill, 01892 782046, www.bestbeech inn.co.uk) has six bedrooms (four en suite), a lounge with a coal fire, and a restaurant serving British dishes and Sunday roasts. The accommodation above Chateaubriand Antiques in the centre of Burwash (01435 882535, www.chateaubriandbed andbreakfast.co.uk) consists of just one double bedroom, a private sitting room and a shower (no bath). It's a characterful, 14th-century timber-framed building, so expect low ceilings and uneven floors.

Church House
High Street, Burwash, TN19 7EH (01435 883282, www.bandbchurchhouse.co.uk). Rates £72-£80 double incl breakfast. No credit cards.
This wisteria-draped Georgian house in Burwash offers two double rooms and one twin room – the latter with a

wonderful Raj-style tiger and elephant mural. Guests have use of the sitting room, which has books and a TV. Expect a proper country breakfast, with local bacon and eggs, and homemade bread and marmalade.

HARTFIELD & ASHDOWN FOREST

Just north of Uckfield is Maresfield, which marks the southern edge of Ashdown Forest and is also home to a Marco Pierre White restaurant/hotel, Wheeler's of St James's Chequers Inn (*see p195*). From here, the A22 heads north through the forest, via Wych Cross and Forest Row, with the village of Hartfield – the centre of Winnie-the-Pooh country – a few miles to the east.

Hartfield

Author AA Milne and his wife moved to Cotchford Farm near Hartfield in 1925 with their son, Christopher Robin; *Winnie-the-Pooh* was published in 1926 and *The House at Pooh Corner* in 1928. Pooh was named after Christopher Robin's teddy bear, and the fictional Hundred Acre Wood where Pooh, Piglet, Eeyore, Owl, Tigger and Rabbit lived was based on Ashdown Forest's Five Hundred Acre Wood. In his biography, Christopher Milne writes: 'Anyone who has read the stories knows the Forest and doesn't need me to describe it.' Pooh's forest and Ashdown Forest are identical.' Even the illustrations by EH Shepard were based directly on the local landscape. (Rolling Stone Brian Jones later owned Cotchford Farm and drowned in the swimming pool in 1969.)

The Pooh connection is nowhere stronger than at Pooh Corner on Hartfield's High Street (01892 770456, www.pooh-country.co.uk), which has,

according to the owners, the largest collection of 'Pooh-phernalia' in the world. Opened in 1978, it's now not only a popular shop, but also a font of Pooh-related knowledge – staff are happy to offer information about the real locations in the Pooh books. 'Smackerals' and 'Tigger's treats' are available in Piglet's tearoom and garden.

Nearby Perryhill Orchards (Edenbridge Road, 01892 770595, www.perryhillorchards.co.uk) is a great place to sample locally produced apple juice, cider and perry. There's also a tearoom, farm shop and the High Weald Craft Centre with items including pottery, wall hangings and jewellery, all made locally.

Things to do

HEATHFIELD & AROUND

Blackberry Farm
On the A22, Whitesmith, BN8 6JD (01825 872912, www.blackberry-farm.co.uk). Open Summer 9.30am-6pm daily. Winter 10am-4pm daily. Admission £6; £4-£5 reductions.

Pony and tractor rides, goat racing and bottle-feeding lambs are some of the activities you can get involved in at Blackberry Farm, just south of East Hoathly. There are plenty of creatures to meet, including pigs, donkeys, guinea pigs, alpacas, tortoises, cows and Shetland ponies. Keen youngsters can become a farmer for the day: after starting bright and early, and getting dressed in their own uniform, they help feed and groom animals, and collect eggs. The extensive outdoor play area caters for all ages, with climbing frames, trampolines and slides.

TEN SUSSEX GOLF COURSES

Brighton & Hove

Devil's Dyke Road, Brighton, BN1 8YJ (01273 556482, www.brightonand hovegolfclub.co.uk). Open times vary; phone for details. Green fees £22-£35.
The oldest club in Sussex (est.1887) is also one of the most beautiful. Situated high on the Downs by Devil's Dyke, this 18-hole course is challenging thanks to the sea breezes, rolling terrain and fast greens. Signature holes are the sixth and 15th, both starting high up. The pleasant clubhouse has views and a snooker room

Crowborough Beacon

Beacon Road, Crowborough, TN6 1UJ (01892 661511, www.cbgc.co.uk). Open 8am-dusk daily. Green fees £35-£45.
Crowborough Beacon dates from 1896 – Sir Arthur Conan Doyle was once captain here – and many Sussex golfers think it's the best course in the county. It's 800 feet above sea level, so there are stunning views, but also a lot of heathland full of ball-eating heather.

Dale Hill

Ticehurst, TN5 7DQ (01580 200112, www.dalehill.co.uk). Open 10am-5pm daily. Green fees £40-£45.
There are two 18-hole courses at Dale Hill, a few miles south-east of Wadhurst. The newer one was designed by Ian Woosnam and is heavily wooded, particularly around the 16th. There's also a driving range, practise putting greens and a modern 35-room hotel.

East Sussex National

Little Horsted, TN22 5ES (01825 880088, www.eastsussexnational. co.uk). Open 8am-dusk Mon-Fri; 11am-dusk Sat, Sun. Green fees £30-£50.
This top-quality golf resort contains a 104-room hotel and a spa, and is popular for business golfing breaks. The two 18-hole championship courses have staged two European Opens and many of the world's best golfers, from Nick Faldo to Colin Montgomerie, have played here. The East Course is the more challenging; the West Course takes a more beautiful route.

Goodwood

Goodwood, PO18 0PN (01243 755168, www.goodwood.co.uk). Open 8am-dusk daily. Green fees £15.50-£20.50.
To complement its racecourse and motor sports circuit, the Goodwood estate has two superb golf courses. The Downs course (originally laid out in 1914) is the hillier but most picturesque option, with views as far as Chichester Cathedral. The Park course winds around Goodwood House and is open to the public. Both have tree-lined fairways and plenty of bunkers.

Ashdown Forest ★

There's evidence of human settlement in Ashdown Forest since the late Palaeolithic period: a stone hand axe dating from 50,000 BC was found here, and later Iron Age sites have also been unearthed. The abundance of trees was crucial to the Weald's iron industry, though even by the 16th century there were concerns over what we would now call deforestation. In 1561, Anne Boleyn's cousin Richard Sackville was appointed Master Forester and engaged in the 'mastership of the Forest and keepership of the wild beasts therin.' Ownership of the forest flip-flopped between the Crown and the aristocracy, and it was used for royal hunts by Henry VIII and others.

Today, the forest covers 20 square miles, of which (despite its name) only 40 per cent is woodland – including oak, birch, beech, coppiced hazel and chestnut and some distinctive clumps of Scots pine. The rest is open heathland, both wet and dry, supporting a great variety of plants; most famous (and now rare) is the blue-purple marsh gentian, which flowers between June and October. The lowland heath attracts stonechat and meadow pipits all year round as well as woodlarks, nightjars and spotted flycatchers in summer. In the wooded areas, look out for stock doves, tawny owls and sparrowhawks. Four species of deer – fallow (the most common), roe, muntjac and sika – live in the forest; take care when driving on local roads, especially at dawn and dusk.

Numerous car parks and picnic areas are dotted across the area, but the best place to start is Ashdown Forest Centre (01342 823583, www.ashdownforest.org, closed Mon-Fri winter), one mile east of the Wych Cross traffic lights on the A22. You can learn about the forest's history, pick up detailed maps (including one of Pooh-related sites) and walking information, and there are regular exhibitions by local artists and photographers.

There's one place in the forest that almost every visitor wants to see: Poohsticks Bridge. Pooh may have been a Bear of Very Little Brain, but the game he accidentally invented is sheer genius. Hardcore fans make a pilgrimage to the humble wooden bridge in Posingford Wood, where AA Milne used to play the game with his son Christopher. Follow the footpath (signposted, if a trifle muddy) from the Pooh car park just off the B2026. Keep a sharp eye out for likely sticks along the half-mile walk as they're often in short supply; better still, bring your own. Drop (don't throw) your sticks over the edge of the bridge, then race to the other side to see which emerges first – a matter of luck, some say, though aficionados might disagree.

Alternatively, if you're feeling Poohed-out, pop into Ashdown Forest Llama Park (*see p190*) or pay a visit to Nutley Windmill, just outside Nutley village. The last open-trestle post mill in Sussex and still in working order, it's open most Wednesdays and on the last Sunday of the month from March to September.

Where to eat & drink

Hatch Inn

Colemans Hatch, TN7 4EJ (01342 822363, www.hatchinn.co.uk). Open 11.30am-3pm, 5.30-11pm daily. Lunch served noon-2.15pm Mon-Fri; noon-2.30pm Sat, Sun. Dinner served 7-9pm Mon-Sat; 6.30-8.30pm Sun.

The Hatch Inn was once a row of three cottages, thought to date from 1430 and apparently a favoured smugglers' haunt. The sense of timelessness continues today, as hours are whiled away chatting to the locals in the tiny bar. You may have to wait for a table to try the excellent food. Dishes range from hearty sandwiches to leek, pea and spinach risotto, and roast pork wrapped in filo pastry; finish with treacle tart or Sussex ice-cream.

Wheeler's of St James's Chequers Inn ★

High Street, Maresfield, TN22 2EH (01825 763843, www.wheelerschequers.com). Lunch served noon-2.30pm Mon-Sat; noon-3pm Sun. Dinner served 6-9pm Mon-Thur, Sun; 6-9.30pm Fri, Sat.

This handsome 18th-century coaching inn is an atmospheric setting for some classic British food courtesy of head chef, and Marco Pierre White protégé, Neil Thornley. The menu shares some dishes with the original Wheeler's fish restaurant in London; pies (fish, steak and ale, shepherd's) figure large, and the marvellously old-fashioned puddings include sherry trifle and eton mess. The restaurant features linen-draped tables and walls decorated with large cartoons and nostalgic photos, while the bar is a more casual affair, with dark beams and a large brick fireplace, and dishes such as smoked haddock kedgeree and corned beef hash.

Where to stay

Of the 12 rooms at Wheeler's of St James's Chequers Inn (*see above*) in Maresfield, it's the two suites that most impress. The Wellington Suite channels old-school grandiose with its four-poster bed and period furniture, while the Shelley Suite is a stylish contemporary space with dramatic floral-patterned wallpaper and curtains. All the rooms (£59-£135 double incl breakfast) were refurbished in 2010, and should be ready to welcome guests by spring 2011.

Buxted Park Hotel

Buxted, TN22 4AY (0845 072 7412, www.handpicked hotels.co.uk/hotels/buxted-park). Rates £126-£183 double incl breakfast.

Illustrative of Buxted Park's idiosyncratic history is the very large chandelier in the bar, which was looted during World War II by the then owner Basil Ionides (also interior designer of London's Savoy hotel). Built in 1722, this grand Palladian house is now part of Hand Picked Hotels' portfolio and, following a thoughtful restoration and refurbishment, is enjoying a deserved renaissance. The 44 rooms vary from simply decorated 'classics' to sumptuous suites with lovely views. The extensive grounds include three large lakes (fishing permitted – borrow a rod from reception), woods, a deer park and a walled garden. It's a popular conference and wedding destination, but time your visit well and you'll discover a peaceful corner of lovely English countryside.

Rookwood

Robin Hood Lane, Warnham, RH12 3RR (01403 252123, www.rookwoodgolf course.co.uk). Open Summer 8am-6.30pm daily. Winter 9am-5pm daily. Green fees £20-£28.

A pay-and-play public course on the edge of Horsham, with a 6,621-yard, 18-hole course and a nine-hole pitch and putt. The Sussex Barn, a bar-restaurant in a huge traditional barn with extensive outdoor terrace, is a pleasant place for a meal or a drink after a round.

Royal Ashdown Forest

Off Chapel Lane, Forest Row, RH18 5LR (01342 822018, www.royalashdown. co.uk). Open times vary; phone for details. Green fees £66-£81.

Voted one of the best 100 golf clubs in the country, Royal Ashdown Forest Golf Club was founded in 1888. It has two 18-hole courses, the Old and the West. Both are famously bunker-free, but remain challenging; the Old course is little changed in 75 years.

Royal Eastbourne

Paradise Drive, Eastbourne, BN20 8BP (01323 744045, www.regc.unospace. net). Open times vary; phone for details. Green fees £25-£45.

There are two courses at this venerable club, founded in 1887: the 18-hole Devonshire (the Duke of Devonshire is the club's president) and the nine-hole Hartington. The views are fabulous: Eastbourne lies directly beneath and on a clear day you can see as far as Dungeness. The clubhouse has recently modernised.

Singing Hills

Off the B2117, Albourne, BN6 9EB (01273 835353, www.singinghills. co.uk). Open Summer 7.30am-10pm daily. Winter 7.30am-5pm daily. Green fees £20-£27.50.

The three nine-hole courses here – the River, the Valley and the Lake – are set in a lovely part of West Sussex, with the Downs rising in the distance. The green at the second hole on the Lake course is surrounded by a moat and known as the 'Island Hole'. Practise facilities include a driving range and putting green.

West Sussex

Golf Club Lane, Wiggonholt, RH20 2EN (01798 872563, www.westsussexgolf. co.uk). Open times vary; phone for details. Green fees £70-£100.

Deemed one of the best 100 golf clubs in the country, West Sussex opened in 1930. Ranging over sandy heathland, the course was designed to be as natural as possible, with trees and lakes providing the challenges. The mock Tudor clubhouse has fine views of the South Downs.

Lewes & Around

Lewes is a handsome county town, set amid the South Downs, whose elegant Regency architecture and manicured lawns echo a bygone era. But behind its well-heeled veneer, the town has a subversive edge. Remnants of its anarchic past and hints of its liberated spirit are much in evidence, from quirky bookshops steeped in local history to conspiratorial pubs and a sprinkling of right-on artist co-operatives.

The town is so independently minded, in fact, that in 2008 retailers introduced their own currency, the 'Lewes pound', with the aim of encouraging people to spend locally (17th-century agitator and revolutionary Thomas Paine, a former resident, is the figurehead on the notes). The town's behind-doors revolutionary spirit – you feel that locals would happily embrace a republic of Lewes – spills out on to the street once a year for the Lewes Bonfire Night, a bacchanalian celebration that draws thousands of revellers.

When it's not being set alight in drunken merrymaking, Lewes is a quiet and beautifully preserved town – perhaps the most lovely in Sussex. On its High Street, independent shops outnumber chain stores, and there are plenty of cosy pubs, all serving Harveys, whose brewery dominates the High Street.

Around Lewes, tiny Tudor hamlets such as Firle and Glynde are glorious spots to stop along the many walking routes in the area (the South Downs Way passes through Lewes), while tourist draws in the Low Weald include the Bluebell Railway and 'Capability' Brown's gardens at Sheffield Park. Charleston, the country retreat of the Bloomsbury Group, is an unmissable destination for lovers of the arts and literature.

LEWES

Lewes Castle (see p200), a striking 11th-century stone motte-and-bailey fortification, is the centrepiece of the town. A hike to the top of the tower rewards you with breathtaking views across the steep sweep of the Downs, stretching out to the coast – particularly lovely at sunset. William the Conqueror first bequeathed the land to William de Warenne in 1066, and the castle was built some 300 years later on the site of a Saxon castle. With his wife, Gundrada, William also founded Lewes Priory (see p200). Lewes became a mint town after the Norman invasion, and later a prosperous little port with docks along the River Ouse, trading in grain and wool.

In 1264, the Battle of Lewes was fought in fields around the town, as Henry III's army clashed with Simon de Montfort's men during the Second Barons' War: the king was captured, and forced to concede to his rebellious barons' demands. The most infamous event in Lewes' history, however, was the Marian Persecutions between 1555 and 1557, which took place during the reign of the devoutly Catholic Mary I (Bloody Mary). In Lewes, 17 Protestants were burned at the stake in front of the Star Inn, now Lewes Town Hall, on the High Street. Among them was iron-maker Richard Woodman, whose account of his arrest was recounted in Foxe's Book of Martyrs: 'I ran down a lane that was full of sharp cinders, the men following me with swords drawn, shouting "strike him, strike him!" I was a good way ahead, but the words made me look back, and this in turn led to my capture, for I stepped on a cinder... Had I had my shoes on I could have escaped, but it was not God's will.'

Lewes's spectacular Bonfire Night celebrations, known locally as the Fifth, commemorates the 17 martyrs. It's a riotous affair, with parades of Bonfire Societies in carnival dress walking the streets, each member holding aloft a burning lantern. Effigies of current public enemies are burnt (George Bush and bankers were recent victims), but it's the traditional burning of the Pope that generally stirs up the most controversy.

Lewes' high street (called Cliffe High Street until it crosses the river, then simply High Street from the river up to the castle and beyond) and idiosyncratic shopping scene are a joy to those seeking refuge from the anodyne British chain store. By the river, Harveys Brewery & Shop (see p200) is the home of Sussex's most famous real ale, and a Lewes institution. (When the Lewes Arms was bought by Greene King, a boycott ensued until the pub put at least one Harveys ale on tap.) The beguiling Bill's Produce Store & Café (see p202) is just opposite, stacked with colourful fruit and veg and rows of own-made condiments.

The town has the middle-class foodie market covered, from upmarket confectioners to specialist fromagerie Cheese Please (46 High Street, 01273 481048, www.cheesepleaseonline.co.uk, closed Sun), where delights run from Sussex blue and lord

Chapel Hill

Lewes Castle. See p200.

Bonfire Night. See p196.

Bill's. See p202.

High Street

Harveys Brewery. See p200.

Gardener's Arms. See p202.

Places to visit

Middle Farm

LEWES

Anne of Cleves House
52 Southover High Street, BN7 1JA (01273 474610, www.sussexpast.co.uk) March-Oct 10am-5.30pm Tue-Sat; 11am-5.30pm Mon, Sun. Admission £4.40; £2.20-£3.90 reductions; £11.80 family.
The one that got away, Anna von Jülich-Kleve-Berg, was Henry VIII's fourth wife. They were married all of seven months when the marriage was annulled on the grounds of non-consummation. Unlike most of Henry's other wives, Anne managed to keep her head – and in 1541 received a generous divorce settlement, which included this house. Although Anne never lived here, it is a fine example of Tudor architecture.

Harveys Brewery
The Bridge Wharf Brewery, 6 Cliffe High Street, BN7 2AH (01273 480209, www.harveys.org.uk). Open Shop 9am-5pm Mon-Sat.
Synonymous with Lewes and the River Ouse, Harveys is Sussex's oldest independent brewery – and is still a family run business. Besides the signature rich ales, it also produces a range of seasonal draft brews, such as the dark Christmas Ale (at a jolly 8% strength) and the mellower honey-malted Harveys Kiss on Valentine's Day; pick up a bottle or two at the Brewery Shop. Alternatively, you can pop in for a pint at the adjacent John Harvey Tavern.

Lewes Castle
169 High Street, BN7 1YE (01273 486290, www.sussexpast.co.uk). Open 11am-5.30pm Mon, Sun; 10am-5.30pm Tues-Sat. Closed Mondays in Jan. Admission £6.40; £3.20-£5.70 reductions; £17 family.
For almost 1,000 years, Lewes Castle has played a pivotal role in the development of the town. William the Conqueror bequeathed the land to William de Warenne in 1066, and the motte-and-bailey castle was built some 300 years later. The Barbican gatehouse is now a bookshop and gift shop, and home to the Museum of Sussex Archaeology, while a climb to the top of the keep is rewarded by stellar views.

Lewes Priory
Priory Park, Cockshut Lane, Southover, (no phone, www.lewespriory.org.uk).
Norman baron William de Warenne and his wife Gundrada founded the Priory of St Pancras between 1078 and 1082. The first priory in England that was run by the Benedictine Order of Cluny, it became immensely wealthy, and was a popular stop for pilgrims on their way to Canterbury. After the Dissolution of the Monasteries in the 1500s, it was partly demolished, and the land fell into the hands of Oliver Cromwell; the house he built here for his son, Lord's Place, is long gone. After a long closure and massive restoration work, the priory opened to the public at the end of 2010.

FIRLE & GLYNDE

Charleston Manor ★
Firle, BN8 6LL (01323 811265, www.charleston. org.uk). Open Apr-Oct 1-5.30pm Sun. Tours 1-6pm Wed-Sat. Admission House & grounds £9; £5-£8 reductions; £23 family. Friday tours £10; £25 family.
This handsome, mellow farmhouse was once home to artists Vanessa Bell and Duncan Grant – hence its extraordinary interiors. See p203 **Do the Charleston**.

Middle Farm ★

Firle, BN8 6LJ (01323 811411, www.middlefarm.com).
Open 9.30am-5.30pm daily. Admission (farm) £3.
Home to the National Collection of Cider and Perry,
Middle Farm stocks over 100 varieties of apple-
based tipple – including its own potent Pookhill
cider. Connoisseurs head for single-variety brews
like Kingston Black, brave souls can opt for the
Naish brothers' Honest to Goodness, and everyone
should sample the house cider/perry blend, Little
Red Rooster. Once you decide on a purchase, fill
up your selected vessel and take it to the counter.

If you don't like cider, a tempting array of fresh
apple juices, sloe gin, country wines and Sussex ales
ensures there's something for everyone. In autumn,
visitors can bring a bag of their own apples to be
pressed: the cloudy, delicious juice is a world away
from the shop-bought version. The farm shop has local
cheeses and vegetables, as well as a superb butcher
with locally shot game. Youngsters will be amply
entertained while you shop by the rabbits, guinea pigs,
patrolling geese and noisy peacocks in the open farm.

THE LOW WEALD

Sheffield Park ★

Sheffield Park, TN22 3QX (01825 790231, www.
nationaltrust.org.uk/main/w-sheffieldparkgarden).
Open Garden Jan-mid Feb, Nov, Dec 10.30am-4pm
daily. Mid Feb-Oct 10.30am-5.30pm daily. Admission
£7.80; £3.90 reductions; £19.50 family.
Many gardens are at their best in spring, but Sheffield
Park comes into its own in autumn, when four linked
lakes offer dramatic reflections of the vivid reds, golds
and yellows created by the wealth of Japanese maples,
nyssa, swamp cypresses, birches and tupelo trees.
The garden was landscaped by 'Capability' Brown in
the 18th century, while the third Earl of Sheffield, who
inherited the estate in 1876, installed a cricket field
(the site of the first England vs Australia international
cricket match in 1884) and an arboretum. In 1910 it
was bought by Arthur Soames, whose passion for
horticulture was matched by an ample fortune; he
imported a huge variety of exotic trees and shrubs.
Although the house has now been divided into luxury
apartments, the garden is National Trust-owned.

SEAFORD TO SALTDEAN

Newhaven Fort

Fort Road, Newhaven, BN9 9DS (01273 517622,
www.newhavenfort.org.uk). Open Mar-Sept 10.30am-
6pm daily. Oct 10.30am-5pm daily. Admission £6;
£4-£5 reductions; £18 family.
Newhaven Fort was built in the 1860s to defend
England – and the port at Newhaven – against the
French navy. Massive guns line its ramparts, while
tunnels dug into the cliffs lead down to the magazine.
The fort played an important role during World War II,
but was left to decay after being decommissioned in
the 1960s. Following restoration work, it has become
a family-friendly attraction. The emphasis is on World
War II, with displays portraying life in the fort during
the war and a Blitz street shelter simulation. The Fort
hosts numerous events, including 1940s music and
dance nights, and children's sleepovers.

Newhaven Fort

SUSSEX

of the hundreds (a hard sheep's cheese, similar to manchego) to continental imports.

There are also some great antique shops, with eclectic curios and art deco lamps at Southdown Antiques (48 Cliffe High Street, 01273 472439), and more fashionable reclaimed salvage pieces at Cliffe Antiques Centre (47 Cliffe High Street, 01273 473266). May's General Store (49 Cliffe High Street, 01273 473787) is also worth a nose around for its herbs, hand-made soaps and health foods.

For beautifully packaged and expensive-looking gifts, drop by Wickle (24 High Street, 01273 487969, www.wickle.co.uk). Along with its own label bath soaks, scrubs and perfumes, it stocks some gorgeous gifts: old-fashioned sweeties from Hope & Greenwood, wonderfully retro children's nightlights, little leather satchels and all manner of homewear, toys and stationery. Head along Market Street and into West Street to find the Needlemakers complex (no phone, www.needlemakers.co.uk), with its arty shops and delightful café (01273 486258).

West up the High Street from the war memorial the architecture is particularly picturesque, especially if you go for a stroll in the twittens (narrow alleyways). Head south on Station Street and you'll stumble on some interesting shops, including Tash Tori Arts & Crafts (no.29, 01273 487670, www.tashtori.co.uk, closed Sun) and second-hand record shop Si's Sounds (4A, 01273 483983).

North of the High Street and opposite Station Road, follow Fisher Lane to Commercial Passage, a short alleyway on the left, and on to Castle Ditch Lane. Turn left down the lane to reach the rambling set of Victorian and Edwardian buildings that house the Star Brewery complex, which has become a creative hub. Illustrators, jewellery-makers, bespoke picture-framers, artists, bookbinders and even an acoustic guitar and mandolin-maker occupy its studios, many of which welcome visitors: check www.starbrewery.co.uk for details. Here, too, is the Hop Gallery (Castle Ditch Lane, 01273 487744, www.hopgallery.com); one of the finest arts venues in the area, it mixes modern and contemporary art across a range of mediums.

Some five minutes' walk north-east of here, on North Street, the artist-run Chalk Gallery (no.4, 01273 474477, www.chalkgallerylewes.co.uk) also deserves further exploration.

For men's clothing and accessories, pop into Paul Clark Clothiers (70 High Street, 01273 477160, closed Sun). It's as appealingly old-fashioned as its name would suggest, with vintage hand mirrors adorning the walls, wooden shelves of neatly folded shirts (Hackett, J Lindeberg, Oliver Spencer), chunky knits from Folk, Hudson shoes and grooming gear from Penhaligon's, Geo F Trumper and DR Harris.

Further up the High Street, beyond the castle, a stroll up the tiny Pipe Passage brings you to a bijou, nameless bookshop run by the affable David Jarman. It houses a fine selection of second-hand art books and fiction, ranging from 50p to £100 (for a hardback set of Sir Walter Scott). For collectable children's books, try the labyrinthine Fifteenth Century Bookshop (99-100 High Street, 01273 474160, www.oldenyoungbooks.co.uk, closed Sun winter).

Near the castle, the handsome, timber-framed Bull House (92 High Street) is the former home of the town's most famous resident, Thomas Paine, who would later make his name as one of the fathers of the American Revolution. The Sussex Archaeological Society (01273-486260, www.sussexpast.co.uk) has its offices here, and runs guided tours by advance request.

Southover

Head past the castle and Bull House then down Keere Street to reach the postcard-perfect Southover area of Lewes. The Anne of Cleves House (see p200), given to Henry VIII's former wife in 1541 as part of her divorce settlement, occupies a 15th-century townhouse on Southover High Street. If it's a sunny day and you're in no mod for museums, admire the exterior while lazing in the lush, romantic surrounds of Southover Grange Gardens (Southover Road, 01273 484999). It's perfect for a picnic, so come with supplies or invest in a recycled wool picnic rug at Wickle (see left) and stock up on provisions at Bill's (see below).

The north wing of the adjacent 17th-century Southover Grange manor house is home to the Sussex Guild Shop (01273 479565, www.the sussexguild.co.uk). It may look disconcertingly like a museum, with products marooned on white surfaces and hidden away in glass cabinets, but there is some great stuff in here. Look out for beautifully crafted bowls made by local wood turner John Plater, and Louise Bell's intricate quilts.

Where to eat & drink

Pelham House (see p207) is a smart option for afternoon tea on the terrace, lunch in the impressive Garden Room, with its eau de nil walls and magnificent views across the gardens, or dinner in the ornate Panelled Room. Head chef Peter Winn has created a simple but appealing menu; try the wood pigeon and beetroot remoulade or chicken liver parfait for starters, the rib-eye steak or smoked confit garlic soufflé for mains, and leave room for the utterly delicious desserts.

Bill's

56 Cliffe High Street, BN7 2AN (01273 476918, www.billsproducestore.co.uk). Open 8am-6pm Mon-Sat; 9am-5pm Sun.

This upmarket produce store and café has become one of Lewes' favourite haunts for wholesome breakfasts, hearty lunches and mid-afternoon little somethings – which means getting a table can be a scramble. Top-quality comfort food is the order of the day here, from bubble and squeak with fried eggs, hollandaise sauce and ham to highly superior fishfinger sandwiches; more sophisticated palates may prefer the goat's cheese tartlet or seasonal vegetable risotto. The menu may look a bit pricey, but there's top quality produce on your plate – and the results are delicious.

Gardener's Arms ★

46 Cliffe High Street, BN7 2AN (01273 474808). Open 11am-11pm Mon-Sat; noon-10.30pm Sun. No credit cards.

Do the Charleston

Artist Vanessa Bell set up house at Charleston, near Firle, in 1916 – accompanied by her lover Duncan Grant, his lover, David Garnett, and her two children. It was Vanessa's sister, the writer Virginia Woolf, who first stumbled on the old, dilapidated farmhouse and urged Vanessa to move there, in spite of its overground gardens ('all now rather run wild'), tatty decor ('the wallpapers are awful') and lack of hot water.

Undeterred, Duncan and Vanessa set about reinventing Charleston, painting every available surface with murals, from the fireplaces and furniture to the doors and walls. Textiles, ceramics and art – including works by Picasso (who visited) and Sickert – added to the glorious welter of colour and textiles. Outside, Grant and Bell reworked the walled garden to designs by the artist and critic Roger Fry, with mosaics, artfully placed sculptures, box hedges, a grid of gravel pathways and tile-bordered ponds; in 1936, Vanessa described it as a 'dithering blaze of flowers and butterflies and apples'.

The Bloomsbury set and their satellites (including Vanessa's husband, the art critic Clive Bell) descended to enjoy the results and take in the country air, while Vanessa revelled in the rural freedom. As Virginia wrote, 'Nessa seems to have slipped civilisation off her back, and splashes about entirely nude, without shame, and enormous spirit. Indeed, Clive now takes up the line that she has ceased to be a presentable lady – I think it all works admirably.'

The house, now open to visitors from April to October, looks as fantastic today as it did 90 years ago: a gloriously uninhibited explosion of colour and creativity. The annual Charleston Festival keeps its intellectual history alive: in 2010, literary heavyweights in attendance included Bill Bryson, Alan Bennett, Zadie Smith and Philip Pullman. There are many other events throughout the year including the Small Wonder short story festival. It also holds courses and literary weekends; consult the website (see p200) for details.

Guided tours are available Wednesday to Saturday, while on Sunday and bank holiday visitors are free to roam the house and gardens. The house is a bit of a trek from Glynde, the nearest train station; Countryliner service 125 runs from Lewes from Wednesday to Saturday, but a car is an easier option.

Bluebell Railway

LEWES

Spring Barn Farm
Kingston Road, Lewes, BN7 3ND (01273 488450, www.springbarnfarmpark.co.uk). Open Park Apr-Oct 9am-5.30pm daily. Nov-March 9am-4.30pm daily. Shop 9am-5.30pm Mon-Sat; 10am-5.30pm Sun. Admission £6.50; £5.50 reductions.

In summer, the big attraction at Spring Barn is its themed maize maze. A haystack, playgrounds, zip wire and pedal go-carts should burn off any remaining energy, and there are special events around Easter, Halloween and Christmas. Animals to see include alpacas, Shetland ponies, goats and, from March until May, newborn lambs. A shop sells gifts, meat from the farm and local ice-cream and cheese, while the Farmhouse Kitchen offers sturdy, wholesome fare and own-made cakes. There's a small campsite, open from April to September.

FIRLE & GLYNDE

Airworks Paragliding Centre
Old Station, Glynde, BN8 6SS (01273 858108, www.airworks.co.uk). Open by appointment. One-day introductory course £130.

This long-established centre offers courses in hand gliding, paragliding and paramotoring. Thanks to the contours of the South Downs, there are almost always good flying conditions. A one-day introduction can get you airborne by lunchtime; check the website for details of longer courses.

Glyndebourne
Glyndebourne, BN8 5UU (01273 812321, www.glyndebourne.com). Open Box office 10am-6pm daily. Tickets £7-£250.

Glyndebourne is one of the country's most important opera houses, and renowned worldwide. It was founded in 1934 by John Christie who owned Glyndebourne House and is now run by his grandson, Gus. The Glyndebourne festival runs from May to August and has a programme of six operas. There are two restaurants open during events, but many visitors bring a picnic.

Walk the Old Coach Road
There's a great walk from Firle to the village of Alfriston, along the Old Coach Road. This beautiful track is centuries old (and haunted by a black dog, according to popular legend), and is open to walkers, cyclists and horseriders. Follow the road past the Ram (*see p207*), towards the Downs, and the Old Coach Road is signposted. Some sections are concreted, although parts can get very muddy. In Alfriston, reward your endeavours with a pint at the 14th-century George Inn (01323 870319, www.the george-alfriston.com). You can return via the South Downs Way, along the top of the ridge.

THE LOW WEALD

Bluebell Railway ★
Sheffield Park Station, TN22 3QL (01825 720825, www.bluebell-railway.com). Open check website for timetable. Fares Return to Kingscote £13; £6.50 reductions; £35 family.
The romance of the steam era lives on in Sussex, where the UK's first preserved standard gauge passenger railway can be found. For £13 return you can puff along the old London & South Coast line between Sheffield Park and Kingscote, half an hour away. Ride one of more than 30 locomotives, including the Golden Arrow Pullman, which recreates the glamorous dining train that once linked London with Paris. Equally quaint is the 1920s Sussex Belle Pullman, which serves old-fashioned cream teas (call for dates). The best time to visit is when bluebells carpet the countryside in spring, but it's scenic at any time of year.

East View Riding Centre & Fruit Farm
Tanyard Lane, Danehill, RH17 7JL (01825 740240, www.ridinginsussex.co.uk). Open times vary; phone for details. Rides £20/hr. No credit cards.
Catering for all abilities, from age seven up, this reliable riding centre offers weekend and weekday rides throughout the year and evening rides in summer. There are no lessons, just escorted rides and treks along bridle paths, in the Ashdown Forest and across the owners' farm. Strawberries and raspberries from the farm are on sale between May and October.

Lavender Line
Isfield Station, nr Uckfield, TN22 5XB (01825 750515, www.lavender-line.co.uk). Open 9am-5pm Sun & bank hols. Fares £8; £5-£7 reductions; £26 family.
At just a mile long, the Lavender Line offers an endearing 15-minute round trip from Isfield to Little Horsted and back. The signal box is open to visitors and there's a model railway and an exhibition coach detailing the line's history. It's only half an hour's drive from the Bluebell line, and there's a decent pub on site, as well as a picnic area. Special services are laid on during the school holidays; check online for details.

SEAFORD TO SALTDEAN

Saltdean Lido
Saltdean Park Road, Saltdean, BN2 8SP (01273 888308, www.saltdean.info). Open May-Sept 7am-9pm Mon-Fri; 10am-6pm Sat, Sun. Admission £4; £3 reductions. No credit cards.
In the 1930s, lidos – an idea adopted from Venice's glamorous bathing spots – were all the rage, and art deco shrines to swimming and sun-worshipping sprang up across the land. The lido at Saltdean is a particularly glorious example, with its elegant, curved lines – rather like a stately ocean liner. An inviting alternative to Brighton's pebbly beach, it's also a family-friendly spot, with a shallow children's pool, a sandpit and a picnic lawn. The Grade II-listed lido is currently under threat; for updates go to www.saltdeanlidocampaign.org.

This tiny boozer has all the bonhomie of a village pub, and it's often a struggle to get a seat. The decor is functional, with beer mats stuck to the bar and a slightly grubby carpet, but that's why you come here – to escape the focaccia-munching, latte-quaffing hordes. There's a superb choice of real ale and cider, with Harveys bitter on tap and five guest beers and ciders. No-frills bar snacks include pasties and pies from the local butcher.

Lewes Arms
1 Mount Place, BN7 1YH (01273 473152, www.the lewesarms.co.uk). Open 11am-11pm Mon-Thur, Sun; 11am-midnight Fri, Sat. Lunch served noon-3pm Mon-Fri; noon-5pm Sun. Dinner served 5.30-8.30pm Mon-Fri. Food served noon-9pm Sat.
Hidden in the backstreets behind the castle, the Lewes Arms remains a welcoming, unpretentious place for a pint. Victorian fireplaces, shelves of battered books and cosy wood panelling exude a homely charm, while the commendable selection of real ale includes local Harveys bitter and seasonal ales. There's a small terrace area for summer afternoons, and a simple menu: mackerel pâté on toast, say, or own-made chilli and chips. For over ten years, the pub has hosted the annual World Pea Throwing Championship, run by the Friends of the Lewes Arms. The size and weight of the peas are strictly invigilated; if you want to start training, bear in mind that the current record is 127 feet.

Real Eating Company
18 Cliffe High Street, BN7 2AJ (01273 402650, www.real-eating.co.uk). Breakfast served 9am-noon Sat. Lunch served noon-4pm daily. Dinner served 6-9.30pm Tue-Sat.
Open from breakfast-time until dinner, the Real Eating Company is a slick, all-day operation, serving well-sourced, supremely fresh dishes. Menus and specials constantly rotate, reflecting the chain's organic, locally sourced credentials. Brunch is a forte, but everything sounds good: fisherman's pie with a poached egg and kale on the side; macaroni cheese with truffle oil and gremolata, or a plate of Sussex ham, free-range eggs and chips. The light-filled space, stripped wooden floors and friendly staff make this a welcoming spot, and there's a rear decked terrace.

Snowdrop Inn
119 South Street, BN7 2BU (01273 471018, www.thesnowdropinn.com). Open noon-midnight Mon-Sat; noon-11pm Sun. Food served noon-9pm daily.
Five minutes' walk from the High Street, the Snowdrop is a much-loved establishment, known for its quirky interior and excellent food. There's a wide selection of real ales, including brews from the excellent Dark Star brewery and Harveys, and music on Mondays, Wednesdays and Saturdays. The food is locally sourced (they have their own pigs and cattle) and vegetarians are well provided for.

Where to stay
Given the popularity of the town, it's curiously lacking in accommodation. Berkeley House B&B (2 Albion Street, 01273 476057, www.berkeleyhouselewes. co.uk) offers three en suite rooms in a Georgian terraced townhouse; its friendly owners are happy to offer recommendations and cook up a fine breakfast.

SUSSEX

Firle

Firle Cricket Club

In Offham, just outside Lewes, Mill Laine Barns (01273 475473, www.milllainebarns.co.uk) comprises six smartly converted farm buildings, and offers B&B in the Old Wash House.

Pelham House

St Andrews Lane, BN7 1UW (01273 488600, www.pelhamhouse.com). Rates £120-£240 double incl breakfast.

With its tasteful decor, period features and attentive service, his 16th-century manor house turned boutique hotel is as artful and discreet as any private members' club. The 31 newly refurbished rooms are decorated in tasteful neutrals, with splashes of colour and hand-made oak furniture; most have lovely views over the tranquil gardens and the South Downs beyond. The owner's art collection is much in evidence in the public rooms, and the restaurant (*see p202*) occupies the lovely Panelled Room and Garden Room.

Shelleys

135-136 High Street, BN7 1XS (01273 472361, www.the-shelleys.co.uk). Rates £145-£210 double incl breakfast.

The Shelleys' premises date from the 1520s, when it was called the Vine (the original sign is in the Anne of Cleves house; *see p200*). It's now a 19-room, family-run hotel, oozing discreet charm (think Regency-stripe sofas and wallpapers, tassel-tied floral curtains and Penhaligon's toiletries in the en suite bathrooms); there's also a bar and restaurant. Unsurprisingly, it's popular with wedding parties.

FIRLE & GLYNDE

Firle

The picturesque village of Firle lies just off the busy A27 that links Eastbourne with Lewes. Just outside the village, at the foot of Firle Beacon, Middle Farm (*see p201*) is home to the National Collection of Cider and Perry, a family-friendly open farm and a spectacularly well-stocked shop. From Middle Farm, it's a short drive into Firle; you can walk, but there's an unpleasant stretch along the main road.

The village of Firle, mentioned in the Domesday Book as Ferla, grew up around the Firle Estate – the centerpiece of which is Firle Place (01273 858307, www.firle.com). Built in Tudor times but given an imposing new limestone façade in the 18th century, Firle is every inch the grand country house, and supposedly provided the inspiration for Pointz Hall in Virginia Woolf's novel *Between the Acts*. Although it is still privately owned and managed by the Gage family, certain rooms are open to the public between June and September, by guided tour only. The art collection is sublime, taking in paintings by Raphael, Van Dyck and Fra Bartolommeo. Call before visiting, as serious structural repairs may mean the house is closed to visitors for 2011.

Along with its pretty, flint-studded cottages, the village is home to St Peter's Church, with a glorious John Piper stained glass window depicting William Blake's tree of life. Opposite the village hall is Little Talland House, which Virginia Woolf rented in 1911 and lived in for a year (although she flatly declared it to be 'an eyesore'). Bloomsbury acolytes can also visit the graves of Vanessa Bell, Quentin Bell and the painter Duncan Grant in the churchyard at St Peter's, though the main place is pilgrimage in these parts is nearby Charleston (*see p203*). The Bloomsbury Group's country retreat is a wonderful mellow old farmhouse, described by Vanessa Bell as: 'most lovely, very solid and simple, with flat walls in that lovely mixture of brick and flint that they use about here, and perfectly flat little windows in the walls and wonderful tiled roofs'. Inside, the rooms are covered with murals, filled with art, and still wonderfully evocative.

Founded in 1758, Firle Cricket Club is thought to be one of the oldest in the country. Ringed by huge oak trees, the cricket ground still hosts regular matches in summer; after catching some of the action, head to the Ram Inn (*see below*) for a pint and some excellent food. Firle is also the start (or finish) of the remaining part of the Old Coach Road that runs along the foot of the Downs to Alfriston. It's a fabulous walk or cycle (*see p204*) through rape and wheat fields, which ripple like water with the slightest breeze.

Glynde

Around four miles east of Lewes, and accessible by train on the Lewes to Eastbourne line, is Glynde. It's little more than a hamlet, with a parish church and a pub, the Trevor Arms (*see below*). The stately Elizabethan manor house of Glynde Place (01273 858224, www.glynde.co.uk) sits at the top of the village, with magnificent views across the Weald. Home to the 7th Viscount and Viscountess Hampden, it can be visited on guided tours in summer, though was closed for building work at the time of writing; call before planning a visit.

St Mary the Virgin, a comparitively recent addition to the village, was built in the 1800s using the readily available flint, as were the houses around the church. Glynde also still retains a traditional blacksmiths, Tyhurst & Son (Glynde Forge, The Street, 01273 858191, www.wonderfulweather vanes.co.uk), which forges everything from fire-baskets to gates and garden furniture, and offers workshops at the weekend. The village is best known, though, for Glyndebourne (*see p204*), one of the country's pre-eminent opera houses.

Where to eat & drink

In Glynde, a tearoom next to the village shop opens from April to September on Friday, Saturday and Sunday, serving light snacks and cream teas. The village pub is the Trevor Arms (01273 858208, www.trevorarms.co.uk), with Harveys cask ales, pub grub and plans afoot to open its own microbrewery. It also has an enormous beer garden with views over the Downs.

Ram Inn ★

The Street, Firle, BN8 6NS (01273 858222, www.the ram-inn.com). Open 11.30am-11.30pm Mon-Sat; noon-10.30pm Sun. Lunch served noon-3.30pm Mon-Sat; noon-4pm Sun. Dinner served 6.30-9.30pm Mon-Sat; 6.30-9pm Sun.

On top of the world

From the vantage point of Ditchling Beacon (*see p211*), the undulating contours of what Rudyard Kipling called the 'blunt, bow-headed, whale-backed Downs' stretch as far as the eye can see. To the west, the South Downs Way (www.southdownsway.co.uk) dips and climbs the chalk escarpment for some 50 miles, back to Hampshire; eastwards on the horizon lies the hazy, blue-grey outline of the cliffs at the Seven Sisters, where the Downs finally reach the sea.

The Victorians, like many modern-day visitors, preferred the drama of nearby Devil's Dyke, five miles along the ridge – a plunging, vertiginous gulf, carved from the chalk strata as the Ice Age snowfields retreated. But the Beacon, rising steeply above the villages and farmland of the Weald on one side, then sloping gently southwards towards the sea, has its own quiet pleasures and oblique charms.

It is a landscape shaped by centuries of sheep grazing – the most profitable use for these bare, precipitous inclines, with their shallow, chalky soils. The constant grazing soon put paid to any saplings or taller plants that took root on the close-cropped slopes, letting shorter, less showy species thrive.

Wild marjoram and thyme grow alongside lacy salad burnet leaves and harebells. Rosette-shaped dwarf thistles stud the turf, and yellow bird's-foot trefoil, purple autumn gentian and the vivid blue unfurlings of round-headed rampion (the 'pride of Sussex') sprinkle the slopes with colour. The flowers, in turn, bring butterflies: common blues and painted ladies, rare silver-spotted skippers or the sudden, iridescent flash of a chalkhill blue.

Ditchling Beacon's role has always been protective: an Iron Age hill fort – now a series of grassy hollows – once stood on its summit, and in 1588 the beacon that gives the hill its name was lit here, warning of the Spanish Armada's approach. Narrow, ancient bostalls (Anglo-Saxon for hill path) climb the slope from the tiny parishes down in the Weald; once used by villagers grazing their sheep, they have been engraved into the hillside by centuries of use.

Running along the crest of the hill, the South Downs Way was once a drovers' route to the great sheep fairs at Findon and Lewes. One of the dew ponds where the shepherds watered their flocks lies on a hillside to the west of the Beacon: a perfectly round, shallow dimple, lined with clay and guarded by twisted hawthorns. Further on are the 19th-century Clayton windmills, known as Jack and Jill, half-hidden behind a tangled copse. From the Beacon, it's a pleasant walk to the windmills; Jill (www.jillwindmill.org.uk) is open from 2pm to 5pm most Sunday afternoons from May to September.

Most exhilarating of all, though, are the sudden steep ascents, on paths that are little more than a series of chalky footholds hewn into the sheer slope. And at the top? No café, no toilets, and certainly no cable car: just the spirit-lifting sweep of the Sussex Weald and the white ribbon of the South Downs Way, entering its homeward straight.

SUSSEX

FIVE SUSSEX ALES

1648 Signature
The East Hoathly-based 1648 microbrewery has some excellent beers and laudable local community spirit; it even produced a beer for Eastbourne's Lammas Festival. Signature is its top seller – a robust yet refreshing pale ale. Seasonal specials such as summer's honey-infused Bee-Head are also worth looking out for on the pumps.

Beachy Head Original Ale
Of the Beachy Head brewery's beers, the Original is still the best, in our eyes – although the award-winning Legless Rambler is not to be sniffed at either. It's served at the Tiger Inn in East Dean (see p186), where it seems perfectly suited as lingering summer tipple. The taste is of cut grass, with a hefty hop kick.

Dark Star Hophead
Now based in the village of Partridge Green, Dark Star is a consistently brilliant brewery: everything they touch turns to a golden, highly drinkable beer. Light and pale, the wonderful Hophead packs quite a floral punch.

FILO Ginger Tom
The First In Last Out brewery is a tiny operation in its namesake pub in Hastings (see p156). Ginger Tom, a ginger-infused light ale, is our favourite. If that's not for you, order a pint of Crofters (an amber ale, and the brewery's biggest seller) or Cardinal – a dark and nutty Sussex porter.

Harveys Best
Sussex beer stalwarts Harveys (see p200) are part of the fabric of the county – when Harveys was pulled from a Lewes pub, the furore made national news. Harveys Best is the brewery's most popular beer, making up 90% of its brewing capacity; look out too for Star of Eastbourne, a powerful, aromatic India pale ale.

At the centre of Firle, this 17th-century inn has been carefully updated according to 21st century sensibilities, with shabby chic decor, tastefully muted paintwork and even the odd chandelier. Bar staff pull pints of Harveys Best, guest ales and ciders, while the menu offers polished gastropub-style dishes: rump of Hankham Farm lamb with sautéed new potatoes and roast veg, say, or pan fried sea bass. There's a lovely beer garden and orchard, with a play area for children, and four fabulous rooms (£95-£145 double incl breakfast) above the pub; see below.

Where to stay
Most visitors to the area stay in Lewes (see pp205-207) or Eastbourne (see p169).

In Glynde, Caburn Cottages (Ranscombe Farm, BN8 6AA, 01273 858538, www.caburncottages.co.uk) offer eight self-contained holiday cottages, with one to three bedrooms. It's a new development, but sensitively built in flint and brick.

In Firle, the Ram Inn (see above) has four swish guestrooms. Up in the eaves, you can sleep among the beams in Beacon View and wallow in the impressive double-ended bath, while the smaller Bo Peep has calming white and soft grey decor, a charming white-painted iron bed and a roll-top bath.

Sheffield Park

THE LOW WEALD

Sheffield Park & around

Heading directly north on the A275 from Lewes, you descend into the Low Weald, whose gently sloping patchwork of copses and fields lies between the Downs and the High Weald.

It's a gorgeous part of Sussex, filled with quaint villages such as Danehill and Fletching (home to the renowned Griffin Inn; *see p213*). The Bluebell Railway (*see p205*) sedately chugs its way through the countryside, accompanied by the gentle rattle of teacups in saucers and puffs of steam.

The reason for the line's original closure by British Rail back in the 1950s is partly what makes the railway's journey so special: it ran through underpopulated countryside, and the route has remained relatively untouched. As you travel through the rolling hills of the Weald, through woods and open farmland and past elegant houses and rustic cottages, the views have a timeless quality. Autumn is especially beautiful: orange and gold trees line the route, and the carriages feel wonderfully cosy as twilight descends. Come May (bluebell season), you can glimpse vivid carpets of blue in the woodland glades.

Almost directly across the road from the Bluebell Railway's Station is the entrance to Sheffield Park, a private manor house surrounded by National Trust land (*see p201*). Lancelot 'Capability' Brown designed the vast, undulating parkland to showcase a wide variety of trees and shrubs. It's one of the best place in the country to see the autumn leaves change colour, though it's stunning all year round.

Ditchling & Ditchling Beacon

At the foot of the South Downs, around 20 minutes' drive north-west of Lewes, Ditchling is a beautiful village, with a charming flint church at its centre. As local author Esther Meynell wrote in 1947: 'If St Margaret's church was snatched up by a giant hand and set down in Warwickshire or Somerset – county of stately Perpendicular towers – it would cry "Sussex" so loudly that it would have to be put back again without any delay.'

Among the village's half-timbered houses are two pubs (*see p212*), a tearoom and a handful of small shops and boutiques. There are also one or two galleries, reflecting Ditchling's longstanding links with the arts. In 1907, sculptor and typographer Eric Gill moved to the village, and in 1921 founded a

Griffin Inn

Catholic community of artists and craftsmen here. The village became a hub of creativity; in the churchyard, look out for the stones carved by Gill and his apprentice, Joseph Cribb.

Overlooking the village, Ditchling Beacon ★ (*see p208* **On top of the world**) is one of the most spectacular sites in the South Downs, and its highest point. Note that twisting, narrow Beacon Road, which runs between Ditchling village and the Beacon, is unsafe for pedestrians; you'll need to wend your way up on footpaths if you plan to walk between the two. Alternatively, there's a pay-and-display National Trust car park at the summit and a small car park at the base of the hill on Underhill Lane. The seasonal 79 bus service from Brighton (01273 292480) runs on Sundays and bank holidays throughout the year, and on Saturdays from Easter to September.

Places to eat & drink

Across the road from the Bull (*see below*) in Ditchling, the General (01273 846638) is a café-restaurant with a sunny little courtyard garden. It does a sterling line in breakfasts, cakes (all made in house) and afternoon teas, along with inventive home-cooked meals (stuffed fig salad with pancetta, chestnuts and apples, say, or fried halloumi with wilted spinach and chickpeas).

Dolly's Pantry (6 West Street, 01273 842708) is an old-fashioned tearoom, while the White Horse (16 West Street, 01273 842006, www.whitehorse ditchling.com) has Dark Star on tap, a compact seasonal menu and a handful of understated, white-painted B&B rooms. On Ditchling Beacon itself, all you'll find is an ice-cream van in the car park during the summer.

Head to the Half Moon (Ditchling Road, 01273 890253, www.halfmoonplumpton.com) in nearby Plumpton for log fires and excellent British food (pig's head terrine, local venison haunch with juniper-spiked port sauce). Another option is the Shepherd & Dog (01273 857382, www. shepherdanddogpub.co.uk) in Fulking – a 17th-century inn set at the foot of the Downs, with low, beamed ceilings and a glorious beer garden.

Over in Danehill, the Coach & Horses (School Lane, 01825 740369, www.coachandhorses.danehill.biz) is handy for a visit to Sheffield Park and the Bluebell Railway. The food is locally sourced and excellent, while the guest ales change every week. For superb views and a children's play area, head for the front garden; the suntrap rear terrace is reserved exclusively for grown-ups.

The Bull

High Street, Ditchling, BN6 8TA (01273 843147, www.thebullditchling.com). Open 11am-11pm Mon-Sat; 11.30am-10.30pm Sun. Lunch served noon-2.30pm, dinner served 6-9.30pm Mon-Fri. Food served noon-9.30pm Sat; noon-9pm Sun.

Decked with overflowing flowerboxes, this dapper inn takes pride of place on Ditchling's narrow high street. It has been smartened up considerably over the years, although its low ceilings, timber beams and cask ales still have plenty of

SUSSEX

authentic charm. Food has become a real focus; local lamb is a good bet, if it's on the menu, and the Sussex cheeseboard comes with crusty sourdough bread. There are four luxurious rooms upstairs (£80-£100 double incl breakfast).

Griffin Inn ★
Fletching, TN22 3SS (01825 722890, www.thegriffin inn.co.uk). Open noon-midnight Mon-Thur, Sun; noon-1am Fri, Sat. Lunch served noon-2.30pm Mon-Sat; noon-3pm Sun. Dinner served 7-9.30pm Mon-Sat.

From the Griffin's expansive garden, the uninterrupted views of the Ouse Valley are idyllic – and best appreciated with a flute of brut or a succulent mouthful of Fletching fillet of beef. If the weather isn't so good, the inn also has three quaint drinking rooms and a two-room restaurant with white tablecloths and a superb à la carte menu (pan fried cod with chorizo, cherry tomatoes and cannellini bean stew, perhaps, or pork chop with roast celeriac, fennel, pancetta and salsa verde). The bar menu is slightly cheaper, and there are regular summer barbecues. If you fall in love with the place, there are 13 rooms (£85-£145 double incl breakfast).

Jolly Sportsman
Chapel Lane, East Chiltington, BN7 3BA (01273 890400, www.thejollysportsman.com). Open phone for details. Lunch served noon-2.30pm Mon-Sat; noon-3.30pm Sun. Dinner served 6-9.30pm Mon-Thur; 6-10pm Fri, Sat.

Over in East Chiltington, some five miles from Lewes, the Jolly Sportsman serves some of the best food in the area (book in advance). It's hard to fault: a modern but unpretentious interior, a pretty terrace and lovely garden, a sterling wine list, beers from assorted microbreweries and exemplary cooking. On the à la carte menu, mains might include harissa coated mackerel with lime and coriander crushed potato or roast grouse, game chips, buttered greens with wild mushroom and blackcurrant sauce, while simpler ploughman's lunches and soups are advertised up on the blackboard. All this comes at a price, although the fixed lunch menu is a more affordable option.

Places to stay

In Ditchling, the four rooms at the Bull (*see left*) are plushly appointed and individually decorated; with its red red walls, sleigh bed and roll-top bath, Ruby is the largest. The Griffin Inn (*see above*) in Fletchling is another good bet, with rooms divided between the main inn and the coach house, as well as the adjacent Griffin House, which has the nicest rooms (the cream-painted antiques and pastel colour schemes are effortlessly chic).

The Low Weald is also great camping territory. Along with Blackberry Wood and the Wowo Campsite (for both, *see below*), Safari Britain (07780 871996, www.safaribritain.com) lets out canvas bell tents and a 'living yurt' to groups (a maximum of 18 people). Its site occupies a lovely spot beneath Firle Beacon from May to September, and its owners can arrange all sorts of guided activities, from foraging to falconry.

Blackberry Wood ★
Street Lane, nr Ditchling, BN6 8RS (01273 890035, www.blackberrywood.com). Rates Tent £5. Double-decker

bus £60. Gypsy caravan £35. Retro caravan £20. All plus £5-£9 per adult, £2.50-£4.50 3-12s.

Blackberry Wood is one of the campsites that made sleeping in a tent fashionable again. The setting, at the foot of the South Downs ridge near Ditchling Beacon, is magical, and the atmosphere wonderfully intimate and homely. Its 20 pitches are set in small clearings amid a tangled woodland of hawthorn, oak and ash trees, interspersed with brambles and shrubs. If pitching tents and untangling guy ropes isn't for you, alternative options include a converted 1960s London bus and two tiny caravans (a traditional wooden wagon and a '60s Dutch model called Bubble).

Newick Park Hotel & Country Estate
Newick, BN8 4SB (01825 723633, www.newick park.co.uk). Rates £165-£285 double incl breakfast.

This Grade II-listed Georgian pile is surrounded by 255 acres of parkland, and set near the village of Newick. It's now a privately owned hotel with 16 bedrooms (13 are in the main house, while three are in the Granary). The rooms are decorated in traditional country house style, with views across the impressive grounds; where possible, the hotel's restaurant uses fruit and vegetables from the walled garden and game from the estate.

RECEPTION
← LOOS + SHOWERS

Blackberry Wood

Wowo Campsite

Wapsbourne Manor Farm, Sheffield Park, TN22 3QT (01825 723414, www.wowo.co.uk). Rates Tent £10 adult; £5 child. Yurt 2 nights £136 for 2 people.

Between the hamlets of Danehill and Fletchling, Wapsbourne Manor Farm's green and pleasant campsite, known as Wowo, flanks Pellingford Brook. The site was originally a strawberry farm, but the friendly Cragg family turned the land over to campers, with instant and immense success. If you're looking for solitude, book one of the eight pitches set along the 'tipi trail' in pretty woodland (a £10 supplement applies); the three yurts offer an even more secluded stay. Campers can explore the 200 acres of farmland, interspersed with woodland and teeming with foxes, rabbits and birds. Rope swings hang from branches, and enchanting paths lead into dark groves. Families dominate the site in the holidays and there's plenty of space for kids to run, cycle and get dirty.

SEAFORD TO SALTDEAN

To the south of Lewes, the stretch of coastal road that runs between Seaford and Saltdean is a rather underwhelming experience. Although certain sections are attractive, for the most part it involves driving (or getting the number 12 bus) through unremarkable new housing. There are some nice spots on the cliffs, but run-down towns such as the port of Newhaven and the bland Peacehaven have little appeal for most visitors. There are often traffic jams, too, especially heading towards Brighton (which lies about five miles west of Saltdean) around rush hour.

One of the major ports in England during the Middle Ages, sleepy Seaford is now a retirement haven, and is also popular with bird-watchers. Its long shingle seafront is unsullied by amusement arcades or even hotels. In fact, there's very little on the esplanade – and therein lies its appeal. To the east it rises towards Seaford Head and the golf course, which then descends into the Cuckmere Valley. The Martello tower on the seafront houses Seaford Museum (The Esplanade, 01323 898222, www.seafordmuseum.co.uk, open Wed, Sat, Sun summer; Sun winter), which charts the town's role in the Cinque Port confederation, the raids it suffered at the hands of dastardly French pirates, and its development into a modern-day seaside town.

From Seaford, the A259 descends into Newhaven harbour, where the River Ouse meets the sea. Newhaven is a frankly unlovely town, although some new housing is being built back on to the Downs, and Newhaven Fort (*see p201*), built in the mid 19th century, is popular with families. From the port here, LD Lines (0800 917 1201, www.ldlines.co.uk) operates two crossings daily to Dieppe.

Next up along the coast is the town of Peacehaven, which was founded in 1916 by entrepreneur Charles Neville. The ever-resourceful Neville ran a competition in the *Daily Express* to name the town and raise publicity for his scheme; New Anzac-on-Sea won, but the name was changed to Peacehaven after the rout at Gallipoli involving Australian and New Zealand Army Corps (ANZAC) soldiers. The town's only other claim to fame comes courtesy of Graham Greene's *Brighton Rock*, as Pinkie Brown falls to his death from its cliffs.

Just beyond Peacehaven is Saltdean, another relatively new development (there was nothing here in 1920). The town is most famous for the fabulous art deco Saltdean Lido (*see p205*). The lido has struggled to stay open and its future is far from certain, but there's enough will in the town to keep it running. For a blustery stroll, a short promenade called Undercliff Walk can be accessed by some stairs opposite the lido.

Wowo Campsite

Brighton & Hove

With its bracing sea air and whiff of scandal, Brighton has a charm all of its own. It may have started life as a humble fishing village, but when the Prince Regent came here for his first 'season' in 1783, its status as a fashionable seaside resort was sealed. As William Thackeray wrote, 'It is the fashion to run down George IV, but what myriads of Londoners ought to thank him for inventing Brighton!'. Its Regency heyday left the town with stately seafront terraces and squares to rival those of Bath – along with its one-of-a-kind Royal Pavilion, a study in architectural excess.

Despite its kiss-me-quick seaside attractions, Brighton is a city that shuns the mainstream and embraces counterculture. It has an ebullient gay scene and a packed arts calendar, culminating in the three-week arts extravaganza of the Brighton Festival. It's also home to a laid-back but fiercely independent shopping scene, encompassing flea markets, art galleries, jewellery shops and delis.

Just along the coast, neighbouring Hove is a more genteel proposition, but equally lovely for a leisurely day of boutique browsing and café-hopping.

BRIGHTON

Central Brighton has many faces. North Laine and the Lanes comprise its creative and culinary heart – a fantastical bubble where niche shops selling bonsai trees, comics or vegetarian shoes do a thriving trade, and 'organic' and 'vintage' are the buzzwords of the day. The so-called Cultural Quarter, meanwhile, is a small district surrounding the Royal Pavilion and the Brighton Dome complex.

While the Lanes have their chic boutiques and North Laine remains custodian of Brighton's hippy soul, the often-overlooked City Centre has its own appeal. Turn an unassuming corner or climb a steep residential hill and you'll find yourself in a different world – home to many of the best pubs in the city, various independent theatres and galleries and plenty of unusual shops.

Brighton's main attraction, though, remains the seafront. Wherever your wanderings take you, all roads lead irresistibly to the sea, and the famously pebbly beach. This is where all of Brighton comes out to play in the summer, until the sun sets spectacularly over the wave-lashed remains of the West Pier – a broodingly beautiful spectacle.

Just back from the seafront, beyond the bright lights of Brighton Pier, Kemp Town is the city's gay quarter, and one of its liveliest areas. Further east, at the end of the quaint Volk's Electric Railway, are the boats and smart apartment complexes of Brighton Marina.

To the west of Brighton, Hove (see p225) has a more relaxed, sedate feel, and is home to some fine restaurants and independent shops.

North Laine ★

From the station down to the sea, bounded by Trafalgar Street and North Street, lies a rainbow maze of quirky cafés, clothes shops and brimming record stores. In full swing, it's as chaotic as it is colourful, as diners chowing down on falafel wraps spill across the pavement, intertwining with street stalls, shoppers and the odd guitar-toting musician.

In the evening, there's drinking, dining and music: you'll find big international names at the Brighton Dome, alternative, world and folky tunes at Komedia (see p233) and local talents at the Prince Albert (48 Trafalgar Street, 01273 730499).

It wasn't always thus. The word 'laine' means open field, and this was once arable land. The late 1700s and early 1800s saw the area evolve into a pocket of dilapidated urban sprawl, despite its proximity to the Royal Pavilion, and slums and slaughterhouses stood where Brightonians sip organic cider and superfood smoothies.

Head left out of the station, down Trafalgar Street, and you're plunged straight into North Laine's narrow streets. Three main shopping drags thread through its heart – Sydney Street, Kensington Gardens and Gardner Street – although forays into the terrace-lined backstreets can also reap rich rewards.

Locals love a bric-a-brac fix, and tat and treasures abound in the famous Snooper's Paradise (7-8 Kensington Gardens, 01273 602558). Squeeze through the turnstile to browse its myriad stalls, crammed with everything from bags of buttons and Bakelite telephones to stylish 1960s lamps. For vintage clothes, head for To Be Worn Again (12 Kensington Gardens, 01273 687811) or the super-stylish Hope & Harlequin (31 Sydney Street, 01273 675222, www.hopeandharlequin.com), whose swing coats and lace '50s frocks ooze old-school glamour.

If the allure of vintage starts to wane, Tribeca (21 Bond Street, 01273 673755) has a beautifully edited selection of womenswear labels, with an understated, grown-up feel: Isabel Marant is a favourite here, along the likes of Vanessa Bruno, American Retro and Paige jeans. For a more quintessential Brighton look, drop by Vegetarian Shoes (12 Gardner Street, 01273

NEWHAVEN to Dieppe — 4 hrs

685685, www.vegetarian-shoes.co.uk, closed Sun), or try a kitsch Mexican skull-print frock for size at Get Cutie (33 Kensington Gardens, 01273 688575, www.getcutie.co.uk). There may not be enough vinyl for music geeks' liking at nearby Resident (28 Kensington Gardens, 01273 606312, www.resident-music.com), but clued-up staff offer recommendations on releases old and new, and this is the place to get gig tickets in Brighton. (If you are into vinyl, *see p219*.)

In a city long associated with dirty weekends, it seems only right to drop by sex toy boutique Lust (43 Gardner Street, 01273 699344, www.lust.co.uk). To get into Brighton's mod vibe, meanwhile, men's clothes shop Jump the Gun (36 Gardner Street, 01273 626333, www.jumpthegun.co.uk) is nirvana for anyone who owns a Fred Perry shirt or ever had designs on a Lambretta – there's always one parked outside. For the pork pie hat to complete the look, head to Mad Hatters (89 Trafalgar Street, 01273 688488, www.madhattersandfriends.co.uk), which stocks all manner of hand-made headgear.

Cultural Quarter
North Laine offers a salient contrast to Brighton's most iconic building, the opulent Royal Pavilion (*see p226*). Designed by John Nash, the Prince of Wales' seaside home is an extravagant mix of chinoiserie, baroque and Gothic – and if you think the exterior looks a bit OTT, wait until you venture inside. The banqueting room alone, with its extraordinary chandelier, is worth the admission fee. The pleasure-loving Prince decamped here to escape his father's watchful eye and pursue a life

of drinking, riding, bathing, womanising and gambling – and fashionable Londoners followed in droves.

After emerging from the Pavilion, stroll through the gardens towards the pedestrianised New Road. It's here that the Prince Regent celebrated his 33rd birthday in 1795 with a vast firework display. Straight ahead is the Theatre Royal (35 Bond Street, 0844 871 7627, www.ambassadortickets.com), which opened in 1807 with a performance of *Hamlet* starring Drury Lane favourite Charles Kemble.

On the right is the Brighton Dome complex. Once the stables for 60 horses and the quarters of the Prince Regent's grooms and stable boys, it's now one of the city's most important cultural venues, encompassing the Corn Exchange, Concert Hall and Pavilion Theatre. Also in the building is the Brighton Museum & Art Gallery (*see p226*). The complex is also the centrepiece of the Brighton Festival each May – a month of culture and partying.

Nearby are Pavilion Parade and the grassy expanse of Old Steine, with its imposing Regency fountain. It's here that Brighton society would parade in all their finery, attempting to catch the eye of royalty.

Along the seafront
It was the mid 18th-century fashion for spas and sea bathing that first drew the Prince Regent to Brighton, 'the Queen of the Watering Places'. Lewes physician Dr Richard Russell was one of the medical champions of the 'sea-cure', publishing his influential *Dissertation of the Use of Sea Water in Diseases of the Glands* in 1750 – a big seller, despite its unwieldy title.

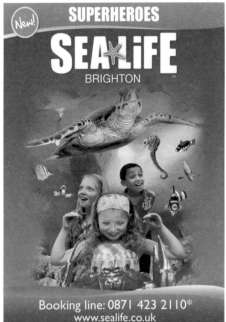

To preserve their modesty, visitors got changed in wooden coaches that were drawn into the sea by horses, known as bathing machines. The coaches were controlled by 'dippers', mostly female, who touted for business along the Steine. The most famous was Martha Gunn, who was favoured by the Prince himself and was, according to her gravestone at St Nicholas' Church, 'Peculiarly Distinguished as a bather in this Town nearly 70 Years'.

The bare frame of the Victorian West Pier, which burnt down in 2003, is a poignant reminder of the past – but the seaside's appeal has endured, despite Brighton's resolutely stony beach. On the shore by the ruined pier, work has begun on the Brighton i360 (www.westpier.co.uk), a 150m-tall observation tower, masterminded by the team that built the London Eye. If all goes to plan, it will open in 2012.

Jutting out into the English Channel to the east, meanwhile, is Brighton Pier (see p226). Also known as Palace Pier, it's a riot of bright lights, garish amusements, candyfloss, kiss-me-quick hats and haunted houses, where kids shriek, coins teeter on the two-penny falls and Elvis croons softly in the background.

Between the two piers, the wide lower esplanade is bordered by pebble beaches and the art galleries, shops, museums, pubs and clubs that inhabit the King's Road Arches, built in the late 1800s as fishing huts and boat builders' sheds. Fittingly, Brighton Fishing Museum (see p226) occupies

Vinyl heaven

Music fans, and vinyl junkies in particular, should consider making a special trip to Brighton. In addition to Rounder (see p231) and Resident (see p216), there are a number of places where the LP is king. On Trafalgar Street there's Wax Factor (01273 673744, www.thewaxfactor.com, closed Sun), great for second-hand vinyl and books, with a rock 'n' roll café attached. Across the Tracks (01273 677906, www.acrossthetracksrecords.com) on Gloucester Road is also a good source of second-hand records. The Record Album (Terminus Road, 01273 323853, www.therecordalbum.com, closed Sun), the grandaddy of record stores in Brighton, is a leading supplier of film soundtracks as well as second-hand records, while Borderline (01273 818611) on Gardner Street has a selection of more unusual CDs and new vinyl. Over on Baker Street, near London Road, Monkey Music Emporium (07814 955217, closed Sun) sells vintage hi-fi as well as vinyl.

several arches, offering an evocative glimpse of the Brighton of old; in May, the museum is the focal point for the Annual Mackerel Fayre and the Blessing of the Nets ceremony. The arches are also home to the delightfully quirky Mechanical Memories Museum (see p227), with its one-arm bandits, clairvoyant machines and other vintage amusements.

SUSSEX

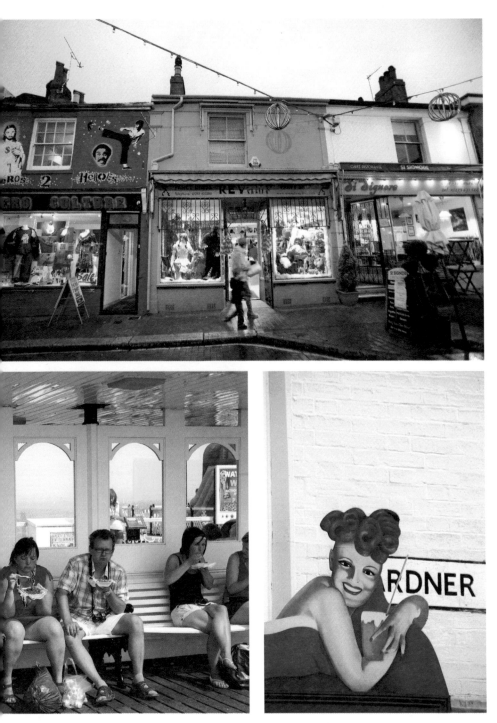

TEN PUBS & BARS

Basketmakers Arms
For listings, see p228.
This cosy corner pub is everything a traditional boozer should be. Cask ales from Fuller's, carefully chosen guest ales and a 100-strong selection of whiskys (including a 'malt of the month') are among the tipples – and that's before you've even started on the bottled beers.

Bedford Tavern
30 Western Street, BN1 2PG (01273 739490). Open noon-midnight Mon-Thur, Sun; noon-1am Fri, Sat. Food served noon-6pm Sun.
There are plenty of original features at this 200-year-old pub, including exposed beams and an open fire, and many a ghost story too. Following a period in the doldrums, it has been restored to its former glory by the team behind North Laine's Brighton Tavern.

Black Dove
74 St James's Street, BN2 1PA (01273 671119). Open 4pm-midnight Mon-Thur, Sun; 4pm-1am Fri, Sat.
This recent addition to the Kemp Town drinking scene is one of the most singular and sophisticated. Decorated with intriguing junk and striking bespoke artwork, it stocks an impressive array of drinks, from beers to good organic wines.

Brighton Rocks
6 Rock Place, BN2 1PF (01273 600550, www.brightonrockspub.com). Open noon-11pm Mon-Wed; noon-midnight Thur; noon-1am Fri, Sat; noon-10.30pm Sun. Food served 6-10pm Thur, Fri; noon-3pm, 6-10pm Sat; 12.30-6pm Sun.
This stylish Kemp Town bar has a decked area out back, and an intimate, cosy vibe inside. A wide-ranging wine list, quality cocktail list and inspired bar snacks and tapas add to the appeal.

Cricketers
15 Black Lion Street, BN1 1ND (01273 329472, www.goldenliongroup.co.uk). Open 11am-11pm Mon-Wed, Sun; 11am-midnight Thur; 11am-1pm Fri, Sat. Food served noon-9pm Mon-Thur; noon-7pm Fri-Sun.
This cosy, historic pub invariably accommodates gaggles of blokes, clusters of shoppers and local employees on their lunch breaks – as well as the odd solitary literary soul, attracted by mention of the place in *Brighton Rock* by former regular Graham Greene.

Dover Castle
43 Southover Street, Hanover, BN2 9UE (01273 688276). Open 9am-midnight Mon-Sat; noon-midnight Sun. Food served noon-3pm, 6-9.30pm Mon-Fri; noon-9.30pm Sat; noon-8pm Sun.

At no.165, Castor & Pollux (*see p230*) is a friendly little gallery, specialising in prints; it's always worth popping in to see the latest exhibition, and to browse the superbly stocked book and gift shop. Finally, for a taste of the sea beyond the chippies, call in at Jack & Linda Mills Traditional Fish Smokers (no phone) for hot mackerel rolls or a crab sandwich to eat on the beach.

Further east, beyond Brighton Pier, the Sea Life Centre (*see p227*) is the oldest operating aquarium in the world, while Volk's Electric Railway (*see p233*) is the oldest operating electric railway. It has been shuttling tourists between the pier and what is now Brighton Marina since 1883. The stop is by the thoroughly 21st-century Yellowave Beachsports (*see p233*); a patch of sandy Los Angeles on pebbly Brighton beach, Yellowave is a beach volleyball and beach soccer court, with weekly barbecues, a bar and a climbing wall.

The Lanes
Sitting pretty by the sea, the Lanes are Brighton's labyrinthine jewellery quarter. Once lined with tiny fisherman's cottages, the narrow alleys (or twittens) can be a real squeeze, so be prepared for bottlenecks. As you'll invariably get lost anyway, the wisest approach is to wander by the glittering window displays with no fixed plan, eyeing the antique emerald-set rings and diamond-studded bracelets.

There's beautiful art deco, Victorian and Edwardian jewellery at Fidra (47 Meeting House Lane, 01273 328348, www.fidra.com); for something more modern, the collection of charms at Jeremy Hoye (22A Ship Street, 01273 777207, www.jeremy-hoye.com) includes a miniature Brighton Pavilion and a tiny copy of Graham Greene's *Brighton Rock*.

On Dukes Lane, Jewel Thief (26 Dukes Lane, 01273 771044. www.jewelthiefgallery.com) has a keen eye for rising talent: Grainne Morton's delicate butterfly bracelets are particularly lovely. It's also close to two chocolate shops, Montezuma's (*see p231*) and Choccywoccydoodah (*see p230*) – the latter's owners also run a nearby café, Bar du Chocolat (27 Middle Street, 01273 732232).

There are plenty of pubs to duck into, including the Cricketers (*see right*), and even more restaurants. Food for Friends (*see p229*) and Terre à Terre (*see p234*) are two standout vegetarian eateries, while Riddle & Finns (*see p231*) does a fine line in seafood, from Pernod-soaked rock oysters to own-made fish pie.

City centre
At the centre of Brighton is the Jubilee Clock Tower, constructed in 1888 to commemorate Queen Victoria's Golden Jubilee. From the clock tower, club-filled West Street runs south towards the seafront, awash with alcohol, aftershave and hen parties. To the west, meanwhile, are the crowded shopping areas of Western Road and Churchill Square. Although Churchill Square Shopping Centre (01273 327428, www.churchillsquare.com) isn't the kind of place to get the pulse racing, it does cover a lot of ground: Urban Outfitters, Zara, Habitat and an Apple Store are among its 80 shops.

But there's more to the city centre than brash clubs and mainstream shopping. Steer away from the main drag and you'll find all manner of unexpected gems, from hidden boutiques and innovative art galleries to quirky cafés and beautiful buildings. Just off Dyke Road, for instance, the cartoonishly gothic, grey-painted Wykeham Terrace was a refuge for 'fallen' women in the 1830s.

Follow Dyke Road north and you'll come to Seven Dials (a quaint name for what is essentially a roundabout). It's a compact, alternative shopping spot crammed with delis and independent gift shops, such as Sixty Seven (67 Dyke Road, 01273 735314, www.shopatsixtyseven.co.uk). As the vintage lips-shaped sofa in the window suggests, this place has more style than your average card and candle shop: stock might run from old-fashioned children's colouring books to the odd piece of '60s Ercol furniture. At no.84, floral and interior designer Kate Langdale (84 Dyke Road 07944 756277, www.katelangdale.com, closed Mon-Sun) has set up a deliciously pretty showroom, with lampshades, soft furnishings, nightwear and baby toys made from vintage fabrics – all very country-garden chic.

Meanwhile, Upper North Street and adjoining Montpelier Place are slowly developing into a little artists' quarter. The modest row of shopfronts now accommodates various studio-boutiques, including rug- and bag-makers Steve & Alistair (47 Upper North Street, 01273 777523), where Alistair McCready sits making shoulder bags at his sewing machine, among piles of rugs sourced from Iran and Afghanistan. On Montpelier Place, Lmnop (no.17, 01273 911288, www.lmnopshop.com) showcases self-published and handmade work by some of the city's illustrators, typographers, print-makers and comic-book writers. Just off Upper North Street, at no.34 Hampton Place, the cramped Billies Café (01273 774386) attracts queues along the pavement on Sunday mornings for its enormous, lavishly-topped potato hashes.

The area between Western Road and the sea is home to most types of eaterie, from the fish-focused Regency Restaurant (131 King's Road, 01273 325014, www.theregencyrestaurant.co.uk), which has overlooked the West Pier since the 1930s, to atmospherically windswept cafés such as the Bucket & Spade Beach Café (26-28 King's Road Arches, 01273 220222), and the takeaway joints of Preston Street.

Kemp Town

East of the Old Steine, Kemp Town is home to an enticing jumble of grand Regency crescents, bric-a-brac shops, enticing delis, cosy cafés and pubs; it's also Brighton's gay quarter. There's a naturist beach, discreetly shielded by the shingle, and a lively nightlife scene, with the larger gay clubs and bars set along the seafront strip. Otherwise, the action centres on the long and colourful St James's Street, which leads to the quieter, calmer Kemp Town village.

The best shopping is along Upper St James's Street, where the neon sign of Brighton Flea Market at no.31A (01273 624006, www.flea-markets.co.uk) is a beacon for bargain-hunters. Antique and vintage

Hanover may be slightly off the beaten track, but it's worth a detour. If you drop by in the daytime, you'll also find the little Muesli Mountain Market (www. mueslimountainmarket.co.uk, Mon-Sat 9am-4.30pm) in full swing in the car park. Come the evening, the pub's dimly lit interior is unassuming, but the vibe is effortlessly cool. It's a Shepherd Neame pub, with a choice of four ales, plus some interesting bottled beers. Food is upmarket, contemporary pub grub.

Evening Star
55-56 Surrey Street, BN1 3PB (01273 328931, www.eveningstarbrighton. co.uk). Open noon-11pm Mon-Thur, Sun; 11.30am-midnight Fri, Sat. Food served noon-3pm Mon-Sat.
Set near the station, this is a haven for real ale types, with Hobbit-friendly ceilings and occasional live music. The owners run a microbrewery of the same name, so there's a rotating selection of fine house brews and seasonal ales. A host of Flemish tipples by the bottle will also delight aficionados.

Greys
105 Southover Street, Hanover, BN2 9UA (01273 680734, www.greyspub. com). Open 4-11pm Mon-Wed; 4-11.30pm Thur; 4pm-12.30am Fri; noon-12.30am Sat; noon-11pm Sun. Lunch served noon-4pm Sun. Dinner served 6-9pm Tue-Thur.
A little local on Southover Street, known for its exceptional music programme; you'll need to buy a ticket. Acoustic and folk musicians from as far afield as Nashville, Memphis and Vancouver have performed here. Monday is gig night. The rest of the time it's a popular pub with Harvey's on tap and excellent food.

Hand in Hand
33 Upper St James's Street, BN2 1JN (01273 699595). Open noon-midnight Mon-Sat; noon-11.30pm Sun.
This tiny, traditional Kemp Town boozer attracts a more mature, discerning clientele, thanks to an outstanding range of ales. Order a pint of Kemp Town ale, brewed on the premises in the microbrewery (Brighton's oldest), and squeeze in alongside the regulars (it really is small).

Hop Poles
13 Middle Street, BN1 1AL (01273 710444). Open noon-midnight Mon-Thur, Sun; noon-1am Fri, Sat. Food served noon-9pm Mon-Sat; noon-7pm Sun.
For a refreshing, well-kept pint in a charming pub, a stone's throw from the seafront, you can't go far wrong with the Hop Poles. Consistently excellent food is its main selling point, though, with an ever-changing menu that might run from hefty burgers and Greek mezzes to sterling weekend roasts.

West Pier. See p219.

Marwood Café. See p230.

shops cluster along the street: for furniture, lighting and ceramics, try In Retro Spect (37 Upper St James's Street, 01273 609374, closed Mon-Wed) or Metro Deco (38 Upper St James's Street, www. metro-deco.com). For vintage clothes, drop by the charming Margaret's at no.30A (01273 681384, closed Mon-Wed, Sun). If you're looking for canine couture, check out the diamanté collars at Doggy Fashion (98 St James's Street, 01273 695631, www.doggyfashion.co.uk, closed Sun).

By now you'll probably be in need of a rest: head back to the murky, much-loved Hand in Hand (*see p223*) for a restorative pint of its own-brewed ale, or to Metro Deco for tea and cake. If you have a dog in tow (kitted out with resplendent new togs, naturally), note that they also serve home-made doggie treats.

Hove

Hove, the burial place of Bronze-age kings and playground of Regency Princes, has every right to claim distinction. The famous phrase beloved by Hovians, 'Hove, actually', supposedly stems from residents' nose-in-the-air response at being asked where in Brighton they come from: when the town merged with its noisy neighbour in 1997 to become Brighton & Hove, the phrase came to encapsulate local resistance to the plan.

Western Road segues seamlessly from Brighton city centre into Hove, crossing the old parish boundary at Little Western Street. IGigi (31A Western Road, (01273 775257, www.igigigeneralstore.com) is one of the first shops you'll come to in Hove – although you won't notice the difference. It sells

Places to visit

Brighton Royal Pavilion

Booth Museum Of Natural History
194 Dyke Road, BN1 5AA (03000 290900,
www.brighton-hove-rpml.org.uk). Open 10am-5pm
Mon-Wed, Fri, Sat; 2-5pm Sun. Admission free.
This wonderfully old-school, 'dead things in glass
cases'-style museum was built to house the collection
of Victorian ornithologist (and gun enthusiast) Edward
Booth. Behind the small red doors you'll find over
half a million insects, animal skeletons, and stuffed
birds, posed – rather ghoulishly to modern eyes – in
re-creations of their natural habitats. A favourite with
children, artists and ironists, its most popular exhibits
include the 'mer-man' (a Victorian fake, cobbled
together from a fish and a monkey) and the 140-
million-year-old bones of a Sussex dinosaur.

Brighton Fishing Museum
201 King's Road Arches, BN1 1NB (01273 723064,
www.brightonfishingmuseum.org.uk). Open 10am-5pm
daily. Admission free.
The hub of Brighton's fishing quarter, down in King's
Road Arches, this volunteer-run museum documents
the city's maritime history with photographs, film clips
and memorabilia. Once you're done, take a stroll along
the promenade, or pop into the Brighton Shellfish and
Oyster Bar (www. brightonshellfish.co.uk) at no.199 for
a sea-themed snack.

Jubilee Library
Jubilee Street, BN1 1GE (01273 290800, www.city
libraries.info). Open 10am-7pm Mon, Tue; 10am-5pm
Wed, Fri, Sat; 10am-8pm Thur; 11am-4pm Sun.
A stunning, eco-friendly, award-winning building that
operates as a library but also has a shop, with a
wide range of classy gifts (including stationery, cards,
puzzles and posters), reading and writing groups
and a rare books collection.

Brighton Museum & Art Gallery
Royal Pavilion, 4-5 Pavilion Buildings, BN1 1EE
(03000 290900, www.brighton-hove-rpml.org.uk).
Open 10am-5pm Tue-Sun. Admission free.
Located in the Royal Pavilion gardens, the Brighton
Museum houses a variety of galleries and exhibitions.
There's pottery, fine art, and contemporary paintings,
as well as galleries dedicated to performance art and
fashion. The shop sells an interesting mix of souvenirs
and gifts, and there's a café too.

Brighton Pier
Grand Junction (01273 609361, www.brightonpier.
co.uk). Open 11am-5pm Mon-Fri; 10am-10.30pm
Sat, Sun. Admission free.
Brash, brassy Brighton Pier is brilliant fun: let any
notions of good taste and decorum go, and surrender
to its flashing fairground rides and amusements,
candyfloss kiosks and hook-a-duck booths. At dusk,
linger at the seafront to watch flocks of starlings
swarm around the pier.

Brighton Royal Pavilion ★
BN1 1EE (03000 290900, www.royalpavilion.org.uk).
Open Apr-Sept 9.30am-5.45pm daily. Oct-Mar 10am-
5.15pm daily. Admission £9.80; £5.60-£7.80
reductions; £25.20 family.
The Prince Regent's outlandish country farmhouse-
turned-mock-Mughal palace was designed by John
'Marble Arch' Nash between 1815 and 1822. The
assemblage of minarets, balconies and domes freely
mixes Indian, Chinese and Gothic notes in the pursuit
of ornate excess, and the Prince's illicit love nest never
ceases to amuse and amaze. The interiors are equally
intriguing, and even more lavish, with magnificent
chinoiserie, columns topped with palm fronds, writhing
gilded dragons and an imitation bamboo staircase.

SUSSEX

Brighton Toy Museum
52-55 Trafalgar Street, BN1 4EB (01273 749494, www.brightontoymuseum.co.uk). Open 10am-5pm Tue-Fri; 11am-5pm Sat. Admission £4; £3 reductions; £12 family.
Under the arches of Brighton Station, this modest museum is a nostalgia-inducing experience for grown-ups, with its slightly spooky wooden puppets, brightly painted Tri-ang cars, gleaming train sets and doll's house furniture. There are some lovely vintage toys for sale in the shop, along with new toys and books.

Hove Museum & Art Gallery
19 New Church Road, BN3 4AB (03000 290900, www.brighton-hove-rpml.org.uk). Open 10am-5pm Mon, Tue, Thur-Sat; 2-5pm Sun. Admission free.
Occupying an Italianate Victorian villa, Hove's museum is home to all manner of treasures. Its contemporary craft and decorative arts collections are superb, running from contemporary designs by Ron Arad and Philippe Starck to an original Dalí 'Mae West' sofa. The fine art collection is wonderfully wide-ranging, taking in works by Constable, Hogarth, Gainsborough, Stanley Spencer and William Blake. It also features exhibitions of 18th-century toys and early movie-making memorabilia, as well as photos and artefacts from Hove through the ages.

Mechanical Memories Museum
250C King's Road Arches, BN1 1NB (no phone, www.mechanicalmemoriesmuseum.co.uk). Open noon-6pm weekends and school hols only – times vary depending on weather. Admission free.
A working museum, Mechanical Memories offers a charming diversion from the mass of seafront tack in the vicinity, paying homage to the automated entertainments of yester-year. The vintage slot machines date from the early 1900s until around 1960; buy old-fashioned pennies to play on the likes of fortune-tellers, horse racing games and One-Armed Bandits. Kids can stamp their name on to aluminium strips (like dog tags), and giggle at the saucy What the Butler Saw machines.

Old Police Cells Museum
Town Hall, Bartholomew Square, BN1 1JA (01273 291052, www.oldpolicecellsmuseum.org.uk). Open times vary; phone for details. Admission free.
Underneath the Town Hall, the Old Police Cells Museum charts the history of policing in Brighton. You can peek into the bleak cells, see the room in which the Chief Constable was murdered in 1844 (a suspect he was questioning seized a poker from the fireside and bludgeoned him to death), and learn about some of the mods and rockers who briefly incarcerated here after violence on the beaches. Police uniforms, rattles and radios round off the collection.

Preston Manor
Preston Drove, BN1 6SD (03000 290900, www. brighton-hove-rpml.org.uk). Open Apr-Sept 10.15am-4.15pm Tue-Sat; 2.15-4.15pm Sun. Admission £5.50; £3.10-£4.50 reductions; £14.10 family.
Home to the Stanford family for over a century, Preston Manor is an evocative re-creation of Edwardian life, with an *Upstairs, Downstairs* mix of elegant reception rooms and bedrooms and more

humble kitchens, sculleries and servants' quarters. It is allegedly one of Britain's most haunted houses, with a long history of supernatural experiences; book a place on one of the late-night ghost tours if you want to see for yourself.

Preston Park
Preston Road, BN1 6HL (www.brighton-hove.gov.uk). Open 24hrs daily.
Formally opened in 1884, the expansive green spaces of Preston Park provide some much needed-peace amid the bustle of Brighton. There's a charming rose garden by the 1920s Rotunda tea pavilion, and a romantic walled garden; the winding Rookery Rockery, meanwhile, is the largest municipal rock garden in the country. There's plenty for more active types too: eight tennis courts, four football pitches, three bowling greens, two cricket pitches, a softball pitch and a 500m velodrome.

Sea Life Centre
Marine Parade, BN2 1TB (01273 604234, www.sealifeeurope.com). Open 10am-5pm daily. Admission £15.50; £10.50-£13 reductions; £45 family.
Just by Brighton Pier, the Sea Life Centre is the world's oldest operating aquarium. There's a rock pool where you can touch the resident crabs and starfish, an underwater tunnel with sharks cruising by, and displays of seahorses, piranhas and translucent moon jellyfish. Taking star billing among the sea creatures, though, is Lulu the giant sea turtle.

Brighton Pier

tastefully muted homewear and quality menswear (labels include Albam and Ally Capellino), and incorporates a decent café; womenswear is sold a few doors down, at no.37.

City Books ★ (23 Western Road, 01273 725306, www.city-books.co.uk) is a local literary institution, thanks to its intelligent selection of titles, friendly service and roster of special events; when Hove resident Nick Cave released *The Death of Bunny Munro*, Will Self interviewed him here. At no.54, Rume (01273 777810, www.rume.co.uk) is a seriously good contemporary furniture shop. Run by second-generation designer and craftsman Richard Baker, it sells two of its own furniture lines (think clean, edgy takes on quintessentially English styles), along with selected pieces from SCP.

Further along Western Road towards Hove, cafés and restaurants dominate the street. The Real Eating Company (86-87 Western Road, 01273 221444, www.real-eating.co.uk/hove) is a popular lunch spot, serving wholesome, locally sourced food, while Meadow (*see p230*) is good for an upmarket dinner. After Western Road turns in to Church Road, look out for Treacle & Co (no.164, 01273 933695, www.treacleandco.co.uk). After supplying gorgeous gooey cakes to Brighton eateries for some time, its owners decided to open this place. The diminutive premises are piled high with cookbooks, old china tea-sets and shabby chic furniture, but it's the buns and cakes that are unmissable.

Brighton Marina

Brighton Marina, a ten-minute bus ride from the city centre, is home to a cluster of shops, restaurants, bars and markets, along with a waterfront outpost of the Hotel Seattle (*see p234*) chain. Opened in the 1970s and architecturally somewhat bland, it is the UK's largest marina.

Many visitors come here for the water sports (*see p232*), but there's also a cinema, bowling alley and casino. Each weekend, the Mermaid Market takes over Marina Square (11am-4pm), showcasing arts and crafts, jewellery and fresh produce. At the marina's eastern edge is a plush residential swathe of balconied flats and houses, sandwiched between colossal white cliffs and the outer harbour; many residents have boats bobbing outside.

There are more than 20 bars and restaurants, the majority lining the upper level 'Board Walk' of the waterfront, with gorgeous views over the harbour. Best placed for a scenic cocktail or meal is the Seattle Bar & Restaurant (Hotel Seattle, 01273 679799, www.hotelseattlebrighton.com). Amid the chain bars and eateries here are a scattering of independents, such as the Gourmet Fish and Chip Company (18 Waterfront, 01273 670701, www.gourmetfishandchipcompany.com, closed Mon).

Similarly, high street shops are juxtaposed with smaller establishments, such as Pebble Beech (Unit 45, 07594 229747, www.pebblebeech.co.uk), which sells ethically traded homeware and accessories from around the world. Some are only open from Friday to Sunday, including Fiery Foods (Unit 30, Marina Square, 01273 705606, www.fieryfoodsuk.co.uk), whose sole raison d'être

would appear to be to set your mouth on fire with everything from chilli sauce to chilli chocolate. For a less fiery chocolate kick, Chocoholly (7 Marina Walk, 07780 975068, www.chocoholly.com, closed Mon-Thur) sells cardamon-infused organic chocolate bars, chunky buttons and rich truffles; its owner also runs two-hour chocolate-making workshops at the weekend.

Brighton Dive Centre (*see p232*) offers diving and snorkelling from its base here, while coastal cruises, fishing trips and powerboat-style soakings can be arranged through Ross Boat Trips (Pontoon 5, 07958 246414, www.watertours.co.uk).

Where to eat & drink

The Parisian-style bistro attached to the Hotel du Vin (*see p235*) is an excellent proposition for an upmarket lunch or dinner. Service is polished, while the menu offers classic bistro fare and fine wines.

The Restaurant at Drakes (*see p234*), meanwhile, is a dimly lit, plush little hideaway. The service and food are as polished as the surrounds: think pan-roasted scallops with butternut squash and vanilla velouté to start, perhaps, followed by red mullet with cuttlefish risotto and braised baby fennel, and Earl Grey panna cotta with poached prunes to round things off.

Bardsley's (Baker Street, 01273 681256, www.bardsleys-fishandchips.co.uk, closed Mon, Sun) is the place to go for quality fish and chips, eat in or takeaway.

For our pick of Brighton's finest boozers, *see p222*.

Basketmakers Arms ★
12 Gloucester Road, BN1 4AB (01273 689006, www.thebasketmakersarms.co.uk). Open 11am-11pm Mon-Thur; 11am-midnight Fri, Sat; noon-11pm Sun. Food served noon-8.30pm Mon-Fri; noon-7pm Sat; noon-4pm Sun.

Beloved by ale enthusiasts, and set close to the North Laine area, the Basketmakers stocks a comprehensive selection of cask ales, with guest ales and Fuller's brews. The other passion here is whisky, with over 100 different bottles on offer. The best pub in Brighton? Quite possibly.

Bill's
The Depot, North Road, BN1 1YE (01273 692894, www.billsproducestore.co.uk). Open/food served 8am-10pm Mon-Sat; 9am-10pm Sun.

At Bill's organic deli and restaurant, diners feast amid baskets of fresh leafy veg, and breathe the aroma of fresh-baked bread. During the day, the long communal tables are packed with regulars tucking into syrup-drizzled buttermilk pancakes, salads and superior hamburgers. In the evening, it's all about wholesome, satisfying dishes such as Thai spiced pumpkin and coconut curry or rosemary and garlic chicken with spring onion mash. The queues can be long.

Due South
139 King's Road Arches, BN1 2FN (01273 821218, www.duesouth.co.uk). Lunch served noon-3.30pm, dinner served 6-10pm daily.

Brighton Pride. See p16.

See p16.

Few spots are more romantic than the table by the arched upstairs window at this seafront restaurant. Contemporary art lines the walls, and the menu is pleasingly seasonal and locally focused: pan-roasted Court Garden lamb, perhaps, or Sussex goat's cheese tart. A great selection of dessert wines can lead you to fork out more than planned.

Fishy Fishy
36 East Street, BN1 1HL (01273 723750, www.fishyfishy.co.uk). Food served noon-11pm daily.
Owned by TV presenter Dermot O'Leary, this laid-back brasserie has earned a good reputation for no-nonsense seafood dishes. Whether it's baked lemon sole with herb and parmesan crust or hot smoked mackerel with artichoke salad, quality is assured. All of the seafood is from sustainable sources, and most of it is caught off the Sussex coast. There's outside seating if the sun shines.

Food for Friends
17-18 Prince Albert Street, BN1 1HF (01273 202310, www.foodforfriends.com). Food served noon-10pm Mon-Thur, Sun; noon-10.30pm Fri, Sat.
The vibe is relaxed and the food excellent at this renowned vegetarian restaurant, set in the South Lanes. Globally influenced dishes such as aubergine and spinach yoghurt curry or spiced parsnip and and carrot rösti are stuffed with fresh local produce, and there are plenty of vegan and gluten-free choices. The wine list includes organic options.

Gingerman
21A Norfolk Square, BN1 2PD (01273 326688, www.gingermanrestaurants.com). Lunch served 12.30-1.45pm, dinner served 7-9.30pm Tue-Sun.
The original Gingerman (the family also own three local gastropubs) is an elegant little restaurant, specialising in

SUSSEX

modern British dishes. The lunch menu is good value, while indulgent options at dinner might include cumin-spiced lamb rack with black cardamom or roast pheasant with game jus, followed by plum tarte tatin and amaretto ice-cream or Cointreau chocolate mousse.

Jamie's Italian
11 Black Lion Street, BN1 1ND (01273 915480, www.jamieoliver.com). Food served noon-11pm Mon-Sat; noon-10.30pm Sun.
The Brighton branch of Mr Oliver's affordable string of Italian eateries is everything you'd expect from Brand Jamie: bright, slick, and radiating good cheer. Plump green olives chilled on a bed of ice (modestly labelled World's Best Olives) are wonderfully smoky, and even the simple bowls of spaghetti bolognaise are aromatic and comforting. Note that it doesn't take bookings, so there may be a wait.

Lion & Lobster
24 Silwood Street, BN1 2PS (01273 327299, www.thelionandlobster.co.uk). Open 11am-1am Mon-Thur; 11am-2am Fri, Sat, noon-midnight Sun. Food served Restaurant 5-10pm Mon-Fri; noon-10pm Sat, Sun. Bar noon-10pm daily.
This cosy, three-floor backstreet pub (think deep red walls and paintings of huntsmen) incorporates a restaurant on the first floor, and a roof terrace for alfresco pints. There are jazz jams on Sundays and sport on the TV throughout the week, and it manages to suit real ale fans, late drinkers and lingering lunchers alike. Food ranges from chips and cheese to proper mains and generous Sunday roasts, with bar food served until closing time. One of the most popular pubs in Brighton, the Lion & Lobster soon fills up after work, with drinkers spilling on to the pavement in summer.

Marwood Café ★
52 Ship Street, BN1 1AF (01273 382063, www.the marwood.com). Open 8am-8pm Mon-Fri; 10am-8pm Sat, Sun.
For the coffee alone, it would be worth walking across the city (the baristas turn out carefully brewed coffees, with antipodean-style flourishes); the superb chocolate brownies clinch the deal. The decor is a kitsch mish-mash of junk, art and 1970s album covers, and the free Wi-Fi, together with comfortable seating and a relaxed atmosphere, make this place a favourite.

Meadow
64 Western Road, BN3 2JQ (01273 721182, www.themeadowrestaurant.co.uk). Breakfast served 9.30am-12.30pm Tue-Sat; 9.30am-noon Sun. Lunch served noon-2.30pm Tue-Sat; noon-3pm Sun. Dinner served 6.30-9.30pm Tue-Thur; 6.30-10.30pm Fri, Sat.
Set near the seafront in Hove, the Meadow occupies a former bank. Light floods through the enormous windows, and a little shop sells fresh produce, bread and distinctly superior ready meals. Head chef Will Murgatroyd trained under Marcus Wareing, and his talent shines through in dishes like home-cured salmon gravlax with Portland crab cake and confit lemon mayonnaise, or roasted turbot with braised oxtail, swiss chard and cockles. For afters, there might be a fruity crumble, buttermilk crème caramel, or chocolate mousse with salted caramel sauce, ice-cream and hazelnuts.

BRIGHTON'S SHOPS

Beyond Retro
42 Vine Street, BN1 4AG (01273 671937, www.beyondretro.com). Open 10am-6pm Mon-Wed, Fri, Sat; 10am-7pm Thur; 11am-5pm Sun.
Delve into a kaleidoscope of clothes and accessories at this enormous vintage emporium. Battered cowboy boots, spangly jumpsuits, polka-dot frocks and '70s leather jackets might be among the spoils – just turn up and have a rootle through the full-to-bursting rails.

Castor + Pollux ★
165 King's Road Arches, Lower Promenade, BN1 1NB (01273 773776, www.castorandpollux. co.uk). Open 10am-5pm daily.
This charming gallery and shop crams all sorts of treasures into its modest seafront premises. Exhibitions showcase rising printmakers (look out for Jonny Hannah's playful linocuts) and more familiar names such as papercuts artist Rob Ryan, while the shop is a temple to gorgeous design: contemporary ceramics, glowing, hand-made glass vases and contemporary porcelain jewellery may be among the spoils, alongside quirky cards and stationery.

Choccywoccydoodah
24 Duke Street, BN1 1AG (01273 329462, www.choccywoccydoodah. com). Open 10am-6pm Mon-Sat; 11am-5pm Sun.
The outlandish chocolate creations here run from kitsch kittens and gothic skulls to great slabs of rich Belgian chocolate, embedded with marshmallows. The shop is most famous, though, for its flamboyant chocolate cakes, piled high with gold dragees, frou-frou chocolate fans and chocolate hearts.

Dave's Comics
5 Sydney Street, BN1 4EN (01273 691012, www.davescomicsuk. blogspot.com). Open 10am-6pm Mon-Wed; 11am-7pm Thur; 10am-6pm Fri, Sat; 11am-5pm Sun.
An intriguing treasure trove of comics, graphic novels and manga titles awaits at Dave's North Laine shop, which often hosts author signing sessions. And if you don't get what all the fuss is about, check out the blog.

Medicine Chest ★

*51-55 Brunswick Street East, BN3 1AU (01273
770002, www.themedicinechest.co.uk). Open 9am-
11pm Tue-Thur, Sun; 9am-1am Fri, Sat. Lunch
served noon-3pm, dinner served 7-10pm Tue-Sun.*

The newest addition to Hove's bar scene is this lovely
speakeasy-style cocktail bar, tucked in the basement of the
former Sanctuary Café. It serves exceptional dry martinis,
while mixologist Mike Mason has also blended his own
set of 'elixirs', using fine botanicals, fruit and cordials: a
lemon drop martini, perhaps, or a moreish home-made
gooseberry syrup-laced Sussex 75. The low-lit bar gets
buzzy as the cocktails flow, and there's a wide-ranging
tapas menu.

Regency Tavern

*32-34 Russell Square, BN1 2EF (01273 325652).
Open 11am-midnight Mon-Sat; noon-11pm Sun. Food
served noon-2.30pm, 6-9pm Mon-Fri; noon-8pm Sat;
noon-5pm Sun.*

Where else could you find six real ales on tap and a disco
ball in the gents? Tucked in the twitten between two
squares, this Shepherd Neame pub (so old it used to charge
a toll for people walking through the twitten) is a celebration
of seaside baroque, complete with striped silk wallpaper,
gilt mirrors, chandeliers and gold cherubs. It really comes
into its own at Christmas, when the owners go all out with
the decorations.

Riddle & Finns

*12 Meeting House Lane, BN1 1HB (01273 323008,
www.riddleandfinns.co.uk). Food served noon-10pm Mon-
Thur; noon-11pm Fri; 9.30-11.30am, noon-11pm Sat;
9.30-11.30am, noon-10pm Sun.*

This ambitious champagne and oyster bar sees diners share
marble-topped tables as they pair immaculately presented
seafood with crisp glasses of fizz. Oysters come hot or cold,
rock or native, with various hot and cold sauces, while
mains include crab, rocket and chilli linguine and pan-fried
sea bass with bubble and squeak.

Terre à Terre ★

*71 East Street, BN1 1HQ (01273 729051, www.terrea
terre.co.uk). Food served noon-10.30pm Mon-Fri; noon-
11pm Sat; noon-10pm Sun.*

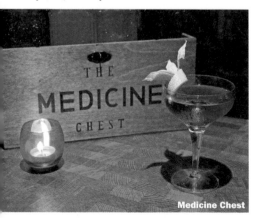

Medicine Chest

Montezuma's

*15 Duke Street, BN1 1AH (01273
324979, www.montezumas.co.uk).
Open 9.30am-6pm Mon-Sat; 11am-
5pm Sun.*

A Brighton institution, Montezuma's
is less outwardly ostentatious than
nearby Choccywoccydoodah (*see
left*), but equally devoted to all things
chocolatey. Its subversive streak lies
in its unexpected flavour combinations,
among them chilli and lime, orange and
geranium and peppermint and vanilla.

Purl

*16 Upper Hamilton Road, BN1 5DF
(01273 248642, www.purl-brighton.
co.uk). Open 10am-6pm Tue-Sat.*

Skeins of gorgeously hued wools and
yarns line the walls at Purl, the brightest
and best knitting shop in Brighton. Along
with knitting books, patterns, needles
and ceramic buttons, it sells jaunty
tea-cosies, sweet crocheted toys
and other kitsch gifts. The owners
also run 'stitch and bitch' sessions
on Thursday evenings.

Rounder

*19 Brighton Square, BN1 1HD (01273
325440, www.rounderbrighton.co.uk).
Open 9.30am-6pm Mon-Sat; 10.30am-
6pm Sun.*

A huge selection of vinyl is Rounder's
USP, plus in-store turntables – much
as you'd expect from one of Brighton's
oldest record stores. Rounder still holds
its own with a great selection of old and
new records, and staff know their stuff.

Snooper's Paradise

*7-8 Kensington Gardens, BN1 4AL
(01273 602558). Open 10am-6pm
Mon-Sat; 11am-4pm Sun.*

Paradise indeed: lose an afternoon at
this busy fleamarket, amid Snooper's
joyous jumble of retro coffee tables,
antiques, clothes, royal memorabilia
mugs, tarnished trumpets and 1950s
'Dainty but Daring' smutty slides, then
emerge blinking into the light.

SUSSEX

Komedia

Brighton Centre

King's Road, BN1 2GR (01273 290131, www. brightoncentre.co.uk). Box office 10am-5.30pm daily. Tickets £20-£65.
With a major redevelopment project now scheduled for 2012, the concrete bunker-like Brighton Centre isn't the most appealing-looking venue. Still, it continues to pull in the big touring acts, thanks to its impressive audience capacity. *X-Factor* stars, respected rock bands, comedians and international DJs all feature on the programme, along with child-pleasing acts such as the Wiggles.

Brighton Dive Centre

37 The Waterfront, Marina Village, BN2 5WA (01273 606068, www.thebrightondivecentre.co.uk). Open Summer 10am-6pm Mon-Sat; 11am-5pm Sun. Winter 10am-6pm Mon, Wed-Sat; 11am-5pm Sun. Prices vary; phone for details.
Based in the Marina Village, the Dive Centre offers PADI training courses, equipment hire, escorted shore and boat dives at local sites, and the chance to dive with sharks at the Brighton Sea Life Centre (*see p227*).

Brighton Dome

Church Street, BN1 1UE (01273 709709, www.brightondome.org). Box office 10am-6pm Mon-Sat. Tickets £4-£105.
A music and arts complex with three venues in one, the Brighton Dome is the main player in the city's mainstream music scene. Big names and large-scale productions impress in the Concert Hall – initially intended as stables for the Prince Regent's horses, but transormed into a plush concert venue in the mid 1800s. The adjacent Corn Exchange hosts a lively mix of bands, touring dance companies and comedians, while the Pavilion Theatre puts on everything from children's theatre to musicals. The Dome also runs the Brighton Festival (www.brightonfestival.org), the annual arts extravaganza that announces the start of summer.

Brighton & Hove Albion

City centre office, 44 North Road, BN1 1YR (01273 695400, www.seagulls.co.uk). Tickets £24-£27.50.
Talk sport in Brighton and it's Brighton & Hove Albion, and, more precisely, the club's stadium that dominate conversation. The Seagulls have bounced from League One to the Championship and back, but stories off the pitch have generated just as much interest – especially regarding the club's home. For the 2011/12 season, the team will move from their temporary ground at Withdean Stadium to the brand new Falmer Stadium (officially, the American Express Community Stadium), set just outside the city near the University of Sussex.

Brighton Racecourse

Freshfield Road, BN2 9XZ (01273 603580, www.brighton-racecourse.co.uk). Tickets £13-£17.

Brighton Racecourse holds regular meetings between April and October, while the three-day Brighton Festival of Racing is at the beginning of August; ladies sport head-turning hats and frocks, hooves thunder on the turf, and everyone has a rip-roaring time.

Coral Brighton & Hove Greyhound Stadium
Nevill Road, Hove, BN3 7BZ (01273 204601, www.brightonandhovegreyhoundstadium.co.uk). Open check website for race times. Admission free Wed, Fri, Sun; £5 Thur; £6 Sat.
If you fancy a flutter, try your luck at the greyhound stadium in Hove. Get up close to the track or book one of the tiered tables in the Skyline restaurant, which afford an overview of the action.

Duke of York's Picturehouse
Preston Circus, BN1 4NA (0871 902 5728, www.picturehouses.co.uk). Box office 9.30am-8.30pm daily. Tickets £8-£13; £7-£12 reductions.
The Duke of York's cinema sits at the top of London Road overlooking Preston Circus, to the north of the city centre. Opened to the public in 1910, it has remained in continuous operation ever since. Little changed over the years, the Grade II-listed building oozes elegance – although the stripy legs poking out on the roof are a bit of a surprise. The programming doesn't shy away from mainstream movies, but mixes them with a healthy proportion of arthouse films and curios, along with introductions and Q&A sessions featuring notable actors and directors. Upstairs there's a small, pleasant bar, with coffee and cakes.

Komedia ★
44-47 Gardner Street, BN1 1UN (0845 293 8480, www.komedia.co.uk). Open times vary; phone for details. Tickets £6-£29.
This quirky venue provides a platform for a wealth of quality fringe and alternative acts. Gigs, cabaret, children's theatre and stand-up comics keep things enjoyably varied, while the Krater Comedy Club is a regular fixture.

New Venture Theatre
Bedford Place, BN1 2PT (01273 808353, 01273 746118 box office, www.newventure.org.uk). Tickets £6-£9.
This community theatre has been putting on amateur productions of popular plays since 1956, and has recently taken to programming more experimental work in the smaller, downstairs studio space (the gorgeous 100-seat proscenium theatre upstairs is currently closed awaiting funding). Quality is varied, but it's fun to listen in on the luvvies in the bohemian saloon bar, which sometimes hosts cabaret performances.

Nightingale Theatre
Above Grand Central pub, 29-30 Surrey Street, BN1 3PA (01273 702563, www.nightingaletheatre.co.uk). Tickets £4-£12.
A fantastic pub-theatre, the Nightingale has Steven Berkoff as its patron and Steven Brett (formerly of Ballet Rambert and London's experimental Spill Festival) as its new artistic director. Here, you can catch some of the best local and international fringe theatre (as well as comedy, dance, poetry and work in development) in a wonderfully intimate setting.

Proud Brighton Ballroom
83 St George's Street, BN2 1EF (01273 605789, www.brightonballroom.com). Open 7pm-2am Wed-Sat. Tickets £4-£12. No credit cards.
There are plenty of cabarets and burlesque shows in Brighton, but none quite like this. The venue, run by London-based company Proud, invites leading event organisers to create unique soirées, from black and white balls to kitsch themed nights. The supper club combines a three-course meal with live entertainment; Broadway Musical Cabarets, say, or White Mink nights, described as 'electro swing versus speakeasy jazz'.

Sussex Cricket Ground
County Ground, Eaton Road, Hove, BN3 3AN (0844 264 0202, www.sussexcricket.co.uk). Tickets £15-£20.
The reassuring thwack of leather on willow still rings across Sussex Cricket Ground in Hove, which fields the county's first division squad. With buildings dating from 1872, and some recent stand additions, it's a charming mix of old and new.

Theatre Royal
35 Bond Street, BN1 1SD (0844 871 7627, www.ambassadortickets.com). Box office 10am-8pm. By phone 9am-10pm. Tickets £10-£30.
The Grade II-listed Theatre Royal may be one of Brighton's more mainstream venues, but it's certainly not shy of putting on alternative comedy or controversial productions. It's also a key venue during the Brighton Comedy Festival.

Volk's Electric Railway
Aquarium Station, Madeira Drive (www.volkselectricrailway.co.uk). Return ticket £2.80; £1.40-£1.80 reductions. Closed winter.
Since 1883, Volk's railway has trundled between the pier end of Madeira Drive and near what is now Brighton Marina. The world's oldest operating electric railway, it was designed by pioneering British engineer Magnus Volk, a Brighton resident. It's a quirky way to travel to the Marina, and is fun for children; the only stop along the way is Halfway Station, near Yellowave (see below).

Yellowave Beachsports
299 Madeira Drive, BN2 1EN (01273 672222, www.yellowave.co.uk). Open May-Sept 10am-10pm Mon-Thur; 10am-8pm Fri-Sun. Nov-Feb 10am-9pm Tue-Thur; 11am-5pm Fri; 10am-5pm Sat, Sun.
In summer, Yellowave's six beach volleyball courts soon fill with Brightonians bouncing volleyballs, keeping up footballs, hurling Frisbees and throwing rugby balls. As well as the sandy area that alternates between volleyball courts and a football pitch, there's a bouldering wall and a café serving home-made soups and salads. Courts can be hired for £20 an hour, but there are also drop-in sessions, coaching programmes for all levels, league games, children's clubs and taster sessions.

Inventive vegetarian cooking in relaxed surrounds is the trademark at Terre à Terre, whose enjoyably eclectic menu encompasses everything from cheddar cheese soufflés to fragrant curries, battered halloumi and chips or neeps, tatties and haggis (meat-free, of course). To start, try the corn cake fritters, served with chilli jelly and guacamole. It's not cheap, but prices reflect the quality and the care taken in the kitchen.

Wine Shop & Tasting Room

9 Jubilee Street, BN1 1GE (01273 567176, www.ten greenbottles.com). Open 11am-11pm Mon-Sat; noon-10pm Sun.

You're in safe hands here: the team specialise in European wines from small producers, and supply heavyweights of the London restaurant scene (J Sheekey, Locanda Locatelli and the River Café, just for starters). Pop in to pick up a bottle, or, for a flat £5 drink-in charge, quaff it at the bar. Charcuterie, cheese and crostini are available, and the menu is set to expand to larger plates.

Where to stay

Alias Hotel Seattle

Brighton Marina, BN2 5WA (01273 679799, www. aliashotels.com). Rates £150-£170 double incl breakfast.

The Hotel Seattle has 70 spacious, modern rooms, half facing on to the Marina. The overall feel is professional but relaxed, with original vintage film posters and 1960s screenprints adding character to the place. The restaurant and bar are open to non-residents; order a cocktail and take a seat on the decked waterside terrace to enjoy the glorious Brighton sunsets.

De Vere Grand

97-99 King's Road, BN1 2FW (01273 224300, www.devere.co.uk). Rates £90-£210 double incl breakfast.

A Victorian masterpiece, the Grand was built in a prime seafront position in the 1860s; to make the most of its setting, make sure you ask for a sea view. The 201 rooms are comfortably appointed, all with an elegantly traditional feel, although concessions to modernity include satellite TV and complimentary broadband. There's a gym, a restaurant and the Victoria Lounge, where cream teas are served.

Drakes ★

43-44 Marine Parade, BN2 1PE (01273 696934, www.drakesofbrighton.com). Rates £105-£210 double.

It's luxury all the way at this hugely popular high-end designer hotel. Snag an expansive bedroom with a view overlooking Brighton Pier and you can sink into a free-standing bath set beside the floor-to-ceiling sea-facing windows. All 20 rooms have been individually decorated, with plenty of little luxuries: Egyptian cotton sheets, goose- and duckdown duvets, flatscreen TVs, free Wi-Fi and White Company toiletries. The in-house restaurant (*see p228*) is highly recommended, and there's a swish cocktail bar for after-dinner drinks.

Hotel Pelirocco ★

10 Regency Square, BN1 2FG (01273 327055, www.hotelpelirocco.co.uk). Rates £95-£160 double incl breakfast.

Terre à Terre. See p231.

SUSSEX

Describing itself as 'England's most rock 'n' roll hotel', the Pelirocco pays tribute to Brighton's long association with illicit weekends: one of the rooms has a mirror on the ceiling and a pole dancing area, while Betty's Boudoir is dedicated to 1950s pin-up Betty Page, with a leopard-print chaise-longue on which to recline. There's a PlayStation 2 in each room to help recovery from a night in the bar sipping cocktails with Brighton music types.

Hotel Una

55-56 Regency Square, BN1 2FF (01273 820464, www.hotel-una.co.uk). Rates £95-£210 double incl breakfast.
Owned by architect Zoran Maricevic, this boutique hotel melds contemporary furniture and lighting with the building's Regency history. Each of the 19 rooms has a very different feel and appeal, so have a look at the website before making your choice: Danube has a freestanding bath with a view, Aragon has a sauna, and Gaula has a private patio. There are six price structures, but check online for some good midweek specials. There's a great cocktail bar too.

Hotel du Vin

2-6 Ship Street, BN1 1AD (01273 718588, www.hotelduvin.com). Rates £125-£250 double.
Brighton's Hotel du Vin is set in a jumble of mock-Tudor and Gothic revival buildings, just on the edge of the Lanes, and close to the seafront. The 49 rooms are thoughfully kitted out, and each is slightly different: the loft suite, Cristal, has an eight-foot-square bed and its own little private roof terrace, but even the standard rooms are comfortable. All feature fine Egyptian linen, drench showers as well as baths, plasma TVs and DVD players, and air conditioning. The bistro (*see p228*) is good enough to attract non-residents (do book), while a carefully chosen cellar supplies the equally popular wine bar.

Myhotel Brighton

17 Jubilee Street, BN1 1GE (01273 900300, www.myhotels.com). Rates £59-£120 double.
In keeping with its North Laine location, Brighton's Myhotel is a playful affair, with bright, jewel-like colours and artworks set against curvaceous white walls. Rooms are sleekly equipped with plasma TVs, an MP3 connection, wonderfully comfortable beds and free Wi-Fi; the Carousel room even has an antique fairground horse. There's a futuristic-looking cocktail bar, and the Chilli Pickle Indian restaurant is promised soon. The treatment room dispenses massages, soothing body wraps and Aveda facials.

Oriental

9 Oriental Place, BN1 2LJ (01273 205050, www.orientalbrighton.co.uk). Rates £59-£170 double incl breakfast.
Thirty seconds from the sea and two minutes from the bustle of Western Road, this fine Regency townhouse is ideally placed in the relative quiet of Oriental Place. As one of the original boutique hotels in the city, the decor is suitably quirky but still modern and stylish. Its nine en suite rooms are understated but chic, with silk headboards, crisp with linen and subtle colour schemes, while the public areas and bar feature an ever-changing selection of artwork. The excellent breakfasts, made from local produce, will also put a spring in your step.

Hotel Pelirocco

SUSSEX

Coastal West Sussex

On the border of East and West Sussex, Brighton has long monopolised the limelight along this stretch of coastline. Westwards of the 'Queen of the Watering Places', though, lie a string of classic resorts and quieter, unspoilt corners, stretching all the way to Chichester Harbour, some 25 miles away.

Inspired by Brighton's success with the Regency fashionable set, pretenders to the crown hastily began building. Worthing, Littlehampton and Bognor Regis all expanded rapidly during the 18th century, although none achieved the same success as Brighton. Worthing's genteel charms remain popular with a loyal coterie of visitors, while Littlehampton is starting to reinvent itself, with a pair of architect-designed seafront eateries and a redeveloped harbour. Bognor, meanwhile, is bolder and brasher: home to Butlins, gaudy amusement arcades and a welter of fish and chip shops.

Much of the stretch between Brighton and Chichester Harbour, though, comprises little more than a path, coastline and striking views of the English Channel, quiet even at the height of summer. Although shingle predominates, there are gently shelving sands around the Manhood Peninsula and, in particular, the sheltered, family-friendly beach at West Wittering.

Beyond the Witterings, Chichester Harbour is an Area of Outstanding Natural Beauty, and best explored by foot, bike or boat. Its excellent restaurants, picturesque quays, miles of footpaths and abundance of birdlife exude a timeless charm, offering a very different side of Sussex by the Sea.

SHOREHAM-BY-SEA & WORTHING

Shoreham-by-Sea

Shoreham-by-Sea has always sat in the sizeable shadow of its famous neighbour – flamboyant, brash Brighton, just 15 minutes' drive away along the coastal road. A sea port in Victorian times, set on the estuary of the River Adur, its natural harbour is still in use, lending an industrious air to the town. The harbour is formed by Shoreham Beach, a shingle bank to the south of town that grew up over the centuries and has now been built on. Adjacent to it, a gaily painted line of houseboats are often stranded on the mudflats. Along with bohemian boat-dwellers, the mudflats attract a multitude of birds – gulls, redshank, lapwing and cormorants.

The Marlipins Museum (see p252) has a small display on archaeology and local history, but it's the checkerboard façade that really marks it out. The programme at the impressive Ropetackle Arts Centre (Little High Street, 01273 464440, www.ropetacklecentre.co.uk) includes regular comedy nights, literary talks, world cinema and music.

If anything, though, Shoreham is known for its airport (see p252) – a Grade II-listed beauty founded in 1910. From here, you can take flying lessons, or watch aerial feats of derring-do at Shoreham Airshow in August.

Worthing

Cross the Norfolk Bridge out of Shoreham and follow the A259 along the coast to Worthing. Property is significantly cheaper here than in Brighton, a mere 20 minutes away by train, so Worthing has seen an influx of workers willing making the short commute. As a result, the town is starting to show signs of regeneration, and one or two independent shops have opened. For the most part, though, it remains a place to enjoy a vast expanse of beach in relative peace and quiet.

Until the mid 1700s, Worthing was a small fishing village, much like Brighton. When the fashion for sea-bathing flooded London society, though, it was transformed into a smart Georgian seaside resort. The first lodging house was built here in 1759 – and while Brighton was favoured by the Prince Regent, his sisters, Princess Amelia and Princess Augusta Sophia, preferred Worthing's quieter charms, and were regular visitors. Oscar Wilde would later stay here in the summer of 1894, when he wrote *The Importance of Being Earnest* – hence the surname of the play's lead character, Jack.

With its mild climate, staid reputation and cluster of convalescent homes, Worthing provided a more sedate alternative to Brighton. As the *Black's Guide to Seaside Resorts*, not a publication given to hyperbole, observed in 1861: 'The temperature is well adapted to invalids, the sea-scapes are beautiful, and the town is, in all respects, identical with other popular sea-side resorts.'

Littlehampton . See p238.

In 1862, the town's first pier was built. It still stands, despite being blown down in 1913, destroyed by fire in 1933 and partially blown up in 1940 (by the British, lest Hitler should use it as a landing point). These days it's home to the flashing lights of the amusement arcade and the Pavilion Theatre (Marine Parade, 01903 206206, www.worthingtheatres.co.uk). There are two more theatres in Worthing: the art deco Connaught Theatre and the Assembly Hall, home to the largest Wurlitzer organ in Europe.

Opposite the pier is the Edwardian Dome Cinema (01903 823112, www.domecinema.co.uk), which celebrated its centenary in 2011; it's in fine condition inside and out, after massive restoration in 2005. Next door is Macari's ice-cream parlour (*see p239*), little changed since it opened in 1959.

The shopping precinct and the Montague and Guildbourne shopping centres are inland along South Street, directly in front of the pier. High-street chains predominate, although there are one or two intriguing independents: on Bath Place, Delish (no.7, 01903 369533, www.delishbeauty.co.uk, closed Wed, Sun) is a lovely little store selling hand-made cosmetics and beauty products. The adjacent Park Life Food & Coffee Bar (*see right*) is a popular spot for coffee and cupcakes.

Worthing Museum & Art Gallery (Chapel Road, 01903 221447, www.worthingmuseum.co.uk) has an impressive costume collection, with pieces dating from the 17th century to the present day. It also has an abundance of vintage teddy bears,

toys and over 1,000 dolls. The exhibition space hosts around four temporary exhibitions a year.

On the eastern edge of town, towards Brighton, Beach House Park is a relic of the town's glory days. Edward VII stayed in the grand Regency-era Beach House several times between 1907 and 1910; today, only the grounds are open to the public. At the centre of the formal gardens is a memorial to the carrier pigeons used during World War II. One stone is engraved: 'In memory of warrior birds who gave their lives on active service 1939-45 and for the use and pleasure of living birds.'

Where to eat & drink

Behind the neoclassical façade of the old Town Hall in Shoreham, Chambers Bistro (High Street, 01273 446677, www.chambersbistro.co.uk) has plenty of tried-and-tested favourites on its menu, from no-nonsense burgers and own-made fish pie to sirloin steaks and confit duck. Beef Wellington is the signature dish, but you have to order it ahead. The Red Lion (Old Shoreham Road, 01273 453171) is a pleasant pub, famous for its links to an 18th-century mail coach robbery. Two local men were hanged for the crime, a sorry tale recounted in Tennyson's poem *Rizpah*.

In Worthing, Parklife Food & Coffee Bar (6 Bath Place, 01903 207777, www.parklifefood.co.uk, closed Sun) has excellent coffee and even better cakes, along with sandwiches and milkshakes. Indigo Restaurant in the Ardington Hotel (Steyne

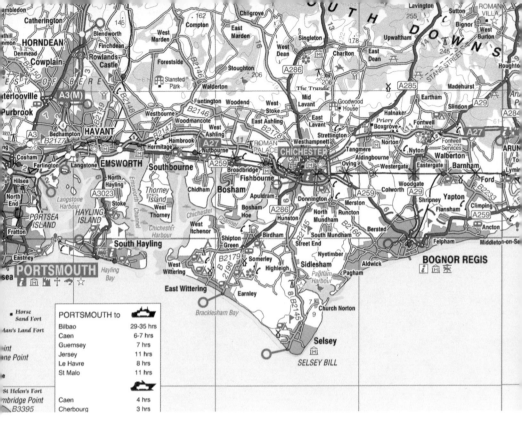

Gardens, 01903 230451, www.indigorestaurant.
info) has a reasonably priced Modern British menu.

Macari's

24-25 Marine Parade, Worthing, BN11 3PT
(01903 532753, www.macarisrestaurant.co.uk).
Open 9am-9pm daily.

On the promenade next to the Edwardian Dome cinema,
this classic ice-cream bar opened in 1959 – and has never
looked back. The flavours change daily, but mainstays
include honeycomb, maple and walnut and Turkish delight,
along with various whipped cream and chocolate sauce-
slathered sundaes. There's also a restaurant menu that
runs from breakfast fry-ups to toasties, salads and classic
pasta dishes

Where to stay

There are dozens of places to stay in Worthing, many
of them old-school B&Bs. Owned by the same family
since 1928, the Ardington Hotel (Steyne Gardens,
01903 230451, www.ardingtonhotel.co.uk) is a
good choice, with friendly service and a good location
overlooking Steyne Gardens. Its rooms were being
updated in a coolly contemporary style at the time of
writing, and there's a pleasant ground-floor restaurant.

Across Steyne Gardens, the Chatsworth Hotel
(01903 236103, www.chatsworthworthing.co.uk)
occupies fine Georgian premises. Its 98 rooms,
some of which have sea views, are comfortably
appointed, with traditional decor.

LITTLEHAMPTON

Vogue may have hailed Littlehampton as the 'coolest
British seaside resort' back in 2006, but many who
visit struggle to believe the hype; the town still has
some way to go before it becomes Sussex's
equivalent of Whitstable. But for many visitors,
herein lies the appeal: with its pretty coastline,
faded promenade, colourful beach huts, retro
chippes and old-school fairground, it exudes a
ramshackle, down-to-earth charm. The town is
also the slightly unexpected site of some striking
modern architecture, in the shape of its pair of
beachfront cafés.

It may be difficult to imagine the place as it used
to be – the seaside stamping ground of artists and
writers such as Byron, Constable and Coleridge, but
Littlehampton is a good place to head to if you're
after the simple pleasures of a British seaside
resort. Come here on a balmy summer's day, head
straight for the seafront and you may well fall for
its low-key charms. Annual events include the Arts
Festival in May and June and the carnival and
Seafront Festival in July. Thanks to its laid-back
vibe and strong winds, the town has also become
a popular destination for wind- and kitesurfing; in
midsummer, the Kitesurfing Championships provide
spectacle by day and beach-party entertainment
at night. If you fancy having a go, there are various
watersports schools (see p246).

Coastguards Beach is good for swimming,
particularly if you head eastward past the groynes.

Best of all, the shingle fades into sand so you don't stub your feet in the shallows. The Blue Flag area of the beach stretches from the Coastguards Tower, on the east bank of the River Arun, to the wonderful East Beach Café (*see p241*), whose undulating, driftwood-inspired outline is a beacon for architecture buffs as well as diners from Brighton and beyond.

In summer, families can hitch a ride on board the Seafront Promenade Train, which runs between Coastguards Tower and Norfolk Gardens, and seafront entertainment might include Punch and Judy shows, music and magic shows. The promenade is also home to Britain's longest bench, unveiled in 2010. The sinuous, 324-metre bench comprises hundreds of plain and brightly painted slats, made from reclaimed wood, and looks like a ribbon of colour weaving around the seafront.

Rows of scruffy shops run off the promenade, though there is fun to be had hooking a duck, gambling pennies in the arcade or bingeing on candyfloss; bordered by the River Arun and the beach, Harbour Park (*see p246*) is a giddy whirl of slot machines, dodgems and crazy golf.

From the little 1940s-built lighthouse at the end of the beach, by Harbour Park, a riverside walkway runs along the River Arun to the East Bank Riverside Development. There's a fine collection of boats to admire in the harbour along the way, together with any number of swans that have learned to love chips and cornets. Once made up of derelict wharves and storage yards, the regenerated riverside is now

home to the Look & Sea Visitor Centre (*see p252*), with its permanent exhibition, Visitor Information Centre and viewing tower, along with the Youth Hostel (*see p241*) and lifeboat station, where a boathouse tour is available on request.

The town centre is two minutes' walk away, with its nautically themed pedestrian precinct and familiar high street names. Alternatively, cross the footbridge to the other side of the River Arun, which is much less developed than its eastern flank. Upriver is the marina, while a 20-minute stroll down Rope Walk and a riverbank footpath will take you past gently decaying moorings and jetties and around the yacht club's headquarters to the west beach.

Part of a designated nature reserve, it's far quieter and more rugged than the east beach, and backed by wild dunes. For those in search of peace and quiet, this is seaside heaven – a long stretch of unadulterated sand, free from neon clutter and with a horizon that seems to run forever. Pack a picnic blanket and a hamper, or better still buy some gourmet fish and chips and own-made ice-cream from the stylish, seasonally opening West Beach Café (*see p241*). You can also hire binoculars for £1.

Climping

Westward along the coastal path from Littlehampton, Climping Beach offers nothing except itself – pebbles at high tide, and a vast swathe of dark, densely packed sand at other times. Quiet and starkly

River Arun, Littlehampton. See p239.

beautiful, it's got next to nothing in the way of amenities, though there is a car park by the beach, and you can stroll up to the Black Horse (*see below*) for a pint.

A leaflet available at the Visitor Information Centre at Look & Sea (*see p252*) details a lovely 4.5-mile circular walk from west beach to Climping, past the golf course and through the woods inland, then back along the beach, past wind-stunted blackthorn bushes, clumps of hardy marram grass and, from June to August, the bright splash of yellow-horned poppies.

Avoid any fenced-off areas. Climping is one of only three small sand dune systems in West Sussex, and a protected Site of Special Scientific Interest (SSSI), for plants, birds, molluscs, insects, reptiles and mammals living and feeding on the sand flats, shingle and secluded sand dunes.

Where to eat & drink

Around five miles from Littlehampton, in the village of Angmering, the Spotted Cow (1 High Street, 01903 783919, www.spottedcowangmering.co.uk) has a boules pitch, a no-nonsense menu and well-kept ales.

The Oyster Catcher in Climping (Yapton Road, 01903 726354, www.vintageinn.co.uk/theoyster catcherclimping) is a thatched pub with a pleasant garden, a flagstone floor and a wide-ranging menu that runs from mezze and mixed grills to Jamaican stew or scampi and chips. Closer to the beach, the Black Horse (01903 715175, www.black horseclimping.co.uk) is a pleasant place for a pint and lunch.

For fine dining in a country house setting, try the quiet, romantic Tapestry Restaurant in the Bailiffscourt Hotel & Health Spa (*see right*). Well executed seasonal British dishes might include wood pigeon and wild mushroom terrine with celeriac remoulade for starters, with braised venison bourguignon or roasted sea bass with white bean and vanilla purée to follow.

East Beach Café ★
Sea Road, Littlehampton, BN17 5GB (01903 731903, www.eastbeachcafe.co.uk). Open Summer 10am-5pm, 6.30-9pm daily. Winter 10am-3.30pm Mon-Wed, Sun; 10am-3.30pm, 6.30-9pm Thur-Sat.
Designed by architect Thomas Heatherwick's studio, this seafront café represents a bold departure for the town. The organic curves of the low-lying, steel-framed building have a sculptural, organic quality, like a piece of driftwood or a giant clam shell. Inside, it feels more boutique restaurant than beachside café, with contoured white walls and floor-to-ceiling windows overlooking the sea. The menu runs from simple classics (fish and chips, soup of the day, Welsh rarebit with watercress salad) to more ambitious Modern British offerings: warm rabbit and chestnut salad with a mustard dressing, perhaps, or mussel, gurnard and salmon saffron chowder. Breakfast is served at weekends, and there are splendid cakes and flapjacks come teatime.

47 Mussel Row
Pier Road, Littlehampton, BN17 5LP (01903 715966). Summer Lunch served noon-2.30pm, dinner served 6-9pm Mon-Fri. Food served noon-9pm Sat; noon-7pm Sun.

Winter Lunch served noon-2.30pm, dinner served 6-9pm Thur, Fri. Food served noon-9pm Sat; noon-7pm Sun.
Among the restaurants along the harbour, 47 Mussel Row stands out for its fresh seafood: mussels served with triple-cooked chips, say, or pan-roasted fillet of local bream with new potatoes. The views across the river are lovely at sunset.

West Beach Café ★
West Beach, Rope Walk, Littlehampton, BN17 5DL (01903 718153, www.eastbeachcafe.co.uk). Open Summer 10am-5pm Mon-Fri, Sun; 10am-7pm Sat. Winter 10am-4pm Sat, Sun.
Although it's less showy than its East Beach sister, this place is still a cut above the standard beachside café. Its compact premises were designed by Asif Khan, an up-and-coming young architect; it's a simple but delightful space, with light pouring in through the floor-to-ceiling windows. On sunny days, the entire frontage opens out on to the beach. The menu is perfectly sited to the surroundings: think salmon and parsley fish cakes, toasted sandwiches and very good fish and chips with minty mushy peas. It's licensed, but also does a nice line in piping-hot mugs of tea.

Where to stay

Bailiffscourt Hotel & Health Spa
Climping Street, Climping, BN17 5RW (01903 723511, www.hshotels.co.uk). Rates £210-£650 double incl breakfast & dinner.
Bailiffscourt is one-of-a-kind: a palimpsest of English architectural styles in a secluded spot near the coast. It was built in 1927 for Walter Guinness, who commissioned the antiquarian and architect Amyas Phillips to construct a country manor house in the medieval style. Crucially, Phillips used stones, fireplaces, doors, windows and woodwork salvaged from medieval ruins around the country, imbuing the house with character. It's now a hotel, with 38 rooms divided between the main house, various outbuildings, and a new wing; there's also a charming restaurant (*see left*) and a spa with an indoor and outdoor swimming pool, steam room, sauna, treatment rooms and a jacuzzi. The 30-acre grounds, shared with several peacocks, are a delight. It's a short walk to Climping Beach.

Littlehampton Youth Hostel
63 Surrey Street, Littlehampton, BN17 5AW (0845 371 9670, www.yha.org.uk). Rates from £16 for 1 person.
Opened in April 2003 as part of the development of Fisherman's Wharf on the east bank of the river Arun, this purpose-built 32-bed hostel is a YHA gem. There are plenty of family rooms, most of which are en suite, and double beds aren't so rare as in other hostels. Facilities include a TV lounge, laundry and drying room and cycle store; it's self catering only, but there is an eclectic array of restaurants just outside the front door. The beach is five minutes' away.

BOGNOR REGIS & FELPHAM

Bognor Regis
If West Wittering (*see p247*) is resolutely uncommercial, Bognor Regis, just east, is a shameless people-pleaser. Its safe bathing and five-mile stretch of sand and shingle have been

West Wittering. See p247.

drawing the crowds for decades, though these days its modesty-protecting bathing machines and genteel boarding houses have given way to gaudy seaside pleasures: amusements galore, chippies, a miniature train, trampolines and crazy golf. It also hosts an imaginative year-round programme of events, starting with the Clowns Convention in March – though safety concerns sometimes stop September's International Bognor Birdman Competition from taking wing.

Officially the sunniest place in Britain, Bognor has long traded on its clement climate. The first entrepreneur to recognise its potential, back in 1787, was a wealthy London hatter named Richard Hotham. He built a health resort to attract the aristocracy to the area, and is credited with tranforming Bognor from a modest fishing village into a fashionable resort. His house – now converted into private apartments – still stands at Hotham Park (01243 830262, www.hothampark.co.uk), while the 22-acre grounds are a public park, with an 18-hole putting green and crazy golf course, miniature railway and boating lake.

In 1929, King George V came to recuperate here following a lung operation, drawn by the town's health-restoring reputation. Duly recovered, the King bestowed a royal honour upon the place and renamed it Bognor Regis. His alleged last words were about the little seaside town, too, though they are less than complimentary; on being assured that he would soon be well enough to return there, his retort was 'bugger Bognor!'

Nowadays, the seafront offers all the trappings of a traditional English holiday, with its bustling promenade, Grade II-listed pier, endless fish and chip shops, music in the bandstand and a summer funfair. The beach is predominantly pebbly, although a stretch of sand emerges at low tide. Indeed, the sandcastle-building competition is an integral part of the one-day Sands of Time Festival (www.sandsoftime.co.uk), which also takes in donkey rides, Punch and Judy and a cavalcade of vintage cars.

The town has been home to Butlins' flagship resort (see p252) since 1960 – though the chain's latest innovation, a modern, multi-million pound spa hotel, is a long way from Billy Butlin's original back-to-basics wooden chalets. The resort also features an enormous water park, which is handy for families on rainy days; even if you're not staying here, day tickets are available (see p252). The Bognor Regis Museum (69 High Street, 01243 865636, closed Mon & all Nov-Mar) packs a more educational punch, and offers free admission.

Felpham

Set on the coastal road to the east of Bognor Regis, heading towards Littlehampton, is the village of Felpham. Its most famous resident was William Blake, who moved here in 1800 at the invitation of his wealthy patron, the poet William Hayley. During his three years in the village, Blake penned sections of his epic poem *Milton*, and was inspired by its beauty and tranquillity. In one of his letters, he wrote a poem in its honour: 'Away to sweet Felpham, for Heaven is there/The Ladder of Angels descend thro' the air/On the turret its spiral does softly descend/Thro' the village then winds, at my cot it does end.'

His cottage can still be seen in the village – though Blake's rural idyll came to an abrupt end after an altercation with a soldier, John Scofield, who was billeted at the nearby Fox Inn (Waterloo Road, 01243 865308, www.thefoxfelpham.co.uk). According to Blake's account, he was driven to retaliate when Scofield threatened to 'knock out' his eyes: 'It affronted my foolish Pride. I therefore took him by the Elbows & pushed him before me till I had got him out. My landlord compell'd the Soldiers to go in doors, after many abusive threats against me & my wife from the two Soldiers.'

Humiliated by the exchange, Scofield and his companion retaliated by accusing Blake of sedition – namely damning 'the King of England, his country and his subjects'. It was a damaging case which saw the poet tried for high treason in Chichester; after being acquitted, he returned to London.

Where to eat & drink

Bognor is not a culinary beacon, although there are plenty of takeaways and chippies. For more choice, drive into Chichester, book a table at the East Beach Café (see p241) in Littlehampton, or head onwards to the Crab & Lobster (see p248) at Pagham.

Dolphin Café

5 Waterloo Square, Bognor Regis, PO21 1TE (07929 597561). Open 7am-3pm daily. No credit cards.
Decorated in crisp blues and whites, this clean, no-frills café a useful spot for an inexpensive lunch, serving sandwiches, jacket potatoes, fish and chips and roasts, with traditional puddings to follow.

Simply Delicious

2 Lennox Street, Bognor Regis, PO21 1LZ (01243 861616, www.simplydeliciousdeli.co.uk). Open 9am-4pm Mon-Sat.
The owners of this delightful deli and café have a real commitment to serving good food and quality produce. Its stock includes cheese from the High Weald Dairy, honey from the South Downs and apple juice from Ringden Farm, while the café menu runs from freshly made soups, panini and Welsh rarebit to splendid rock cakes, scones and hot buttered crumpets. Take-away picnics can be provided on request.

Where to stay

Best Western Beachcroft Hotel

Clyde Road, Felpham, PO22 7AH (01243 827142, www.beachcroft-hotel.co.uk). Rates £88-£129 double incl breakfast.
This friendly, 35-room Best Western hotel occupies a prime beachfront site in Felpham, just east of Bognor Regis. Most of the spacious rooms have glorious views out to sea, and everything is in good condition and spotlessly clean. The indoor swimming pool is a decent size, there's an in-house

East Beach Café. See p241.

Climping. See p239.

SUSSEX

spa and beauty therapist, and the atmosphere in the restaurant is homely and relaxed.

Royal Norfolk Hotel

The Esplanade, Bognor Regis, PO21 2LH (01243 826222, www.royalnorfolkhotel.com). Rates £78-£90 double incl breakfast.

Built in 1830 at the western end of the esplanade, the Royal Norfolk was once a grand hideaway for the likes of Queen Victoria, King Edward VII, the exiled Emperor Napoleon III of France and the Empress Maud of Russia. The decor is rather dated, but its 46 rooms are spacious and light, with big windows and high ceilings. Sitting comfortably in three acres of gardens on the seafront, the hotel offers croquet, bowls and its own car park – something of a rarity in Bognor.

Shoreline & Ocean Hotel

Butlins, Bognor Regis, PO21 1JJ (01243 810099, www.butlins.com). Rates Shoreline £113-£191 family/weekend. Ocean Hotel £113-£191 double/weekend.

Built in 2005 and designed to look like an ocean liner, the Shoreline looms over Bognor's seafront. With its modern facilities, big windows and sunny ambience, the 160-room hotel aims to broaden Butlins' appeal, offering a more luxurious take on the holiday camp experience. Sure enough, its air-conditioned rooms feature all sorts of extra

Things to do

LITTLEHAMPTON

Finkyinc Kitesurfing School

Sea Road, BN16 2LX (01903 731021, http://finkyinc. com). Open by appointment. Taster session £30/hr.

These kitesurfing experts tutor a steady stream of eager learners, as well as more advanced kitesurfers. Radio helmets enable instructors to communicate with pupils, however many waves might come between them, and all trainers are fully certified by either the International Kitesurfing Organisation or the British Kitesurfing Association.

Harbour Park

Windmill Road, The Seafront, BN17 5LH (01903 721200, www.harbourpark.com). Open times vary; check website for details. Admission free. Super Saver Ride Book £15.

This old-school amusement park has free entry, but operates a token system for rides. Family-friendly fairground classics – a waltzer, dodgems and caterpillar coaster among them – predominate, and the very young have their own selection of rides and play areas.

Littlehampton Dutch Bike Company

47 Pier Road, BN17 5LW (01903 730089, www.dutchbikeshop.co.uk). Open 9am-5pm Mon-Sat; 10am-4pm Sun. Hire £10/2hrs; £12 daily; £15 overnight.

Explore the area at your own pace on a bike from the Dutch Bike Company. Bikes come equipped with locks, and child seats can be fitted on request; note that a £50 deposit is required.

BOGNOR REGIS & FELPHAM

Arena Sports Centre

Westloats Lane, Bognor Regis, PO21 5JD (01243 870000, www.arenasportscentre.com). Open 7am-11pm Mon-Fri; 8.30am-6pm Sat; 8.30am-8pm Sun.

It's a tiring task just reading through the list of activities available at this sports centre: aerobics, archery, badminton, basketball, cricket, fencing, football, gymnastics, hockey, martial arts, netball, pool, swimming and table tennis, to name just a few. It's also home to one of the largest climbing walls in this corner of Britain, at more than nine metres high.

MANHOOD PENINSULA

Mulberry Divers

9 Orchard Parade, East Beach, Selsey, PO20 0NS (01243 601000, www.mulberrydivers.co.uk). Open by appointment. Discover scuba session £25.

There are more than 100 shipwrecks to explore off the coast of the Manhood Peninsula; for those new to the sport, Mulberry Divers is also a respected family-run PADI dive centre. The Discover Scuba courses start in a nearby pool, and later move into the open water.

Salterns Way Cycle Path

www.conservancy.co.uk

On summer weekends, the best way to avoid car park queues for the beach at West Wittering is to cycle from Chichester along the Salterns Way Cycle Path. Some 11 miles long, it runs past sleek, gleaming boats at Chichester Marina, along lily-covered waterways and through cool, dim copses before emerging in West Wittering. A map of the route can be downloaded from the Chichester Harbour Conservancy website, above.

Wittering Surf Shop

13 Shore Road, East Wittering, PO20 8DY (01243 672292, www.witteringsurfshop.com). Open 9am-5pm Mon-Fri; 9am-5.30pm Sat; 10am-4pm Sun.

Surfboards, wetsuits and advice can be found at this popular surf shop, along with all manner of beach gear. Boards and wetsuits can also be hired. Group and private lessons are available (April to September).

West Beach Café. See p241.

comforts: the pricier 'Nelson's Staterooms' feature games consoles, flatscreen TVs and DVD players in the children's dens, balconies and large en suites. The 200-room Ocean hotel is even more modern; think bright red walls, vibrant pop art, floor-to-ceiling windows and a spa. A minimum two-night stay is usually required at both hotels.

MANHOOD PENINSULA ★

The splendidly named Manhood Peninsula extends from Pagham Harbour in the east to Chichester Harbour in the west, and includes the parishes of East and West Wittering, Selsey, Sidlesham, Itchenor and Bosham.

West Wittering is the principal destination on the peninsula, but there are some excellent pubs and restaurants in the area, including the Crab & Lobster (see p248); after lunch, take a stroll around the nature reserve at Pagham Harbour (see p252), a designated Site of Special Scientific Interest.

East Wittering & Bracklesham Bay

In the 1950s, Niklaus Pevsner described East Wittering as 'a jumble of bungalows and chalets near the beach in an untidy half grown up state'. The description still rings true; nonetheless, the quiet shingle beach has its own appeal. Among the seafront bungalows are a couple of self-catering holiday lets, built around old railway carriages (see p249) and with decked terraces bordering the beach.

A few miles along the coast, towards Selsey and the tip of the Manhood Peninsula, is Bracklesham Bay. Surrounded by an unlovely sprawl of modern bungalows, the shingle-backed beach may not be as inviting as West Wittering – but there's fine fossil-hunting to be had here. Dark, sea-polished sharks' teeth and fossilised shells wash up regularly, with particularly rich pickings after stormy weather. It's also popular with surfers and windsurfers.

West Wittering

The prime attraction for most visitors is the long, sandy beach at West Wittering. Sheltered by the Isle of Wight and the rolling swell of the South Downs, it enjoys its own benign microclimate, earning it the sobriquet 'God's pocket'. Even on blustery days, there's a chance the sun will still be shining down here – and if not, cups of hot chocolate from the beach café and old-fashioned British stoicism fortify the faithful and their wetsuit-clad offspring.

Thanks to a group of enterprising locals, who pooled resources and bought the beach and surrounding grassland in 1952 to save it from developers, it's an idyllic spot. There are no crazy golf courses or amusement arcades to distract the kids from sandcastle-building; no naff bungalows and caravan parks. Instead, the wide, sloping sands are backed by a tall tamarisk hedge and a row of weathered beach huts and a 20-acre swathe of grassland, occupied by butterflies, picnicking families and wonky lines of parked cars.

Simple pleasures are the order of the day here. At low tide, a quarter of a mile of fine, softly sloping sand emerges, along with shallow tidal pools and a sandbar-sheltered lagoon. Children paddle and drift on dinghies in the smaller pools (there are lifeguards from May to September). The bigger tidal lagoon, meanwhile, is perfect for a sedate swim, and a mecca for kitesurfers and windsurfers – its calm waters are ideal for showing off (the old hands) or falling off (the novices). If you want to spend all day frolicking in the sea, you can get all the necessary gear at Wittering Surf Shop (see p246).

Aside from the surf shop, the beach's sole concession to commercialism is a low block housing a beach shop, a café and two takeaway hatches. Most beachgoers prefer to bring a picnic or spark up a barbecue: come midday, the heady smell of browning sausages wafts across the dunes.

The best way to get to the beach – and bypass the snaking queue for the car park that builds up on summer weekends – is to cycle down from Chichester on the 11-mile Salterns Way Cycle Path (*see p246*). It runs through some beautiful countryside, before finally emerging in West Wittering village, a charming slice of nostalgia with its flint-studded cottages and tiny, peaceful church. If you're coming by train but don't want to cycle, go to Chichester and catch the 53 bus; cars should take the A286 south from Chichester for seven miles.

East Head to Chichester Harbour
Inviting as the clean, gently shelving sands and calm waters of West Wittering may be, that's only half the story. At the western end of the beach, the shifting sand dunes and salt marshes of East Head ★ possess a desolate beauty, and are a haven for wildlife and those in search of solitude.

A sand and shingle spit, East Head marks the entrance to Chichester Harbour. On its seaward side, the sandy strand is narrower than the main beach, but infinitely quieter. Look out for treasures deposited by the sea: pearl-lined slipper limpet shells, razor clams, cockles and whelks. The northernmost tip is the busiest spot, as passing yachts drop anchor for lunch and a dip, and day-trippers sprawl on the sand. Off-season, their place is taken by a colony of harper seals, who swim across from Thorney Island to bask in the winter sunshine. Even at the height of summer, though, there's peace and quiet to be found.

Shaped by the wind and waves, the dunes are constantly shifting, gathering around the clumps of spiky marram grass and forming and reforming into new patterns. Roped-off areas protect ringed-plover nesting sites and dunes where rare silver spiny digger wasps burrow – one of the reasons this is a designated Site of Special Scientific Interest, protected by the National Trust (*see p252*).

On the landward side, the salt marshes are bleakly beautiful at any time of year, and covered with purple sea lavender in early summer. Where East Head meets the mainland, a footpath meanders around the harbour to the sailing village of Itchenor. Along the way is the green triangle of Snow Hill Common and a white-painted row of old coastguard cottages, built to deter the 18th-century smugglers who used Snow Hill Creek to transport contraband. Here, too, is the crabbing pool, where small children (and competitive fathers) gaze into the murky depths, armed with bacon-baited lines.

At Itchenor, summer boat trips explore the harbour, and the footpath stretches onwards to Chichester Marina and beyond. But the handsome, red-brick Ship Inn (*see p249*) beckons, with its outdoor tables, locally brewed real ales and gargantuan portions of fish and chips. It used to be popular with World War II pilots based nearby.

Chichester Harbour is an Area of Outstanding Natural Beauty, sprawled across 22 square miles of estuary and shoreline. Wading birds and wildfowl congregate on the mudflats, walkers explore the 50 miles of footpaths, and it's a tremendously popular spot for sailing and messing about in boats. Chichester Harbour Conservancy (01243 513275, www.conservancy.co.uk) runs a range of guided walking tours throughout the year, along with boat trips and photography courses.

Where to eat & drink
The best fish and chips on the peninsula are to be found at the Boathouse in East Wittering (10 Shore Road, 01243 673386). Just up the road at no.59, Rendezvous restaurant (01243 673584) serves freshly caught fish and tempting meat dishes, as well as family-friendly fodder.

The bright and breezy Beach House B&B (*see p250*) doubles up as a laid-back café-restaurant. Claim a table on the wooden veranda and enjoy some sterling local seafood: Sussex smokies, whole tail scampi, or whatever has come in on the boats.

Crab & Lobster
Mill Lane, Sidlesham, PO20 7NB (01243 641233, www.crab-lobster.co.uk). Lunch served noon-2.30pm, dinner served 6-9.30pm Mon-Fri. Food served noon-9.30pm Sat; noon-9pm Sun.

Bognor Regis. See p241.

Perched by Pagham nature reserve, the Crab & Lobster has a romantic setting – the patio overlooks the marshes – and lots of character (the building is 350 years old), despite the modern dining room. Seafood is the culinary forte, not least the inn's namesake crustaceans. Poached fillet of sea trout with lobster ravioli, citrus crushed potato and shellfish bisque is typical of the kitchen's sophisticated approach. If you don't like seafood, there are meaty alternatives such as duo of Gloucester Old Spot pork belly and braised cheek with rösti potato and carrot and cardamom purée. This is a very popular place, so book ahead – and expect restaurant rather than pub prices. In addition, there are four swish B&B rooms (£140-£180 double incl breakfast) and a two-bedroom cottage (£220-£250 incl breakfast).

Old House at Home

Cakeham Road, West Wittering, PO20 8AD (01243 511234, www.theoldhouseathome.co.uk). Open noon-11pm Mon-Sat; noon-10.30pm Sun. Lunch served noon-2.30pm Mon-Sat; noon-3pm Sun. Dinner served 6.30-9pm daily.

West Wittering's only pub is a good one. Its menu offers hearty classics (sausage and mash, scampi and chips) made with local produce. Inside, three log fires keep things warm in winter; in summer, the deck patio and garden are a good place to enjoy the sea breeze.

Ship Inn

The Street, West Itchenor, PO20 7AH (01243 512284, www.theshipinnitchenor.co.uk). Open 9am-11pm daily. Food served noon-2.30pm, 6.30-9.30pm daily.

This traditional English pub is perched near the shores of Chichester Harbour. Much of the menu comprises immaculately fresh fish – plaice, mackerel, crab and lobster – complemented by local real ales, including Ballards Best, Ringwood Fortyniner, Castle Bitter from the Arundel Brewery and King's Horsham Best (the pub is recommended by CAMRA). If the ale takes its toll, there are two rooms and a cottage to rent on a bed and breakfast basis, starting at £80 a night.

Where to stay

Camping options abound in these parts. The campsite closest to West Wittering beach is Wick's Farm Holiday Park (Redlands Lane, 01243 513116, www.wicksfarm.co.uk), winner of a gold David Bellamy Conservation Award. In East Wittering, the grassy paddock at Stubcroft Farm (*see p250*) is another idyllic spot at which to pitch camp.

For a more luxurious stay, book into the Crab & Lobster (*see p248*) in Sidlesham. The four sleek rooms have views over Pagham Harbour.

In East Wittering, there are a handful of quirky beachfront holiday lets built around old railway carriages. The Dodo (01730 814002, www.thedodo.co.uk) epitomises coastal chic, with its white-painted wooden furniture, pretty floral materials and decked terrace; it sleeps 12 in total, with a mix of doubles, twin beds and bunks.

SIX SUSSEX WRITERS

Hilaire Belloc (1870-1953)
This French-born writer, poet and historian bought a house in Shipley, near Horsham, in 1906 where he lived until his death. Published in 1911, *The Four Men: a Farrago* tells the story of a fictional trip across Sussex from Robertsbridge to the Hampshire border, and is packed with local tales, myths and vignettes of rural life.

William Blake (1757-1827)
The visionary poet and painter lived in a thatched cottage in Felpham, on the coast near Bognor Regis, from 1800 to 1803. Blake wrote parts of his epic *Milton* here, including the stirring preface ('And did those feet in ancient time/ Walk upon England's mountains green/ And was the holy Lamb of God/On England's pleasant pastures seen') that would later become the hymn *Jerusalem*. He was also involved in an unfortunate altercation with a drunken soldier, who was trespassing in his garden; in retaliation, the soldier accused him of cursing the king, and Blake was put on trial at Chichester, though acquitted.

Graham Greene (1904-1991)
Graham Greene's name is forever linked to Brighton, thanks to *Brighton Rock* – a shocking, tightly written foray into the city's seedy underbelly and razor-blade wielding gang culture. The book was published in 1938 and first made into a film in 1947, with a young Richard Attenborough as its sociopathic antihero, Pinkie Brown. A new version, with the action transplanted to the 1960s and Sam Riley as the lead, was released in February 2011.

Peter James (b.1948)
The Brighton-born crime author has used the city as a backdrop for all his bestselling Roy Grace novels, detailing its parks, pubs, courts and criminals with uncanny precision. James regularly spends time with the Sussex police, adding an authentic edge to Detective Superintendent Grace's exploits. And his favourite childhood reading? *Brighton Rock*, of course.

Beach House
Rookwood Road, West Wittering, PO20 8LT (01243 514800, www.beachhse.co.uk). Rates £75-£90 double incl breakfast.
In West Wittering village, 15 minutes' walk from the beach, the Beach House has seven simple, spacious en suite rooms, incliding several family rooms. The residents' lounge is equipped with a fridge and microwave; alternatively, you can eat in the café-restaurant (*see p248*) downstairs. Early booking is essential, and there is a two-night minimum stay during school holidays and weekends from April to September.

Stubcroft Farm Campsite & B&B
Stubcroft Lane, East Wittering, PO20 8PJ (01243 671469, www.stubcroft.com). Rates Campsite £7 per person. B&B £75-£85 double incl breakfast. No credit cards.
Stubcroft Farm is a beauty of a campsite, well within reach of the beach. Set on a family-run farm, it consists of a mown five-acre field, split by tall mixed hedgerows into three small enclosures and one large field. There's usually a good-natured mix of campers in all areas, and also plenty of space for ball games and mooching. It's also eco-friendly, with recycling bins and six eco loos. If the great outdoors gets all too much, there are two B&B rooms in the Victorian farmhouse. Like the campsite, it's run on enviromentally-friendly lines. All around are peaceful private lanes and grounds to explore, making this a delightful countryside retreat. In spring and summer there are lambs and calves on the farm.

BOSHAM
The village of Bosham (pronounced 'Bozzum') is set on one of the tidal creeks off Chichester Harbour, across the water from the Manhood Peninsula. To get there from the peninsula, you'll have to drive around the water, skirting Chichester. Alternatively, a small foot-passenger ferry (07970 378350, www.itchenorferry.co.uk) runs from the jetty at Itchenor to Smuggler's Hard in Bosham, from April to late October.

A mecca for sailing enthusiasts, Bosham is a picturesque little place, dominated by the Saxon tower of the Holy Trinity Church. According to legend, this is where the Danish King Canute attempted – and failed – to turn the waters back. It's also said that his daughter was buried in the church after drowning in the village millstream; in 1865, a small Saxon stone coffin containing a girl's bones was found, and re-interred by the chancel arch.

A tidal creek borders the narrow High Street, which is notoriously prone to flooding; the quaint fishermen's cottages have raised entrances, or boards to keep the water out at high tide. The Anchor Bleu (*see p251*) is a fine old boozer at the heart of the village, with a delightful waterside terrace. On Bosham Lane, Bosham Walk Art & Craft Centre (01243 572475, www.bosham-walk.co.uk) is also worth a look. Set in a former boathouse, its two floors are occupied by small boutiques selling jewellery, textiles, paintings and sculpture, and a tea room.

Running along the water's edge, Shore Road is frequently submerged at high tide; take heed of the warning signs and don't park your car there.

Where to eat & drink

Within easy reach of both Itchenor and Bosham, at Dell Quay, is the Crown & Anchor (Dell Quay Road, 01243 781712, www.crownandanchorchichester. com). Its gravelled terrace is the perfect place for a pint, watching the comings and goings of the little boats and the sun setting over Chichester Harbour, while the menu offers uncomplicated pub grub (cheese and chutney sandwiches, gammon, egg and chips, or sausages and mash for the kids).

Anchor Bleu

High Street, Bosham, PO18 8LF (01243 573956, www. bosham.org/anchor). Open Summer 11am-11.30pm Mon-Sat; noon-10.30pm Sun. Winter noon-3pm, 5.30-10.30pm Mon-Wed; noon-3pm, 5.30-11pm Thur; 11.30am-11.30pm Fri, Sat; noon-10.30pm Sun. Summer Lunch served noon-3pm, dinner served 6.30-9.30pm Mon-Sat. Food served noon-8.30pm Sun. Winter Lunch served noon-3pm daily. Dinner served 6.30-9.30pm Mon-Sat.

With its flagstones, log fires and ample line-up of real ales, the Anchor Bleu is a welcoming spot, with decent food and hearty portions as further pluses. There's a small beer garden at the front, and a fine rear terrace overlooking the water; just be careful where you park, as the road along the seafront is often flooded at high tide.

36 on the Quay ★

47 South Street, Emsworth, PO10 7EG (01243 375592, www.36onthequay.co.uk). Lunch served noon-2pm, dinner served 7-10pm Tue-Sat.

Almost five miles west of Bosham, just over the border in Hampshire, is the village of Emsworth. It's worth a detour for the Michelin-starred 36 on the Quay, set in a 17th-century building on the quayside. There's an emphasis on skillfully-executed fish dishes with fine dining flourishes, although the lunch menu is somewhat simpler. It also offers accommodation, with five B&B rooms (£100-£250 double incl continental breakfast) and a small self-contained cottage (£120 double).

Where to stay

In Emsworth, 36 on the Quay (*see above*) also offers five tastefully appointed rooms; as it's a 17th-century building, some are on the small side. The owners also rent out a 16th-century fisherman's cottage, Cardamom, which is small but very quaint, with a compact sitting room and enclosed garden.

Charters B&B

Bosham Lane, Bosham, PO18 8HG (01243 572644, www.chartersbandb.co.uk). Rates £80-£100 double incl breakfast.

The two bright, welcoming suites at Charters have their own entrances, and feel more like a hotel than a B&B. The Sail Loft is particularly smart, with its roll-top bath, king size bed and underfloor heating. At the weekend, full English breakfasts are cooked on the Aga, with local sausages in pride of place.

Rudyard Kipling (1865-1936)
The author of the *The Jungle Book* lived at Bateman's (*see p190*), a 17th-century sandstone manor house in Burwash, East Sussex, from 1902 until his death. It was here that he wrote *If* and *Puck of Pook's Hill*. Born in British India, Kipling loved Sussex, and even penned an ode in its honour; 'God gave all men all earth to love,/But since our hearts are small/Ordained for each one spot should prove/Beloved over all.' And later continues 'Each to his choice, and I rejoice/The lot has fallen to me/ In a fair ground-in a fair ground –/Yea, Sussex by the Sea!'

Virginia Woolf (1882-1941)
The novelist's country retreat was Monk's House (01323 870001, www.nationaltrust.org.uk), an 18th-century, weatherboard-clad cottage in Rodmell, near Lewes, with a writing hut in the garden. (Opening times are limited, so check before visiting.) Virginia was also a frequent visitor to Charleston (*see p200*), where her sister, the painter Vanessa Bell, created a gloriously bohemian family home and artistic hub in a mellow Wealden farmhouse. As Virginia cheerfully admitted, 'Charleston is by no means a gentleman's house. The atmosphere seems full of catastrophes which upset no one; the atmosphere is good humoured, lively, as it tends to be after three months of domestic disaster.'

SUSSEX

Places to visit

SHOREHAM-BY-SEA & WORTHING

Marlipins Museum
36 High Street, Shoreham-by-Sea (01273 462994, www.sussexpast.co.uk). Open May-Oct 10.30am-4.30pm Tue-Sat. Admission £2; £1 reductions.
The museum is set in a fascinating building, with a wonderful checkerboard façade of Sussex flint and Caen stone, and a two-storey modern annex. Inside you'll find a rundown of local history, covering Shoreham's maritime past, agricultural heritage and, more surprisingly, its once-thriving film studios.

Shoreham Airport
Shoreham-by-Sea, BN43 5FF (01273 441061, www.shorehamairport.co.uk). Open 10am-4pm daily. Tours £3.50. No credit cards.
The modern airport is, by and large, a pretty bleak proposition – but it wasn't always thus. Set in the South Downs, Shoreham's aerodrome captures the glamour of a bygone age. The Grade II-listed terminal, built in 1936, is an art deco gem. Pleasure flights and flying lessons are available, while tours last an hour and must be booked in advance. Exhibits in the visitors' centre range from a World War II bomb to 'Archive Archie' – a touching tribute to the airport's unofficial pet rodent, and there's a restaurant too.

LITTLEHAMPTON

Littlehampton Museum
Manor House, Church Street, BN17 5EW (01903 738100, www.littlehampton-tc.gov.uk). Open 9am-4.30pm Mon-Fri; 10.30am-4.30pm Sat. Admission free.
This museum takes in various permanent collections, ranging from from a hoard of Roman silver coins found at Climping, to a maritime gallery with over 200 model ships. The temporary exhibition programme also showcases work by local artists.

Look & Sea Heritage Exhibition Centre
63-65 Surrey Street, BN17 5AW (01903 718984, www.lookandsea.co.uk). Open 9am-5pm daily. Admission £2; £1-£1.50 reductions.
Interactive exhibits, fascinating facts and surprisingly good food make this riverside complex a good place to

keep the family amused for a couple of hours. The focus is on exploring the local community and its history, from RNLI films showing full scale rescues at sea, to an exhibition on how the town has developed since Tudor times. The highlight, however, is the viewing tower, which offers panoramic views across the harbour.

Tangmere Military Aviation Museum
Tangmere, PO20 2ES (01243 790090, www.tangmere-museum.org.uk). Open Mar-Oct 10am-5.30pm daily. Feb, Nov 10am-4.30pm daily. Admission £7.50; £2-£6 reductions; £17 family.
Try your hand at flying in a special flight simulator and see some wonderful historic aircraft, including the record-breaking cherry-red Hawker Hunter that was flown by fighter pilot Neville Duke. This haven for history buffs and aviation fans was set up in 1982 at Tangmere airfield – one of the UK's key airbases during World War II.

BOGNOR REGIS & FELPHAM

Butlins
Upper Bognor Road, Bognor Regis, PO21 1JJ (0845 070 4770, www.butlins.com). Day pass £17-£25; £8.50-£15 reductions.
The kitsch world of Butlins is still going strong, with its fairground rides, flumes, and cheery staff bounding about in bright red jackets. These days, though, Butlins Bognor Regis has several slick additions that have brought it more in line with the 21st century – notably its pair of modern hotels and spa (see p246). Children will be more impressed by the waterpark, with its slides, water cannons, wave machines and rapids. The site also takes in a funfair, go-karts, adventure golf, playgrounds and a high ropes course, some of which involve extra charges.

MANHOOD PENINSULA

East Head
West Wittering (07799 072593, www.nationaltrust.org.uk). Open 24hrs daily. Admission free.
At the western end of West Wittering beach, the East Head nature reserve is an SSSI (a Site of Special Scientific Interest), an SPA (Special Protection Area) and an SAC (Special Area of Conservation). The sand dunes on the fragile, ever-eroding sand and shingle spit are home to many maritime plants, as well as various sand lizards and butterflies. Birdwatchers will not be disappointed by the dunes and neighbouring salt marsh: migrant wildfowl includes sanderling, redshank, curlew and godwits. Chichester Harbour, which East Head faces, is also a bird haven during the winter, and there are regular nature walks and boat trips run by Chichester Harbour Conservancy (01243 512301, www.conservancy.co.uk).

Pagham Harbour Local Nature Reserve
Selsey Road, Sidlesham, PO20 7NE (01243 641508, www.sussexwt.org.uk). Open Nature reserve 24hrs daily. Visitors' Centre times vary; phone for details. Admission free.
The tidal mudflats of Pagham Harbour attract waders and egrets, as well as a number of rare plants, including chidling pink and the southern marsh orchid.

Mid Sussex

Glancing at Mid Sussex on a map, it would be easy to dismiss the area as a heavily populated and overwhelmingly urban sprawl. With Crawley and Horsham in the north, and East Grinstead, Haywards Heath and Burgess Hill on the easternmost border of West Sussex, Mid Sussex is prime commuting territory, with the M23/A23, the south-east's main traffic artery, pulsing through it to Brighton. But what many miss while hurtling down the motorway or speeding past on the train is the little-visited countryside, speckled with hamlets, pubs, stately manors and some stunning gardens, including Kew's country offshoot, Wakehurst Place. The towns too have more to offer than might first meet the eye: East Grinstead is home to the longest continuous row of Tudor houses in the country, while the cobbled streets around the Carfax shopping precinct in Horsham are an unexpected delight.

Perhaps the loveliest part of Mid Sussex is along the ridge of the South Downs – a stretch that takes in the plunging, precipitous Devil's Dyke. The legend is that the devil, seeing the spires of the Weald, decided to dig a trench to the sea to submerge the churches. His energetic digging woke an old woman, who lit a candle to see what was going on. Seeing the light, the devil thought that morning had come and promptly scarpered, leaving a steep, sweeping valley carved into the landscape.

HURSTPIERPOINT TO WASHINGTON

From east to west, the South Downs Way follows the ridge of the chalk Downs, from Ditchling Beacon (see p211), passing the Clayton Windmills above the villages of Stenying and Bramber, past Chanctonbury Ring and through the village of Washington.

Hurstpierpoint

Seven miles directly north of Brighton, Hurstpierpoint is a well-kept, well-to-do little settlement. At the crossroads of the High Street and Cuckfield Road is Holy Trinity Church. In 1845 it was completely rebuilt by Charles Barry (who designed the Houses of Parliament), although its 13th-century font remains, along with two weathered medieval effigies of knights. In 1313 the village was granted a royal charter to hold the Fair of St Lawrence – it still takes place every year on the first Saturday in July. It's a delightfully traditional shindig, with a tug-o-war between pub teams, assorted stalls, a procession of gaily coloured floats and a funfair.

Continue east along the High Street to the cosy New Inn (see p256) on the right. Opposite, at no.99, Café Murano (01273 835344, closed Sun) sells wholesome food as well as a few trinkets. At no.117, Hampers Delicatessen (01273 833452, www.hampersofhurst.com, closed Sun) is perfect for picnic supplies and sells superb bread. Another standout is South Downs Cellars (no.100, 01273 833830, www.southdownscellars.co.uk, closed Mon, Sun), whose ample stock includes wines from the nearby Plumpton Estate.

Neighbouring Hassocks is less pretty than Hurstpierpoint, though home to the railway station, while nearby Clayton is best known for the two windmills that sit above the village, known locally as Jack and Jill (see p261); the church also has some fine 12th-century wall murals. From Clayton, it's a mile's uphill walk to Wolstonbury Hill – one of the highest points of the Downs, and with magnificent views to match.

Devil's Dyke

The Victorians, like many modern-day visitors, loved the drama of Devil's Dyke – a plunging, vertiginous gulf, carved out from the chalk strata as the Ice Age snowfields retreated. Day-trippers flocked to peer into the abyss; in its tourist heyday at the end of the 19th century, there was even a cable car, perilously strung across the valley.

These day it remains popular with walkers, picnickers, kite-flyers and hang-gliders, who circle above and occasionally swoop incredibly close to the north side of the Downs. Even at ground level the views are sublime; 'perhaps the most grand & affecting natural landscape in the world,' according to John Constable. Although the Devils Dyke pub near the summit is a less than lovely construction, it's a handy stop-off for a pint. There's a National Trust car park, if you're not arriving on foot or bike via the South Downs Way, or aboard the no.77 bus from Brighton.

Bramber & Steyning

In 1926, the splendidly named English landscape painter Reginald Rex Vicat Cole painted the Brooks of Bramber. It shows a bridge over the River Adur near Bramber Castle, with cattle crossing and a dark,

foreboding sky. The pastoral way of life may have changed somewhat since, yet the landscape remains largely unchanged. Walkers can follow the path along the foot of the Downs from the village of Poynings, and cross the River Adur on the bridge that Cole painted.

From here, the remains of Bramber Castle (www.english-heritage.org.uk) hove into view. The stronghold was built in around 1070 by Norman nobleman William de Braose, the first Lord of the Rape of Bramber, in the days when Bramber was an important port and the Adur a hugger-mugger of sea-going vessels. Today the river is the province of a few graceful swans, while Bramber is a sleepy village. The castle is in ruins, although the Church of St Nicholas, the oldest Norman church in Sussex, remains.

The village is also home to the 15th-century, timber-framed St Mary's House & Garden (see p261), originally a monastic inn for pilgrims. The house inspired Sir Arthur Conan Doyle's story *The Musgrave Ritual*, while its former owners Algernon Bourke and his wife Gwendolen were immortalised in Oscar Wilde's *The Importance of Being Earnest*.

Steyning, which has almost consumed Bramber, is equally historic, although substantially larger. The most scenic thoroughfare is the largely residential Church Street, which is dotted with listed buildings, while the shops are concentrated along the High Street. Under the clock tower, Cobblestone Walk (74 High Street, www.cobblestonewalk.co.uk) is a small shopping arcade with around 20 independent shops. Look out for Mary's Vintage & Retro (07917 266365, open Tue, Sat), where stocks runs from silk

gloves and elegant cloche hats to statement sunglasses and 1980s dresses. Steyning Tea Rooms (see p256) is a delight, with wonderful cakes and stylish but cosy decor.

Chanctonbury Ring

Above Steyning on the South Downs, the hilltop Chanctonbury Ring offers fantastic views over the Weald. It has long been used as a look-out: the remains of an Iron Age hill fort have been found, along with Bronze Age pottery. The Romans would later use the ring as a religious site, building two temples here. However, it wasn't until the mid 18th century that the circle of beech trees that make Chanctonbury so distinctive were planted by Charles Goring, following the lines of the ancient fort.

A sense of mystery and foreboding seems to have attached itself to the site, with reports of unusual phenomenon and UFO sightings; in 1979, a strange altar was discovered, with a five-pointed star made out of flint at its centre. It is also said that if you run around the dark trees anti-clockwise seven times on a moonless night, the devil himself will appear.

Where to eat & drink

The pub at the top of Devil's Dyke (01273 857256) is perfectly placed for an after-walk pint or a sunset tipple. For a more picturesque country pub, though, head down into the Weald to the Shepherd & Dog (The Street, Fulking, 01273 857382, www.shepherdanddogpub.co.uk) – a 17th-century inn set at the foot of the Downs, with low, beamed ceilings and a glorious beer garden.

SUSSEX

St Nicholas

Steyning Tea Rooms (32 High Street, 01903 810064) is a real find. The cakes are wonderful (if they're on the menu, try the delicious rhubarb or plum scones), the lunches are own-made, and the panelled interior, decked out with bunting and mismatched wooden furniture, is the epitome of shabby chic.

Chequer Inn

41 High Street, Steyning, BN44 3RE (01903 814437, www.chequerinnsteyning.co.uk). Open 10am-11pm Mon-Thur, Sun; 10am-midnight Fri, Sat. Breakfast served 10am-noon Mon-Sat; 10-11.30am Sun. Lunch served noon-2pm Mon-Sat; noon-2.30pm Sun. Dinner served 6.30-9pm Mon-Sat.

The Chequer Inn has been on this spot since 1440, and, as with many coaching inns, fulfilled multiple functions: in its prime, it incorporated a court room, post office and coroner's office. Those days are long gone, although the hospitable log fires and heavy beams remain. The menu comprises fairly conventional pub grub, but it's of good quality; the eggs in your brie and bacon omelette come from a local farm, while Sussex sausages are served with heaps of mash, peas and own-made onion gravy. To give an idea of the portions, one of the breakfasts is called Armageddon.

Fig Tree

120 High Street, Hurstpierpoint, BN6 9PX (01273 832183, www.figtreerestaurant.co.uk). Lunch served noon-2pm Wed-Sat; 12.30-2.30pm Sun. Dinner served 7-9.30pm Tue-Sat.

Since it opened in 2006, the Fig Tree has built quite a reputation for itself. It's a quietly handsome establishment, with solid wooden furniture and a muted colour scheme; service is impeccable. The regularly changing menu, which is based on seasonal ingredients, mixes modern English and French influences, featuring the likes of bourguignon of venison and ox cheeks with sautéed mushrooms, buttered curly kale and bubble and squeak potato cake.

Ginger Fox

Muddleswood Road, Albourne, BN6 9EA (01273 857888, www.gingermanrestaurants.com). Open noon-11.30pm Mon-Fri; noon-midnight Sat; noon-10.30pm Sun. Lunch served noon-2pm Mon-Fri; 12.30-3.30pm Sat; noon-4pm Sun. Dinner served 6-10pm daily.

Part of the small, locally founded Gingerman restaurant group, the Ginger Fox gives big British flavours a contemporary flourish. Tuck into a starter of saffron and oxtail arancini with parmesan and piquillo pepper purée, a main of roast breast of pheasant with sweet and sour red cabbage, celeriac gratin and cranberry jus, and finish with a lemon and lime posset with poached pears, mulled wine syrup and ginger snaps. It's all delivered with silky smooth service and views over the Downs.

New Inn ★

76 High Street, Hurstpierpoint, BN6 9RQ (01273 834608, www.thenewinnhurst.com). Open 11am-11pm Mon-Sat; 11.30am-10.30pm Sun. Lunch served noon-2.30pm, dinner served 6.30-9.30pm Mon-Sat. Food served noon-9pm Sun.

The wonderful New Inn dates back to 1450, but has been carefully overhauled to suit modern sensibilities. Antlers hang on the walls above plump chesterfield sofas in the low-

lit back bar, while artfully arranged antique clocks, figurines and books add a thoroughly cosy feel. Out back, there's a walled garden with a children's play area. The menu runs from doorstep sarnies to hearty mains: roasted vegetable crumble, perhaps, or honey-roast pheasant, with sautéed parsnips, sugar snap peas and chestnuts.

Nia Café

27 High Street, Steyning, BN44 3YE (01903 879999, www.niacafe.co.uk). Open 10am-4pm, 6.30-10pm Wed-Sun.

This compact café and restaurant is a lovely addition to Steyning's dining scene. The breakfast menu is particularly sumptuous, running from crumpets and croissants to maple syrup-doused pancakes, fry-ups or soft-boiled eggs with soldiers. Lunchtime might bring Sussex cheddar rarebit or salmon and haddock fish cakes with salsa verde, while dinner options nod towards old-fashioned comfort food: cottage pie with purple sprouting broccoli, say, or coq au vin with broad bean mash. Its premises are on the small side, but the south-facing terrace adds extra space in summer.

Whites Bar & Kitchen

23 High Street, Steyning, BN44 3YE (01903 812347, www.whitesbarkitchen.co.uk). Open 10am-11pm Mon-Thur; 10am-midnight Fri, Sat; 10am-10.30pm Sun. Lunch served noon-2.30pm Mon-Sat; noon-3pm Sun. Dinner served 6-9.30pm Mon-Sat; 6.30-9pm Sun.

With its curvaceous chrome bar and cocktail list, the bar at Whites oozes sophistication – and the restaurant is equally polished. Plenty of Sussex eateries may promise locally sourced produce, but this place goes one step further, listing food miles on its menu. Foraged ingredients also feature in dishes such as marbled game terrine with crab apple jelly, smoked wild mushroom tapenade and walnut toast – and that's just for starters. Other dishes have a global influence (pan-roasted sea bass, lemon spinach, basmati pilaf and courgette raita, for example), while vegetarian options are pleasingly inventive.

Where to stay

The bedrooms at the Best Western Old Tollgate (The Street, Bramber, 01903 879494, www.oldtollgate hotel.com) are a tad soulless, but everything is dusted and polished to a good chain hotel standard.

For rural tranquillity, book one of the six B&B rooms at Clayton Wickham Farmhouse (Belmont Lane, 01273 845698, www.cwfbandb.co.uk), just outside Hurstpierpoint. Two of the rooms are set in the main farmhouse, parts of which date from the 14th century, while the others occupy the barn conversion. The three-acre gardens have a croquet lawn and tennis court, and the views over the surrounding fields and woods are glorious.

In Steyning, Springwells (9 High Street, 01903 812446, www.springwells.co.uk) occupies a handsome Georgian merchant's house. Its 11 bedrooms run from simple doubles with shared bathrooms to grander four-poster rooms.

Wickwoods Country Club, Hotel & Spa

Shaves Wood Lane, Albourne, BN6 9DY (01273 857567, www.wickwoods.co.uk). Rates £66.50-£95 double incl breakfast.

Devil's Dyke. See p253.

FIVE SUSSEX VINEYARDS

Bookers
Bolney Wine Estate, Foxhole Lane,
Bolney, RH17 5NB (01444 881894,
www.bookersvineyard.co.uk).
Bookers' offerings – including its
sparkling wines, produced using a
traditional bottle-fermentation method
– have won the winery numerous awards.
The family-run vineyard, ten miles south
of Crawley, spans 22 acres, and, thanks
to a grant from DEFRA, a shiny new
winery was completed in 2005.
Consult the website for details of
tours and tastings.

Breaky Bottom
Northease Farm, Rodmell, Lewes,
BN7 3EX (01273 476427,
www.breakybottom.co.uk).
Head to this popular vineyard, a short
drive from Lewes, for an informative tour
or to lend a hand during picking season.
The main grape grown is the clean-tasting
Seyval Blanc. Visits are by appointment
only, so call ahead.

Carr Taylor
Wheel Lane, Westfield, TN35 4SG
(01424 752501, www.carr-taylor.co.uk).
Guided tours of the vineyard (five miles
inland from Hastings) take in a potted
history of English wine-making, along
with a chance to see the vats, presses
and bottling room, then try the finished
products. The large shop stocks local
produce as well as the vineyard's
impressive array of wines and fragrant
fruit wines.

Nutbourne Vineyards
Gay Street, West Chiltington, RH20
2HE (01798 815196, www.nutbourne
vineyards.com).
Seven types of grape are nurtured at
Nutbourne, where 18 acres of vines
produce the grapes to make between
25,000 and 50,000 bottles a year. As
well as dry whites, Nutbourne produces
a sparkling wine made by the traditional
Champagne method. The vineyard
(which is very close to Nyetimber) is
open weekday afternoons from May
to October; visitors can learn how the
grapes are cultivated, visit the windmill,
and wander the grounds, taking in lakes,
poultry and even llamas.

Nyetimber
Gay Street, West Chiltington, RH20 2HH
(01798 813989, www.nyetimber.com).
Nyetimber's premium sparkling wine
is known the world over, and made
wholly from estate-grown fruit. The
438-acre vineyard surrounds 11th-
century Nyetimber Manor, just east
of Pulborough, but neither are open
to visitors.

Bookers

Set amid 22 acres, facilities at this country club include six floodlit tennis courts, a gym, and a spa with a heated pool, sauna and steam room. Its five rooms are more of an afterthought, but each is well designed, en suite, and with all the amenities you'd expect; at the top of the tree, the 'premier' room features a sleigh bed and a garden view balcony. Note that an additional £10 charge applies for a day's use of the spa and fitness facilities.

BURGESS HILL TO EAST GRINSTEAD

North of Hurstpierpoint is the beginning of a stretch of urban sprawl that runs from Burgess Hill, on the main Brighton-London train line, up to Haywards Heath. Places of interest are scarce, although just over the border in East Sussex are the Bluebell Railway (see p205) and the National Trust's Sheffield Park (see p201). Just north of Haywards Heath, meanwhile, are Borde Hill Gardens (see p261).

Climbing north, the countryside becomes increasingly wooded, and the housing makes way for the open Weald. The stretch of road north of Haywards Heath on the B2028 is through classic Sussex terrain, with rolling, forested hills, little farmhouses and views around every corner; train commuters will tell you that the finest view in Sussex is from the viaduct a couple of minutes outside Haywards Heath.

On the north-eastern outskirts of Haywards Heath, Lindfield is one of the prettier villages hereabouts. Charmingly crooked medieval houses line the gently sloping High Street, which is planted with lime trees and leads up to All Saints' church. At its lower end is the enormous village pond and the common; cricket matches take place in summer, and there's a huge bonfire and fireworks on 5 November. If you're planning on eating or staying over, Limes of Lindfield (see p262) is a friendly, dapper little bistro with rooms.

Just over three miles away, the village of Ardingly is home to the South of England Agricultural Society Showground. It hosts an enormous three-day show each June, where prize pigs, show-jumping spectaculars, food stalls and brass bands jostle for visitors' attention. A mile west of the village, Ardingly Reservoir is a 198-acre body of water that's used for all manner of water sports. Windsurfing, sailing and canoeing sessions can be booked through Ardingly Activity Centre (see p259). Fishing is also popular, with carp, trench and eel all regularly biting. At the north end of the reservoir, Wakehurst Place (see p262) is Kew Gardens' country outpost, and the home of the Millennium Seed Bank.

Drive west through Balcombe to reach High Beeches Gardens and wonderful Nymans (for both see p261).

East Grinstead

With its shops and museum, East Grinstead provides enough distraction for a couple of hours. Its High Street is home to the longest continuous row of 14th-century timber-framed buildings in England, one of which contains the East Grinstead Bookshop

Things to do

HURSTPIERPOINT TO WASHINGTON

Washbrooks Family Farm
Brighton Road, Hurstpierpoint, BN6 9EF (01273 832201, www.washbrooks.co.uk). Open 9.30am-5pm daily. Admission £5; £4.50 reductions; £17 family.
A thoroughly enjoyable time can be had at Washbrooks, meeting all manner of animals: ducks, sheep, chickens, pigs, ponies, rabbits and – somewhat incongruously – wallabies. Indoor and outdoor play areas offer much diversion, and the tearoom whips up old favourites such as cottage pie and macaroni cheese.

BURGESS HILL TO EAST GRINSTEAD

Ardingly Activity Centre
The Lodge, Ardingly Reservoir, Ardingly, RH17 6SQ (01444 892549, www.ardingly activitycentre.co.uk). Open by appointment only. Rates from £69 per 2hrs personal tuition.
From yachting and powerboating to windsurfing and canoeing, there are all manner of water-based activities to get to grips with at this activity centre. Pick up qualifications or hire a kayak and have a gentle splash around. Ardingly Activity Centre also takes fishing seriously, with resident species including roach, rudd, carp, bream, pike and perch.

HORSHAM & AROUND

Holmbush Farm World
Crawley Road, Faygate, RH12 4SE (01293 851110, www.holmbushfarm.co.uk). Open Feb-Oct 10am-5.30pm daily. Admission £7; £5.50-£6.25 reductions; £23 family.
Old-fashioned, wholesome entertainments prevail at Holmbush Farm World, where goat racing and tractor rides are about as radical as it gets. There are various characters to meet, from Rolo the Shetland pony to Winston and Clementine the rare woolly pigs, and animal handling sessions with rabbits, ferrets, guinea pigs and (for more intrepid visitors) rats. In spring, newborn lambs and chicks join the menagerie. A tea barn and indoor and outdoor play areas round off the experience.

Tulleys Farm Maze
Turners Hill, Crawley, RH10 4PE (01342 718472, www.tulleysmaizemaze.co.uk). Open Mid July-mid Sept 10am-6pm daily. Admission check website for details.
On the outskirts of Crawley, Tulleys Farm offers an all-action family day out during the summer holidays, with its giant corn maze, bouncy slides, tractor rides and farm animals. A new maze is designed every year, with almost four miles of pathway to get lost in (there are gallery bridges to help you get your bearings). It's also open on selected Friday and Saturday nights in winter for special torchlight maze nights; check the website for details.

Wakehurst Place. See p262.

HURSTPIERPOINT TO WASHINGTON

Jill Windmill
Mill Lane, Clayton, BN6 9PG (www.jillwindmill.org.uk). Open May-Sept 2-5pm Sun. Admission free.
This 19th-century corn windmill originally stood in Brighton in the early 1800s, but was hauled to its present perch above Clayton in 1852, by a team of oxen. Known as Jill (its partner, Jack, is the privately owned tower mill next door), the mill is now open to the public most Sundays from May to September. It's in full working order, and stoneground wholemeal flour is sometimes on sale, wind conditions permitting.

St Mary's House
Bramber, BN44 3WE (01903 816205, www. stmarysbramber.co.uk). Open May-Sept 2-6pm Thur, Sun. Admission House & gardens £7.50; £4-£6.50 reductions; £18 family. Gardens only £5; £2.50-£4 reductions; £12 family. No credit cards.
Literary connections are at the heart of St Mary's history. Former owner Algernon Bourke and his wife Gwendolen inspired the principal characters in Oscar Wilde's *The Importance of Being Earnest*, while another former owner, Alfred Musgrave, lent his name to *The Musgrave Ritual*, one of Sherlock Holmes' escapades. The house is a 15th-century timber-framed building, with fine wood panelling and an Elizabethan painted room with beautiful gilding. In the five-acre gardens, highlights run from animal topiary to the walled Victorian vegetable garden.

BURGESS HILL TO EAST GRINSTEAD

Borde Hill Gardens
Balcombe Road, Haywards Heath, RH16 1XP (01444 450326, www.bordehill.co.uk). Open Mid Mar-mid Sept 10am-6pm daily. Admission £8; £2.25-£7 reductions; £22 family.
The gardens at Borde Hill are wonderfully diverse, with a series of garden rooms. Among them are the beautiful rose garden, white garden and azalea ring – a mass of vibrant flowers, which reaches its colourful zenith around May. With its rectangular pond, dotted with waterlilies, and views across the Downs, the terraced Italian garden is particularly lovely. The self-service café (01444 458845) has a sheltered sun-trap terrace at the back, and does a very decent line in freshly baked scones, sandwiches and wholesome hot lunches (butternut squash, beetroot and blue cheese tart, perhaps, or Sussex smokie with bread and salad). There's also an adventure playground.

Cuckfield Museum
High Street, Cuckfield, RH17 5EL (01444 473630, www.cuckfield.org). Open Mid Feb-mid Dec 10am-12.30pm Wed, Fri; 10am-4pm Sat. Admission free.
The museum's star attraction is its display on the 'Cuckfield Dinosaurs' and the work of Dr Gideon Mantell, a local obstetrician with a fruitful sideline in paleontology. In 1822, he discovered the first fossilised iguanodon teeth – though some would

have it that they were actually found by his wife. The museum also explores the history of the area's human residents, with photographs, textiles and domestic artefacts.

East Grinstead Museum
Old Market Yard, Cantelupe Road, East Grinstead, RH19 3BJ (01342 302233, www.eastgrinstead museum.org.uk). Open 10am-4pm Wed-Sat; 2-5pm Sun. Admission free.
Delve into the history of this little market town with displays, interactive features and audio and visual presentations. A temporary exhibition area displays new works three times a year. The museum has recently acquired the fascinating collection of the Queen Victoria Hospital, where badly burned airmen from World War II underwent pioneering reconstructive surgery.

High Beeches Gardens
High Beeches Lane, Handcross, RH17 6HQ (01444 400589, www.highbeeches.com). Open Gardens Mar-Oct 1-5pm Mon, Tue, Thur-Sun. Tearoom All year 11.30am-4pm Mon, Tue, Thur-Sun. Admission £6. No credit cards.
There are masses of exotic and unusual plants at this 27-acre woodland and water garden, including a number of species gathered by intrepid Victorian plant-hunters. Everything from bluebells to bananas thrives here; in August, don't miss the bright blue drifts of willow gentian. Another standout feature is the wildflower meadow, which is at its peak in June. The autumn colours are spectacular, and there's a tree trail that you can follow at any time of year.

Nymans ★
On the B2114, Handcross, RH17 6EB (01444 405250, www.nationaltrust.org.uk/nymans). Open House Mar-Oct 11am-3pm Mon, Wed-Sun. Gardens, woods & restaurant Mar-Oct 10am-5pm daily. Jan, Feb, Nov, Dec 10am-4pm daily. Admission £9; £4.50 reductions; £21.50 family.
Three generations of the Messel family cultivated these gloriously romantic gardens, which were bequeathed to the National Trust in 1953. The setting is awe-inspiring and the plants spectacular, and rare – the Messels sponsored the great plant collectors of the day to ensure as wide and interesting a variety of specimens as possible. Part of the house – a 1920s mock medieval manor, designed by the wonderfully named Sir Walter Tapper and Norman Evill – burned down in 1947, and its roofless remains provide an evocative backdrop to the greenery.

Priest House
North Lane, West Hoathly, RH19 4PP (01342 810479, www.sussexpast.co.uk). Open Mar-Oct 10.30am-5.30pm Tue-Sat; noon-5.30pm Sun. Admission £3.50; £1.75-£3 reductions. No credit cards.
Illustrious former owners of this 15th-century timber-framed house include Henry VIII's chief minister, Thomas Cromwell. The unfortunate Cromwell was beheaded after falling out of favour with the hot-

headed king, and ownership passed to Henry's fourth wife, Anne of Cleves, as part of her divorce settlement, although she never lived here. It was first opened to the public in 1908 by its then-owner John Godwin King, who later gave the house and its contents to the Sussex Archaeological Society. Today, the pieces on display include 17th- and 18th-century furniture, embroidery and ironwork. There's also an attractive cottage garden, planted with an enormous array of herbs.

Standen
West Hoathly Road, East Grinstead, RH19 4NE (01342 323029, www.nationaltrust.org.uk/ standen). Open times vary; check website for details. Admission £7.80; £3.90 reductions; £22.50 family.
Standing amid tranquil 12-acre hillside gardens, with peerless views over the High Weald, this stunning Arts and Crafts family home was designed by architect Philip Webb. The interiors were the work of William Morris's company, with superbly crafted metalwork, furniture, ceramics, wallpaper and tapestries. It's a visual feast, even if you're not an Arts and Crafts enthusiast. Meanwhile, true devotees can book a stay in the second-floor apartment (*see p263*).

Wakehurst Place ★
On the B2028, Ardingly, RH17 6TN (01444 894066, www.kew.org). Open Gardens Mar-Oct 10am-6pm daily. Jan, Feb, Nov, Dec 10am-4.30pm daily. Seed bank & mansion Mar-Oct 10am-5pm daily. Jan, Feb, Nov, Dec 10am-3.30pm daily. Admission £10.75; free reductions.
As well as gardens galore, Kew's lesser-known West Sussex site, Wakehurst Place, is home to the amazing Millennium Seed Bank. Its objective? To collect seeds and specimens from more than 24,000 plant species, guarding them against extinction. Learn why and how the seeds are stored in underground vaults, and check out the world's largest seed – the rather saucily shaped coco de mer. You'll never get your arms around the trunky Californian beauty known as *Sequoiadendron giganteum*, located outside the Elizabethan mansion: it's 35 metres tall, and draped with 2,000 fairy lights at Christmas. It's so bright that pilots flying into Gatwick look out for it.

HORSHAM & AROUND

Horsham Museum
9 Causeway, Horsham, RH12 1HE (01403 254959, www.horshammuseum.org). Open 10am-5pm Mon-Sat. Admission free.
There's something for everyone at this well-kept museum. Photography, costume, crime and punishment and natural history are among the topics explored in its galleries, and a steady stream of activity sessions are held throughout the year. Look out for the intriguing Cabinet of Curiosities, whose contents range from skulls and Roman relics to giant shells. The building is fascinating in itself – a medieval timber-framed merchants house, with two walled gardens.

(Tudor House, 22 High Street, 01342 322669, www.eastgrinsteadbookshop.co.uk, closed Sun). The weathered carvings on the exterior are exquisite, while the shop is superbly stocked with new and second-hand literature.

If the buildings spark your interest, the town's museum (*see p261*) outlines the history of East Grinstead and the surrounding villages. Exhibits run from a giant plaster cast of an iguanodon's footprint to a recently donated collection of artefacts from the Queen Victoria Hospital. The hospital was best known for its associations with the Guinea Pig Club – a group of World War II airmen, disfigured in action, who were treated at its burns unit by pioneering plastic surgeon Archibald McIndoe.

Continue along the High Street to the sandstone, Grade I-listed Sackville College (01342 323414, open mid June-mid Sept Wed-Sun), one of the best-preserved Jacobean almshouses in the country. Founded in 1609 and completed ten years later, it has acted as a home for the elderly ever since.

Two miles south of town, Standen (*see left*) is a spectacular Arts and Crafts family home, now run by the National Trust. It has fantastic views across the Weir Wood Reservoir (01342 820650, www.weirwoodreservoir.co.uk), which is a popular spot for sailing, angling and birdwatching.

Where to eat & drink

In East Grinstead, CJ's Coffee House (55-57 High Street, 01342 301910) is a welcoming stop, with the companiable gurgle of the coffee machine and clatter of cutlery. Despite being a chain pub – and feeling like one – the Dorset Arms (58 High Street, 01342 316363, www.gkpubs.co.uk) is still a pleasant place for a drink or some good-value pub food. A generously proportioned old coaching inn, it has booth seating in the main bar and dining tables in much of the rest of the pub.

Limes of Lindfield
67 High Street, Lindfield, RH16 2HN (01444 487858, www.limesoflindfield.co.uk). Open 10am-3pm, 6.30-11pm Mon-Sat. Lunch served noon-2.30pm, dinner seved 7-9pm Mon-Sat.
Limes of Lindfield is a trim contemporary bistro with pared-down decor and a smart, appealingly varied menu – salmon and coriander rosti cakes with lemon crème fraîche and salad at lunchtime, say, or roasted lamb shank with bean cassoulet for supper. It also has four comfortable, bright en suite rooms (£125 double incl breakfast), with their own entrance on the High Street.

Ockenden Manor
Ockenden Lane, Cuckfield, RH17 5LD (01444 416111, www.hshotels.co.uk). Lunch served noon-2pm, dinner served 7-9pm daily.
Set in nine-acre grounds in the pretty Tudor village of Cuckfield, two miles outside Haywards Heath, this Elizabethan manor is now an opulent hotel and fine dining restaurant. Under head chef Stephen Crane, the kitchen has won a Michelin star for its superb seasonal food (winter truffle soup to start, perhaps, followed by wild Balcombe duck breast and confit with colcannon, rainbow chard,

salsify and orange). If you can't quite tear yourself away, there are 22 rooms and suites (£190-£395 double incl breakfast), packed with period charm.

Where to stay

In East Grinstead, three stately double rooms can be found above CJ's Coffee House at Gothic House (55 High Street, 01342 301910, www.gothichouse 55.com), while there are four more modern rooms at Limes of Lindfield (*see p262*).

For an opulent weekend away, book a room or suite at Ockenden Manor (*see p262*) in Cuckfield. It's at the upper end of the price spectrum, and features might include a private staircase, a terrace overlooking the Downs or an expansive four-poster bed. A spa is set to open in late 2011.

Arts and Crafts enthusiasts will be in raptures at Standen (*see p262*), where the National Trust rents out a one-bedroom apartment in the former servants' wing. It's decorated in William Morris prints and textiles, and the setting is sublime.

Alexander House Hotel & Utopia Spa

Turners Hill, East Grinstead, RH10 4QD (01342 714914, www.alexanderhotels.co.uk/alexander). Rates £185-£550 double incl breakfast.
Set in 120 acres of gardens, woods and parkland, just outside East Grinstead, this old mansion is now a smart 38-room hotel and spa. The decor is quietly contemporary rather than country-house chintz – though there is a fine four-poster in the Henley Suite. There are two on-site eateries; AG's Grill Room specialises in high-end slabs of tender meat with thick-cut chips, while Reflections is a sleek brasserie with a courtyard dining area.

Gravetye Manor

Vowels Lane, nr West Hoathly, RH19 4LJ (01342 810567, www.gravetyemanor.co.uk). Rates £200-£430 double incl continental breakfast.
This 17-room luxury hotel, which occupies a fabulous Elizabethan manor, was undergoing refurbishment at the time of writing, but promises great things. Antique furniture, panelled walls, rich floral fabrics and handsome fireplaces are par for the course in an updated take on classic country house styling. The gardens are a delight; the original design was the work of William Robinson, a celebrated gardener and champion of more natural planting and native flowers and trees, who lived here from 1884 until his death in 1935. There's also a smart modern British restaurant; in summer, almost all the fruit and vegetables used in the kitchen come from the walled kitchen gardens.

HORSHAM & AROUND

Horsham

Horsham lies on the border of Surrey. Unlike Crawley and Gatwick, with their largely post-World War II architecture, the town has retained many of its historic buildings, despite the Luftwaffe's best efforts. Its cosmopolitan vibe is helped by the large open pedestrianised shopping centre, in particular the Carfax, a cobbled boulevard with a bandstand,

built in 1892, where bands play every Saturday between April and September.

There are a handful of great shops. Katerina (18 Carfax, 01403 243024, www.katerina.co.uk, closed Mon, Sun) specialises in contemporary handcrafted jewellery and gifts, while Country Produce (44b Carfax, 01403 274136, www. country-produce.co.uk) is an excellent butcher and deli. On Saturdays, there's a local produce market.

South of Carfax is the old Market Square, on which stand the Town Hall and Horsham Museum (9 Causeway, 01403 254959, www.horsham museum.org, closed Sun). Housed in a medieval timber-framed merchant's house, the museum's 26 galleries chart the history of the area. One gallery is devoted to Percy Bysshe Shelley, who was born in nearby Warnham, and there's an interesting programme of temporary exhibitions. Talbot Lane and Pump Alley, leading off the Market Square, have some well-preserved timber-framed buildings. Continuing south, past the museum, are a mix of 15th- and 16th-century buildings. The oldest building in Horsham, though, is St Mary's Parish Church (www.stmaryshorsham.org.uk), built in 1247. Although the interior has been altered over the centuries, it remains a fine example of the Early English style. Opposite the church, the River Arun passes through the very pleasant Memorial Gardens, behind which lies the cricket ground.

At the end of pedestrianised, shop-lined West Street is the dramatic, spherical *Rising Universe* water sculpture, also known as the Shelley Fountain. Unveiled in 1996 – and the subject of some controversy – it commemorates the great Romantic poet, whose family vault is in St Mary's.

A short walk to the north of the town, Horsham Park takes in a playground, tennis courts, a sensory garden, a bandstand and a café (01403 259941). There's also a leisure centre, Pavilions in the Park (Hurst Road, 01403 219200), for rainy days. North again, along Warnham Road, is the Warnham Local Nature Reserve (01403 256890, www.horsham districtcountryside.org), a wooded, 92-acre site with a vast, reed-fringed millpond at its southern end. There's a visitor centre with an exhibition room and a café, and various hides and trails to explore.

St Leonard's Forest

East of Horsham is St Leonard's Forest, a designated Area of Outstanding Natural Beauty that features ancient woodland along with swathes of gorse- and heather-covered heathland and farmland. Legend has it that in the sixth century, St Leonard killed the last dragon in England in the forest – and indeed, Saxon historian Ethelweard wrote in 770 that 'monstrous serpents were seen in the country of the Southern Angles that is called Sussex.'

Iron smelting was a major industry here in the 16th century, with a rich seam of iron ore and plenty of wood to fuel the furnaces and water to drive the hammers and bellows. The ponds remain, along with circular pits from which the ore was extracted. The first part of the 90-mile High Weald Landscape Trail (www.highweald.org/explore/walking-and-cycling) runs through the forest.

TEN SUSSEX GARDENS

Borde Hill Gardens
Each of the distinctive garden rooms at Borde Hill has its own style, and encompass a splendid variety of seasonal colour. Bordered by box hedges and curving pathways, the rose garden is a delight, and there are some glorious rhododendrons and a striking Chinese tulip tree in the romantically named Garden of Allah. *See p261.*

Carpet Gardens
For a more orderly take on gardening, check out Eastbourne's famous Carpet Gardens, on the promenade in front of the pier. Using bedding plants, fabulous patterns are arranged with inch-perfect precision, adding a jaunty splash of colour to the seafront. *See p174.*

Denmans Garden
Small but immensely charming, this sculpture-dotted four-acre plot is a showcase for landscape designer John Brookes' considerable talents. The planting has a gloriously wild, untamed feel, with plants creeping on to the gravel paths and lush, densely planted beds brimming with flowers and foliage. There's also a garden centre and a café. *See p286.*

Great Dixter House & Gardens
Working alongside head gardener Fergus Garrett, the late Christopher Lloyd certainly left his mark at Great Dixter – a place of pilgrimage for gardeners. From the quirky yew topiary to the gloriously profuse long border (at its colourful best in summer), it is full of unexpected delights. *See p162.*

High Beeches Gardens
From May's bluebell-filled glades to glowing autumn colours (the maples are particularly resplendent), High Beeches is a garden for all seasons. It's also home to assorted champion trees (the tallest of their kind in the UK), an idyllic wildflower meadow, and the National Collection of stewartia trees. *See p261.*

South of Horsham

Out of Horsham, the A24 leads directly south to the coast and Worthing. Following the A281 south to Steyning is a much more interesting route, however, passing near the villages of Warninglid, Wineham and Henfield. Quaint as the villages are, the real attraction is the scattering of excellent country pubs. Henfield is the largest of the three villages, and home to a small but charming museum (www.henfield.gov.uk), whose exhibits run from fossils and farming implements to lethal-looking mousetraps and a penny farthing. In the village itself, look out for the thatched Cat House on Church Street. The story goes that its owner, Bob Ward, had a canary that was killed by a cat belonging to the parish priest. In retaliation, Ward painted pictures of the offending moggy and unfortunate bird all over his house, to remind the priest of the crime.

Where to eat & drink

Black Jug
31 North Street, Horsham, RH12 1RJ (01403 253526, www.blackjug-horsham.co.uk). Open 11.30am-11pm Mon-Sat; noon-10.30pm Sun. Food served noon-10pm Mon-Sat; noon-9.30pm Sun.
The Black Jug's extensive menu is ever-changing but consistently good, whether it's a seared tuna salad with fennel, rocket and orange or plate of hearty, red wine-braised beef with shallots and horseradish mash. There's a sizeable wine list, and ales from small breweries. It's a welcoming, laid-back place, with huge wooden tables, Edwardian wood panelling, an open fire and a part-covered leafy courtyard.

Half Moon
The Street, Warninglid, RH17 5TR (01444 461227, www.thehalfmoonwarninglid.co.uk). Open 11.30am-2.30pm, 5.30-11pm Mon-Sat; noon-10.30pm Sun. Lunch served noon-2pm daily. Dinner served 6-9.30pm Mon-Sat.
Set on a crossroads, this Grade II-listed brick and stone pub dates from the 18th century, but has been brushed up considerably to become a thriving gastropub. There are splendid real ales on tap and an inviting seasonal menu that makes good use of local produce (pan-fried pheasant breast with game faggot, creamed leeks and ratte potatoes, perhaps, or beetroot and Sussex cheese risotto).

Red Lion
Lion Lane, Turners Hill, RH10 4NU (01342 715416). Open 11am-11pm Mon-Sat; noon-8pm Sun. Lunch served noon-2.30pm daily.
Toast your feet by a log fire and settle down to a pint of Harveys at this cosy traditional pub. Food is served at lunch only, with a great roast on Sunday, but the real ale flows all day. In summer, the grassy rear garden comes into its own.

Royal Oak ★
Wineham, BN5 9AY (01444 881252). Open 11am-3pm, 5.30-11pm Mon-Fri; 11am-3pm, 6-11pm Sat; noon-4pm, 7-10.30pm Sun. Lunch served noon-2.30pm Mon-Sat; noon-3pm Sun. Dinner served 7-9pm Mon-Sat.

It may be slightly off the beaten track, but the Royal Oak is worth a detour. Built as two cottages in the 13th century, the black and white timbered building has been a pub for at least 200 years. The beer, served from casks, is excellent, and the food superb: once you're settled by the inglenook fireplace in the bar, with a plate of twice-baked soufflé or soft herring roes on toast with lemon and green leaves (or anything else from the daily changing menu), you'll be in no hurry to leave. The glorious beer garden is another draw.

Where to stay

Just over two miles from Horsham, the lakeside Mannings Heath Hotel (Winterpit Lane, Mannings Heath, 01403 891191, www.manningsheath hotel.com) has 19 comfortable rooms and its own nine-hole golf course. It's a popular wedding venue, and can get booked out.

Cisswood House Hotel (Sandygate Lane, Lower Beeding, 01403 891216, www.cisswoodhouse.com) is a rather elegant 1920s property, built for Sir Woodman Burbridge, then the chairman of Harrods. It's now a 51-room hotel with a restaurant, indoor swimming pool, spa treatments and delightful landscaped grounds.

South Lodge Hotel

Brighton Road (A281), nr Lower Beeding, RH13 6PS (01403 891711, www.southlodgehotel.co.uk). Rates £278-£714 double incl breakfast.

Built by Victorian collector and explorer Frederick Du Cane Godman, this grand mansion is set in 93 acres of grounds, with wonderful Wealden views. Now a luxurious country house hotel, it has 89 rooms and suites. Features run from freestanding roll-top baths and wrought-iron beds to private gardens and hot tubs (depending on how much you want to spend), but little luxuries such as the pillow menu and well-stocked tea caddies come as standard. The 22-seater Pass restaurant has a front-row view of the chefs at work in the kitchen, and specialises in tasting menus, running from four to eight courses. Dishes might include the likes of celeriac velouté with roasted scallop and apple, confit salmon with pickled beetroot and smoked eel, or pork belly with cauliflower purée. The Camellia Country Kitchen is geared towards more traditional tastes: think thyme-braised lamb shank and lyonnaise potatoes, or smoked haddock with saffron mash and garden greens, topped with a poached egg.

Tottington Manor Hotel

Edburton, nr Henfield, BN5 9LJ (01903 815757, www.tottingtonmanor.co.uk). Rates £100 double incl breakfast.

Dating from 1604, this historical bolthole a few miles south of Henfield makes for a fascinating stay. During World War II, it became part of Churchill's secret Auxiliary Unit, with seven bunkers built below the building, and escape tunnels leading into the fields that remain to this day. Above ground, the five en suite bedrooms enjoy bucolic country views, and there's a restaurant serving hearty dishes in no-nonsense portions (own-made steak, kidney and mushroom suet pudding, say, or pepper-crusted monkfish with herb mash and creamed spinach). There's also an appealing children's menu.

Merriments Gardens

The delightfully named Merriments Gardens are perhaps the most colourful in all Sussex, particularly the 'hot' border. Cooler shades prevail in the peaceful Blue Gravel garden, while the deliberately untamed wildlife area attracts a profusion of birdlife and butterflies. See p163.

Nymans Garden

Run by the National Trust and planted around a romantic ruin, Nymans is home to an astonishing variety of plants. Along with rose, heather and rock gardens, there are woodland walks and a beautiful bulb meadow. See p261.

Sheffield Park

Landscaped by 'Capability' Brown and centered on four magnificent lakes, Sheffield Park is perhaps the best place in the country to see the leaves turn in autumn. In spring, the bluebells and daffodils take centre stage, closely followed by vividly hued azaleas and rhododendrons in early summer. See p201.

Wakehurst Place

Kew's place in the country, Wakehurst is also the home of the Millennium Seed Bank, where more than 24,000 plant species are stored. After learning about the project, wander the 465-acre estate, complete with ornamental gardens and woodland. See p262.

West Dean Gardens

Refreshingly, vegetables are the focus of the superb gardens at West Dean (though there are lovely spring plantings, glorious bulbs and wildflowers, and an Edwardian pergola entwined with clematis, rose and honeysuckle). The walled kitchen gardens, raised beds and Victorian glasshouses are beautifully tended – and you can sample some of the produce at the on-site restaurant. See p288.

Arundel & the Arun Valley

A formidable sense of history permeates life in Arundel. Every corner of this attractive, compact town provides a glimpse into the past: a ruined medieval priory, Tudor dwellings, a Victorian coaching inn. Georgian townhouses sit alongside traditional Sussex cottages on the narrow streets. Dominating everything is the star attraction: Arundel Castle, first built during William the Conquerer's reign. Yet the town is far from being marooned in the past; its restaurants and, in particular, its independent shops and art galleries offer a wealth of contemporary interest for visitors.

North of Arundel, the Arun Valley weaves through the lowlands around Amberley and up into the Weald. Amberley is a quaint village with a couple of good pubs and one spectacular hotel; the South Downs Way runs through here too. The Romans enjoyed the area, building a villa at Bignor and leaving behind some marvellous mosaics. To the north-west is Petworth, a well-preserved medieval town that is to antiques what Hay-on-Wye is to bookshops. It's also home to a splendid manor house containing some of the National Trust's most treasured paintings.

ARUNDEL

With its hilltop castle and cathedral and the River Arun running beneath, Arundel looks more like a stage set for a medieval period drama than a real town. It's easy to understand why visitors in search of historic England are so drawn to it.

The vicinity has been inhabited for thousands of years, as the many tumuli (burial mounds) on the South Downs attest. But it was the Romans who first realised the benefits of Arundel's position atop the first inland hill. It was perfect for repelling marauders from the sea and from the River Arun, which is navigable until at least Amberley nine miles inland (as late as the 1920s Arundel was a working port, with large ships heading up the river). They built huge villas in the town, as they did across West Sussex; remains are still being unearthed. The last Romans quit England at the beginning of the fifth century and Arundel seemed destined to remain a small Saxon market town. But then Arundel Castle (see p272) was built, and life changed.

The first castle was constructed in 1067, part of William the Conqueror's sea defences across Sussex that included castles at Bramber, Pevensey, Dover and Carisbrooke on the Isle of Wight. It was granted to Roger de Montgomery, Earl of Arundel, along with a third of Sussex. Since 1138, with the occasional reversion to the Crown, the castle has passed directly within the same aristocratic family via the d'Albinis, FitzAlans and Howards. A succession crisis in 1580 was averted after Lady Mary FitzAlan (there was no male heir) married Thomas Howard, the 4th Duke of Norfolk, and the castle has belonged to the Duchy of Norfolk ever since.

The oldest remaining features are the Norman motte and gatehouse. Much of the fortifications visible today were, in fact, created between 1875 and 1900 by the 15th Duke of Norfolk. Inside, however, many of the astonishingly opulent furnishings are much older. A tour of the castle is a revelation, not only into its history, but how it still functions as a family home – one of the reasons it's open only between April and October. (The current Duke of Norfolk, incidentally, is the Earl Marshall, responsible for the organisation of state funerals and coronations, and also Britain's highest-ranking peer.)

The castle is Arundel's main attraction, of course, but the town has plenty of other delights. The Roman Catholic Arundel Cathedral (see p272) was built in 1873 to a French Gothic design by Joseph Hansom (inventor of the hansom cab). It's a bold gesture and rather overshadows 14th-century St Nicholas Church (see p273) across the road, but the latter is both beautiful and historically significant. Also of major appeal is the WWT Arundel Wetland Centre (see p273), encompassing reed beds, lakes and other habitats and is visited by thousands of migrating and local birds, some very rare. Even those turned off by the words 'bird reserve' will enjoy the excitement of being surrounded by bizarre-looking ducks keen to get to your bag of food.

Despite the prevalence of coach parties and weekenders during the summer, Arundel has a pleasing sense of being at ease with itself. Many of the antiques shops for which it was once known have gone – try Petworth instead – but it has an impressive range of intriguing, independent shops, and a disproportionate number of good eateries and wine bars. Accommodation options lag behind, but there are a couple of excellent small hotels.

The town is busy throughout the summer, especially during the ten-day Arundel Festival at the end of August. Focusing on music, drama and visual art, the festival encompasses a vast range of events and activities, including Shakespeare performances in the castle's garden, free gigs,

SUSSEX

street entertainers and open-air film screenings. Drip Action Theatre Company holds an international competition for 30-minute plays, resulting in the eight day Theatre Trail: eight plays in eight locations – in the past, venues have included pubs, gardens, restaurants and even a kitchen. Similarly, the ever-growing Gallery Trail opens the doors of 50 homes, galleries, pubs and shops to show work by more than 100 artists. Old-fashioned fun includes the Marbles Tournament, and there are numerous family-friendly events.

Another key event is the Feast of Corpus Christi, also known as the Carpet of Flowers, which has been celebrated in Arundel Cathedral for over 100 years. Talking place 60 days after Easter, it involves a 93-foot floral display on the floor of the nave and a procession around town.

The town centre

Old Arundel sits to the north of the River Arun and the A27, which bypasses the town; the cathedral and castle give away its position, especially if you're coming from the east. The car park on Mill Lane next to the castle entrance is a good starting point for a walking tour. The railway station is about half a mile south of town.

In the car park is the History Store, a temporary home for the Arundel Museum Society (01903 882456, www.arundelmuseum.org.uk) that contains a small display of quality tile work and other artefacts from the Roman occupation of Sussex. Plans are afoot for a new visitor centre and museum to create a 'heritage hub' in Arundel. If funds are forthcoming, it will probably open in 2012-13. Turn left from the car park to see the

Arundel Castle. See p272.

Things to do

ARUNDEL

Arundel River Cruises

Arundel Boatyard, Mill Road, BN18 9PA (01903 882609, www.riveraruncruises.com). Open Mar-Oct 10am-4pm daily. Fares 1hr cruise £7; £4 reductions.
The River Arun is the reason Arundel exists and the town was a working port until the early 20th century. Today, it's only leisure cruisers that ply the river. Arundel Boatyard offers one-hour trips upriver on 12- or 28-seater wooden boats. Shorter trips can be taken to Bridge Old Port for £4. The Riverside Tea Gardens are open from February to October, weather permitting.

Arundel Jailhouse & Ghost Experience

The Undercroft, Arundel Town Hall, Maltravers Street, BN18 9AP (www.arundeljailhouse. co.uk). Open Easter & summer hols noon-6pm daily. Rest of year noon-6pm Sat, Sun. Admission £5; £3-£4 reductions. No credit cards.
The Arundel Jailhouse was built in 1836 to house those sentenced in the court room directly above. Nowadays it has many facets, all slightly bizarre. The Ghost Experience – a spooky 20-minute candlelit tour of the cells – has been an established attraction for a while, but new owners have added comedy nights, murder mystery evenings and monthly Jailhouse Blues music evenings. The website warns: 'Not suitable for babies and toddlers or persons of a nervous disposition or with heart complaints.' Check the website for details of upcoming events.

AMBERLEY, PETWORTH & BILLINGSHURST

Wey & Arun Canal

The Granary, Flitchfold Farm, Loxwood, RH14 0RH (01403 752403, www.weyandarun.co.uk). Boat trips Easter-Oct 12.30pm, 1.30pm, 2.30pm Sat; 12.30pm, 1.30pm, 2.30pm. 3.30pm Sun, bank hols. Fares £4-£12; £2-£6 reductions.
Formed in 1970, the Wey & Arun Canal Trust has worked tirelessly to restore navigable links between the Rivers Wey and Arun. Twenty-one bridges, two aqueducts and 11 locks have now been restored and boat trips leave from the jetty behind the Onslow Arms pub at Loxwood. The standard 35-minute trip costs only £4, but enthusiasts can book 3.5-hour trip for £12.

Woodland Skills

Woodland Yurting, Keepers Barn, Tittlesfold, The Haven, RH14 9BG (01403 824057, www.woodlandskills.com).
Based at Woodland Yurting (*see p281*), woodsman Clive Cobie offers bushcraft sessions from basic skills to in-depth courses in everything from coppicing to rural crafts. An events calendar is available on the website, but bespoke courses can be booked.

Arundel Cathedral. See p272.

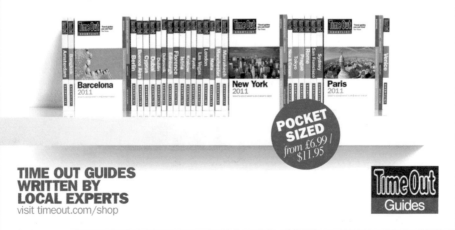

remains of a 13th-century Dominican priory, known as Blackfriars. It was destroyed, along with many other buildings in the town, during the Dissolution of the Monasteries. Take a right past the mock-Tudor post office (built in 1895) to reach the High Street. Nearly all Arundel's best shops, pubs and restaurants are within a ten-minute walk of here.

Arundel House hotel and restaurant (see p275) is on the left in a Georgian merchant's house. Straight ahead is the old market square and war memorial. Watching over the tiny cobbled square are two long-established shops. Pallant of Arundel (see p275) has been a grocer for more than 100 years; it's now an upmarket deli serving local produce and fine French cheeses, Spanish meats and other international goods. The wine selection includes bottles from Sussex vineyards. Next door is the traditional Arundel Butcher (01903 882270, closed Sun), which supplies many of the town's restaurants and pubs.

There are plenty of other shops worth investigating. Kim's Bookshop (no.10, 01903 882680, www.kimsbookshop.co.uk) stocks more than 30,000 new, second-hand and antiquarian books. If you need walking or camping equipment, Peglers (nos.18-20, 01903 883375, www.peglers.co.uk) is a very successful outdoors shop, with two branches in town. Squibbly Biskit (no.21, 01903 884427, www.squibblybiskit.co.uk, closed Sun) sells wooden toys and designer togs for children. Spencer Swaffer Antiques (no.30, 01903 882132, www.spencerswaffer.co.uk) is an Arundel institution, with a wonderful display of furniture, lighting and other interior design pieces. 'Many call it the best shop in England,' according to Architectural Digest. Next door is the Book Ferret (no.34, 01903 885727, www.thebookferret.co.uk), a relatively new addition, with a monthly book club.

Pubs on the High Street include the Swan Hotel (nos.27-29, 01903 882314), an expansive Fuller's pub, and the estimable Red Lion (see p276). The Norfolk Arms Hotel (see p276) is a coaching inn built in the late 1700s, while the Town House (see p276) is one of Arundel's best restaurants, and also offers accommodation.

Towards the top of the High Street, take a left into picturesque Maltravers Street, with its Georgian and Victorian townhouses that change hands for more than £1 million. At the crooked Bakers Arms Cottage, turn left again, into cobbled Bakers Arms Hill, to reach Tarrant Street – the main shopping street. On the right, Sparks Yard ★ (no.18, 01903 885588, www.sparksyard.com) occupies an attractive red-brick building. This popular two-storey shop sells fine kitchenware, garden items, posh gadgets, cookery books and wooden toys, and stocks brands such as Alessi, Emma Bridgewater and Vita audio equipment. Its café serves Illy coffee, ice-cream milkshakes and sinful cakes.

Head in the other direction, back towards the High Street, to find the Victoria Institute (no.10, 07787 056272, www.thevictoriainstitute.org), the nearest thing the town has to a community centre. It hosts a roster of events from jazz gigs and dance classes to plays by Drip Action Theatre

Arundel

(www.dripaction.co.uk). Check the institute's website for details.

There are a couple of contemporary art galleries on Tarrant Street. Zimmer Stewart (no.29, 01903 885867, www.zimmerstewart.co.uk, closed Mon, Sun) presents paintings, sculpture, ceramics and textiles by local and international artists. Across the road is newcomer Square 1 Art (1 Tarrant Square, 01903 884468, www.square1art.co.uk, open Wed-Sat winter; Tue summer), housed within the shell of a Tudor house. Prints, sculpture, ceramics, urban art and paintings are on show, alongside work by owner and sculptor Andrea Schulewitz.

The Old Printing Works (www.theoldprintingworks.co.uk) is a Victorian-themed arcade set back from Tarrant Street; look out for the Walking Stick Shop (01903 883796, www.walkingstickshop.co.uk) and Arundel Teddy Bears (01903 884458, www.arundelteddybears.co.uk, closed Wed). Long-established Castle Chocolates (no.11, 01903 884419) makes its own fudge and chocolate, and has an extraordinary range of confectionery, from sugar mice and old-fashioned boiled sweets to toffees and liquorice in all its guises. Owner Clive Gardner spreads good cheer as he beams out from behind the counter in his colourful bow tie and straw boater. Next door is Antiquities (no.5, 01903 884355, www.antiquitiesarundel.com), run by Ian and Christina Fenwick. It sells, as seems the norm in Arundel, large pieces such as 18th-century English and French furniture and fittings.

WWT Arundel Wetland Centre

ARUNDEL

Arundel Castle ★

High Street, BN18 9AB (01903 882173, www.arundel castle.org). Open Aug 10am-5pm daily. Apr-July, Sept, Oct 10am-5pm Tue-Sun. Admission £7.50-£16; £7.50-£13.50 reductions; £36-£39 family.

Arundel Castle originated at the end of the 11th century and has been the family home of the Dukes of Norfolk and their ancestors for more than 850 years. Aside from the occasional reversion to the throne, it's one of the longest inhabited aristocratic houses in England. In 1643, during the Civil War, the castle was besieged by General Waller (for Parliament) and the defences were partly demolished. Happily, many of the original features – such as the crenellated Norman keep, gatehouse and barbican, and the lower part of Bevis Tower – survived. The house was almost completely rebuilt in the late 19th century.

The castle is definitely worth exploring (despite the high admission price) for its collection of paintings by Van Dyck, Gainsborough and Reynolds, among others, as well as its tapestries and furniture, and the gorgeous FitzAlan Chapel. Other treasures include a 14th-century two-handed sword, a jousting saddle (thought to be the only one in existence) and a silver icon of the Virgin and Child by Fabergé. A new formal garden opened in 2008 and is a tribute to Thomas Howard, 14th Earl of Arundel (1585-1646), known as 'the Collector'. An organic kitchen garden has been re-created, but the over-the-top decorations are based on what 'the Collector' is thought to have enjoyed at his house in London. There's also a restaurant, café and gift shop. At weekends, outdoor events include medieval-style encampments with jousting and archery displays.

Arundel Cathedral

Parsons Hill, BN18 9AY (01903 882297, www.arundelcathedral.org). Open 9am-6pm daily.

The Roman Catholic Cathedral of Our Lady and St Philip Howard was completed in 1873 in the French Gothic style; it started out as a parish church and became a cathedral only in 1965. It's best viewed from a distance, but if you do decide to get close, there's a fine rose window over the west door and, inside, the shrine of St Philip Howard, 13th Earl of Arundel, who converted to Catholicism. He was

captured while fleeing abroad and sentenced to death, but died in 1595 aged 39 after languishing 11 years in the Tower of London.

St Nicholas Church

London Road, BN18 9AT (01903 882262, www.stnicholas-arundel.co.uk). Open 9am-6pm daily.
The Domesday Book mentions a church on this site, but it fell into ruin after the Black Death of 1349 (when there was a shortage of labourers) and was rebuilt in 1380. It became barracks and stables for the Parliamentarians during the Civil War – their guns laid siege to Arundel Castle from the church tower. Unusually, as well as serving as the Anglican parish church, the building also incorporates the castle's private Roman Catholic chapel. The wall dividing them was removed in 1969 and now a glass wall and iron grille separates the two sections; it's opened for ecumenical special occasions. The carved stone pulpit is one of only six pre-Reformation examples in the country.

WWT Arundel Wetland Centre ★

Mill Road, BN18 9PB (01903 883355, www.wwt.org.uk). Open Apr-Oct 9.30am-5.30pm daily. Jan-Mar, Nov, Dec 9.30am-4.30pm daily. Admission £9.36; £4.68-£7.82 reductions; £24.95 family.
Overlooked by looming Arundel Castle, this impressive 65-acre wetland reserve is a beauty. A network of trails weaves through various habitats, including a newly expanded reed bed (along a wooden boardwalk), an 'Arctic tundra' section and a variety of enclosures for waterfowl from around the world. There are also hides and an unusual building made of reeds that contains a camera obscura. Buy a bag of feed and enjoy the onslaught of ducks and geese that follow you around in hope of a snack. Wildfowl & Wetlands Trust (WWT) founder Peter Scott saved the Hawaiian goose from almost certain extinction; it now eats out of your hand. The visitor centre houses a café with wall-to-ceiling windows over bird-busy Swan Lake. Don't miss the free guided boat trips (11am-4.30pm daily): you might spot a kingfisher or one of the water voles that have been reintroduced here. Children will enjoy the play areas, daily bird-feeding and pond dipping, where they can examine the contents of their net under a microscope.

Places to visit

AMBERLEY, PETWORTH & BILLINGSHURST

Amberley Museum & Heritage Centre

Amberley, BN18 9LT (01798 831370, www.
amberleymuseum.co.uk). Open Apr-Oct 10am-
5.30pm Tue-Sun (daily during school hols). Admission
£9.60; £6.10-£8.60 reductions; £29.50 family.
This 36-acre open-air museum near the South
Downs Way features more than 30 different
buildings and hundreds of exhibits from bygone
days. Displays cover transport, printing,
telecommunications and electricity, and there's
a variety of working craftspeople in residence,
including a potter, clay-pipe maker and broom-
maker. You can travel around the site on a vintage
bus and a narrow-gauge train. Children will enjoy
the nature and woodland trail, playground and the
fact that there's plenty of space to run around in.
In all, it's a wonderful conglomeration of England's
artisan and industrial history, splendidly laid out.
Watch the introductory video at the Hayloft Theatre
before drawing up a plan of action for the day.

Bignor Roman Villa

Bignor, RH20 1PH (01798 869259, www.bignor
romanvilla.co.uk). Open June-Aug 10am-6pm daily.
Mar-May, Sept, Oct 10am-5pm daily. Admission
£5.50; £2.50-£4 reductions; £14 family.
If you can't get to Fishbourne, there is some splendid
and remarkably well-preserved Roman flooring at
Bignor Roman Villa. The finest mosaics depict
Ganymede, cup-bearer to the gods, in characteristic
Phrygian bonnet, a portrait of Venus (or possibly
the lady of the house), and a snake-haired head
of Medusa, located in the changing room of the
bathhouse. The remains were discovered in 1811
and opened to the public in 1815. The mosaics are
still housed in the small thatched Georgian buildings
that were originally erected to protect them. The site
is set in open farmland, with beautiful views of the
South Downs and plenty of footpaths nearby.

Fishers Farm Park

Newpound Lane, Wisborough Green, RH14 0EG
(01403 700063, www.fishersfarmpark.co.uk).
Open 10am-5pm daily. Admission prices vary;
check website for details.
Fishers is consistently voted one of the country's
top ten countryside attractions for families, mostly
because it's run like clockwork, looks gorgeous and
has so much to do. This is a place where families
with children aged up to about 12 could quite happily
spend an entire day. The variety and quality of the
rides, giant sandpits, climbing/clambering features,
soft play areas and general activities is quite
astounding, though you'll also find the usual cuddly
animals that are happy to be stroked. In addition,
there are pony and tractor rides, a ghost tunnel,
bumper boats, pedal karts, a mini adventure golf
course and seasonal shire horse shows and pig
racing. Prices vary according to season.

Parham House & Gardens ★

A283 between Storrington & Pulborough, RH20 4HS
(01903 744888, www.parhaminsussex.co.uk). Open
House Aug 2-5pm Tue-Fri, Sun. Apr-July, Sept 2-5pm
Wed, Thur, Sun. Oct 2-5pm Sun. Gardens May-Aug
noon-5pm Tue-Fri, Sun. Apr, Sept noon-5pm Wed,
Thur, Sun. Oct noon-5pm Sun. Admission House
& gardens £8.50; £4-£8 reductions; £24 family.
Gardens only £6.50; £3-£6 reductions; £17 family.
Parham House is a rare example of a large Elizabethan
manor house that has been restored according to
mid 20th-century ideas. It was first opened to the
public in 1948 by Clive and Alicia Pearson, and
remains in the same family. Simon Jenkins wrote of
it, 'Nothing in Parham is superfluous, nothing unloved.
This is a house of magic.' Highlights are the 160-foot
Long Gallery (with a beautiful 1968 ceiling by
renowned stage designer Oliver Messel) and the Great
Hall with its fine Elizabethan and Jacobean furniture.
The grounds include a deer park, a beautiful walled
flower garden designed for for long periods of colour,
a herb garden and an orchard. In the landscaped
Pleasure Grounds you'll find a lake, a summer house
and a modern maze whose design is based on a 16th-
century embroidery found in the house.

Petworth House & Park ★

Petworth, GU28 0AE (01798 342207, www.national
trust.org.uk). Open House mid Mar-Oct 11am-5pm
Mon-Wed, Sat, Sun. Pleasure Ground mid Mar-Oct
11am-6pm Mon-Wed, Sat, Sun. Mid Feb-mid Mar
10.30am-3.30pm Mon-Wed, Sat, Sun. mid Nov-mid
Dec 10.30am-3.30pm Wed-Sun. Admission House
& grounds £10.40; £5.20 reductions; £26 family.
Pleasure Ground £4; £2 reductions.
Built in the late 17th century and set in a 700-acre
deer park landscaped by Lancelot 'Capability' Brown,
Petworth House was immortalised in paintings by
JMW Turner. These days, it houses works by Van Dyck,
Gainsborough, Titian, Bosch and Blake as well as
carvings by Grinling Gibbons and assorted sculptures,
making up the National Trust's largest art collection.
There's a lot to take in, especially if you're also
visiting the Pleasure Ground (a 30-acre woodland
garden), taking a peek at the servants' quarters or
attending one of the open-air plays or concerts.
The ten-minute Welcome to Petworth talk is a good
general introduction to the house and grounds,
before you choose what to focus on. Don't miss
the Turner paintings, 1592 Molyneux globe (the
earliest English globe in existence) and 15th-century
decorated vellum manuscript of the Canterbury Tales.
The grounds are home to the largest herd of fallow
deer in England.

RSPB Pulborough Brooks

Wiggonholt, 2 miles south of Pulborough on A283
(01798 875851, www.rspb.org.uk). Open Visitor
Centre 9.30am-5pm daily. Trail dawn-dusk daily.
Admission Visitor Centre free. Trail £3.50; £1-£2.50
reductions; £7 family.
This RSPB nature reserve within the Arun Valley in
the South Downs National Park attracts redshanks,
lapwings, duck, geese, swans and many other species
to its heathland and flooded meadows. Listen for
nightingales in late April and May. There are hides
and trails to explore, and a café and gift shop. Guided
walks take place throughout the year; phone or check
the website for details.

SUSSEX

For a final antiques fix, head down the High Street and across the river to Arundel Eccentrics (Old Brewery Building, 2A Fitzalan Road, 07973 968446, www.arundeleccentrics.com, open Sat & by appt). Owner Brenda Nassarian restores, paints and decorates Victorian furniture and other vintage items; the results are unusual and beautiful. Pieces range in size from buckets and bowls to chests of drawers.

Also across the river is Arundel Lido (01903 882404, www.arundel-lido.com, open May-Sept). With its two heated pools, large grassed areas and views of the castle, it's one of England's most idyllic locations for open-air swimming. Young children will enjoy the Flying Fortress indoor play area (01903 733550, www.flying-fortress.co.uk) in Ford, a few miles south of town. It also has a teenage-friendly pool and football tables, and comfortable sofas and a café for tired parents.

Where to eat & drink

Despite being relatively small, Arundel has a wide selection of restaurants, tearooms and pubs. For snacking, Pallant of Arundel (17 High Street, 01903 882288, www.pallantofarundel.co.uk) can provide French cheeses, charcuterie, bread and a bottle of Sussex wine. The King's Arms (36 Tarrant Street, 01903 882312) is the oldest pub in town (built c1625) and is the locals' pub of choice. It has a dartboard, a quiz night, no food (although you can bring in your own), a sun-trap beer garden, good ales and friendly staff. On the same street is the Eagle (no.41, 01903 882304), a lovely little inn with log fires and a dining area. At no.25, Butler's Restaurant & Bar (01903 882222,

www.butlersarundel.co.uk) has good-value set lunches and dinners, Sunday roasts and a bar.

The newest and most stylish of the town's wine bars is Osteria Pappardelle (41 High Street, 01903 882025, www.pappardelle.co.uk). With long copper-topped tables and stools, it's a pleasant place for a coffee and pastry in the morning, and there are more than 60 wines by the glass and 40 grappas. The Italian influence comes from the long-established Pappardelle restaurant upstairs. Also on the High Street and also Italian is La Campania (no.51, 01903 884500, www.la-campania.co.uk). It's popular with families and larger groups. Jazzmins Wine Bar (no.63, 01903 883029) has regular live music in the evenings.

Don't forget the Black Rabbit (01903 882828, www.hall-woodhouse.co.uk) on Mill Road in Offham, past the Wetland Centre. A large family-friendly pub, it's a good base for a walk around the area.

Arundel House ★

11 High Street, BN18 9AD (01903 882136, www. arundelhouseonline.com). Lunch served noon-2pm, dinner served 7-9.30pm Tue-Sat.

High-quality Modern British cuisine is on offer at Arundel House, a restaurant with rooms (£75-£140 double incl breakfast; *see p276*) inside a Georgian merchant's house. There are only a few tables, making for an intimate meal. Expect the likes of crisp pheasant leg confit on parsnip purée with juniper-scented sauce to start, and cannon of Sussex lamb on polenta cake with wilted spinach as a main. The menu changes seasonally and each course has a fixed price. Note that children are not permitted.

Bay Tree

21 Tarrant Street, BN18 9DG (01903 883679, www. thebaytreearundel.co.uk). Lunch served 11.30am-3pm

SUSSEX

George & Dragon. See p278.

Tue-Fri; 10.30am-4.30pm Sat, Sun. Dinner served 6.45-9.15pm Tue-Fri; 6.45-9.45pm Sat.
This intimate restaurant serves uncomplicated, bistro-style dishes such as grilled, herb-crusted Arundel trout with white wine sauce, and pan-fried lamb cutlets with garlic and rosemary. It's also the relaxed surroundings and sunny terrace that keep the regulars coming back – that and the goat's cheese crème brûlée. The menu changes every couple of months, and there are lighter bites during the day including paninis, soup and salads.

George & Dragon ★
Main Street, Burpham, BN18 9RR (01903 883131, www.georgeanddragoninnburpham.com). Open noon-3.30pm, 6-11pm daily. Lunch served noon-2pm Mon-Fri; noon-3pm Sat, Sun. Dinner served 6.30-9.30pm daily.
Follow a winding road from Arundel to the quaint village of Burpham (pronounced 'Burfam'), complete with a rose-clad lychgate in front of the 12th-century flint church (writer and illustrator Mervyn Peake is buried in the churchyard). Now a renowned gastropub, the George & Dragon is 300 years old, and was once used by smugglers as a spot to divide the spoils that came up the river. An 18th-century spinning jenny is set in the ceiling. Modern European dishes are served in the elegant dining room: terrine of pigeon, duck, guinea fowl and chicken with apple chutney to start, followed by bacon-wrapped monkfish with colcannon, fine beans and a chive and crayfish buerre blanc. Excellent thick-cut sandwiches are available from the bar and there are several tables dedicated to drinkers (beers come from the Arundel Brewery).

Red Lion
45 High Street, BN18 9AG (01903 882214, www.redlionarundel.com). Open 11am-11pm Mon-Thur, Sun; 11am-midnight Fri, Sat. Lunch served noon-3pm, dinner served 6-9pm Mon-Fri. Food served noon-9pm Sat, Sun.
With an open fire, large sofas, real ales, a summer terrace and a separate dining area, the Red Lion effortlessly covers all bases. It has a light, airy and modern feel that makes for a relaxing coffee or pint. The menu offers good pub food at reasonable prices. The steak and Hammerpot porter pie uses meat from Arundel Butcher across the road and porter from the nearby Hammerpot brewery. It's a family-friendly pub, with a sandpit at the back. Evenings attract a younger crowd, and there are live music events a couple of times a month.

Town House ★
65 High Street, BN18 9AJ (01903 883847, www.the townhouse.co.uk). Lunch served noon-2.30pm, dinner served 7-9.30pm Tue-Sat.
The Town House has an excellent reputation locally. The elegant dining room within the Grade II-listed Regency building mixes a stunning 16th-century Italian walnut ceiling with modern touches. Head chef Lee Williams uses mainly local ingredients to produce a sumptuous Modern European menu; typical dishes include local cep soup with truffle oil, followed by grilled supreme and confit leg of guinea fowl with braised lentils and pearl barley. It's a set price, and very reasonable for cooking of this quality. There are also four bedrooms (£95-£130 double incl breakfast; *see right*).

Where to stay
Apart from a couple of notable exceptions, accommodation in Arundel hasn't kept up with its innovations in shopping and dining.

However, two of the town's best restaurants also have rooms. The Town House (*see left*) has four elegant bedrooms, awash with white and gold, with ornate plasterwork ceilings and antique furniture. Both the suite and large double room have four-poster beds and views over the castle walls. It's a charming boutique option, eschewing the vogue for the modern touch.

Of the five smart, contemporary rooms at Arundel House hotel ★ (*see p275*), the largest is split-level with a bed above, and a large bathroom and dressing area below. None of the rooms is huge, but they have superb waterfall showers (no baths) and decor is modern and calming. Note that children are not allowed.

For a list of B&Bs, visit the informative community website www.arundel.org.uk.

Arundel Youth Hostel
Warningcamp, BN18 9QY (01903 882204, www.yha.org.uk). Rates £16-£20 per person; £12-£16 reductions.
Located at the end of a private road, this handsome, cream-coloured Georgian mansion has a spacious front lawn and plenty of room for children. It has 62 beds in total, most of them in four- or six-bed rooms. It's well equipped, with a licensed restaurant as well as a self-catering kitchen, barbecue facilities in the extensive grounds, camping spaces and, for rainy days, a big lounge plus pool table, table tennis and bar football.

Billycan Camping
Manor Farm, Tortington, BN18 0BG (01903 882103, www.billycancamping.co.uk). Rates 2 nights weekend £195 for 2/3-person tent; £235 for 4/5-person tent.
Set among 650 acres of working farmland, Billycan Camping doesn't lack space. All the accommodation is in canvas bell tents, which come with rugs, chairs, pots and pans, mugs, cutlery, an airbed and, of course, a billycan. All you need to bring is bedding, towels, a torch and food. The price includes a barbecue or stew on Friday night and a breakfast hamper (coffee, eggs, bacon, bread) on Saturday morning, all from local producers. The shower block and toilet have solar lighting – there's no electricity on site. A communal campfire is lit every night.

Norfolk Arms Hotel
22 High Street, BN18 9AB (01903 882101, www.norfolkarmshotel.com). Rates £81-£155 double incl breakfast.
Built in 1783 as a coaching inn for the 10th Duke of Norfolk, this imposing hotel dominates the centre of Arundel. Its crowning glory is the ballroom (now used for conferences and other events) with its minstrels' gallery and huge original mirrors. The hotel is part of the Forestdale Group, which runs 18 other hotels up and down the country and offers family-friendly rates in all. Of the 33 rooms, the premier grade ones are the most spacious; the decor is a little chintzy, but they're comfortable. The hotel also welcomes all manner of animals – including dogs, cats and even the odd parrot.

AMBERLEY, PETWORTH & BILLINGSHURST

Amberley

From Arundel, it's only a short drive to Amberley, on the other side of the River Arun – it's also accessible via the water courtesy of Arun Cruises (*see p268*). Head north on the A284, turn right at the first roundabout and through the hamlet of Houghton, lined with flint and timber-framed houses. The George & Dragon (*see p278*) once sheltered the future Charles II on the run from Cromwell's army. Continue east, briefly parallel to the River Arun and the low-lying meadow, and cross the bridge.

A hundred men once worked at the lime and cement works that is now the Amberley Museum & Heritage Centre (*see p274*), also known as Amberley Working Museum, next to the train station. It traces the working heritage of the region with the help of numerous craftsmen who demonstrate everything from blacksmithing to clay-pipe making. Exhibits include narrow-gauge locomotives and a vintage bus collection.

Turn off the B2139 into Amberley itself to find Amberley Castle and St Michael's church. Both were completed shortly after the Norman conquest by Bishop Luffa, using French masons who had been brought over to England to build Chichester Cathedral. The castle – one of three country palaces for the Bishops of Chichester – was considered necessary to defend the prelates from fractious peasants and marauding pirates. Today, the castle is an exclusive hotel (*see p281*).

In *Off the Beaten Track in Sussex*, written by Arthur Stanley Cooke in 1912, he calls the village 'Amberley God knows'. He explains the origin thus:

'In winter, if you ask an Amberley man where he dwells, he says "Amberley, God help us". In summer he says, "Amberley, where *would* you live?". "Amberley, God knows" is, however, the name it is known by and called of Sussex country folk.' However, he also wrote 'Amberley folk are credited with being web-footed' – although that may have something to do with the low-lying marshes rather than any genetic reason.

A few miles further east is Parham House (*see p274*), a beautifully kept Elizabethan manor house with an exquisite flower garden.

Petworth ★

Head north from Arundel on the A284, go straight over the first roundabout and on to the A29. Bignor, home to the remains of the Roman villa (*see p274*), is signposted to the left. Further north, just before the hamlet of Watersfield, is Sussex Farm Foods (01798 831985, www.sussexfarmfoods.co.uk), a lovely store with local cheese, meat, fruit and vegetables, and a little coffee shop. A few miles further on is Pulborough, worth stopping in if you arrive in July for the 12-hour Pulborough Lawnmower Race, a Le Mans-style endurance event whereby competitors keep going for 12 hours on assorted mowers. Alternatively, turn on to the B2138 at Sussex Farm Foods and head directly to the gorgeous little town of Petworth.

Petworth contains almost 30 antiques shops. These aren't curio-style shops; there is, for example, one that specialises in 16th- to 18th-century oak furniture. The Petworth Antiques & Decorative Arts trading association has more details on its website, www.paada.com. There's also a good selection of independent shops, but it's the majesty and confidence of the town's architecture that is its principal attraction. The downside is the constant heavy traffic along the narrow, winding streets.

A sense of grandeur is imposed by Petworth House (*see p274*) – a palatial 17th-century mansion on the edge of town. The high walls surrounding the house and Capability Brown-designed gardens also seem to enclose Petworth itself, almost making the town feel part of the same complex.

The centrepoint of the town has been the Market Square since at least 1541; today, it's a busy intersection. The most eye-catching building being Leconfield Hall (www.leconfieldhall.org.uk); built in 1794, the former courthouse is now used for markets, book sales and occasional film screenings. Opposite is Astarte Gallery (Old Bank House, 01798 342305), one of the few galleries in town selling contemporary art, sculpture and jewellery. Walk south to the corner with Saddlers Row to find Woodcock Antiques (Tudor Cottage, 01798 342125, www.woodcockantiques.com, closed Sat, Sun), specialising in oak and country furniture from the 16th to 18th centuries with many large-scale pieces in beautiful condition.

Richard Gardner (Swan House, 01798 343411 www.richardgardnerantiques.co.uk, closed Sun) opposite is one of the best antiques shops in town

SUSSEX

and has the accolades to prove it. The large premises are full of statement furniture, silverware and Staffordshire figures. Turning left at the end of Saddlers Row, you'll come to Augustus Brandt Antiques (Newlands House, Pound Street, 01798 344722, www.augustus-brandt-antiques.co.uk, closed Sat, Sun), one of the biggest players in Petworth. Its breathtaking showroom focuses on large items of furniture.

On the other side of Market Square is Golden Square, home to Hennings Wine Merchants (01798 343021, www.henningswine.co.uk, closed Sun) with an extensive range of fine wines. Curl round into the little arcade for the Bay Tree Bakery (01798 342260, closed Sun) and Petworth Bookshop (01798 342082, closed Sun).

The most atmospheric street in Petworth is Lombard Street, leading north off Golden Square. Once the town's busiest thoroughfare, full of butchers, bakers and grocers, nowadays it's a pretty cobbled lane with a few restaurants and shops. Chequers Antiques (Playhouse Gallery, 01798 343813, www.chequersantiques.com, closed Sun) specialises in silver, glassware, lighting and china. At the end of the street is St Mary's Church. Built in the 14th century, it underwent significant reconstruction by Sir Charles Barry (who designed the Houses of Parliament) in the 1820s. It occasionally hosts classical concerts and is also the principal venue for the Petworth Festival (www.petworthfestival.org.uk) in July. The focus is on classical music and jazz, but there are forays into comedy and world music. To the left of the church is the entrance to Petworth House.

To get a sense of life in the town 100 years ago, visit Petworth Cottage Museum (346 High Street, 01798 342100, www.petworthcottagemuseum.co.uk, open Apr-Oct Tue-Sat). The small cottage has been refurbished to look just as it did in 1910, when Mrs Mary Cummings lived there while working as a seamstress at Petworth House.

Billingshurst

The countryside around the Surrey/Sussex border, on the edge of the South Downs and the High Weald, is upmarket commuter territory. The wealth is evident in the smart, manicured villages and posh inns – you're as likely to meet a Rolls on the country lanes as a tractor. One of the main attractions north of Petworth are boat trips along the Wey & Arun Canal (see p268), which has been restored by a group of passionate enthusiasts.

Billingshurst has little to recommend it, but there's a bank and a few shops including a Budgens. Westons (Fulfords Road, 01403 791228, www.westonsfarmshop.co.uk), off the A264 towards Horsham, sells everything from fruit and veg to chutneys and ginger cordial.

To the east of the town on the A272, is Coolham, a hamlet known for its 'Blue Idol' meeting house for Quakers, once prominent in the village. The timber-framed building is thought to have been built around 1580 and it's likely that William Penn, the Quaker founder of Pennsylvania, worshipped here. A little further down the A272 is King's Mill in Shipley

(www.shipleywindmill.org.uk). Hilaire Belloc, writer and Sussex enthusiast, bought this white smock mill, the largest in the county, in 1906 and lived in it until he died in 1953. Used as the home of the title character of the BBC TV series *Jonathan Creek*, it's closed to the public.

Where to eat & drink

Real ale aficionados should seek out the Black Horse at Amberley (High Street, 01798 831700), handy for walks along the South Downs Way and the banks of the River Arun.

Petworth doesn't have a great selection of eateries. The Star (Market Square, 01798 342569, www.thestarpetworth.co.uk) is a pleasant place with a modern interior that looks like a chain pub (it's tied to Fullers) despite being built in the 16th century. The restaurant section serves pub-grub favourites and has leather sofas around a log fire. There's live music every other Saturday and on occasional Fridays. The Coco Café & Sugar Lounge (Saddlers Row, 01798 344006, www.cococafeandsugarlounge.com) is a lovely coffee house and sweet shop filled with old-school candied delights and artisan chocolate.

Around Billingshurst there's a pub on every village corner, it seems. Among the best is the Blue Ship (01403 822709) in the Haven, just north of Billingshurst. It's a proper country boozer, festooned with flowers on the outside, low-ceilinged and unpretentious inside. King & Barnes Sussex Bitter is served from a hatch, and no-nonsense food (jacket potatoes, macaroni cheese, treacle pudding) is available. The Onslow Arms (01403 752452), next to the canal at Loxwood, a ten-minute drive away, is a good choice for lunch if you're planning to join one of the canal boat trips.

Fox Inn

A281, Bucks Green, RH12 3JP (01403 822386, www.foxinn.co.uk). Open 11am-11pm daily. Food served noon-10pm daily.
The 16th-century Fox Inn is an upmarket option with a garden and a restaurant specialising in hefty plates of fish and seafood. It's packed most nights with well-groomed locals tucking into lemon sole fillets or seafood paella, and occasionally more exotic offerings. You can also get takeaway fish and chips.

George & Dragon

Houghton, BN18 9LW (01798 831559, www.thegeorgeanddragonhoughton.co.uk). Open Summer 11am-11pm Mon-Thur; 11am-11.30pm Fri, Sat; noon-11pm Sun. Winter 11am-3pm, 6-11pm Mon-Thur; 11am-11.30pm Fri, Sat; noon-11pm Sun. Lunch served noon-2.30pm Mon-Sat; noon-3pm Sun. Dinner served 6.30-9pm Mon-Sat.
On 14 October 1651, this flint and half-timbered house served a pint to one of history's more notable characters: the future Charles II. He was fleeing to France after Oliver Cromwell had beaten the Royalists in the Battle of Worcester and brought the English Civil War to a close. The pub retains much of its original character, and serves decent food and some fine ales. There's a large garden too.

Amberley Castle. See p281.

SUSSEX

TEN SUSSEX BREWERIES

Arundel, dominated by its 11th-century Norman castle and large Gothic cathedral, is one of the most historically important places along the South Downs Way and where there is war, soldiers and garrisons, there is usually a sizeable brewing culture. The ancient 'Arundel Saga', a poem thought to be translated from inscriptions on Celtic drinking vessels, states: 'So take to heart this moral wherever you may be, in city, town or country, or beside the briny sea. The palate that is jaded will find there's much to choose among the rich enticements of Arundel's fine brews.' Beer is still made in Arundel today, and across the county.

Adur Brewery
Adur Business Centre, Little High Street, Shoreham-by-Sea, BN43 5EG (01273 467527, www.adurbrewery.com).
Available from Middle Farm (*see p201*) and other selected establishments, the Adur Brewery is a fast-rising concern, especially considering it only launched in 2007. A list of suppliers can be found on the website.

Arundel Brewery
Unit C7, Ford Airfield Estate, Arundel, BN18 0HY (01903 733111, www.arundelbrewery.co.uk).
Founded in 1992, the award-winning Arundel Brewery is the best-known brewer in the area. There are six core beers, plus at least two seasonal ales every month. Its most famous beer is Sussex Gold (4.2%), a golden ale available at various supermarkets. The brewery has off-sales.

Ballard's Brewery
Old Sawmill, Nyewood, GU31 5HA (01730 821301, www.ballards-brewery.co.uk).
Ballard's was founded in 1980 in a farm in West Sussex; it now operates in larger premises in nearby Nyewood (just over the border in Hampshire). Its first two brews, Best Bitter (4.2%), a copper-coloured beer with fruity flavours, and Wassail (6%), a knee-bendingly strong ruby-coloured ale, are still favourites in local pubs. The brewery shop sells the beers and associated merchandise.

Beachy Head Brewery
Tiger Inn, East Dean, BN20 0DA (01323 423313, www.beachyhead.org.uk/brewery.html).
Despite the Legless Rambler (5%) winning in the 'good name awards', the Original Ale (4.5%) is the best of this microbrewery's beers. Tasting of cut grass with a hefty hop kick, it's served at the Tiger Inn – where the brewery was established in 2006. The beers are increasingly found across Sussex, but particularly around Eastbourne.

Woodland Yurting

Stag
Balls Cross, GU28 9JP (01403 820241, www.the staginn.org.uk). Open 11am-3pm, 6-11pm Mon-Sat; noon-2.30pm, 7-10.30pm Sun. Lunch served noon-2pm Mon-Sat; noon-2.30pm Sun. Dinner served 7-9pm Mon-Sat.
The Stag, located three miles north of Petworth, is one of those real untouched country pubs. No pan-fried scallops here. It's beloved by CAMRA which praises its range of real ales and interior, which is largely untouched since it was a coaching inn in the 17th century. There's a large inglenook fireplace, skittles and other bar games.

White Horse
The Street, Sutton, RH20 1PS (01798 869221, www.whitehorse-sutton.co.uk). Open noon-3pm Mon; noon-3pm, 6-11pm Tue-Sat; noon-4pm Sun. Lunch served noon-2pm daily. Dinner served 7-9pm Tue-Sat.
Cream walls, dark wooden floors and open fireplaces; this is a sophisticated gastropub – all designer logos, wine lists and fresh flowers. Which is by no means a bad thing: the locals still pile in thanks to the cosy candlelit evening atmosphere and real ales on tap. The menu is classic upmarket country pub food, with dishes such as game casserole and wild boar terrine. There are tables outside and five smart en suite bedrooms. Each room (from £85 per double incl breakfast) is individually designed, with high-quality furnishings; the best contains a lovely four-poster.

Where to stay
Several pubs offer good accommodation around Amberley, including the upmarket White Horse (*see above*). The Thatched House (Hog Lane, 01798 831329, www.thatchedhouseamberley.co.uk) is a four-star B&B – credit cards not accepted, though.

There are also some fine choices between Petworth and Midhurst, which appear in the chapter Chichester & Around (*see p282-299*).

Just east of Petworth, Arundel Holt Court (Wakestone Lane, Bedham, 01798 805426, www.arundelholtcourt.co.uk) has three sparkling rooms and a comfortable beamed lounge area. The Old Pond Cottage (Billingshurst Road, 01403 701110, www.oldpondcottage.com) is a friendly B&B with two rooms in Wisborough Green, a few miles west of Billingshurst.

Amberley Castle ★

Amberley, BN18 9LT (01798 831992, www.amberley castle.co.uk). Rates £230-£520 double incl breakfast.

This astonishing hotel is housed in a mansion within the crenellated walls and moat of a medieval castle. Buildings on the site date back to 1103, when Bishop Ralph de Luffa (who also oversaw the building of Chichester Cathedral) ruled the area. Since then, Henry VII, Charles II and Queen Elizabeths I and II have all stayed the night. As a Royalist stronghold, Amberley Castle was high on Cromwell's list of places to destroy; fortunately, much of the original fortifications remain. Tapestries, ancestral portraits and weapons hang from the walls, and suits of armour look as though they're about to walk away. The portcullis is still ceremonially raised and lowered daily. The 19 rooms and suites are superb, featuring four-poster beds and antique furniture, and open fires in winter. Service is unobtrusive and flawless. The restaurant's head chef, James Duggan, creates modern twists on British classics. The grounds include a tree-house (which can be hired for two to dine in), a tennis court, a croquet lawn, an 18-hole putting green and strolling peacocks.

Linacre Lodge

Baynards, Rudgwick, RH12 3AD (01403 823522, www.linacrelodge.co.uk). Rates £85 double incl breakfast. No credit cards.

There are just two rooms at Linacre Lodge. Bristow is a large en suite double with sunshine yellow walls and lovely views, while the More suite has an enormous bed and its own little sitting room. The owners have put a lot of care and attention into this place: free Wi-Fi, thick bathrobes and home-made biscuits on the hospitality tray are among the appealing extras. The lodge stands on the edge of the Baynards Park estate, so there are plenty of footpaths to explore. There's also excellent access to longer walking and cycling trails, including the Down's Link and Sussex Border Path; Linacre's friendly owners can provide packed lunches on request.

Old Railway Station

Petworth, GU28 0JF (01798 342346, www.old-station.co.uk). Rates £92-£198 double incl breakfast.

For an unusual place to stay, try this converted Grade II-listed railway station, built in 1892, and four restored Pullman train carriages. There are ten rooms in all; the brown and cream carriages with their gleaming wood and brass fittings are most fun, and retain the luxurious air of their original use.

Woodland Yurting ★

Keepers Barn, Tittlesfold, The Haven, RH14 9BG (01403 824057, www.woodlandyurting.com). Open Apr-Sept. Rates £60 per night midweek double yurt; £140 weekend retreat (Fri-Sun). No credit cards.

Woodland Yurting, which opened in spring 2009, has been an instant hit. It's easy to see why: it's a beautiful, tranquil spot and although planes pass overhead and the hum of traffic is audible, it feels very remote. Five yurts are tucked higgledy-piggledy amid the trees, beside a large meadow that's perfect for kickabouts or just lolling in the sun. The Chinese-made yurts are functional rather than pretty, furnished with beds, kitchen equipment and crockery. On arrival, you're given a lantern, a one-ring gas stove and a cooler box with ice-packs. There are also bushcraft taster sessions (*see p268*).

Dark Star Brewing Co

22 Star Road, Partridge Green, RH13 8RA (01403 713085, www.darkstarbrewing.co.uk).

Dark Star is a consistently brilliant brewery that started in the mid 1990s in Brighton's Evening Star pub. The bestseller among the seven main brews is Hophead (3.8%), a light, pale gold ale with a strong floral aroma.

Fallen Angel Brewery

14 Carriers Way, East Hoathly, BN8 6AG (01825 841307, www.fallenangelbrewery.com).

Naughty Nun and Karma Sutra are among the come-on labels from this small East Sussex outfit. The ales are all natural – meaning they are carbonated by living yeast in the bottle. They can be bought from Cooden Cellars in Eastbourne or online.

FILO Brewing Company

4-15 High Street, Hastings, TN34 3EY (01424 425079, www.thefilo.co.uk).

Mike Bigg and Tony Champion started this microbrewery, based at the First In Last Out (FILO), in 2000. Crofters (3.8%) is the main beer, but four others are regularly brewed, including Ginger Tom (4.5%) an organic, light-coloured ale infused with ginger and lemon.

Harveys of Lewes

Bridge Wharf Brewery, 6 Cliffe High Street, Lewes, BN7 2AH (01273 480209, www.harveys.org.uk).

Founded in 1790, Harveys is part of the fabric of Sussex – when their beer was pulled from a Lewes pub, the furore made national news – and the handsome Georgian brewery still dominates the centre of town. Sussex Best is its best-known and most popular bitter.

1648 Brewing Co

Old Stables Brewery, Mill Lane, East Hoathly, BN8 6QB (01825 840830, www.1648brewing.co.uk).

Based behind the King's Head pub, the tiny 1648 Brewery was founded in 2002. Its key beer is the 1648 Original (3.9%) but it's the pale, crisp Signature (4.4%) that's won the most awards. It also brews a beer for Eastbourne's Lammas festival, where it always has a stall.

White Brewing Company

Pebsham Farm Business Park, Pebsham Lane, Bexhill-on-Sea, TN40 2RZ (01424 731066, www.white-brewing.co.uk).

Started in 1995, this fun-loving brewery – if the labels are anything to go by – offers assorted cask and bottled beers. Popular brews include amber-coloured, hoppy-flavoured 1066 Country Bitter (4%), and Blonde (4%), a pale ale with a lemon finish. Tours can be booked, and there's a small shop on the premises.

Chichester & Western Sussex

The Romans called Chichester Noviomagus Reginorum, and designated it the capital of the kingdom of Civitas Reginorum. A 56-mile Roman road ran from here to London, and the city's main streets still follow the cross pattern the Romans laid out. Two miles outside the city centre, the famous murals and palatial remains at Fishbourne Roman Palace are an evocative reminder of Chichester's ancient riches.

Today, Chichester is an affluent market town, with a wealth of perfectly preserved Tudor buildings. The focus is the Cathedral, founded in 1076, whose magnificent spire can be seen from miles around. Home to some astonishing 20th-century artworks, including Marc Chagall's stained-glass window, it remains at the forefront of Chichester's rich cultural life, along with the Pallant Gallery and the Festival Theatre. Further evidence of the city's thriving artistic scene can be found in its boutiques, stocked with pieces by local artisans.

Around Chichester is the Sussex that makes even hardened city dwellers go misty-eyed. Quaint old villages are hidden among the lush folds of the South Downs, along with flint-built 16th-century coaching inns, ancient dry stone walls and fine Norman churches, with over 2,500 miles of public footpaths to explore. Goodwood is a major draw, with its sculpture park, vintage car rallies and racecourse, while the lovely Tudor town of Midhurst is not to be missed – and is in the fortuitous position of being surrounded by many excellent country pubs.

CHICHESTER & AROUND

The compact, historic city of Chichester exudes a peaceful, quietly prosperous charm. It's a lovely setting, between the South Downs and the sea: as the mournful cry of seagulls will remind you, the water isn't far away.

Chichester was founded in AD 70 by the Romans, who laid out an orderly street plan and built the original city walls, which were rebuilt in flint in medieval times. The main streets of the city – called, with unimpeachable logic, North, South, East and West Streets – slice it neatly into four areas. The Cathedral dominates the south-west sector, while the finest of the Georgian buildings are in the south-east, in the streets known as the Pallants.

It may look fantastically quaint and well tended now, but it wasn't always so. In 1596, with the wool trade in decline, a petition to the Lord Treasurer of England bemoaned that 'the citty of Chichester doth so fast decay and run to ruine, and the multitude inhabiting there so fast growe to beggory that except for remedy thereof some speedy order be taken'.

The Cathedral (see p286) is the centre of the city. Visible from miles away and immortalised by Turner in his painting of the Chichester Canal, it's a striking structure, best known for its Chagall stained-glass window and impressive spire. As

architecture critic Ian Nairn wrote in 1965: 'No other English cathedral, not even Lincoln, exerts such a continuous presence on the flat surrounding countryside. And it is the continuity which is the important thing; the spire becomes as invariable and natural as the sky and sun'. Concerts are held here regularly; call 01243 782595 or visit www.chichestercathedral.org.uk for details.

By the Cathedral and the main shopping area is an impressive Tudor-era Market Cross. Made from intricately carved Caen stone, it is widely regarded as the finest in Sussex, if not the country.

On North Pallant, just off East Street, is the Pallant House Gallery (see p288). Housed in a stately Queen Anne townhouse and strikingly modern contemporary wing, its outstanding collection of 20th-century British art takes in works by Henry Moore, Peter Blake, Bridget Riley, Lucian Freud and Barbara Hepworth. The programme of contemporary art shows here also proves that the gallery has its finger firmly on the pulse.

Shopping

North, East, South and West streets extend from the Market Cross, each lined with shops and some fine Georgian façades. High street chains dominate East Street, although there is an outpost of Sussex-based chocolatiers Montezuma's (01243 537385, www.montezumas.co.uk) at no.29. Its forte is

unusual flavour combinations, including white chocolate with ginger and chilli. At no.56A is Dartagnan (01243 539491, www.dartagnan menswear.co.uk), an upmarket men's boutique selling such brands as Paul Smith, Nudie Jeans and Vivienne Westwood.

At the end of East Street is the Hornet, a splendidly named street with some offbeat shops. The Almshouse Arcade (no.19, www.almshouse arcade.co.uk) houses a cluster of antique and curio shops, and the delightful Buttons & Bows (www. buttonsandbows-shop.com, closed Mon, Tue, Sun) selling hand-made toys, jewellery and accessories. A few doors along from the Arcade, Beyond the Fringe (21 the Hornet, 01243 513343, closed Mon, Fri, Sun) is a treasure trove of vintage clothes, while Hornet Provisions (no.23, 01243 790999, closed Sun) is a pleasant little deli specialising in high-quality Italian goods and international wines.

Down South Street you'll find a couple of good jewellers; Smith & Ralier (no.64, 01243 380024, www.jewellers-chichester.co.uk, closed Sun) and

Cred (no.41, 01243 773588, www.credjewellery. com, closed Mon, Sun), which only sells jewellery made from ethically sourced metals, diamonds and gemstones. Take a detour along Coopers Street for womenswear boutique Strawberry Clothing (01243 773700, www.strawberry-clothing.co.uk, closed Sun) and, next door, the recently opened Pretty Scruffy Shop & Gallery ★ (01243 779715, www.prettyscruffy.com, closed Mon, Sun). It's a delightful mix of jewellery, ceramics, furnishings and arty bits and bobs.

Back on South Street, at no.53, Chichester Toys (01243 788055) is a capacious, traditional toyshop. The Tourist Information Centre is at no.29A (01243 775888, www.chichester.gov.uk, closed Sun): the street numbers along South Street are not in logical order, and it's about halfway down the road.

Past the Cathedral, West Street is bordered by picturesque Georgian townhouses. At nos.40-41 is Peter Hancock Antiques (01243 786173, closed Mon, Sun), a small shop filled with curios, antiques

Events at Goodwood. See p290.

SUSSEX

Pallant House Gallery. See p288.

CHICHESTER & AROUND

Cass Sculpture Foundation

Goodwood, PO18 0QP (01243 538449, www. sculpture.org.uk). Open Apr-Oct 10.30am-5pm Tue-Sun. Other times by appointment. Admission £10; free-£5 reductions.

In a bid to safeguard the future of British sculpture, the Foundation commissions large-scale works from emerging and established homegrown talents. Eighty pieces – by the likes of Tony Cragg, Andy Goldsworthy, Elisabeth Frink and David Mach – are displayed at any one time amid 26 leafy acres of the Goodwood Estate. Anyone's welcome to visit, though serious collectors should take their chequebooks: the sculptures in this enormous, ever-evolving exhibition are for sale.

Chichester Cathedral ★

West Street, Chichester, PO19 1RD (01243 782595, www.chichestercathedral.org.uk). Open Summer 7.15am-7pm daily. Winter 7.15am-6pm daily. Tours 11.15am, 2.30pm Mon-Sat. Admission free. Tours £3 suggested donation.

The magnificent Cathedral was built by the Normans and consecrated in 1108. Since then, numerous buildings have been added, including the cloisters, which now house a café. Volunteers are on hand around the Cathedral to answer questions about its turbulent 900-year history, and free tours run at 11.15am and 2.30pm Monday to Saturday. The Cathedral is known for its artistic works, including John Skelton's stone and copper font and Graham Sutherland's painting *Noli Me Tangere*. The highlight is a glowing stained-glass window, designed by Marc Chagall in 1978. The Shrine of St Richard (canonised in 1262) was venerated by pilgrims until Henry VIII destroyed it in 1533, but pilgrims have returned in recent times. The Cathedral also hosts a forward-thinking series of concerts, exhibitions and talks.

Chichester District Museum

29 Little London, Chichester, PO19 1PB (01243 784683, www.chichester.gov.uk/museum). Open 10am-5.30pm Thur-Sat. Admission free.

Learn everything about Chichester that your mind could possibly cram in at this information-packed museum, set in an 18th-century corn store. Exhibitions cover local history, archaeology and geology, and the temporary exhibition gallery sees a changing line-up.

Denmans Garden

Denmans Lane, Fontwell, BN18 0SU (01243 542808, www.denmans-garden.co.uk). Open Summer 9.30am-5pm daily. Winter 9.30am-4pm daily. Admission £4.95; £3.95-£4.75 reductions.

Four acres of verdant escapism await at Denmans Garden, home to colourful shrubs, venerable trees and winding pathways. Despite its relatively modest proportions, the garden has plenty of points of interest, from the artful scattering of statues to the gently wild nature of the walled garden. As well as being a shelter for more sensitive plant life, the newly revamped conservatory is home to some chirpy budgerigars.

Fishbourne Roman Palace

Salthill Road, Fishbourne, PO19 3QR (01243 789829, www.sussexpast.co.uk). Open Mar-Oct 10am-5pm daily. Feb, Nov, Dec 10am-4pm daily. Jan 10am-4pm Sat, Sun. Admission £7.90; £4.20-£7 reductions; £21 family.

Only rediscovered in 1960, Fishbourne Roman Palace was quite possibly once the finest residence north of the Alps. It was constructed in the first century AD for King Tiberius Claudius Togidubnus, and contained around 100 rooms. The foundations of a quarter of them can still be seen in the north wing, and there are some marvellous mosaics, including the well-known Cupid on a Dolphin. There are 3-D reconstructions, a formal garden to explore, and the chance to handle priceless remains.

It's fun for children too: admiring historic mosaics is all very well, but having a go at making them, writing with a stylus on a wax tablet, or playing centuries-old games like knucklebones or counters is much more diverting. Call for details of ceramics and mosaic-making workshops (adults only).

Goodwood House ★

Goodwood, PO18 0PX (01243 755000, www.goodwood.co.uk). Open Aug 1-5pm Mon-Thur, Sun. Mid Mar-Sept 1-5pm Mon, Sun. Tours 1.20pm, 1.45m, 2.15pm, 2.45pm, 3.15pm, 4pm. Admission (incl tour) £9.50; £4-£8.50 reductions; £22 family.

This beautifully restored Regency mansion, set amid the immense Goodwood Estate, is still the home of the Earl of March, whose family has lived here for some 300 years. The resplendent State Apartments include paintings of London by Canaletto, magnificent depictions of horses by George Stubbs and several Van Dyck portraits. The exquisite Sèvres dinner service, painted with exotic birds, is another highlight, as are the 18th-century French tapestries.

The wider Goodwood Estate includes the Cass Sculpture Foundation (*see left*), and some lovely walks to the south and east of the racecourse – host, of course, to the annual Glorious Goodwood meeting.

Otter Gallery

University of Chichester, College Lane, Chichester PO19 6PE (01243 816098, www.chiuni.ac.uk/ottergallery). Open Term time 9am-9pm Mon-Thur; 10am-5pm Fri-Sun. Out of term 9am-5pm Mon-Fri. Admission free.

With the University of Chichester's focus on the arts, it's no surprise that there's an excellent gallery on campus. There are around ten exhibitions a year, of primarily contemporary art. The gallery also holds a fine permanent collection of 20th-century art, with pieces by Henry Moore, Graham Sutherland, Jacob Epstein, Patrick Heron and Paul Nash.

SUSSEX

Places to visit

Oxmarket Centre of Arts
St Andrews Court, off East Street, Chichester, PO19 1YH (01243 779103, www.oxmarket.com). Open 10am-4.30pm Mon-Sat. Admission free.
The Oxmarket Centre of Arts, which occupies the deconsecrated St Andrew in Oxmarket church, has six exhibition spaces. Generally showcasing artists from the locality, it has up to 150 different shows and exhibits a year, running from jewellery through to ceramics, sculpture to photography.

Pallant House Gallery ★
9 North Pallant, PO19 1TJ (01243 774557, www. pallant.org.uk). Open 10am-5pm Tue, Wed, Fri, Sat; 10am-8pm Thur; 11am-5pm Sun. Admission £7.50; free-£4 reductions; £17 family.
This wonderful gallery has an outstanding collection of 20th-century British art, featuring works by Henry Moore, Peter Blake, Bridget Riley, Lucian Freud, Walter Sickert, Graham Sutherland and many more. Exciting contemporary art shows and installations and a gallery dedicated to printmakers add to the appeal. The extensive bookshop specialises in modern British art and has a large selection of rare out-of-print books, while the restaurant, Field & Fork (*see p290*) is a gem.

Weald & Downland Open Air Museum
Singleton, PO18 0EU (01243 811363, www.weald down.co.uk). Open Apr-Oct 10.30am-6pm daily. Mar, Nov, Dec 10.30am-4pm daily. Jan, Feb 10.30am-4pm Wed, Sat, Sun. Admission £9.50; £5-£8.50 reductions; £26 family.
An utterly extraordinary place, this outdoor museum sprawls across 50 acres of Sussex countryside. It's a soothing place for a wander, dotted with 50 fascinating buildings that date from the 13th to the 19th centuries. Rescued from destruction, the buildings have been painstakingly dismantled, restored and rebuilt here in their original form, some with period gardens. Visitors can see bread, pottage and sweetmeats being prepared in the working Tudor kitchen, marvel at the working water mill where stoneground flour is produced daily, admire the skills of early carpenters and watch the heavy horses at work in the fields. Plenty of other farm animals await inspection, and there are daily craft activities and special events for children during the school holidays.

Uppark House & Garden
South Harting, Petersfield, GU31 5QR (01730 825857, www.nationaltrust.org.uk). Open Mid Mar-Oct
12.30-4.30pm Mon-Thur, Sun. Mid Nov, Dec 11am-3pm Sun. Admission House & garden £8; £4 reductions; £20 family. Garden only £4; £2 reductions.
Run by the National Trust, this Georgian beauty was painstakingly restored after a devastating fire swept through the upper storeys in 1989. The splendid Grand Tour collection takes in paintings, ceramics and furniture, and there's a marvelous 18th-century dolls' house. Down in the basement are the beautifully preserved servants' quarters: author HG Wells' mother was the housekeeper here in Victorian times, and the rooms are pretty much as they were in her day. Leave time to explore the gardens, with their sweeping lawns, mellow stone walls and dainty foliage.

West Dean Gardens
West Dean, PO18 0QZ (01243 818210, www.westdean.org.uk). Open Mar-Oct 10.30am-5pm daily. Feb, Nov, Dec 10.30am-3.30pm daily. Admission Summer £7.50; £3.50-£7 reductions; £18.50 family. Winter £4.75; £2.25-£4.25 reductions; £11.75 family.
If you want to see how to grow your own vegetables, or simply revel in some gloriously productive gardens, West Dean Gardens is the pinnacle of vegetable perfection. Its pristine glasshouses, perfect cold frames and immaculate raised beds display the finest edibles. Edward James, a generous patron of the Surrealist movement, once owned West Dean: two of his tree sculptures stand in the spring garden, and his simple, slate-topped grave is in the arboretum.

MIDHURST & AROUND

Cowdray Ruins ★
River Ground Stables, Cowdray Park, Midhurst, GU29 9AL (01730 810781, www.cowdray.org.uk). Open Mid Mar-Oct 10.30am-4pm Mon-Thur, Sun. Admission £6; £3.50-£5 reductions; £14.50 family.
It may have been largely destroyed by fire in 1793, but Cowdray remains an impressive example of the kind of abode occupied by wealthy Tudors. The house dates back to the 1520s, and was passed along a stream of Viscounts and Earls; today, the ruins are owned by the current Viscount Cowdray, who opened them to the public in 2007. The crenellated towers and soaring, roofless remains are a poignant sight, set on a grassy site on the north bank of the River Rother. The audio tour has more on Cowdray's long history, and there's a visitor centre and café.

and rare books. Hidden Nature (no.51, 01243 784884, closed Sun) is dedicated to all things nature-related, from gardening to tree identification. Aimed at both adults and children, it works brilliantly, and has superb cakes in the café.

Pedestrianised North Street starts with banks and big chains, but soon becomes much more interesting. Chichester Butter Market is an imposing, colonnaded building designed by John Nash – though ambitious renovation plans seem to have stalled. At no.81 is the Swallow Baker, selling sumptuous cupcakes, great coffee and milkshakes. Thru the Looking Glass (nos.55-56,

01243 538133) deals in bold 20th-century vintage pieces and contemporary furniture, accessories and lighting. Number Forty-Three (no.43, 07786 912734, closed Mon, Sat), meanwhile, is a quirky little store selling 'upcycled' furniture and accessories. The designers can often be seen working on their latest discoveries, and the service is relaxed but attentive.

Goodwood & Around
North of Chichester, the flat coastal plain rises gently into the South Downs and perhaps the most beautiful part of West Sussex. It is bisected by a

Goodwood Hotel. See p291.

30-mile section of the South Downs Way (*see p182*), which runs from South Harting to Storrington; it would take two or three leisurely days to walk this stretch, but there are plenty of shorter routes to give a taste of the sweeping views and captivating woodland. Most of the ancient trading route is also a bridleway, and accessible to horseriders and mountain bikers as well as walkers.

Ten minutes' drive from Chichester, Goodwood House (*see p287*) is an immaculately restored Regency mansion with a glorious collection of paintings. Surrounding the house is an immense, 12,000-acre estate, encompassing a sculpture park (*see p286*), two beautifully landscaped 18-hole golf courses, a celebrated motor circuit and a racecourse. The highlight of the race season, which runs from May until October, is the five-day Glorious Goodwood Festival in July. Other major events held at the estate run from the Festival of Speed to the Goodwood Revival weekend, a race meeting of 1940s, '50s and '60s cars. Attendees dress to the nines in vintage clothes, and modern motors are banned.

A few miles north of Goodwood, Singleton is home to the Weald & Downland Open Air Museum (*see p288*) – a highly unusual collection of 50 historic buildings that have been rescued, rebuilt and restored to offer a fascinating journey through the area's architecture over the past 500 years. Afterwards, lunch in style at the 16th-century Partridge Inn, or the Fox Goes Free (for both, *see below*) in Charlton.

The small but pretty nearby village of West Dean is dominated by the imposing, flint-built West Dean House, once home to the poet Edward James. A passionate and generous patron of the Surrealist movement (Dalí and Magritte were among the artists he helped), James bequeathed the house and estate to a trust in 1964, and it's now home to the arts and crafts-focused West Dean College. In the grounds, the inspiring West Dean Gardens (*see p288*) are open to the public. Figs, nectarines, peaches and grapes flourish in the Victorian greenhouses, while the Edwardian pergola is entwined with clematis and honeysuckle; the site also takes in a 49-acre arboretum, along with sunken gardens and a spring garden and summerhouse.

Where to eat & drink

In the town centre, the Fountain Inn (29 Southgate, no phone) is one of the oldest pubs in Chichester, and has part of the Roman city wall passing through its restaurant. In the evening, the Chichester Inn (38 West Street, 01243 783185, www.chichester inn.co.uk) is popular with students for its live music; during the day, it's a relaxed, unpretentious pub, with local beers on tap, art on the walls and a cosy log fire.

Four miles east of Chichester in Oving, the idyllic, thatched Gribble Inn (Gribble Lane, 01243 786893, www.hall-woodhouse.co.uk) brews its own ales, including Plucking Pheasant, Pig's Ear and the strong, strictly seasonal Winter Wobbler.

Alternatively, drive four miles north west of the city to East Ashling and the Horse & Groom (01243 575339, www.thehorseandgroomchichester.com) – an equable old country pub with a grassy beer garden, an oak-beamed restaurant and a CAMRA award to its name.

Around Goodwood, the 18th-century Star & Garter (01243 811318) in East Dean prides itself on its food – not least the seafood platter, which features Selsey crab and lobster – and has cheaper lunchtime set menus during the week. In nearby Singleton, the 16th-century Partridge Inn (Singleton Lane, 01243 811251, www.thepartridgeinn.co.uk) has also moved with the times. Run by a former executive chef at the Ritz, it serves well-executed pub classics rather than anything too high-falutin': ploughman's lunches, steak and mushroom pie with hand-cut chips, and crunchy deep-fried whitebait with tartare sauce. There's a good children's menu too (think tasty haddock and bacon fish cakes rather than plain fishfingers).

Comme Ça
67 Broyle Road, Chichester, PO19 6BD (01243 788724, www.commeca.co.uk). Lunch served noon-3pm Wed-Sun. Dinner served 5.30-10.30pm Tue-Sat.
With a chef from Normandy in the kitchen, the food at this Chichester fixture is authentically Gallic (fish soup, moules marinière, smoked duck, foie gras and chateaubriand), but British flavours creep in: Stilton soufflé, say, or local Selsey crab. Finish off with a medley of French cheeses. In the summer, the garden room and patio come into their own.

Field & Fork ★
Pallant House Gallery, 9 North Pallant (entrance on East Pallant), Chichester, PO19 1TJ (01243 770827, www.fieldandfork.co.uk). Open 10am-5pm Tue; 11.30am-3pm, 6-10pm Wed-Sat; 11.30am-5pm Sun. Lunch served 11.30am-3pm Tue-Sun. Dinner served 6-10pm Wed-Sat.
A small restaurant with a big reputation, Field & Fork is set in the Pallant House Gallery. It's run by Sam Mahoney, who left London's Kensington Place to run his own show here. His Modern British menu (steamed fillet of hake, curried shellfish casserole, saffron potatoes and mange tout, or slow-cooked cheek of beef, celeriac and horseradish purée and port-braised shallots) relies heavily on seasonal and local ingredients, but also spans the globe in flavours. Though simpler, the lunch menu is a delight, running from classic eggs florentine to pea, feta and chickpea fritters with toasted pumpkin seed salad. Afternoon tea is served from 3pm, but you have to book.

Fox Goes Free ★
Charlton, PO18 0HU (01243 811461, www.thefoxgoes free.com). Open 11am-11pm Mon-Sat; noon-10.30pm Sun. Food served noon-2.30pm, 6.30-10pm Mon-Fri; noon-10pm Sat, Sun.
A contender for the loveliest pub in West Sussex, this 300-year-old inn was a stopover for William III during his hunting trips to the neighbouring Goodwood Estate. These days, the low dark-timbered nooks and large garden accommodate families and groups of friends enjoying some locally produced pints (including a couple brewed by the pub), perhaps over a game of Trivial Pursuit by the log fire,

or some excellent food. The menu features such dishes as pan-fried calf's liver with red onion marmalade or crispy confit duck with savoy cabbage and plum sauce; there's a bar menu of pub grub too. The Fox also has five B&B rooms (£90-£110 double incl breakfast).

George & Dragon

North Street, Chichester, PO19 1NG (01243 785660, www.georgeanddragoninn.co.uk). Open 9.30am-11pm Mon-Thur; 9.30am-midnight Fri, Sat; 9.30am-10.30pm Sun. Food served 9.30am-3pm, 5-9pm Mon-Fri; 9.30am-9pm Sat; 9.30am-3pm Sun.
This upmarket gastropub is an all-rounder. It serves sterling breakfasts, mid-morning coffees, inviting lunches (bubble and squeak cake with bacon, gruyère and home-made tomato and ale chutney) and a compact but well-judged evening menu. There's a decked rear patio, and ten en suite rooms (£80-£90 double incl breakfast) in a converted barn.

St Martin's Organic Tea Rooms

3 St Martin's Street, Chichester, PO19 1NP (01243 786715, www.organictearooms.co.uk). Open 10am-6pm Mon-Fri; 9am-6pm Sat. No credit cards.
In a higgledy-piggledy medieval terraced house with an 18th-century façade, this highly popular tearoom and café serves carefully prepared, organic and mostly vegetarian dishes: soups, salads, quiches, risottos and an outstanding welsh rarebit. A selection of tempting cakes and desserts (apple crumble, banana and walnut loaf) adds a sweet touch. There's a pleasant courtyard for sunny weather, but the peaceful vibe inside makes for an enjoyable hour or two over a pot of loose-leaf tea.

Trents

50 South Street, Chichester, PO19 1DS (01243 773714, www.trentschichester.co.uk). Open/food served 7.30am-10pm Mon-Sat; 8.30am-10pm Sun.

This lively wine bar has a wide-ranging menu of comfort food classics (calf's liver and bacon with bubble and squeak, steak and chips) and lighter Mediterranean dishes such as seafood risotto with mascarpone or smoked chicken and chorizo salad. It's also popular for breakfast, running from porridge and croissants to grilled mushrooms on toast and mighty fry-ups. There are five modern, understated rooms (£85-£99 double not incl breakfast); bear in mind that the wine bar below can be noisy until closing time, especially at weekends.

Where to stay

There is a huge range of accommodation in Chichester and the surrounding towns and villages, from affordable B&Bs to smart country house hotels. Prices throughout the area soar during the Festival of Speed and Glorious Goodwood; book months ahead, or avoid them entirely.

In the centre of Chichester, the George & Dragon has ten rooms in an old flint barn, while Trents (for both, *see left*) offers five guestrooms. On North Street, the 36-room Ship Hotel (no.57, 01243 778000, www.theshiphotel.net) is another central option. Set in a Grade II-listed Georgian manor house, it has conservative decor and an expansive bar and eating area, serving solid simple food. In East Dean, the Star & Garter (*see left*) has six en suite rooms.

Goodwood Hotel

Goodwood Estate, PO18 0QB (01243 775537, www.goodwood.co.uk). Rates from £109 double incl breakfast.
Set amid the Goodwood Estate, this 93-room hotel has plenty of luxury trimmings – not least a health club and spa, with Decléor and Carita treatments. The rooms and suites, meanwhile, combine elegant antiques and rich

SUSSEX

Fox Goes Free

Chichester Cathedral. See p286.

fabrics with modern touches and splashes of colour. The hotel's restaurant is the Richmond Arms, a light-filled former coaching inn. The menu is appealingly seasonal, and some of the ingredients hail from the estate's own farm.

Richmond House
230 Oving Road, Chichester, PO19 7EJ (01243 771464, www.richmondhousechichester.co.uk). Rates £80-£120 double incl breakfast.
Ten minutes' walk from the city centre, this boutique B&B is as stylish as it is welcoming. Each of the three rooms has its own distinctive feel, but Molton Brown toiletries, featherdown quilts and free Wi-Fi come as standard. Room 2 is small but elegant, with a hidden shower room (check behind the bookcase-print panel), room 1 has a big bath and French doors on to the garden, and 3 has a sumptuous four-poster. Breakfasts are top-notch.

Royal Oak Inn
Pook Lane, East Lavant, PO18 0AX (01243 527434, www.royaloakeastlavant.co.uk). Rates B&B £110-£190 double incl breakfast. Self-catering cottages £180-£260.
In the village of East Lavant, within easy reach of Chichester and Goodwood, this 200-year-old coaching inn has a delightfully rural setting. Its six en suite rooms are stylishly decorated and wonderfully welcoming, with down duvets, flatscreen TVs, L'Occitane toiletries and warm, mellow colour schemes. There are also two pretty flint holiday cottages across the road from the pub. The food (herb-crusted hake, free-range Sussex pork with potatoes dauphinoise and calvados cream) is splendid, and there's a terrace for balmy summer evenings.

MIDHURST & AROUND

Midhurst
In 1932, Walter Wilkinson travelled across Sussex with his Punch and Judy cart, writing about his travels in the book *A Sussex Peep-Show*. Although he signally failed to draw a crowd in Midhurst, he had time to admire the town: 'Midhurst, with its Cowdray House, its old timbered inns and gabled houses, is sufficiently a show in itself, and I passed through, admiring, but not admired'. Today, Midhurst seems little changed. The ruins of Cowdray House (*see p288*) are awe-inspiring, and the ancient inns still full of character.

St Mary Magdalene and St Denys' church (Church Hill, www.midhurstparishchurch.net) was built in 1291, around the same time as Midhurst Castle, the foundations of which can be seen at the end of St Ann's Hill. The town flourished in Tudor times, and plenty of well-preserved Tudor buildings remain, particularly around the Market Square and church.

In Elizabeth House, facing the war memorial, a Harveys of Lewes shop sells the brewery's bottled ales and other local tipples. In the same building, with its entrance on West Street, is the Swan Inn (01730 812853, www.theswaninnmidhurst.co.uk). Heading down West Street, the Spread Eagle Hotel (*see p297*) is a former coaching inn that once served the London-Chichester route, and now takes up several buildings. Next door is Jefferson's

(01730 813135, closed Mon and Sun), a traditional butcher and fishmonger. Other independent shops include Black Sheep (01730 812862, closed Sun), a modish knitting shop, and Wine Etcetera (no.7, 01730 813300, www.wine-etcetera.com, closed Sun) next door.

At Rumbold's Hill, walk right towards the main town along North Street. Some of the houses have yellow-painted window frames, which shows they're owned by the Cowdray Estate. The colour was a nod to the Liberal political affiliation of Weetman Pearson (1882-1933), the 2nd Viscount Cowdray. At no.15 is Michael Courtney (01730 813146, www.michaelcourtney-familybutchers.co.uk, closed Sun), an extremely popular old-fashioned butcher. The Angel Hotel (*see p297*) is a 17th-century coaching inn; over the centuries, its illustrious visitors have included Elizabeth I and Hilaire Belloc. Beside the hotel, on Lambert's Lane, is an excellent example of a Tudor house with a Georgian façade. Further down on the right, opposite Midhurst Grammar School (where HG Wells studied), is the Tourist Information Centre (01730 817322, www.visitmidhurst.com, closed Sun winter).

Just off North Street is the delightfully named Knockhundred Row, where Midhurst Library (01730 813564, closed Sun) occupies the best-preserved Tudor property in town – once the home of wealthy silk-makers. Inside, its stunning beamed roof now rises above shelves of books. On the corner by the library, Cabbage White (01730 814555, www.cabbage-white.com, closed Sun) stocks upmarket gardening gear and homeware. Left along Sheep Lane are more Tudor houses, some with Georgian façades, others with beamed, overhanging first floors.

Sheep Lane leads to the Market Square and the old town hall – now home to Garton's Coffee House (01730 817166, www.gartonscoffeehouse.co.uk). With its heavy oak furniture, Wi-Fi and a menu that includes breakfast bagels, toasted crumpets and daily specials, it's an appealingly laid-back hangout. On the north side of the square are the old stocks and pillory, last used in 1859.

Around Midhurst
South and south-west of Midhurst are a series of lovely hamlets, worth visiting for their stellar pubs. Among them are the Keepers Arms (*see p296*) in Trotton; in Chilgrove, the Fish House (*see right*) is a first-rate seafood restaurant in the depths of the Sussex countryside. Just outside South Harting, Uppark House & Garden (*see p288*) is a four-square red-brick manor house owned by the National Trust; seriously damaged by a fire in 1989, it has been meticulously restored.

North-east of Midhurst are the villages of Lodsworth, Lickfold, Lurgashall and Fernhurst. Again, they are sprinkled with fine pubs: the Noah's Ark Inn (*see p296*) in Lurgashall, the Halfway Bridge Inn (*see right*) in Lodsworth and the Duke of Cumberland Arms (*see right*) in Fernhurst. Lurgashall is also home to the Lurgashall Winery (*see right*), which sells fruit wines, meads and liqueurs.

Where to eat & drink

Duke of Cumberland Arms
Henley, Fernhurst, GU27 3HQ (01428 652280, www.dukeofcumberland.com). Open 11.30am-11pm daily. Lunch served noon-2pm daily. Dinner served 7-9pm Tue-Sat.
This wonderfully isolated pub is well known for its local produce and fresh fish (sometimes from the trout pond out back, in the leafy gardens). The lunch menu includes dishes such as pea, prawn and crayfish risotto or pan-seared scallop and bacon salad, while the dinner menu takes in the heartier likes of eight-hour braised lamb shank or smoked haddock with Welsh rarebit and spinach. Local Nyetimber is among the wines, while ales are served straight from the cask.

Fish House
High Street, Chilgrove, PO18 9HX (01243 519444, www.thefishhouse.co.uk). Open 8am-11pm daily. Lunch
served noon-2.30pm Mon-Sat; noon-4pm Sun. Dinner served 6-9.45pm Mon-Sat; 6-9pm Sun.
This sophisticated seafood restaurant and hotel is a slightly unexpected find in such a rural setting. The menu runs from Irish or Jersey oysters, roast king scallops and poached sea bass with fennel and orange salad to simply grilled fish of the day or the house fish pie – though even that involves lobster. A couple of fish-free options slip through the net, particularly for Sunday lunch, and there is a short vegetarian menu. The 15 bedrooms (from £150 double incl breakfast) are equally swish.

Halfway Bridge Inn
Lodsworth, GU28 9BP (01798 861281, www.halfwaybridge.co.uk). Open 11am-11pm Mon-Sat; noon-10.30pm Sun. Lunch served noon-2.30pm daily. Dinner served 6.30-9.15pm Mon-Sat; 6.30-8.30pm Sun.
After a modern makeover, this 300-year-old pub is looking decidedly dapper (think muted paintwork, leather bar stools

Things to do

CHICHESTER & AROUND

Blackdown Farm Riding Club
Lower House Farm, Ropes Lane, Fernhurst, GU27 3JD (01428 654106, www.ruralridesuk.co.uk). Open by appointment. One hour ride £35.
Few activities can banish city blues faster than a day's horseriding, inhaling the pastoral perfume of leather, hay and horses. Blackdown Farm Riding Club offers plenty of off-road hacking, so you get all the exhilaration of charging about the countryside without any of the legwork. Set on an 800-acre farm near the village of Fernhurst, on the wooded slopes of the Western Weald, the club offers unrivalled access to two of the region's highlights: the National Trust land belonging to the beautiful ruins of the Cowdray Estate, and nearby Blackdown, the second highest point in the South-east.

Chichester Canal Boat Trips
Canal Basin, Canal Wharf, Chichester, PO19 8DT (01243 377405, www.chichestercanal.org.uk). Trips Mar-Oct 10.15am, noon, 2pm, 3.30pm daily. Fares £5.50; £3.50 reductions. No credit cards.
Take a trip along the Chichester Ship Canal aboard the 12-seater narrowboat *Egremont*, which goes as far as Donnington. Rowing boats and canoes are also available for hire, if you'd rather explore under your own power, while the four-mile towpath is a peaceful place for a walk or bike ride; look out for the bright blue flash of a kingfisher.

Chichester Festival Theatre
Oaklands Park, PO19 6AP (01243 784437, www.cft.org.uk). Open Box office 10am-8pm Mon-Sat. Tickets £12-£37.
Chichester Festival Theatre has been a leading light in the UK theatre scene ever since it was founded in 1962, with Sir Laurence Olivier as its artistic director. It was the first modern theatre in England with a thrust stage, and the birthplace of the National Theatre. It reaches its annual zenith in festival season – April to September – when a packed programme squeezes in everything from musicals and classic theatre to

contemporary productions, some of which later transfer to the West End (*Enron* was one such success in recent years). During the festival, the theatre also puts on outdoor performances, and special events such as comedy nights.

Downs Golf Course
Goodwood Estate, PO18 0PN (01243 755168, www.goodwood.co.uk). Open 8am-dusk daily. Green fees £15.50-£20.50.
Golf is also very much at the heart of Goodwood. The excellent Downs Course was created by legendary course designer James Braid in 1914; non-members were recently allowed to play here for the first time. Near the Goodwood Hotel, you can pay-and-play on the Park Course, against the dramatic backdrop of Goodwood House.

South Downs Planetarium
Sir Patrick Moore Building, Kingsham Farm, Kingsham Road, Chichester, PO19 8RP (01243 774400, www.southdowns.org.uk/sdpt). Open show times vary; check website for details. Admission £6; £4 reductions. No credit cards.
Cloud coverage and poor viewing conditions can make star-gazing in the real night sky challenging for novices – so planetariums, which project the sky on to a giant dome, are the perfect solution. There's a changing line-up of shows at Chichester's Planetarium, including the ominous-sounding 'When rocks fall from space'.

MIDHURST & AROUND

Lurgashall Winery
Lurgashall, GU28 9HA (01428 707292, www.lurgashall.co.uk). Open 11am-5pm Thur-Sun.
It's a winery, but there's not a grape in sight. This small-scale family-run business produces all manner of liqueurs, using such ingredients as sloes, ginger and black cherry, along with wines made from gooseberry, plum, elderflower and even silver birch. There's also a selection of warming meads, including a potent whisky variant. There's little here besides a shop and café, but the congenial staff will be happy to show you the winery.

SUSSEX

and stylishly stripped-back brickwork). The extensive menu might flit from tagine or Thai-style fish cakes to five-spiced pork belly with sweet potato and ginger mash; traditionalists may prefer the poshed-up pub classics, such as chicken and smoked ham pie with Jersey Royals and seasonal vegetables, or beer-battered fish and chips. The six B&B rooms (from £130 double incl breakfast), housed in a converted barn by the pub, are equally modern, with PlayStations and flatscreen TVs.

Horseguards Inn ★

Upperton Road, Tillington, GU28 9AF (01798 342332, www.thehorseguardsinn.co.uk). Open noon-11pm daily. Food served noon-2.30pm, 6.30-9pm Mon-Fri; noon-3pm, 6.30-9pm Sat; noon-3.30pm, 6.30-9pm Sun.

The tiny hamlet of Tillington, between Midhurst and Petworth, is worth a detour for this wonderful, 350-year-old pub, set in three white-painted cottages. Its snug, low-ceilinged rooms are filled with antiques and trinkets amassed over the centuries, and there are barbecues in the generously proportioned beer garden in summer. Until 1840, it was called the New Star; the change of name is attributed to its popularity with the horseguards posted at nearby Petworth House. The food comprises hearty English cooking, with game in season and herbs from the garden, and there are three bright, comfortable B&B rooms (£80 double incl breakfast), one in the tiny cottage adjacent to the pub.

Keepers Arms

Terwick Lane, Trotton, GU31 5ER (01730 813724, www.keepersarms.co.uk). Open noon-3pm, 6-11pm Tue-Sat; noon-4pm Sun. Lunch served noon-2pm Tue-Sat; noon-2.30pm Sun. Dinner served Summer 7-9.30pm Tue-Sat. Winter 6.30-9pm Tue-Sat.

This upmarket gastropub knows how to serve a sophisticated plate of food. Starters might include ham hock rillette with a burnt chilli and courgette salad, or hazelnut-crusted scallops with raisin purée; to follow, feast on roasted belly and braised shoulder of pork with celeriac dauphinois and carrot and coriander purée. The hearty, more traditional pub offerings scrawled on the blackboard are cheaper than the restaurant menu, with fish and chips or a warming beef stew coming in at just over a tenner. In summer, the parasol-shaded tables are a prime spot for a leisurely pint and a spot of lunch.

Noah's Ark Inn ★

The Green, Lurgashall, GU28 9ET (01428 707346, www.noahsarkinn.co.uk). Open 11am-3.30pm, 5.30-11pm Mon-Sat; noon-9pm Sun. Lunch served noon-2.30pm Mon-Sat; noon-3.30pm Sun. Dinner served 7-9.30pm Mon-Sat.

For a picture-perfect village setting – it sits overlooking the village green – look no further than the Noah's Ark. This charming 16th-century inn ticks every bucolic box, and serves satisfying roasts as well. It's a fine place to forget

Cowdray Ruins. See p288.

about city living and watch the afternoon disappear through the bottom of a pint glass, and equally appealing in winter (log fires, leather sofas, lots of snugs and cosy corners) and summer (masses of outdoor seating).

Royal Oak
Hooksway, PO18 9JZ (01243 535257, www.royaloak hooksway.co.uk). Open 11.30am-2.30pm, 6pm-11pm Tue-Sat; noon-3pm Sun. Lunch served noon-2pm Tue-Sun. Dinner served 7-9.30pm Tue-Sat.
Open fires, real ales and some extremely passable pub grub (pâté and toast with cranberry jelly, say, or an enormous mixed grill comprising steak, pork chop, lamb chop, sausage, bacon and a fried egg), are among the Royal Oak's tangible assets. It also claims to be haunted by the ghost of a 17th-century sheep rustler. William Shepherd, so the tale goes, was shot in the Royal Oak by angry farmers, and his spirit is said still to waft around the pub. See the website for a (some may say dubious) photo, taken by the landlord.

Seven Fish
North Street, Midhurst, GU29 9DJ (01730 716280, www.sevenfish.co.uk). Open 10am-10pm daily.
Opened in 2010, Seven Fish is a large, modern seafood restaurant. Although it opens for breakfast, and as a bar and coffee shop throughout the day, it's the fresh fish and pleasant surrounds that attract regulars. There's a nautical theme, with arty photos of fishing vessels on the

wall and snug wood-burning stoves in winter. In the summer there's a patio just about overlooking Cowdray House. The menu might include fish pie with goat's cheese mash and wilted spinach, and crab, chilli, coriander and spring onion linguine, as well as the non-fishy likes of chicken with fennel, green beans and chorizo. For vegetarians, there are various risottos and pastas.

Where to stay
Fish House (*see p295*) has 15 ultra-modern rooms, with Italian marble bathrooms, reclaimed teak furniture and bold, contemporary textiles and wallpapers; luxurious touches run from espresso machines to gigantic plasma TVs, and there are hot tubs in little gazebos in the grounds.

Plenty of local pubs also offer B&B. The Halfway Bridge Inn (*see p295*) offers six well-appointed rooms in a converted barn to the rear of the pub, with flatscreen TVs, DVD players and PlayStations. The Horseguards Inn (*see left*) also has three appealing rooms to retire to after dinner.

Angel Hotel
North Street, Midhurst, GU29 9DN (01730 812421, www.theangelmidhurst.co.uk). Rates £105-£185 double incl breakfast.
Packed with history and set in the centre of Midhurst, this 17th-century coaching inn hasn't rested on its laurels. Staff are unfailingly helpful, while the antiques-dotted rooms have been brought up to date with flatscreen TVs, CD players and free Wi-Fi. The suites, meanwhile, have wonderful four-poster beds. There's also a first-rate restaurant, Bentleys.

Park House Hotel
Bepton, GU29 0JB (01730 819000, www.parkhouse hotel.com). Rates £160-£215 double incl breakfast.
Just outside Midhurst, in the downland village of Bepton, Park House is a delightfully intimate, family-owned country house hotel, set amid ten-acre grounds. The decor is elegantly traditional, with toile wallpapers, antiques and inviting easy chairs, although free Wi-Fi and iMac TVs and monitors are a 21st-century touch. A croquet lawn, two grass tennis courts, bowls lawn and outdoor heated pool (summer only) are among the on-site sporting diversions, and there's an opulent spa to help you recover from your exertions, along with a polished restaurant.

Spread Eagle
South Street, Midhurst, GU29 9NH (01730 816911, www.hshotels.co.uk). Rates £125-£370 double incl breakfast.
The Spread Eagle is an historic stay, largely in a topsy-turvy Tudor house with old-English decor and 38 bedrooms and suites. The imposing Queen's Suite has its own wig closet and there's a secret passage in the panelled White Room, which is said to have been used by smugglers. Adding a spot of contemporary luxury is the Aquila Health Spa, whose facilities include a hot tub, sauna, steam room and indoor pool. The restaurant has tapestry hangings, romantic candlelight and a smart menu: seared scallop slices with grilled red pepper and courgette tart to start, perhaps, followed by saddle of venison with spiced red cabbage and smoked bacon croquettes.

SUSSEX

Further Reference

USEFUL ADDRESSES
www.english-heritage.org.uk
www.enjoyengland.com
www.heritageopendays.org.uk
www.metoffice.gov.uk
www.nationalrail.co.uk
www.nationaltrust.org.uk
www.ordnancesurvey.co.uk
www.showbus.com/timetables
www.sustrans.org.uk
www.thegoodpubguide.co.uk
www.thetrainline.com
www.ukworldheritage.org.uk
www.visitbritain.com

COAST & COUNTRYSIDE
www.babo.org.uk British
Association of Balloon Operators.
www.bbc.co.uk/coast BBC Coast.
http://camping.uk-directory.com
UK Camping and Caravanning.
www.cpre.org.uk Campaign for
the Protection of Rural England.
www.goodbeachguide.co.uk
www.lidos.org.uk Lidos in the UK.
www.nationalparks.gov.uk
www.nationaltrail.co.uk
www.naturalengland.org.uk
www.ngs.org.uk
National Gardens Scheme.
www.river-swimming.co.uk River
& Lake Swimming Association.
www.ramblers.org.uk
Ramblers Assocation.
www.rya.org.uk
Royal Yachting Association.
www.ukclimbing.com
www.uk-golfguide.com
www.walkingbritain.co.uk
www.walkingclub.org.uk
Saturday Walkers' Club.
www.walking-routes.co.uk
www.wildswimming.com
Wild Swimming.

HOLIDAY HOME COMPANIES
The Big Domain 01326 240028,
www.thebigdomain.com.
Boutique Boltholes 0845 094
9864, www.boutiqueboltholes.co.uk.
Brighton Holiday Homes 01273
624459, www.brightonholiday
homes.co.uk.
Cottages4you 0845 268 0763,
www.cottages4you.co.uk.
Curlew Cottages 01304 619444,
www.curlewcottages.co.uk.
Garden of England Cottages
01892 510117, www.garden
ofenglandcottages.co.uk
Hideaways 01747 828170,
www.hideaways.co.uk.
Landmark Trust 01628 825925,
www.landmarktrust.org.uk.
Superior Cottages
www.superiorcottages.co.uk.

KENT

TOURIST INFORMATION CENTRES
More details can be found at
www.visitkent.co.uk. The main
tourist offices are listed below.
See www.visitkent.co.uk/greeters
for an innovative scheme whereby
a local resident spends an hour
orienting visitors, free of charge.
Canterbury 01227 378100,
www.canterbury.co.uk.
Dover 01304 205108,
www.whitecliffscountry.org.uk.
Maidstone 01622 602169,
www.visitmaidstone.com.
Rochester 01634 843666,
www.visitmedway.org.
Thanet 01843 577577,
www.visitthanet.co.uk.
Tunbridge Wells 01892 515675,
www.visittunbridgewells.com.

USEFUL ADDRESSES
www.bbc.co.uk/kent Local news,
weather and events.
www.insidekentmagazine.co.uk
Bi-monthly magazine, available
free online with features on local
businesses, personalities, dining
and entertainment.
http://isleone.co.uk/do Thanet-
based reviews, features and news
for locals and visitors.
www.kent.gov.uk
Kent County Council.
http://kent.greatbritishlife.co.uk
A monthly guide to life in Kent,
with extensive events listings.
www.kentattractions.co.uk
Association of Tourist Attractions
in Kent.
www.kentcreativearts.co.uk
Art fairs and exhibitions.
www.kentdowns.org.uk Kent Downs
Area of Outstanding Natural Beauty.
www.kentonline.co.uk
Kent's online newspaper.
www.kentwildlifetrust.co.uk
Kent Wildlife Trust.
www.undergroundkent.co.uk
Kent's Napoleonic fortifications
and various underground tunnels.
www.visitkent.co.uk
Official tourist information site.
www.whatsonmedway.co.uk Events
and entertainment in Medway.

FICTION
Frances Hodgson Burnett The
Secret Garden The walled garden
at Great Maytham Hall, where
Burnett lived for many years, is
often credited as her inspiration
for this classic children's story.

Geoffrey Chaucer The Canterbury
Tales A group of pilgrims, travelling
to the shrine of Saint Thomas
Becket at Canterbury Cathedral,
exchange all manner of tales.
Charles Dickens Great Expectations
Rochester and the marshes of the
Medway estuary feature heavily in
the story of Pip's quest to become
a gentleman.
Somerset Maugham Of Human
Bondage Much of Maugham's
masterpiece is based on his
experiences living with his uncle,
the Vicar of Whitstable.
Vita Sackville-West The Edwardians
Vita Sackville-West explores her
childhood at Knole House, presented
here as the House of Chevron.
Virginia Woolf Orlando Knole House
also serves as the setting for this
fantastic, fictional 'biography', which
spans several centuries and was
inspired by Vita Sackville-West.

NON-FICTION
Charles Darwin On the Origin of
Species Darwin lived and worked
at Down House for some 40 years.
He often took long walks around the
grounds, practising the uninterrupted
reflection and observation that
helped him to formulate his ground-
breaking work on evolution.
Paul Harris, Ray Hollands Along the
Kent Coast A pictorial history of the
county's coastline, with atmospheric
black and white photographs

POETRY
Elizabeth Barrett Browning
Complete Poetical Works
Browning depicts the Long Gallery
at Penshurst and muses on the
portraits of the Sydneys in her poem
'The Picture Gallery at Penshurst'.
Thom Gunn Boss Cupid Although he
spent much of his life in California,
Gunn was born in Gravesend and
visited aunts in Snodland, the
setting for one of his most famous
poems, 'The Butcher's Son'.
Ben Jonson The Complete Poems
'To Penshurst' is the model of the
17th-century country house poem,
addressed to the family estate of
poet Philip Sydney.
The Medway Poets A poetry group
founded in Medway with strong punk
associations, later the originators of
the Stuckist art movement.

FILM
Creation (Jon Amiel, 2009) Paul
Bettany played the lead in this
portrayal of Charles Darwin, with
domestic scenes shot at Darwin's
home in Kent, Down House.

Half a Sixpence (George Sidney, 1967) A musical adaptation of HG Wells's novel Kipps: the Story of a Simple Soul with performances on location in Tunbridge Wells.

The Other Boleyn Girl (Justin Chadwick, 2008) Dover Castle, Penshurst Place and Knole House all appeared in this story about King Henry VIII's second wife, Anne Boleyn, and her lesser-known sister.

A Room with a View (James Ivory, 1985) Along with Italy, the village of Chiddingstone provided an idyllic filming location for EM Forster's tale of repression and romance.

War Requiem (Derek Jarman, 1989) Jarman's distinctive garden at his home in Dungeness appears in his adaptation of Benjamin Britten's musical piece on the futility of war; it also starred as the Garden of Eden in The Garden (1990).

TV

The Darling Buds of May ITV, 1991-93 Much of this comic drama, adapted from HE Bates's novels, was shot in the village of Pluckley and surrounding locations.

The Gathering Storm BBC & HBO, 2002 Albert Finney appeared in this study of Winston Churchill's life in the lead-up to World War II, as did Churchill's former home, Chartwell.

Little Dorrit BBC, 2008 Deal Castle was a fliming location for this hugely successful 13-part adaption of Dickens's novel, dressed up as a colourful Marseilles marketplace.

The War Game BBC, 1985 Despite winning an Academy Award in 1966, this documentary-style drama wasn't shown on British TV until 1985. It showed Rochester, RAF Manston and Maidstone barracks hit by nuclear missiles, and was deemed 'too horrifying for the medium of broadcasting'.

MUSIC

The Beatles Magical Mystery Tour Parts of the Beatles' experimental music film were shot around West Malling's RAF airfield (little of which remains today).

Caravan Blind Dog at St Dunstan's The psychedelic band's 1976 album made much of their Canterbury roots. The title refers to the St Dunstan area, whose pubs were frequented by the band, and the cover is a photograph of St Dunstan's Street.

ART

Billy Childish Childish was born in Chatham where he still lives and works. His work takes in painting, writing, film and music.

William Dyce The Scottish artist's most praised painting is Pegwell Bay, Kent – a Recollection of October 5th 1858, now on display at the Tate.

Tracey Emin A Royal Academian and leading light of the Young British Artists, Emin grew up in Margate and studied in Maidstone. She exhibited a series of sculptures in the first Folkestone Triennial, citing social issues in the town as her inspiration.

JMW Turner Turner greatly admired Kent's quality of light and dramatic sunsets, declaring that 'the skies over Thanet are the loveliest in all Europe'. The Kentish landscape features in many of his works; in celebration of the connection, the Turner Contemporary opened in Margate in April 2011.

WALKS & CYCLE TRAILS

Crab & Winkle Way www.sustrans.org.uk A charming, seven-mile walking and cycling trail, running from Canterbury to Whitstable harbour.

Faversham walking www.faversham.org Eight food-related walks, taking in the best of Faversham's countryside and local produce.

Greensand Way www.kent.gov.uk Setting off at Haslemere in Surrey, this 108-mile walking route passes through the Kent Downs before ending at Hamstreet, overlooking Romney Marsh.

North Downs Way www.nationaltrail.co.uk/Northdowns A glorious 153-mile walk across Kent and Surrey, following the North Downs.

Saxon Shore Way www.kent.gov.uk This 160-mile path runs from Gravesend in Kent to Hastings in East Sussex, following the ancient coastline past castles, Martello towers and Iron Age hill forts.

Walking in Kent www.walkinginkent.co.uk Information on walking groups and routes.

White Cliffs Countryside Project www.whitecliffscountryside.org.uk PDFs of walking and cycling routes around Dover, Deal and Sandwich.

SUSSEX

TOURIST INFORMATION CENTRES

More details can be found at www.visitsussex.org. The main tourist offices are listed below.

Arundel 01903 882268.
Brighton 01273 290337, www.visitbrighton.com.
Chichester 01243 775888, www.visitchichester.com.
Eastbourne 0871 663 0031.
Hastings 01424 451111, www.visit1066country.com.
Lewes 01273 483448.
Rye 01797 229049, www.visitrye.co.uk.

USEFUL ADDRESSES

www.theargus.co.uk Brighton and Hove based newspaper.
www.bbc.co.uk/sussex Local news, weather and events.
www.eastmagazine.co.uk A guide to Brighton and East Sussex events.
www.eastsussex.gov.uk East Sussex County Council.
http://sussex.greatbritishlife.co.uk A monthly publication dedicated to Sussex, with features and a comprehensive list of events in the county.
www.sussexbythesea.com Information on events and attractions for visitors to the South Coast.
www.thesussexnewspaper.com The online version of the newspaper that covers the whole of Sussex.
www.sussexwt.org.uk Sussex Wildlife Trust.
www.thisissussex.co.uk News, sports and showbiz with a local focus.
www.vegetarianbrighton.co.uk Website compiling the best vegetarian and vegan eateries in the city.
www.vivalewes.com A weekly online guide to what's happening in Lewes.
www.westsussex.gov.uk West Sussex County Council.

FICTION

Daisy Ashford The Young Visiters Written in 1890 by nine-year-old Daisy Ashford, The Young Visitors was rediscoved and published in 1917, with a foreward by JM Barrie. It drew on Daisy's Lewes childhood, and met with considerable acclaim.

Nick Cave The Death of Bunny Munro The musician's second novel follows an alcoholic salesman and his son on a road trip around Brighton. Many of the locations and events are real, including the fire that destroyed the West Pier.

Arthur Conan Doyle The Valley of Fear Holmes and his faithful assistant, Dr Watson, investigate a mysterious murder at a Sussex manor house.

Graham Greene Brighton Rock The most famous fictional representation of Brighton is a seamy tale of gang culture, murder and double-crossing.

AA Milne Winnie-the-Pooh The story of Pooh, Piglet, Christopher Robin and friends was set in the author's beloved Ashdown Forest.

HG Wells The Invisible Man A desperate scientist has developed the ability to make himself invisible, and wreaks terror in the village of Iping and surrounding areas.

Virginia Woolf Between the Acts Woolf's novel centres on the staging of a play at Pointz Hall, an Elizabethan manor modelled on two grand Sussex houses: Glynde Place and Firle Place.

NON-FICTION

Mrs Henry Dudeney *A Lewes Diary: 1916-1944* The diary of Alice Dudeney, a prolific novelist who was compared to Thomas Hardy by her contemporaries, is a little-known gem.

Lorraine Harrison *Inspiring Sussex Gardeners* This delightful book is part of a series of idiosyncratic, beautifully illustrated books on Sussex, published by the Snake River Press.

Thomas Walker Horsfield *The History, Antiquities and Topography of the County of Sussex* A respected two-volume work providing a comprehensive history of Sussex up to its publication in 1835.

Spike Milligan *The Selected War Memoirs* Posted to Bexhill for two years during World War II, many of Milligan's early war memoirs relate to the area.

POETRY

Hilaire Belloc *Poems* The French-born poet, writer and historian lived in the village of Slindon for much of his childhood. His love of the West Sussex countryside is evident in later poems such as 'The South Country', 'West Sussex Drinking Song' and 'Ha'nacker Mill'.

William Blake *The Complete Poems* The mystic poet's preface to his epic poem *Milton* ('And did those feet in ancient time'/Walk upon England's mountains green'), which would later become the hymn 'Jerusalem', was written when he lived at Felpham. It's believed that the view over the Downs from Lavant lay behind the reference to 'England's green and pleasant Land'.

Rudyard Kipling *The Collected Poems* Kipling adored Sussex, and lived at Bateman's, a 17th-century manor house in the Weald, from 1902 until his death in 1939. He details the county's charms in the poem 'Sussex', which concludes: 'Each to his choice, and I rejoice/ The lot has fallen to me/In a fair ground – in a fair ground –/Yea, Sussex by the sea!'

FILM

Angus, Thongs and Perfect Snogging *(Gurinder Chadha, 2008)* Comical coming of age story set in Eastbourne, as a young girl attempts to get a boyfriend and throw a successful birthday party.

The Birthday Party *(William Friedkin, 1968)* The screen adaptation of Harold Pinter's acclaimed play was shot on location in Worthing.

Brighton Rock *(John Boulting, 1947 & Rowan Joffe, 2011)* Greene's iconic Brighton tale has twice been adapted for the big screen. The 1947 version starred Richard Attenborough as its anti-hero, Pinkie Brown, while Rowan Joffe's 2011 film brought the story forward to 1964, against the backdrop of Brighton's mods and rockers, with Sam Riley in the lead role.

Notes on a Scandal *(Richard Eyre, 2006)* Scenes for this Oscar-nominated psychological drama, starring Cate Blanchett and Judi Dench, were filmed at locations around Beachy Head, including the Cavendish Hotel and 117 Royal Parade.

Quadrophenia *(Franc Roddam, 1979)* Based on the Who's rock opera of the same name, this cult film features a mass brawl between mods and rockers on Brighton Beach; its famed final scene was filmed at Beachy Head.

TV & RADIO

Foyle's War *ITV, 2002-present* In this Hastings-set series, detective Christopher Foyle chases criminals taking advantage of the chaotic aftermath of World War II.

The Goon Show *BBC, 1951-1960* An episode of the surreal radio comedy, written by Spike Milligan, was entitled 'The Dreaded Batter Pudding Hurler (of Bexhill-on-Sea)'; Milligan was posted at Bexhill during the war.

Little Britain *BBC, 2003-2006* Fanciful transvestite Emily Howard walks along Eastbourne promenade claiming 'I'm a lady', in the comedy sketch show created by David Walliams and Matt Lucas.

Only Fools & Horses *BBC, 1992* The Christmas special of the sitcom saw dodgy trader Del Boy filling bottles with tap water and selling them as 'Peckham Spring'. Sales are so good, Del earns enough to take the family to Brighton's Grand Hotel for Christmas.

Stranger on the Shore *BBC, 1961* A five-part serial following a shy French au pair as she tries to acclimate to British life in Brighton.

Sugar Rush *Channel 4, 2005-2006* Based on Julie Burchills's novel of the same name, this Channel 4 production traced the fortunes of a teenage lesbian after moving from London to Brighton.

MUSIC

Claude Debussy *La Mer* Debussy arrived in Eastbourne in 1905, after fleeing Paris to escape the scandal of leaving his first wife. Here, in close proximity to the coast, he was able to complete his masterful orchestral representation of the sea.

Keane The anthemic rockers hail from Battle, and have played a song called 'Sovereign Light Café' at their gigs since 2009. The track refers to a café on Bexhill seafront frequented by the band, and is due to appear on their next studio album.

The Kooks Summer days in Brighton filter through into the music of this popular indie band, based in the city.

Van der Graaf Generator *Pawn Hearts* The cover photograph of this classic prog rock album was taken at band manager Tony Stratton-Smith's house in Crowborough.

ART

Vanessa Bell The astonishing painted interior of artist Vanessa Bell's Sussex home, Charleston, is preserved in all its glory. The 17th-century farmhouse – which became a country retreat for the Bloomsbury Set – was also the subject of several of Bell's paintings.

Edward Burra Although Burra, in his own inimitable style, dismissed Rye as a 'ducky little Tinkerbell towne [....] like an itsy bitsy morgue quayte DEAD', he was a lifelong resident. Scenes from the town featured in several of his watercolours, including the menacing *Soldiers at Rye*.

Duncan Grant Scottish painter and Bloomsbury Group stalwart Duncan Grant decorated Charleston with Vanessa Bell; they also painted the vivid murals in nearby Berwick Church.

Eric Ravilious A prominent artist in Britain in the 1930s, Ravilious was born in Eastbourne and cited the Sussex landscape as a major influence in his work. His watercolours and woodcuts often depict local landmarks, such as Beachy Head and the Long Man of Wilmington.

Sir Anthony van Dyck Born in Antwerp, van Dyck moved to London in 1632 and became the premier portrait painter in the court of King Charles I. He made several evocative pen drawings of Rye, including one of St Mary's Church.

WALKS & CYCLE TRAILS

Cuckoo Trail *www.eastsussex. gov.uk/leisureandtourism* A mostly off-road 11-mile trail, running along a disused East Sussex railway line.

Footprints of Sussex *www.footprintsofsussex.co.uk* A company offering walking holidays on the South Downs Way.

Scenic Sussex Trails *http://scenicsussextrails.com* Information on guided walks around Sussex. Literary walks explore Sussex as it was known to Hilaire Belloc and Lord Alfred Tennyson.

South Downs Way *www.nationaltrail.co.uk/southdowns.*

Sussex Border Path *www.sussexborderpath.co.uk* A 150-mile route, taking in swathes of unspoilt countryside.

Walk and Cycle Sussex *http://sussex.walkandcycle.co.uk* A great source of routes and tips for walkers and cyclists in the county.

Kent Thematic Index

INDEX

INDEX

Kent A-Z Index

INDEX

Where to eat & drink in Kent

INDEX

Where to stay in Kent

INDEX

Sussex Thematic Index

INDEX

INDEX

INDEX

Sussex A-Z Index

Page numbers in *italics* indicate illustrations; **bold** type indicates key information.

INDEX

INDEX

Where to eat & drink in Sussex

INDEX

Where to stay in Sussex

Advertisers' Index

Please refer to relevant sections for addresses and/or telephone numbers